MANGA from the HEART

OTOMEN

STORY AND ART BY AYA KANNO

VAMPIRE KNIGHT

STORY AND ART BY MATSURI HINO

Natsume's **BOOK of FRIENDS**

STORY AND ART BY YUKI MIDORIKAWA

Want to see more of what you're looking for?

Let your voice be heard!

hojobeat.com/mangasurvey

Help us give you more manga from the heart!

ratings.viz.com ratings.viz.com **VIZ** media www.viz.com

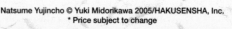

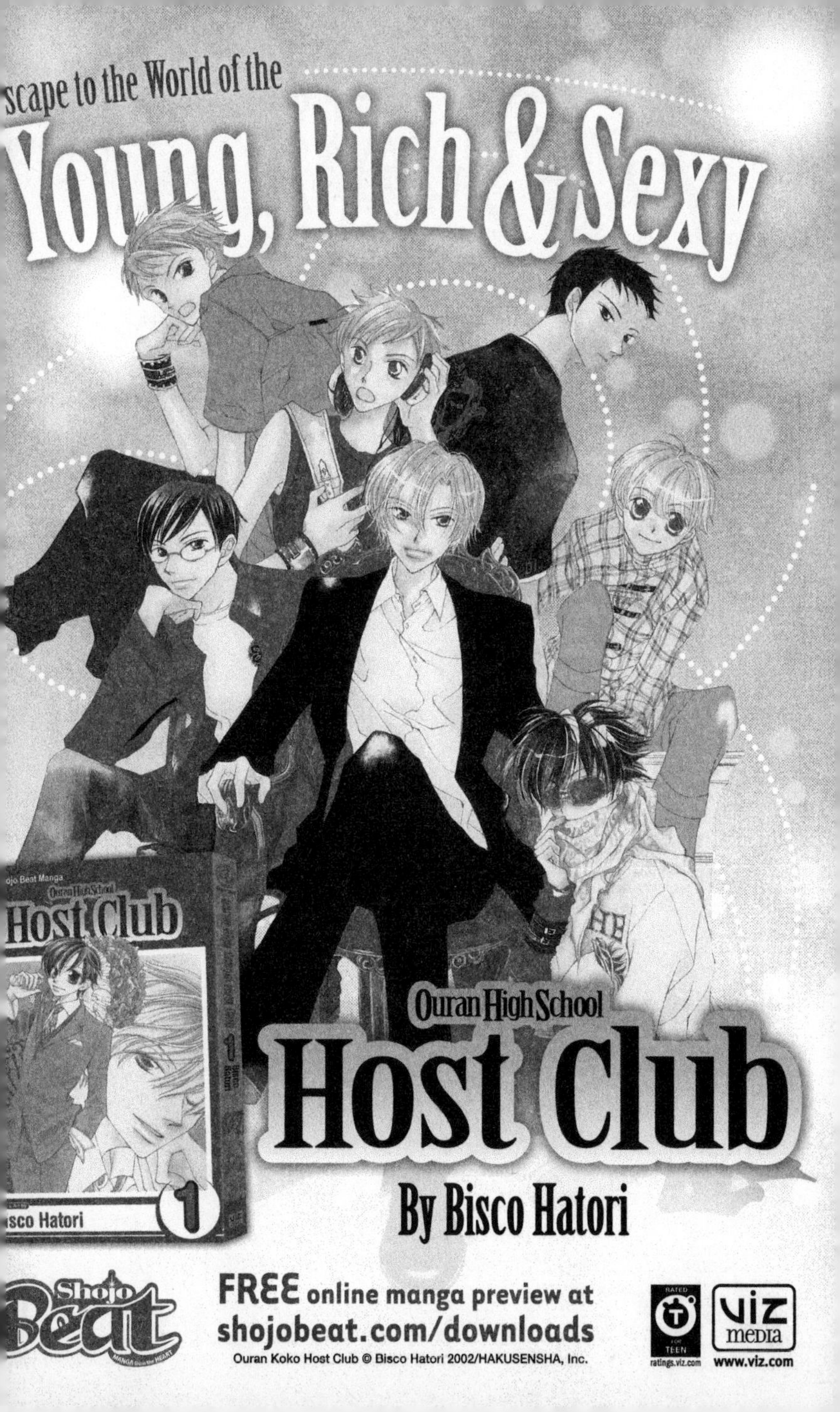
scape to the World of the
Young, Rich & Sexy
Shojo Beat Manga
Ouran High School
Host Club
1
isco Hatori
Ouran High School
Host Club
By Bisco Hatori
Shojo Beat
FREE online manga preview at
shojobeat.com/downloads
Ouran Koko Host Club © Bisco Hatori 2002/HAKUSENSHA, Inc.
RATED T FOR TEEN
ratings.viz.com
VIZ media
www.viz.com

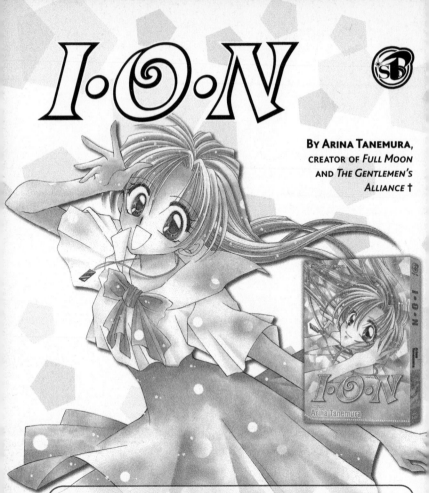

Cactus's Secret

VOL. 4
Shojo Beat Edition

Story and Art by
Nana Haruta

TRANSLATION & ADAPTATION Su Mon Han
TOUCH-UP ART & LETTERING Deron Bennett
DESIGN Courtney Utt
EDITOR Nancy Thistlethwaite

SABOTEN NO HIMITSU © 2003 by Nana Haruta. All rights
reserved. First published in Japan in 2003 by SHUEISHA Inc.,
Tokyo. English translation rights arranged by SHUEISHA Inc.

Printed in the U.S.A.

Published by VIZ Media, LLC
P.O. Box 77010
San Francisco, CA 94107

10 9 8 7 6 5 4 3 2 1
First printing, December 2010

www.shojobeat.com   www.viz.com

Cactus's Secret

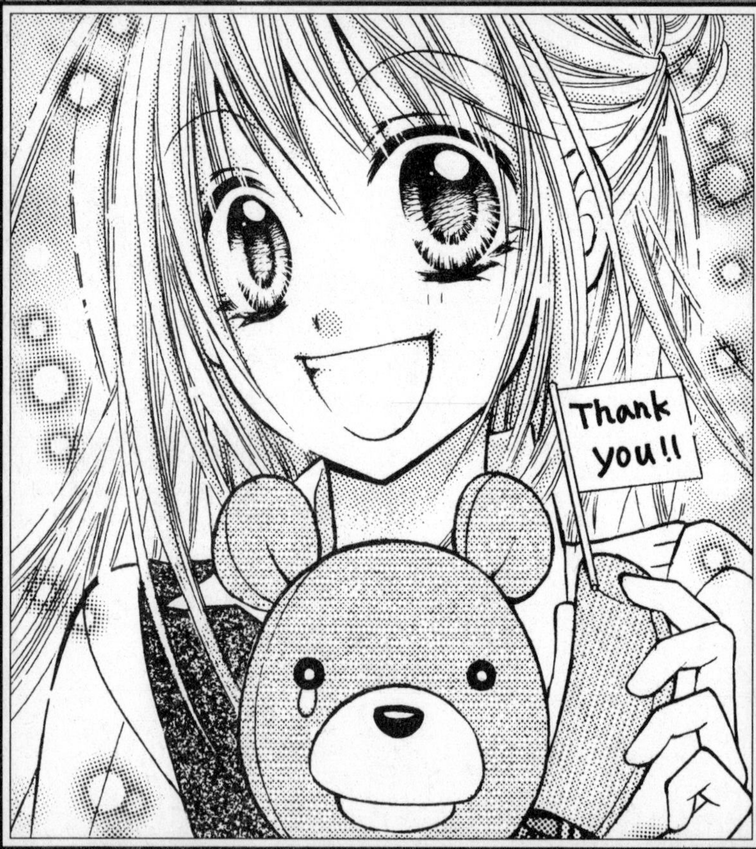
Thank you!!

4 Nana Haruta

Contents

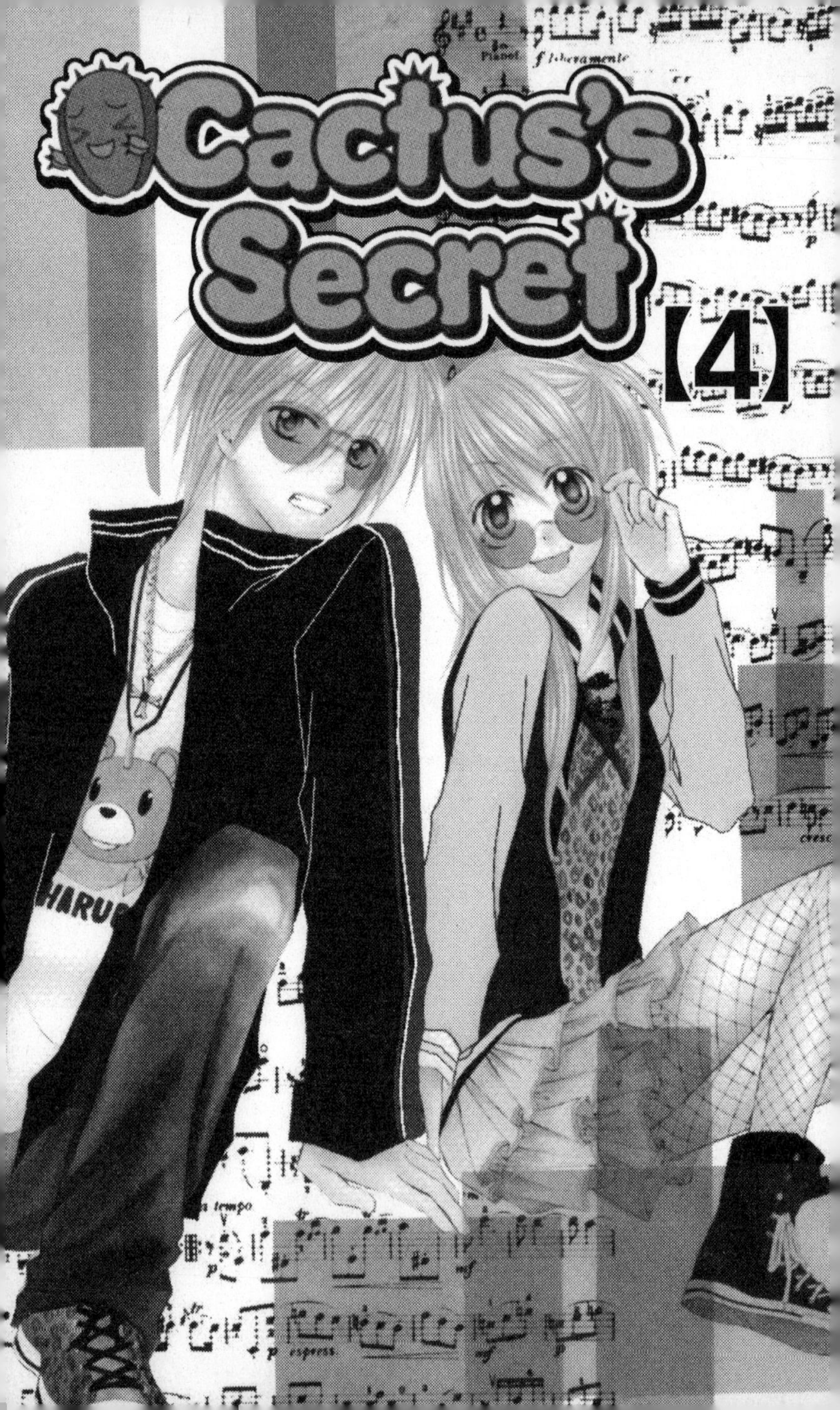
Cactus's Secret
【4】

CAST OF CHARACTERS

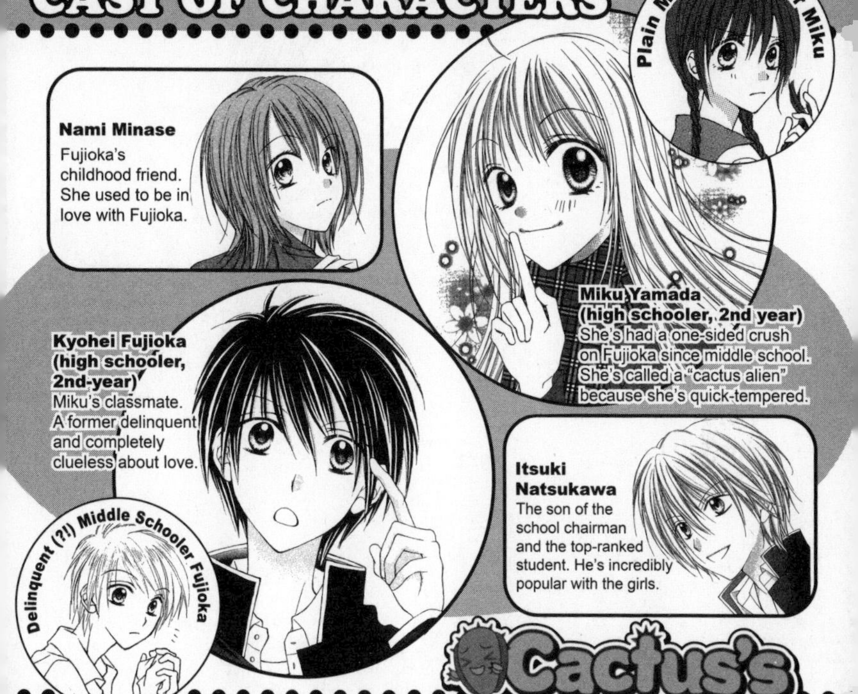
Plain Middle Schooler Miku
Nami Minase
Fujioka's childhood friend. She used to be in love with Fujioka.
Miku Yamada (high schooler, 2nd year)
She's had a one-sided crush on Fujioka since middle school. She's called a "cactus alien" because she's quick-tempered.
Kyohei Fujioka (high schooler, 2nd-year)
Miku's classmate. A former delinquent and completely clueless about love.
Itsuki Natsukawa
The son of the school chairman and the top-ranked student. He's incredibly popular with the girls.
Delinquent (?!) Middle Schooler Fujioka

Cactus's Secret

Since middle school, Miku (currently a high school second year) has had a one-sided crush on Fujioka, a boy who is completely clueless about love. In third quarter of their first year of high school, Miku finally worked up the courage to confess her love to him but was, unfortunately, turned down. Despite that, Miku decides not to give up her efforts to win him over.

Then, when Miku saves Fujioka from being expelled wrongly from school, the two suddenly become very close! ♥ Fujioka tells her to wait just a little longer for him. He even joins the school's Sports Day Planning Committee with Miku, and her hopes rise!

Into this situation comes the mysterious Kudo, who encounters Miku by chance in the street one day. Kudo somehow seems to know Fujioka and lures Miku away with his clever words. Unfortunately, Fujioka spots them leaving together! With that, the good feelings between Miku and Fujioka sour again—or so it seems until an outburst from Fujioka reveals he may actually be jealous!

Their progress seems at a standstill until the Sports Day Festival. When Fujioka continues being ambiguous about his feelings, Miku finally loses her temper and explodes at him! With that, Fujioka finally confesses his love to her in front of the entire school! We also discover along the way that Kudo is Fujioka's older brother. Thus, Miku's efforts and long-lived feelings for Fujioka finally come to fruition! Or...they should have.

The problem this time is Miku herself. Being preoccupied with her new relationship with Fujioka, she forgets to study for the vitally important final exams. Her rank drops below the top 30 for the first time. As she may have lost her chance to request a teacher's recommendation to get into college, Miku is devastated.

Miku resolves to study after school in the library every day until the next National Mock Exam. Fujioka, on the other hand, has never once considered what he wants to do with his future and doesn't want to join Miku with her extra studies. Miku is touched that Fujioka is willing to wait until she's finished studying to walk home with her every day, but with things as they are, will these two really have a future together?!

STORY THUS FAR

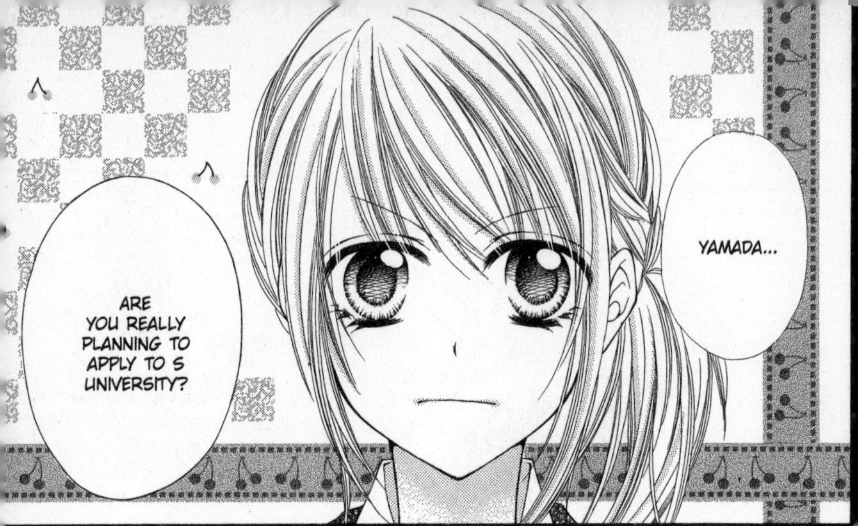
YAMADA...
ARE YOU REALLY PLANNING TO APPLY TO S UNIVERSITY?

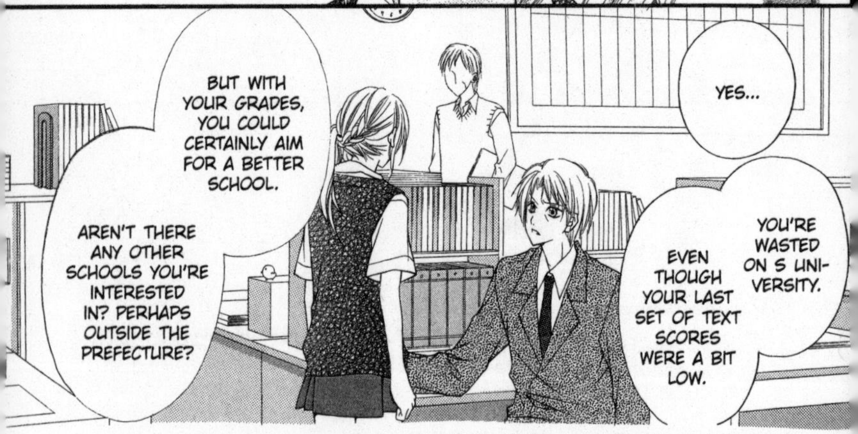
YES...
YOU'RE WASTED ON S UNIVERSITY.
EVEN THOUGH YOUR LAST SET OF TEXT SCORES WERE A BIT LOW.
BUT WITH YOUR GRADES, YOU COULD CERTAINLY AIM FOR A BETTER SCHOOL.
AREN'T THERE ANY OTHER SCHOOLS YOU'RE INTERESTED IN? PERHAPS OUTSIDE THE PREFECTURE?

SMALL TALK ①

I love drawing Nurse Kitamura—she's so much fun! Even though she already had a reputation amongst the folks at Ribon as a bad character even before I started drawing her... ♭
Please pay particular attention to the incredible detail of the shading on her ample bosom in the scene where she takes off her coat. It's all thanks to the amazing efforts of one of my assistants, who is supremely good at screentoning female anatomy!! (laugh)

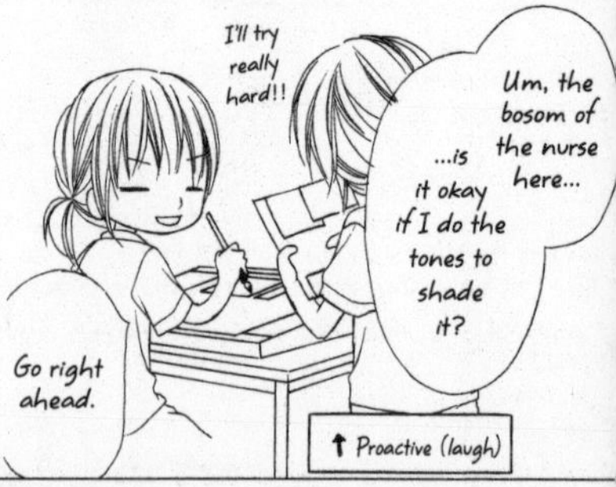
Um, the bosom of the nurse here...
...is it okay if I do the tones to shade it?
I'll try really hard!!
Go right ahead.
↑ Proactive (laugh)

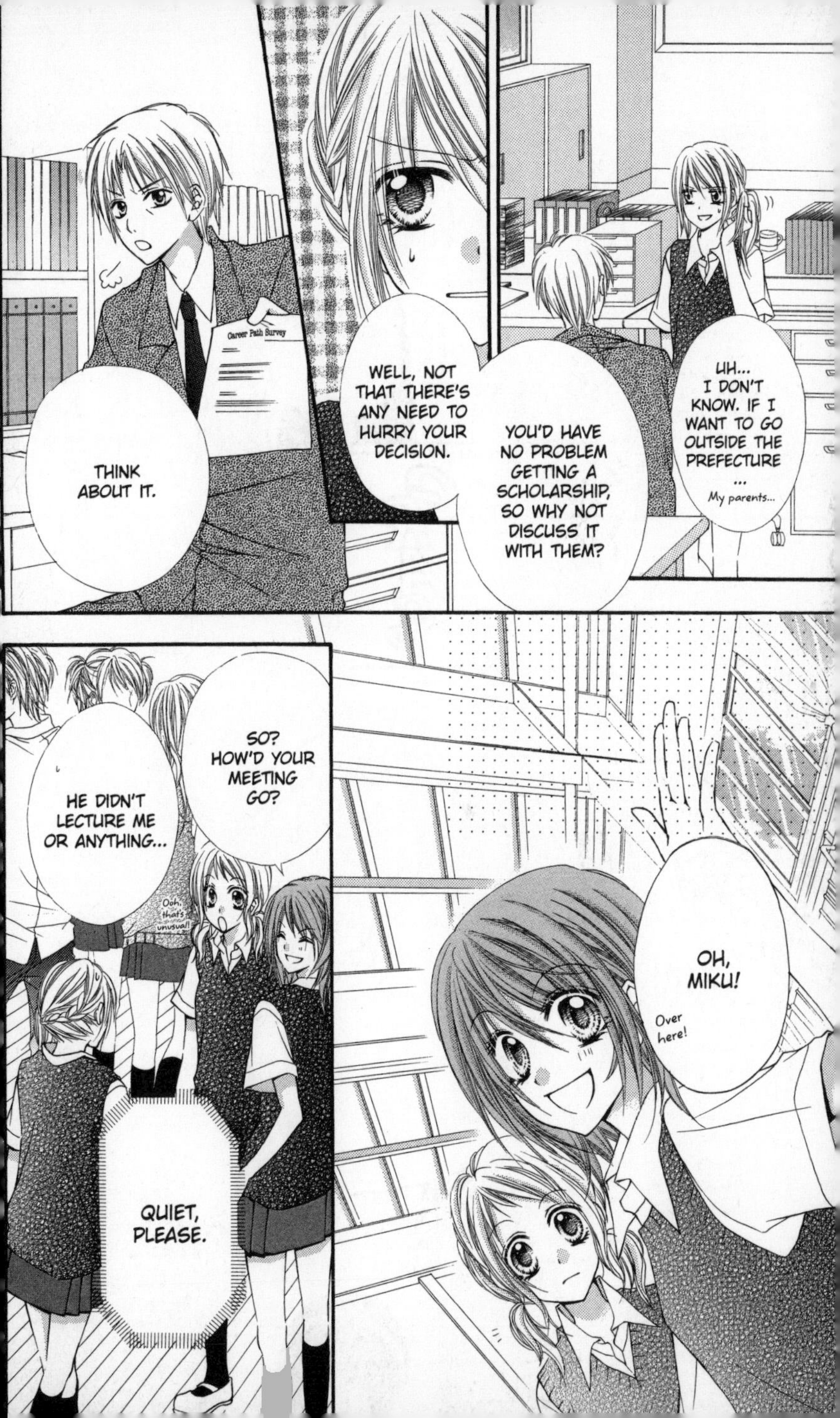
UH... I DON'T KNOW. IF I WANT TO GO OUTSIDE THE PREFECTURE...
My parents...
YOU'D HAVE NO PROBLEM GETTING A SCHOLARSHIP, SO WHY NOT DISCUSS IT WITH THEM?
WELL, NOT THAT THERE'S ANY NEED TO HURRY YOUR DECISION.
Career Path Survey
THINK ABOUT IT.
OH, MIKU!
Over here!
SO? HOW'D YOUR MEETING GO?
HE DIDN'T LECTURE ME OR ANYTHING...
Ooh, that's unusual!
QUIET, PLEASE.

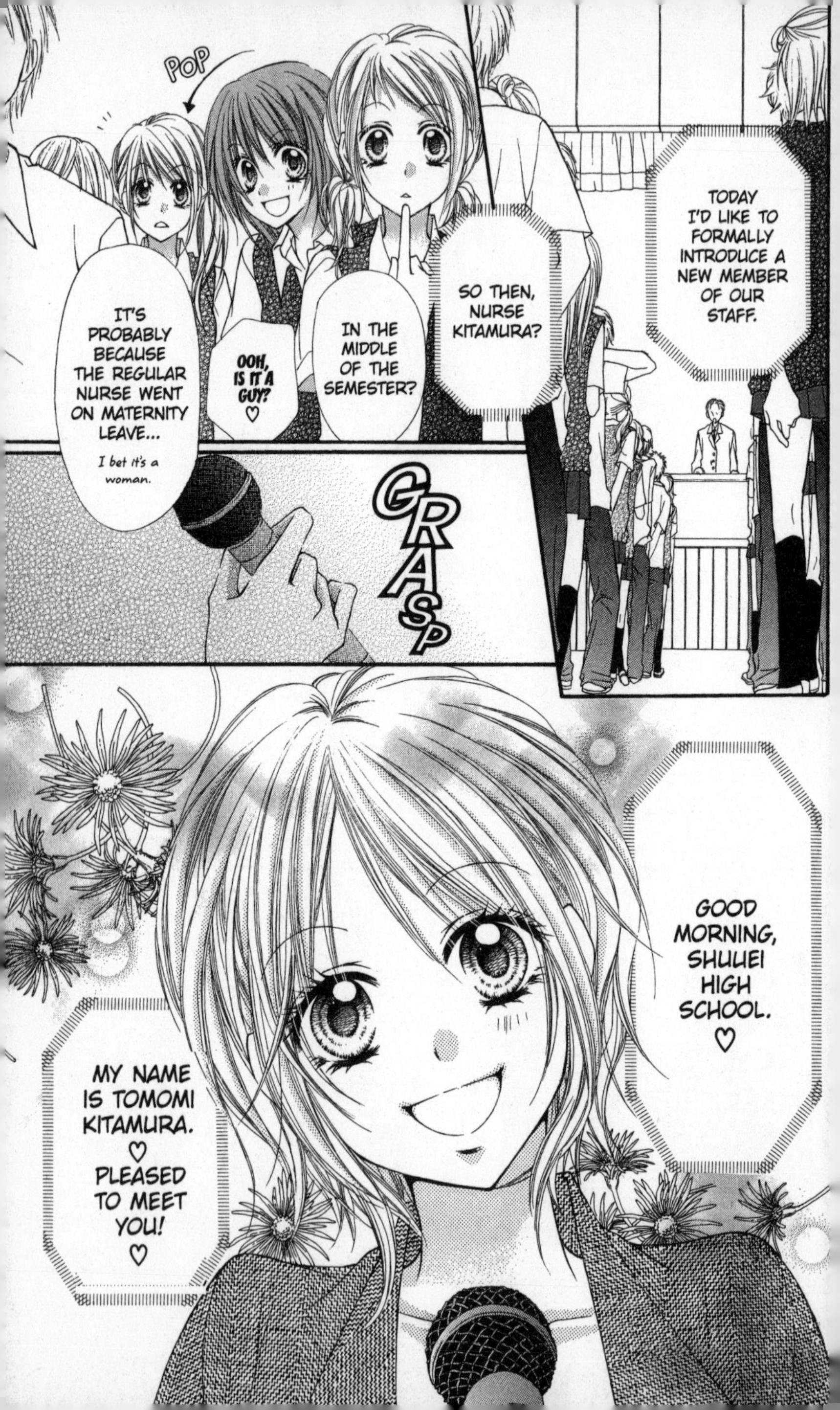
TODAY I'D LIKE TO FORMALLY INTRODUCE A NEW MEMBER OF OUR STAFF.
POP
SO THEN, NURSE KITAMURA?
IN THE MIDDLE OF THE SEMESTER?
OOH, IS IT A GUY? ♡
IT'S PROBABLY BECAUSE THE REGULAR NURSE WENT ON MATERNITY LEAVE...
I bet it's a woman.
GRASP
GOOD MORNING, SHUUEI HIGH SCHOOL. ♡
MY NAME IS TOMOMI KITAMURA. ♡ PLEASED TO MEET YOU! ♡

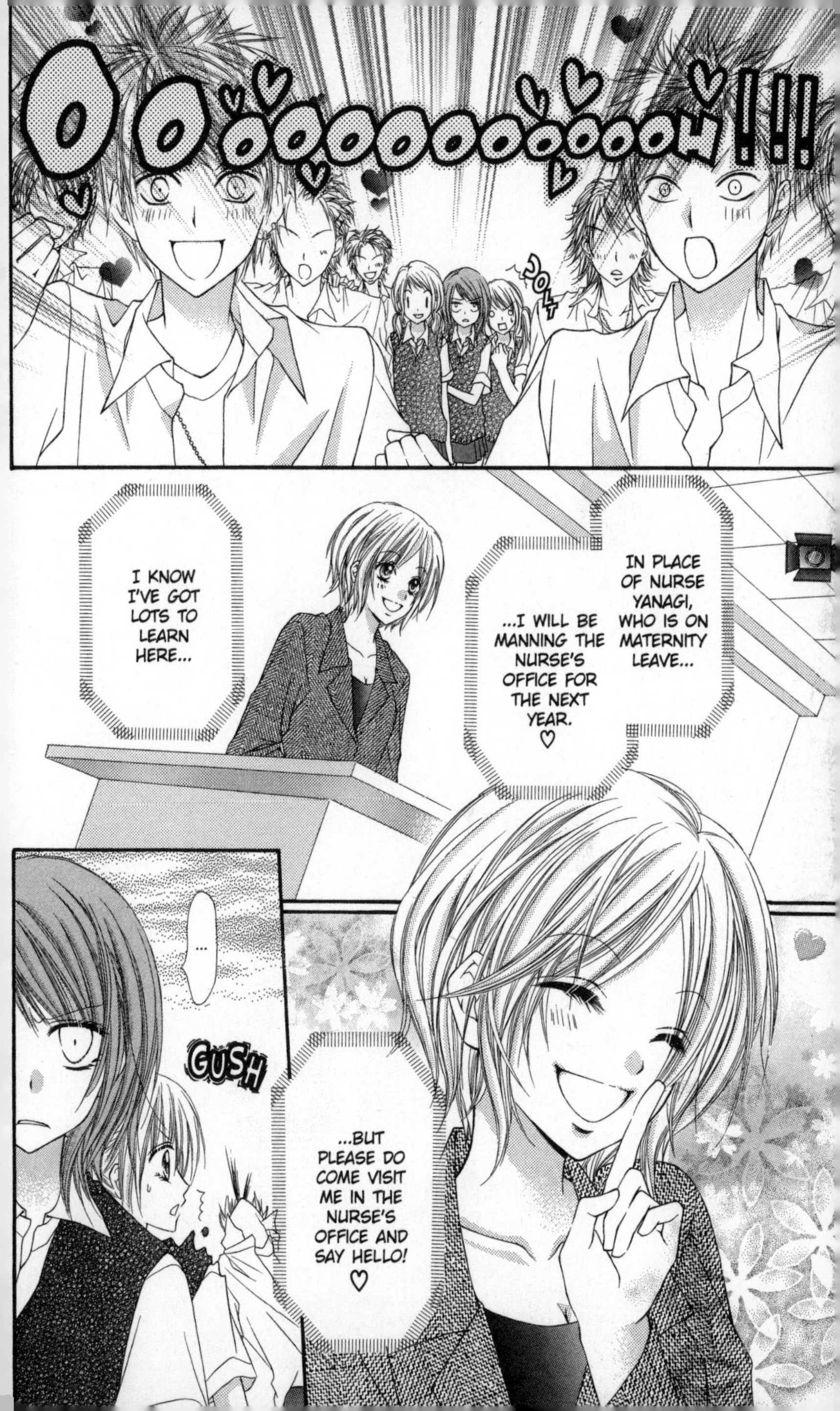
OOOOOOOOOOOOOOOH!!!
JOLT
IN PLACE OF NURSE YANAGI, WHO IS ON MATERNITY LEAVE...
...I WILL BE MANNING THE NURSE'S OFFICE FOR THE NEXT YEAR. ♡
I KNOW I'VE GOT LOTS TO LEARN HERE...
...BUT PLEASE DO COME VISIT ME IN THE NURSE'S OFFICE AND SAY HELLO! ♡
...
GUSH

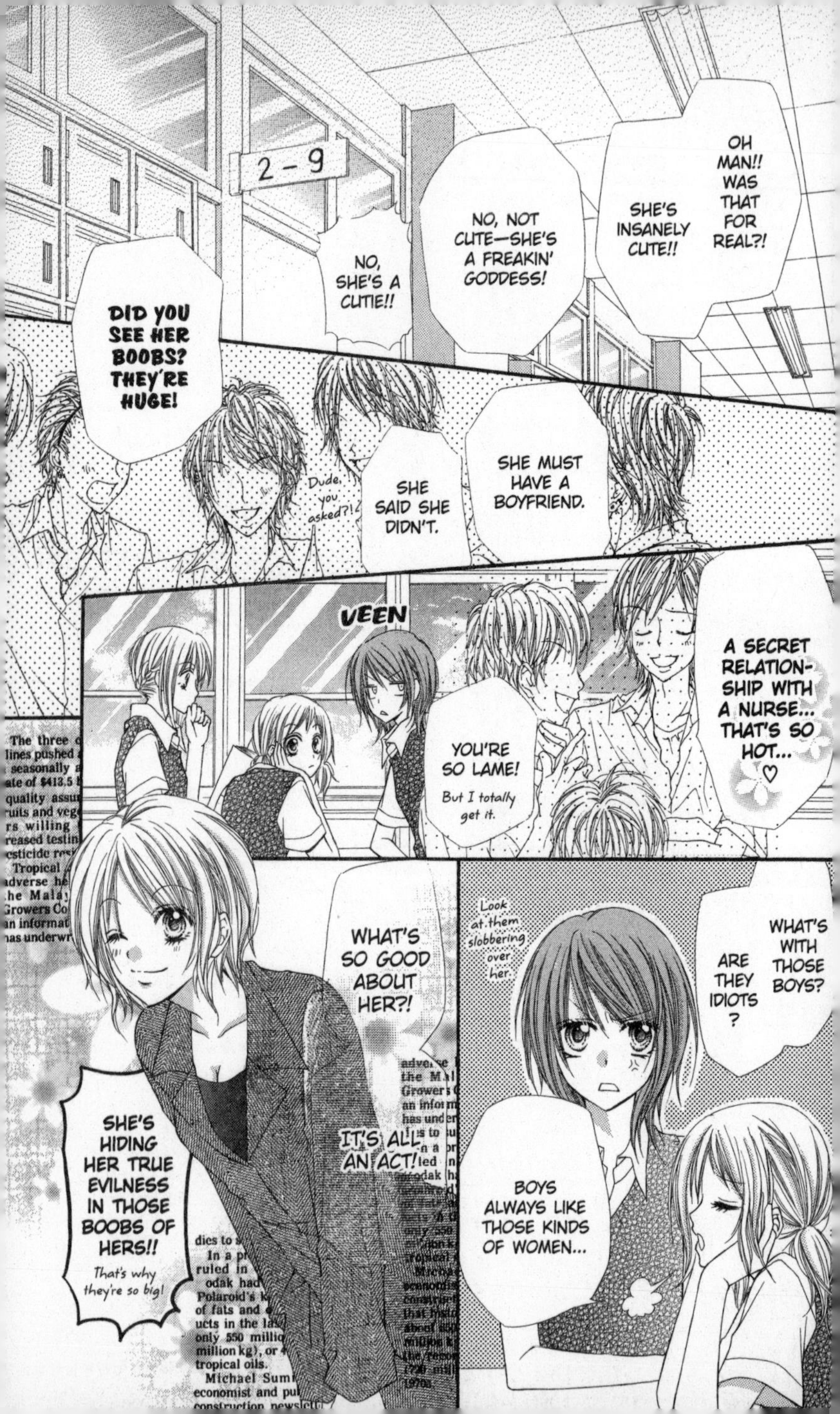
2-9
OH MAN!! WAS THAT FOR REAL?!
SHE'S INSANELY CUTE!!
NO, NOT CUTE—SHE'S A FREAKIN' GODDESS!
NO, SHE'S A CUTIE!!
DID YOU SEE HER BOOBS? THEY'RE HUGE!
SHE MUST HAVE A BOYFRIEND.
SHE SAID SHE DIDN'T.
Dude, you asked?!
A SECRET RELATIONSHIP WITH A NURSE... THAT'S SO HOT... ♡
YOU'RE SO LAME!
But I totally get it.
VEEN
WHAT'S WITH THOSE BOYS?
ARE THEY IDIOTS?
Look at them slobbering over her.
BOYS ALWAYS LIKE THOSE KINDS OF WOMEN...
WHAT'S SO GOOD ABOUT HER?!
IT'S ALL AN ACT!
SHE'S HIDING HER TRUE EVILNESS IN THOSE BOOBS OF HERS!!
That's why they're so big!

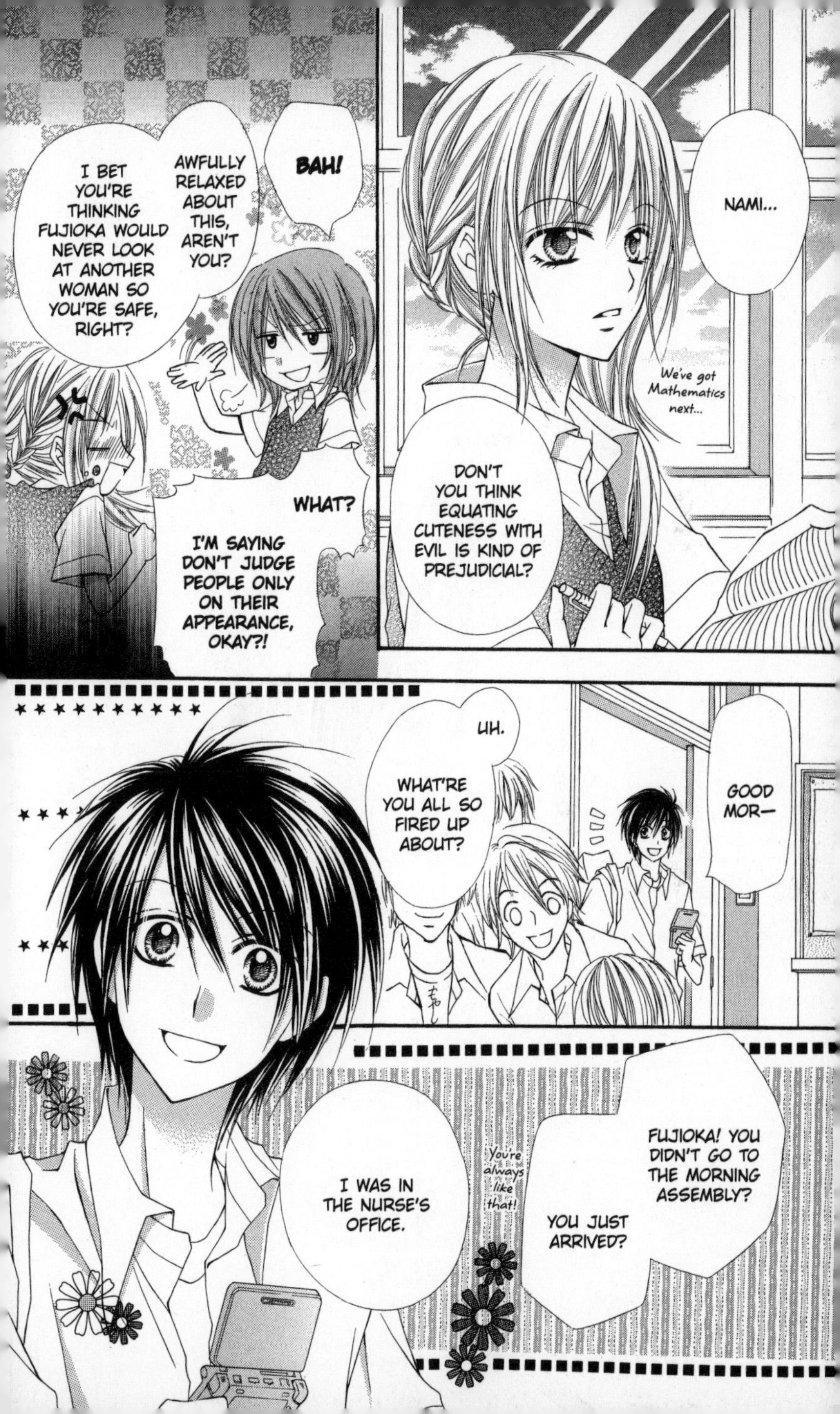
NAMI...
We've got Mathematics next...
DON'T YOU THINK EQUATING CUTENESS WITH EVIL IS KIND OF PREJUDICIAL?
BAH!
AWFULLY RELAXED ABOUT THIS, AREN'T YOU?
I BET YOU'RE THINKING FUJIOKA WOULD NEVER LOOK AT ANOTHER WOMAN SO YOU'RE SAFE, RIGHT?
WHAT?
I'M SAYING DON'T JUDGE PEOPLE ONLY ON THEIR APPEARANCE, OKAY?!
GOOD MOR—
UH.
WHAT'RE YOU ALL SO FIRED UP ABOUT?
FUJIOKA! YOU DIDN'T GO TO THE MORNING ASSEMBLY?
YOU JUST ARRIVED?
You're always like that!
I WAS IN THE NURSE'S OFFICE.

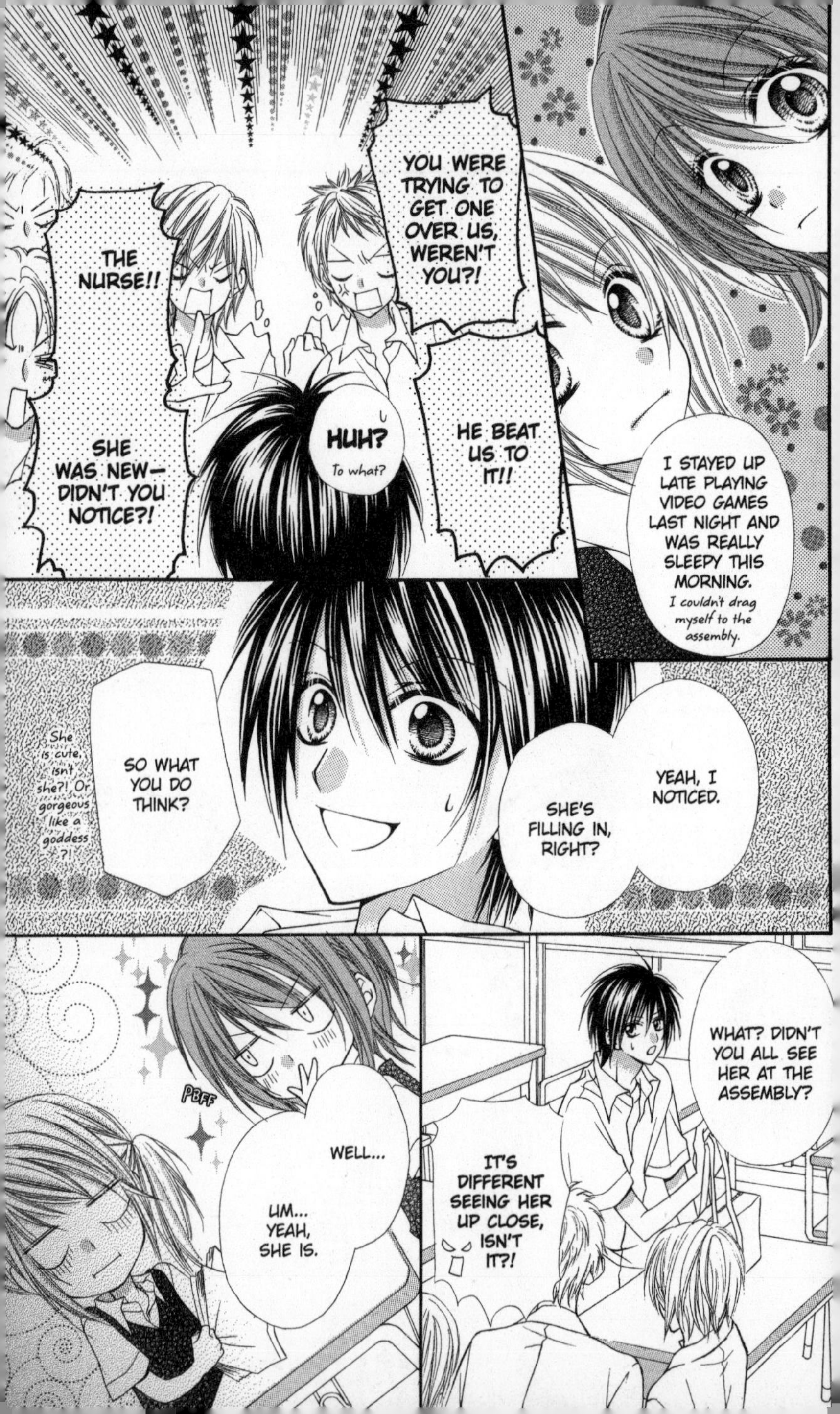
I STAYED UP LATE PLAYING VIDEO GAMES LAST NIGHT AND WAS REALLY SLEEPY THIS MORNING.
I couldn't drag myself to the assembly.
YOU WERE TRYING TO GET ONE OVER US, WEREN'T YOU?!
HE BEAT US TO IT!!
HUH?
To what?
THE NURSE!!
SHE WAS NEW—DIDN'T YOU NOTICE?!
YEAH, I NOTICED.
SHE'S FILLING IN, RIGHT?
SO WHAT YOU DO THINK?
She is cute, isn't she?! Or gorgeous like a goddess ✧?!
WHAT? DIDN'T YOU ALL SEE HER AT THE ASSEMBLY?
IT'S DIFFERENT SEEING HER UP CLOSE, ISN'T IT?!
WELL...
UM... YEAH, SHE IS.
PBFF

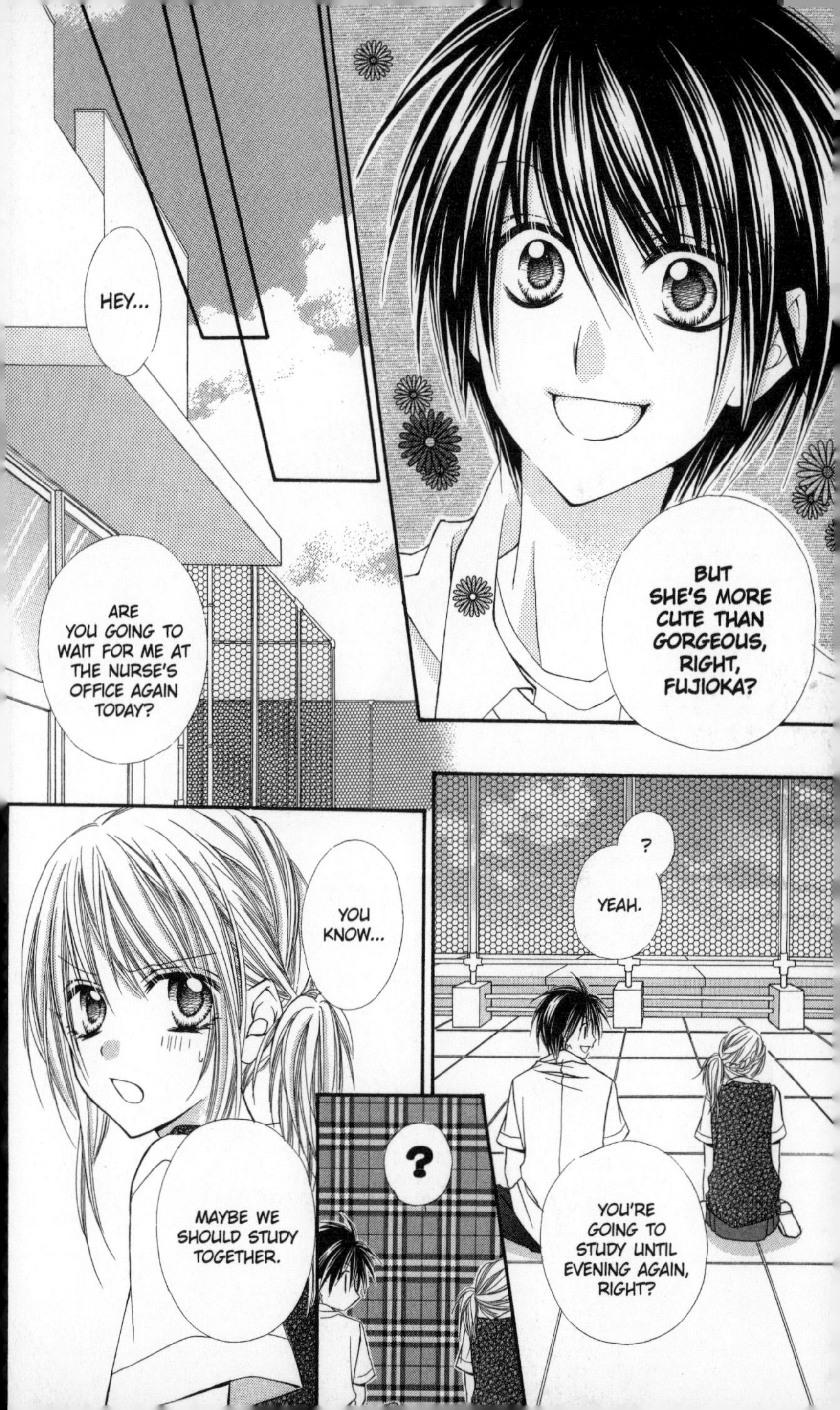
BUT SHE'S MORE CUTE THAN GORGEOUS, RIGHT, FUJIOKA?
HEY...
ARE YOU GOING TO WAIT FOR ME AT THE NURSE'S OFFICE AGAIN TODAY?
?
YEAH.
YOU'RE GOING TO STUDY UNTIL EVENING AGAIN, RIGHT?
YOU KNOW...
MAYBE WE SHOULD STUDY TOGETHER.
?

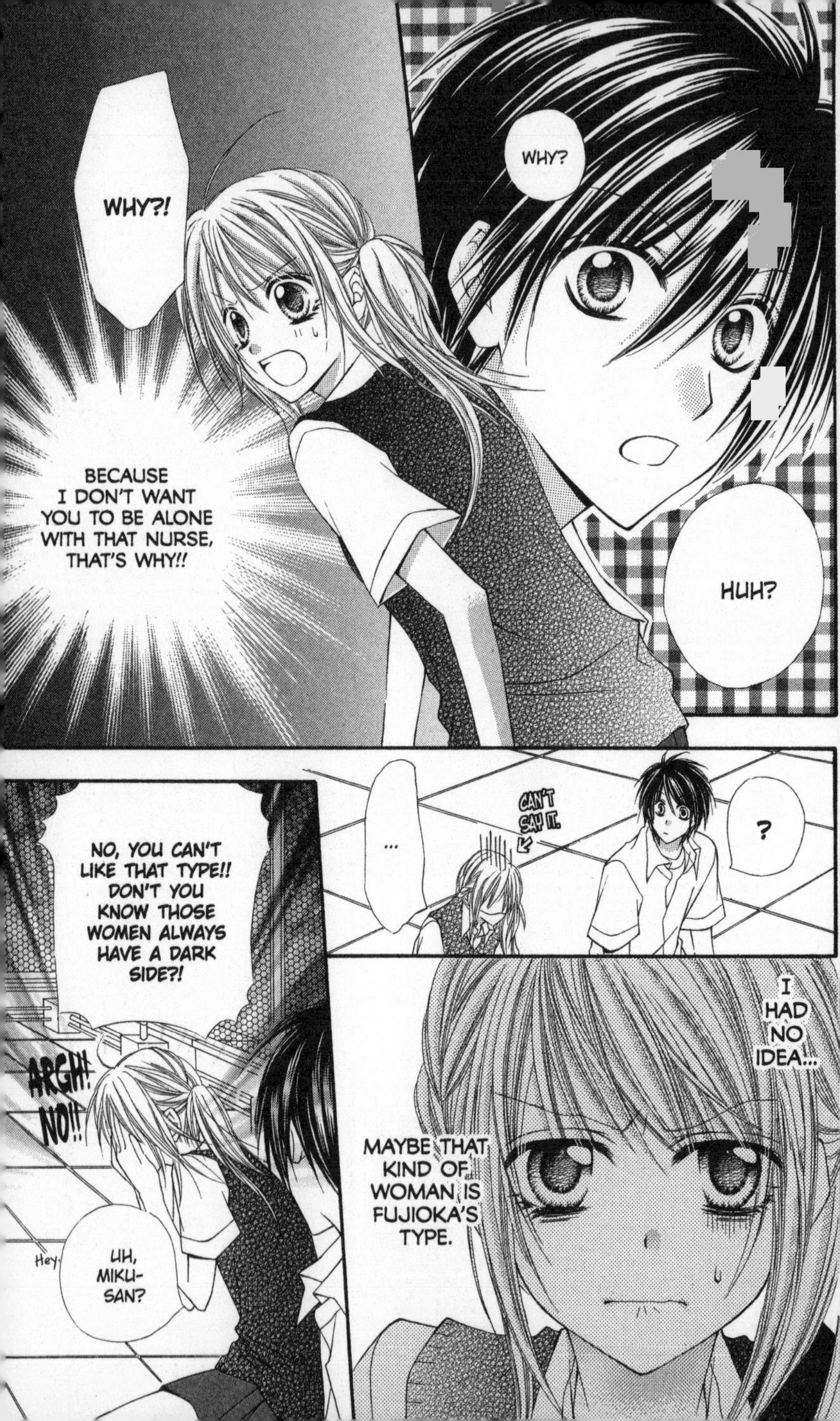
WHY?
WHY?!
BECAUSE I DON'T WANT YOU TO BE ALONE WITH THAT NURSE, THAT'S WHY!!
HUH?
?
CAN'T SAY IT.
...
I HAD NO IDEA...
MAYBE THAT KIND OF WOMAN IS FUJIOKA'S TYPE.
NO, YOU CAN'T LIKE THAT TYPE!! DON'T YOU KNOW THOSE WOMEN ALWAYS HAVE A DARK SIDE?!
ARGH! NO!!
Hey.
UH, MIKU-SAN?

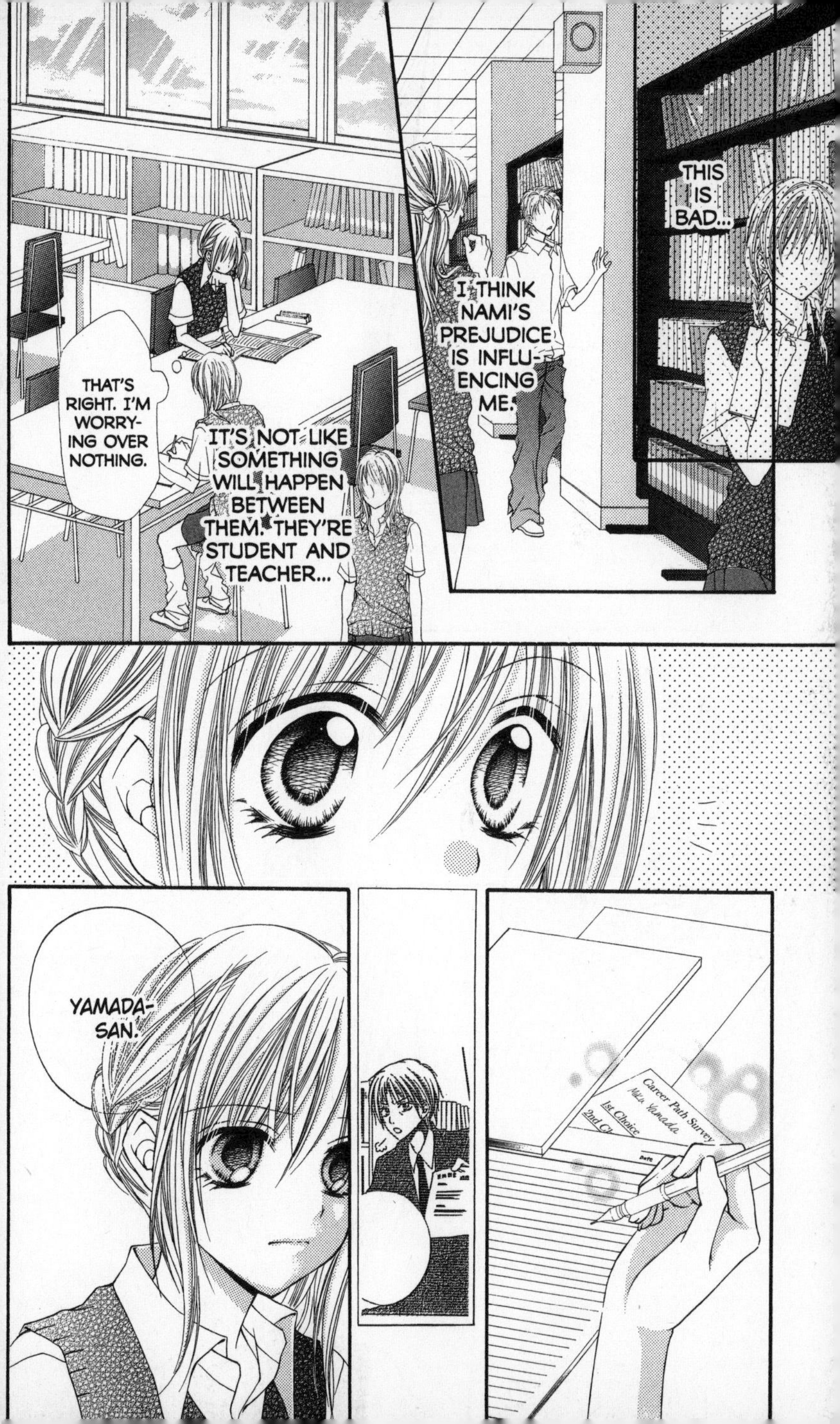
THIS IS BAD...
I THINK NAMI'S PREJUDICE IS INFLUENCING ME.
IT'S NOT LIKE SOMETHING WILL HAPPEN BETWEEN THEM. THEY'RE STUDENT AND TEACHER...
THAT'S RIGHT. I'M WORRYING OVER NOTHING.
Career Path Survey
Miss Yamada
1st Choice
YAMADA-SAN.

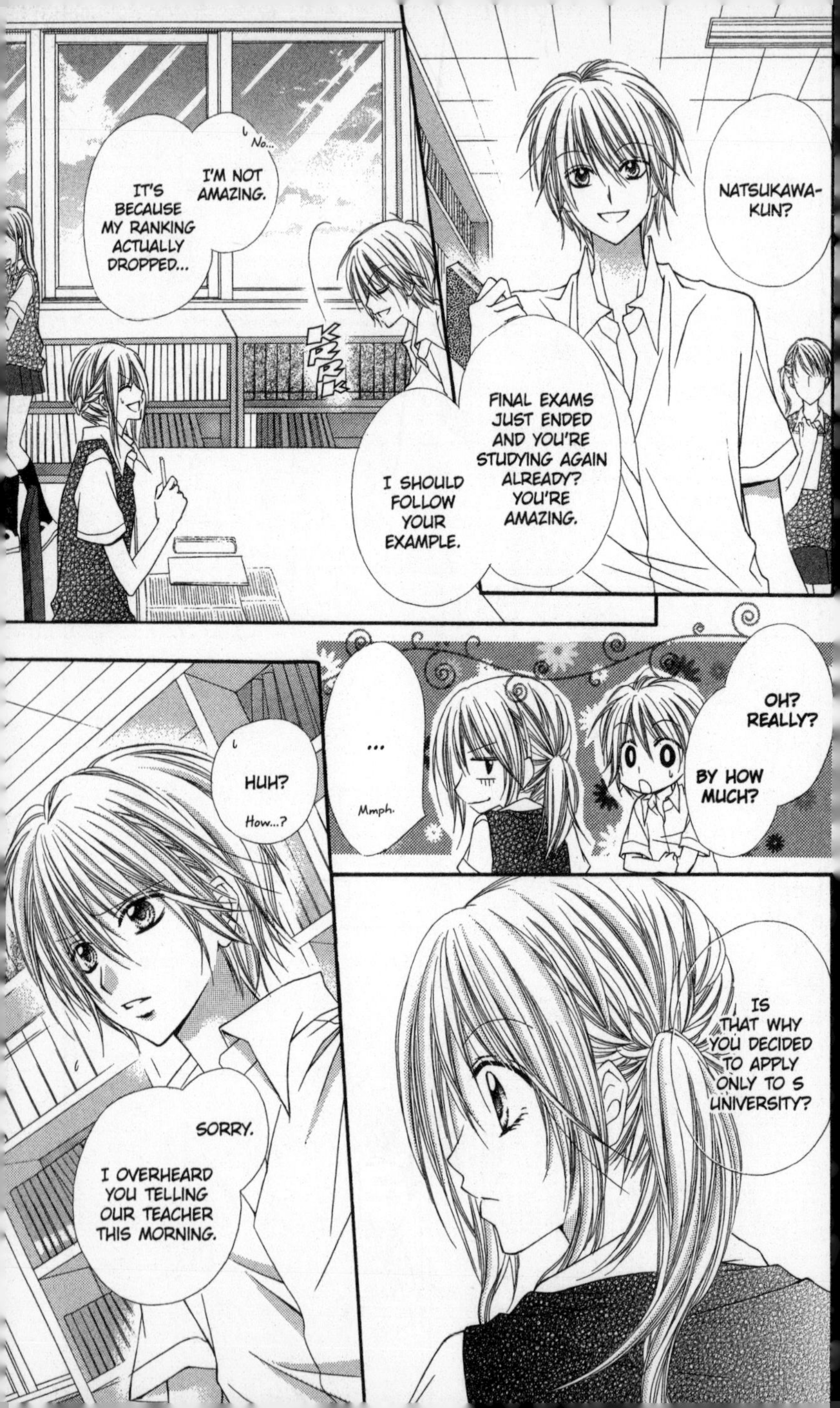
NATSUKAWA-KUN?
FINAL EXAMS JUST ENDED AND YOU'RE STUDYING AGAIN ALREADY? YOU'RE AMAZING.
I SHOULD FOLLOW YOUR EXAMPLE.
No...
I'M NOT AMAZING.
IT'S BECAUSE MY RANKING ACTUALLY DROPPED...
OH? REALLY?
BY HOW MUCH?
...
Mmph.
IS THAT WHY YOU DECIDED TO APPLY ONLY TO S UNIVERSITY?
HUH?
How...?
SORRY.
I OVERHEARD YOU TELLING OUR TEACHER THIS MORNING.

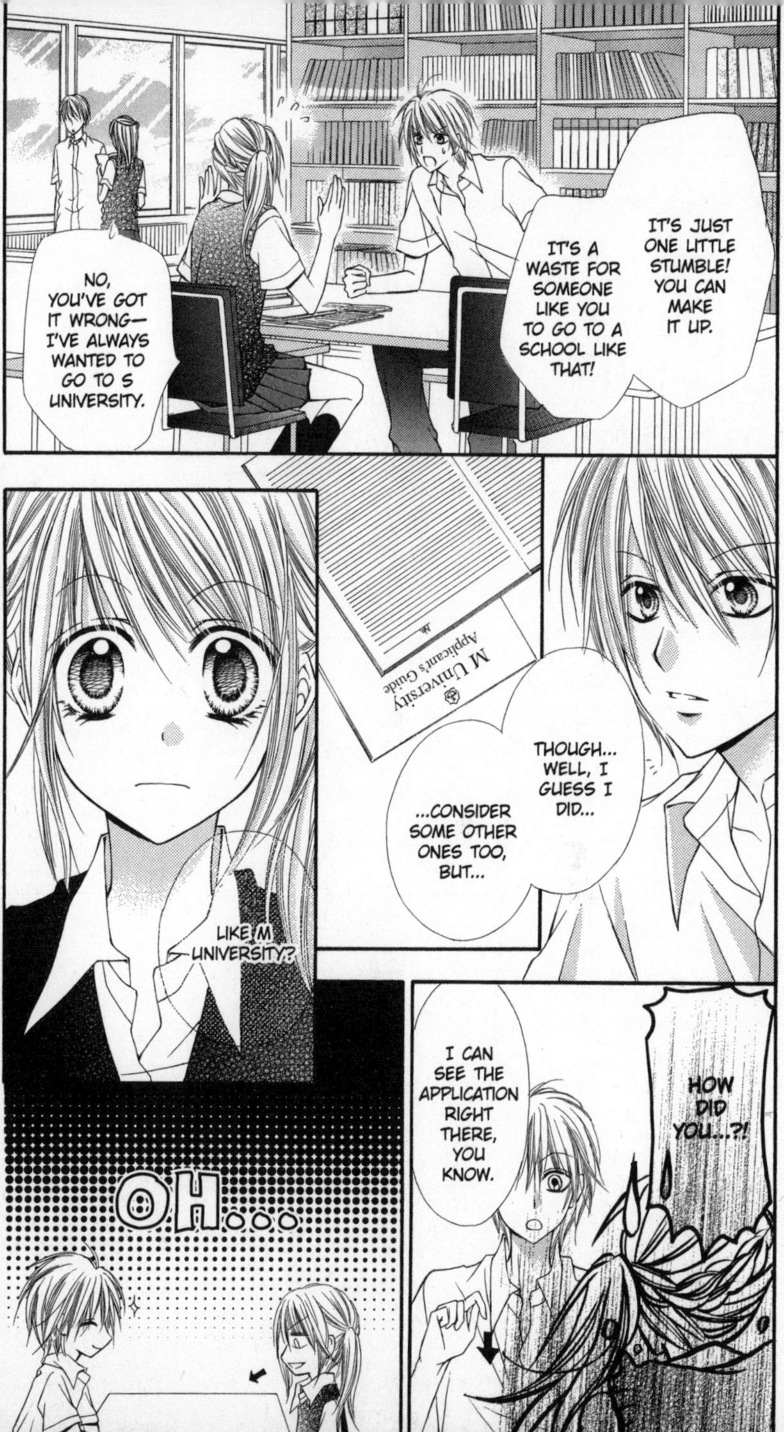
IT'S JUST ONE LITTLE STUMBLE! YOU CAN MAKE IT UP.
IT'S A WASTE FOR SOMEONE LIKE YOU TO GO TO A SCHOOL LIKE THAT!
NO, YOU'VE GOT IT WRONG— I'VE ALWAYS WANTED TO GO TO S UNIVERSITY.
THOUGH... WELL, I GUESS I DID...
...CONSIDER SOME OTHER ONES TOO, BUT...
M University
Applicant's Guide
LIKE M UNIVERSITY?
HOW DID YOU...?!
I CAN SEE THE APPLICATION RIGHT THERE, YOU KNOW.
OH...

1
one

THANK YOU!!!

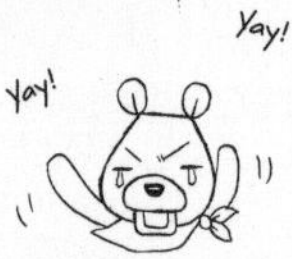
Yay!
Yay!

Hello, everybody! I'm Nana Haruta. Thanks to all of you, we have now reached volume 4, the final volume, of *Cactus's Secret*. Thank you so much for reading along with me to the very end.

Right now I've already started the serialization of my next series, so things are pretty busy around here. But you know, the reason I'm so busy with this new series right from the start is thanks to *Cactus's Secret* and all your support. Just between you and me, there were a few things about this series that I was a little hesitant about (laughs), but I really gained a lot from drawing it. I'll treasure those things always and keep doing my best from here on!

Please enjoy volume 4! ✿✿

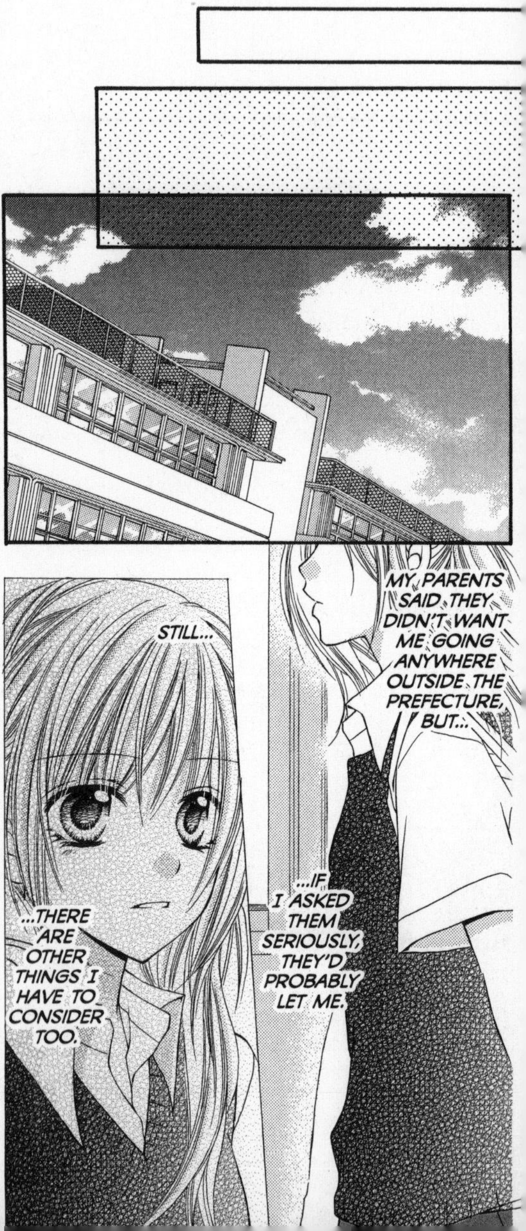
MY PARENTS SAID THEY DIDN'T WANT ME GOING ANYWHERE OUTSIDE THE PREFECTURE, BUT...
...IF I ASKED THEM SERIOUSLY, THEY'D PROBABLY LET ME.
STILL...
...THERE ARE OTHER THINGS I HAVE TO CONSIDER TOO.

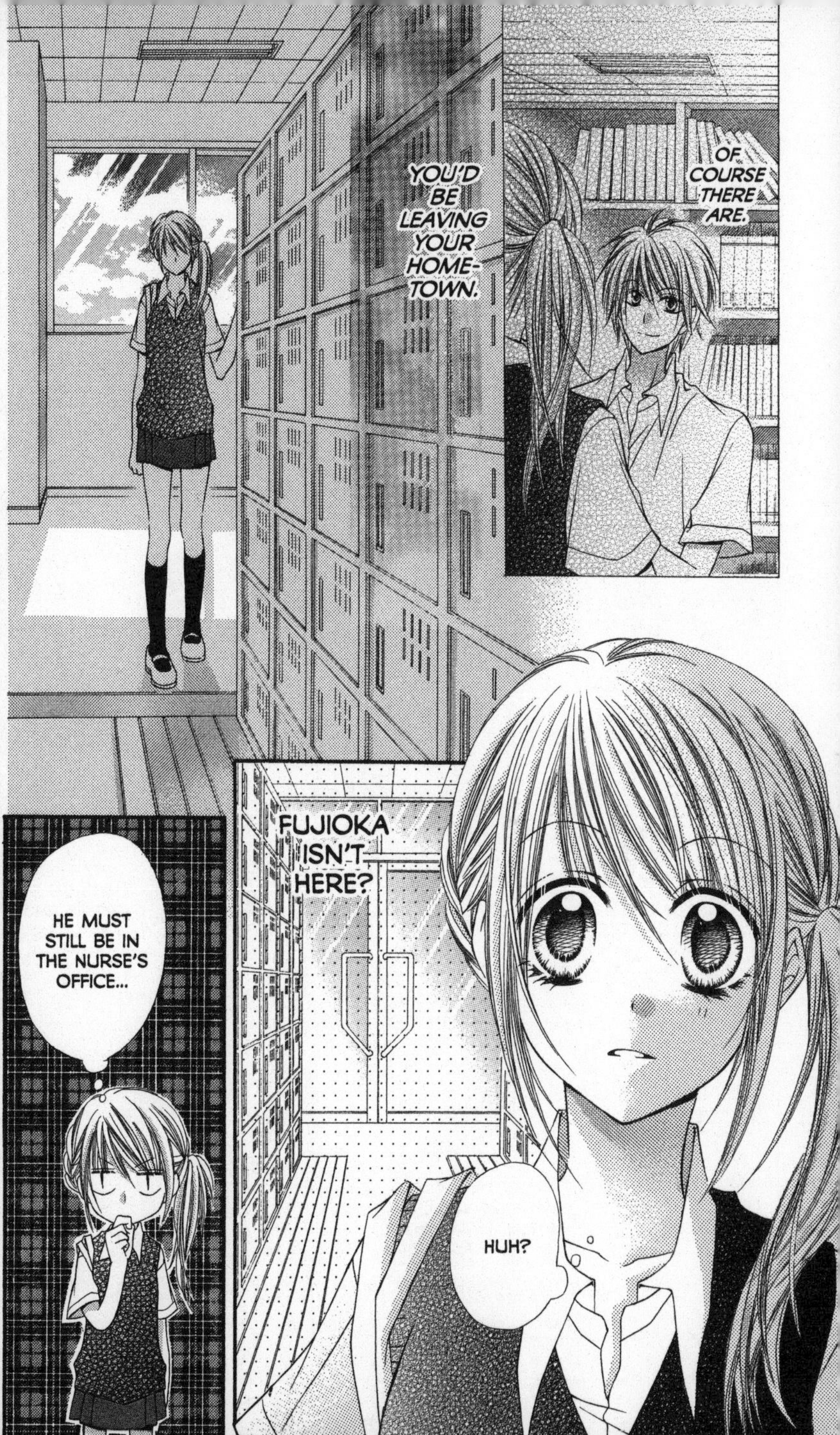
OF COURSE THERE ARE.
YOU'D BE LEAVING YOUR HOME-TOWN.
HUH?
FUJIOKA ISN'T HERE?
HE MUST STILL BE IN THE NURSE'S OFFICE...

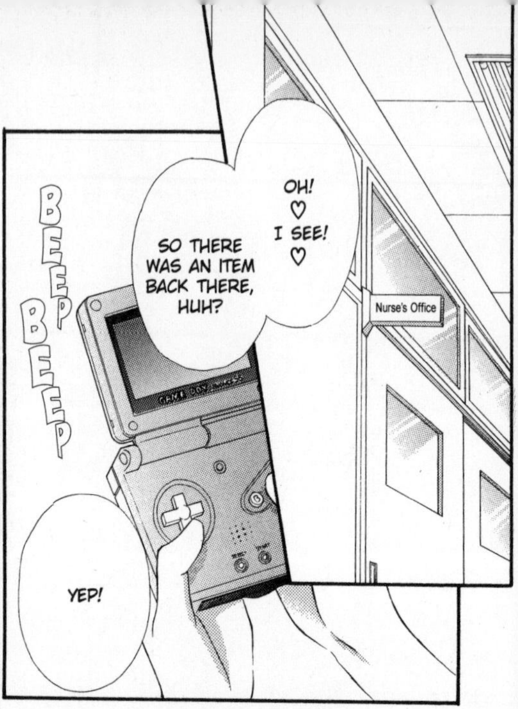
OH! ♡ I SEE! ♡
SO THERE WAS AN ITEM BACK THERE, HUH?
Nurse's Office
BEEP BEEP
YEP!

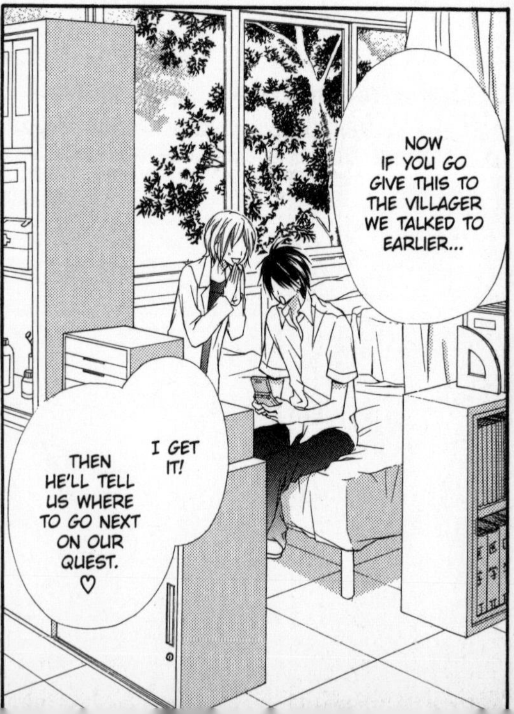
NOW IF YOU GO GIVE THIS TO THE VILLAGER WE TALKED TO EARLIER...
I GET IT!
THEN HE'LL TELL US WHERE TO GO NEXT ON OUR QUEST. ♡

2
two

1 In the first column, I mentioned I'd been "busy." What happened was that I was half-forced into going back home to celebrate Obon. My editor kindly told me, "Yes, go ahead back home and get good and rested! But also be sure to be good and finish the sidebars and bonus pages by the time you get back!" But somehow they're still not done a day before the deadline... What on earth was I doing all the time I was at my parents' house...?!

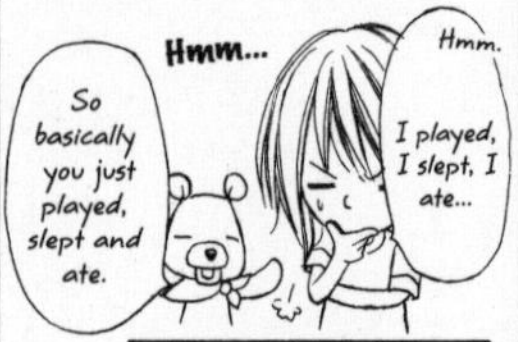
Hmm.
I played, I slept, I ate...
Hmm...
So basically you just played, slept and ate.

Bottom line:
She procrastinated.

Unsurprisingly.

Oh! I also got to play with fireworks for the first time in a long while! Though it was in the middle of a park in the dead of night. But you know, the park was surrounded by these dense woods and there were tons of bugs around. After just a few hours there, I had seven bug bites on me...

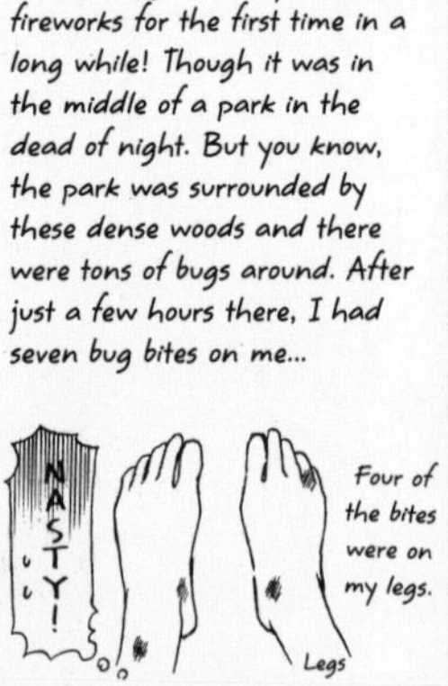
Four of the bites were on my legs.
Legs
NASTY!

And they're so itchy...

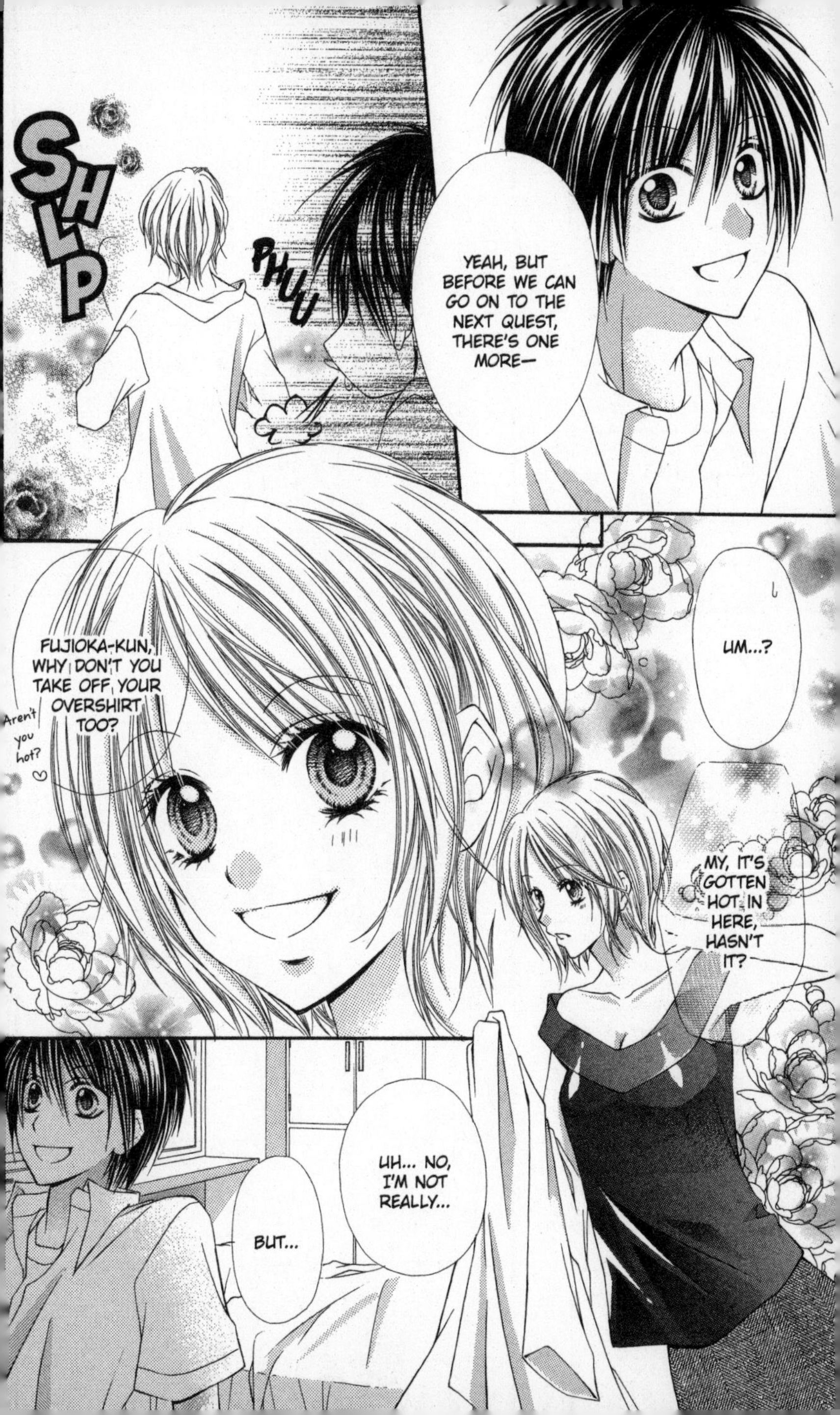
YEAH, BUT BEFORE WE CAN GO ON TO THE NEXT QUEST, THERE'S ONE MORE—
PHUU
SHLP
UM...?
MY, IT'S GOTTEN HOT IN HERE, HASN'T IT?
FUJIOKA-KUN, WHY DON'T YOU TAKE OFF YOUR OVERSHIRT TOO?
Aren't you hot?
UH... NO, I'M NOT REALLY...
BUT...

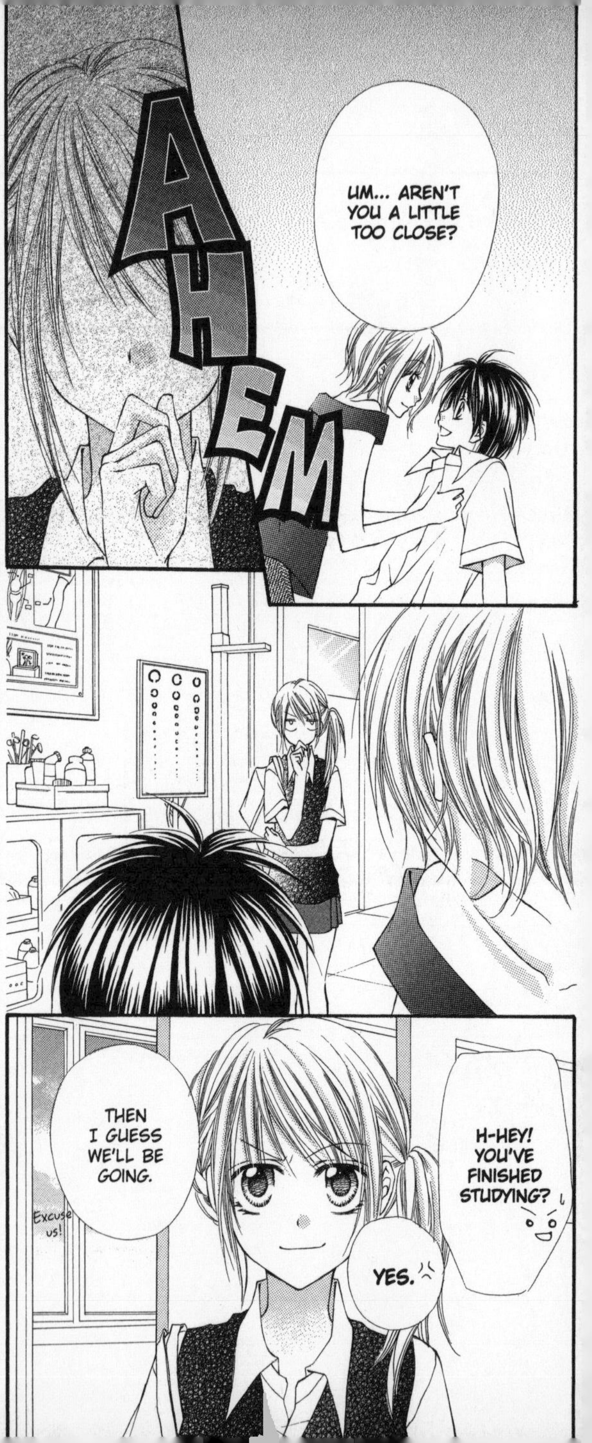
UM... AREN'T YOU A LITTLE TOO CLOSE?
AHEM
H-HEY! YOU'VE FINISHED STUDYING?
YES.
THEN I GUESS WE'LL BE GOING.
Excuse us!

3
three

While I was home, I also dug up a time capsule! But it isn't just any regular old time capsule that you open up again after a certain number of years and that's the end of it.

It's my friend from middle school C-chan's and my "Continuous Time Capsule."

① We place commemorative items and letters into the box.

↓

② We bury the box.

↓

③ 1 year later, we dig up the box.

↓

④ We take a look at what's inside then put it back in, plus new stuff.

↓

⑤ We dig it back up and open it again in one year's time.

Then that isn't really a time capsule, is it?

But it's still tons of fun, and that's the important thing. We've been doing it every year since our third year of middle school, so there's already quite a lot of history in that box. We've even got purikura of us from third year of middle school in there... So embarrassing. (laugh)

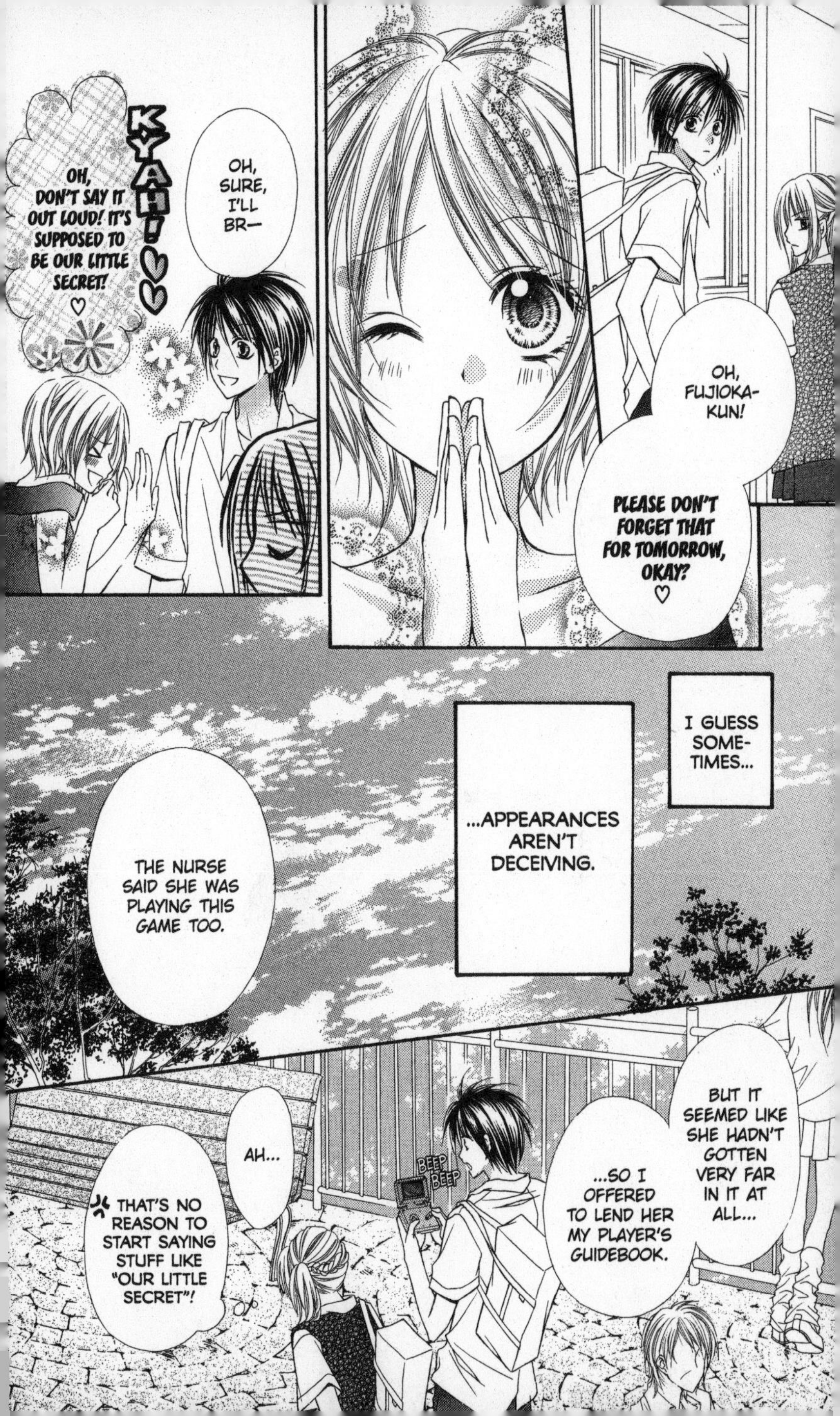
OH, FUJIOKA-KUN!
PLEASE DON'T FORGET THAT FOR TOMORROW, OKAY? ♡
OH, SURE, I'LL BR—
KYAH! ♥♥
OH, DON'T SAY IT OUT LOUD! IT'S SUPPOSED TO BE OUR LITTLE SECRET! ♡
I GUESS SOMETIMES...
...APPEARANCES AREN'T DECEIVING.
THE NURSE SAID SHE WAS PLAYING THIS GAME TOO.
BUT IT SEEMED LIKE SHE HADN'T GOTTEN VERY FAR IN IT AT ALL...
...SO I OFFERED TO LEND HER MY PLAYER'S GUIDEBOOK.
BEEP BEEP
AH...
THAT'S NO REASON TO START SAYING STUFF LIKE "OUR LITTLE SECRET"!

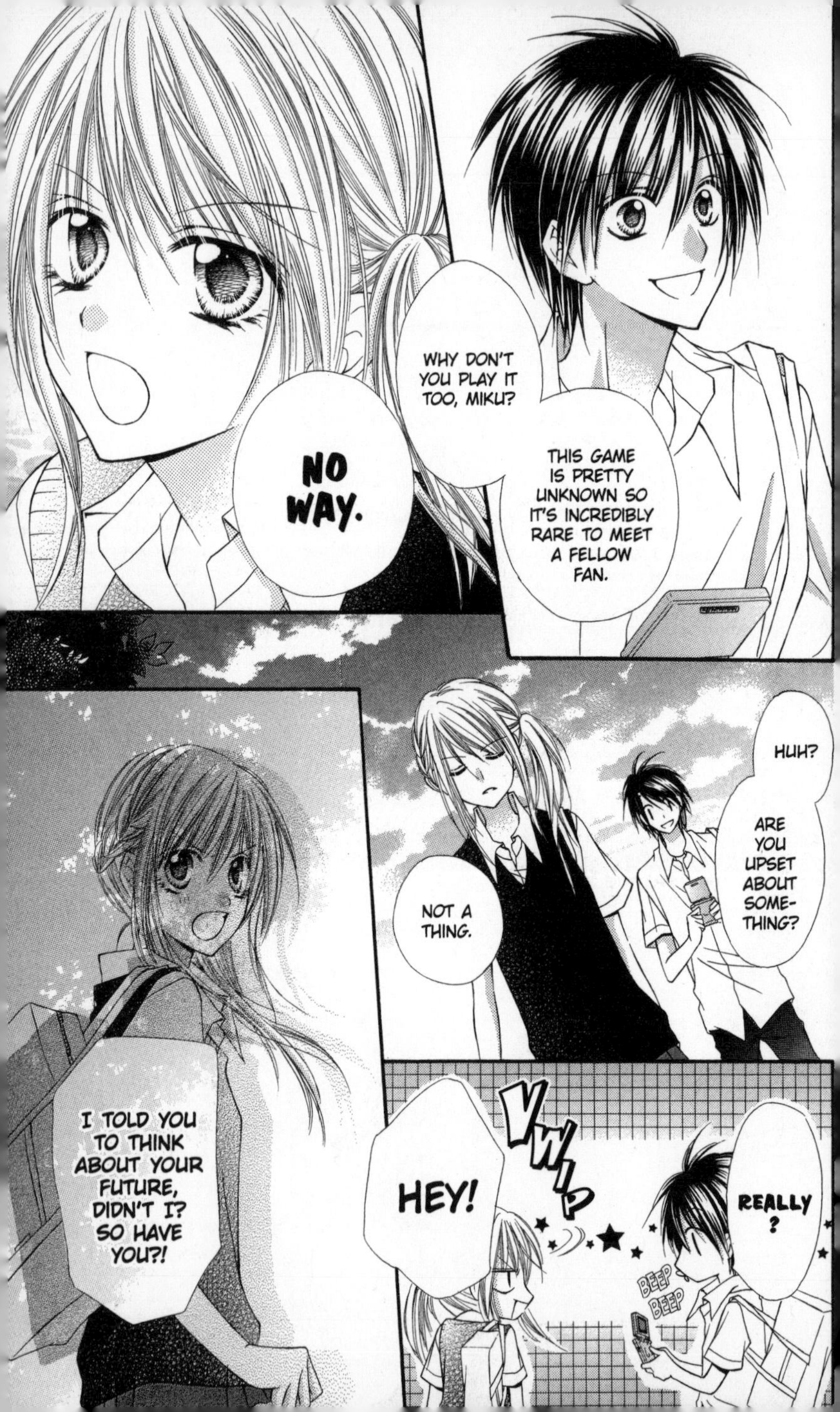
WHY DON'T YOU PLAY IT TOO, MIKU?
THIS GAME IS PRETTY UNKNOWN SO IT'S INCREDIBLY RARE TO MEET A FELLOW FAN.
NO WAY.
HUH?
ARE YOU UPSET ABOUT SOME-THING?
NOT A THING.
REALLY?
BEEP BEEP
VWIP
HEY!
I TOLD YOU TO THINK ABOUT YOUR FUTURE, DIDN'T I? SO HAVE YOU?!

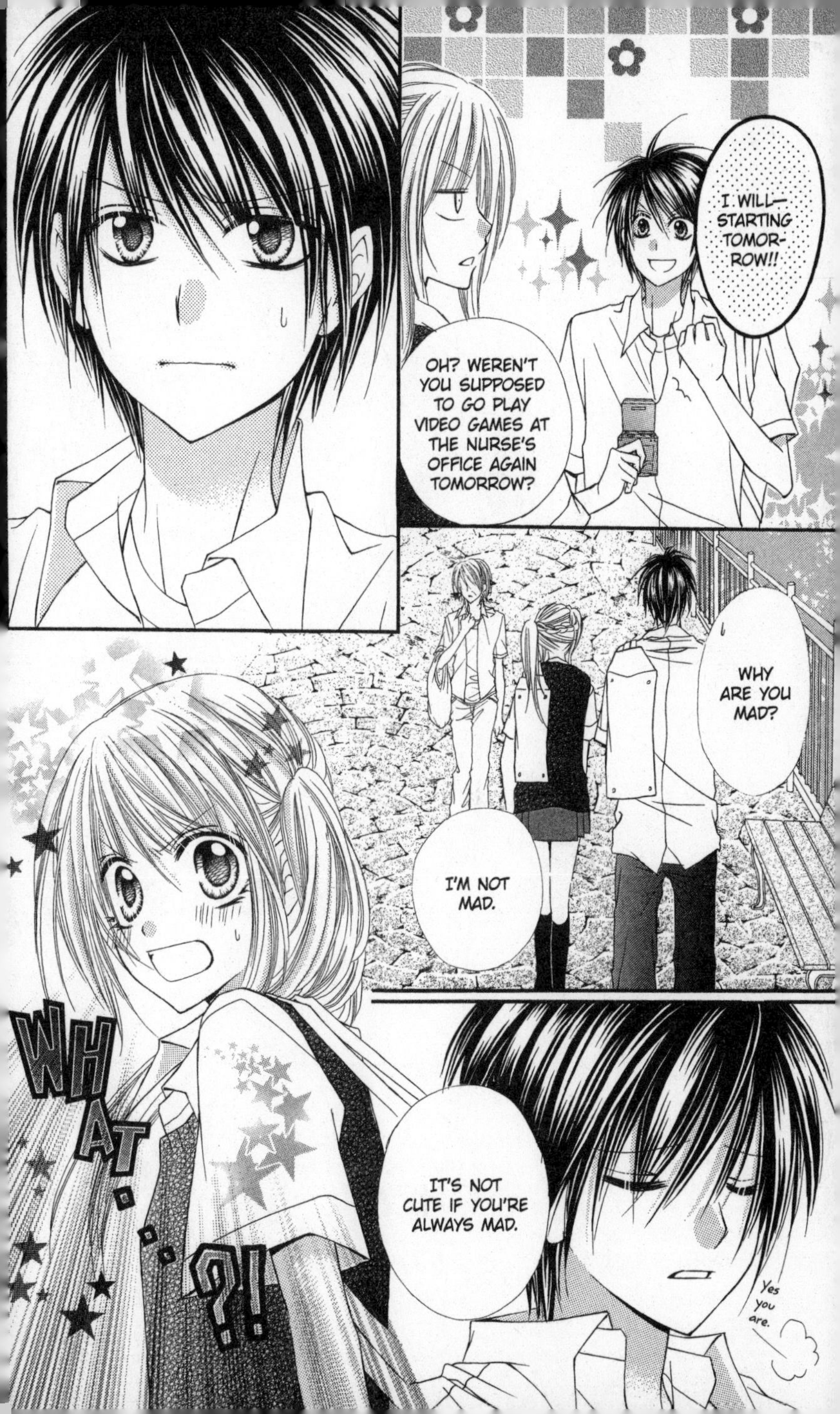
I WILL— STARTING TOMORROW!!
OH? WEREN'T YOU SUPPOSED TO GO PLAY VIDEO GAMES AT THE NURSE'S OFFICE AGAIN TOMORROW?
WHY ARE YOU MAD?
I'M NOT MAD.
Yes you are.
IT'S NOT CUTE IF YOU'RE ALWAYS MAD.
WHAT...?!

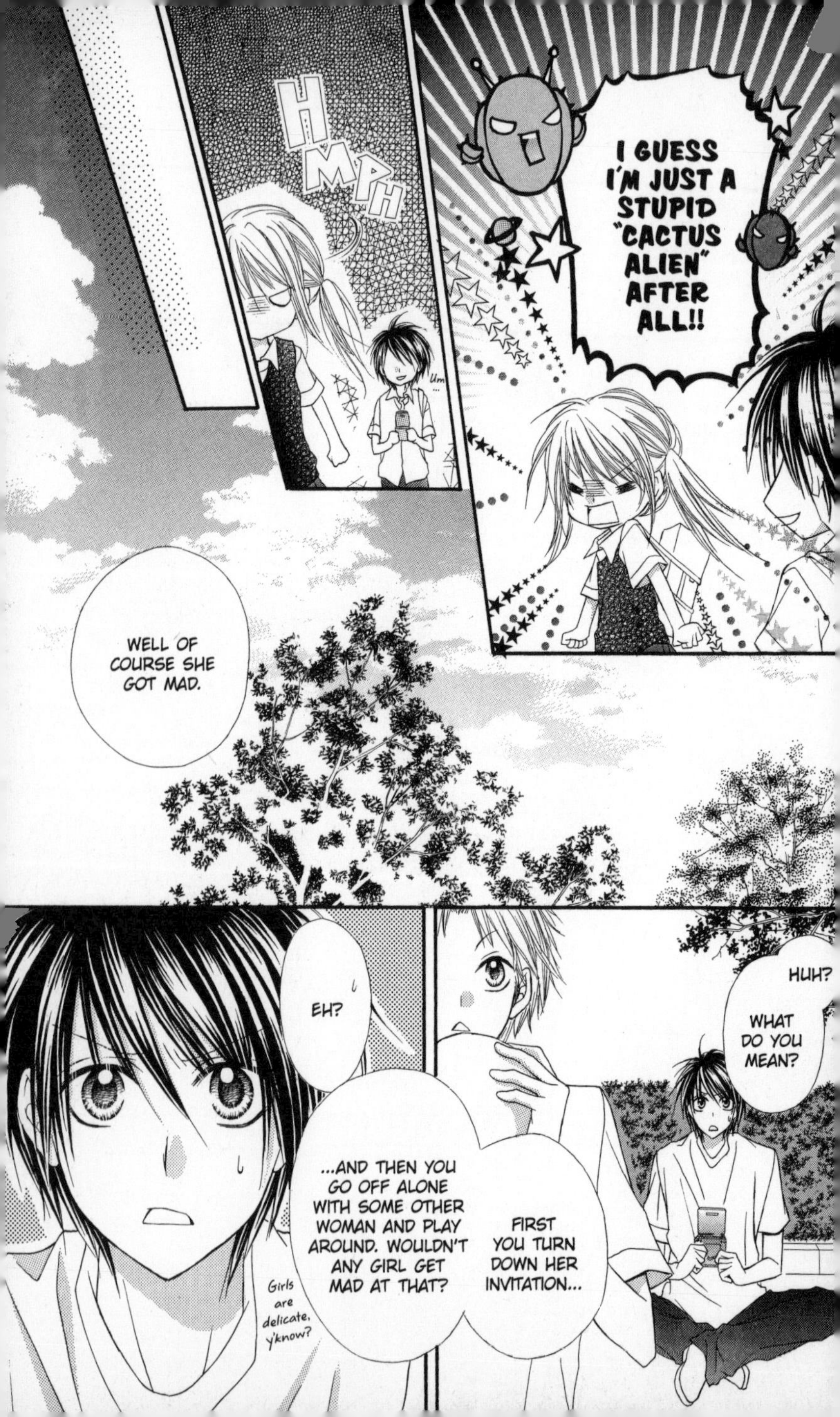
I GUESS I'M JUST A STUPID "CACTUS ALIEN" AFTER ALL!!
HMPH
Um...
WELL OF COURSE SHE GOT MAD.
HUH?
WHAT DO YOU MEAN?
FIRST YOU TURN DOWN HER INVITATION...
...AND THEN YOU GO OFF ALONE WITH SOME OTHER WOMAN AND PLAY AROUND. WOULDN'T ANY GIRL GET MAD AT THAT?
Girls are delicate, y'know?
EH?

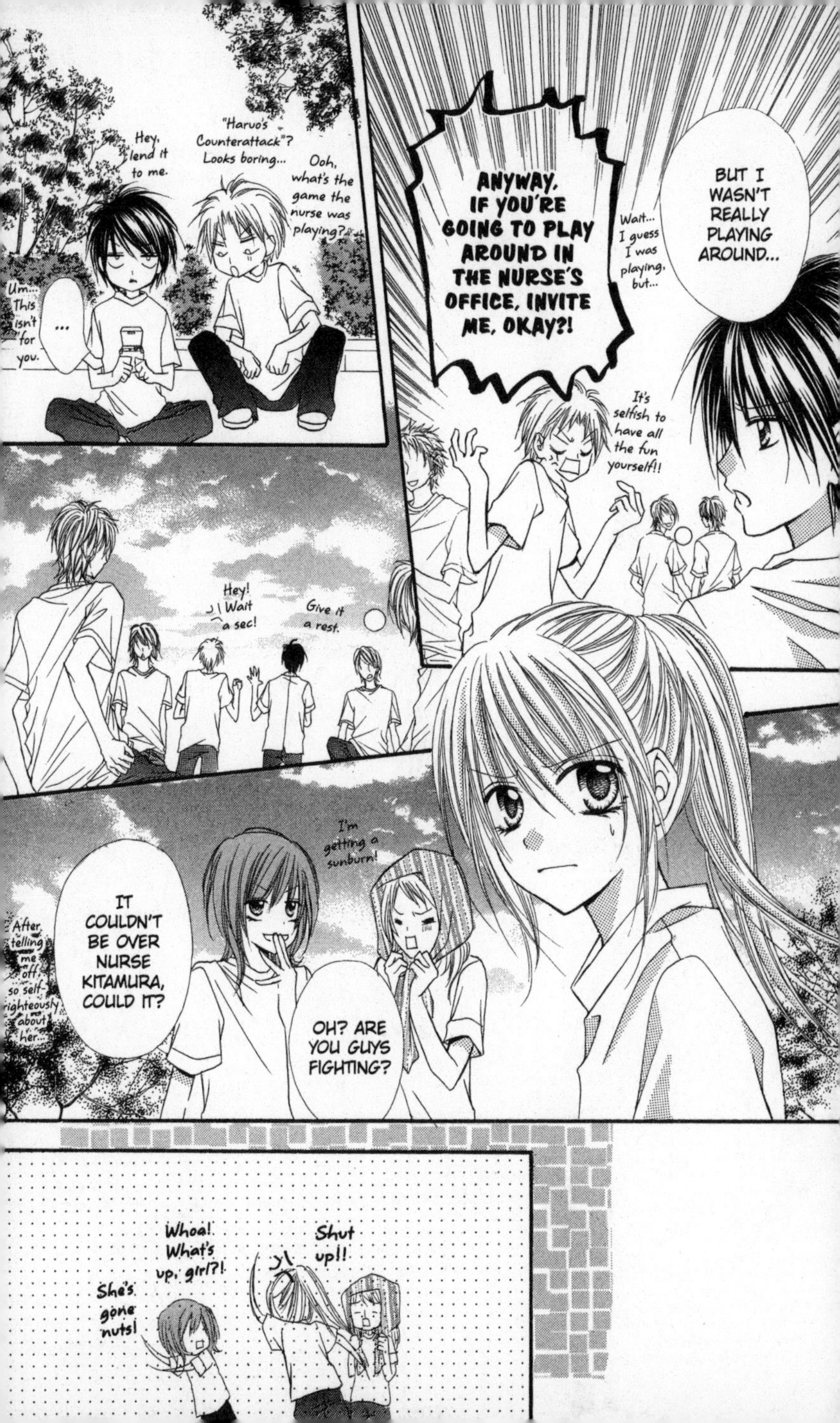

BUT I WASN'T REALLY PLAYING AROUND...
Wait... I guess I was playing, but...
ANYWAY, IF YOU'RE GOING TO PLAY AROUND IN THE NURSE'S OFFICE, INVITE ME, OKAY?!
It's selfish to have all the fun yourself!!
Ooh, what's the game the nurse was playing?
"Haruo's Counterattack"? Looks boring...
Hey, lend it to me.
...
Um... This isn't for you.
Give it a rest.
Hey! Wait a sec!
I'm getting a sunburn!
OH? ARE YOU GUYS FIGHTING?
IT COULDN'T BE OVER NURSE KITAMURA, COULD IT?
After telling me off so self-righteously about her...
Shut up!!
Whoa! What's up, girl?!
She's gone nuts!

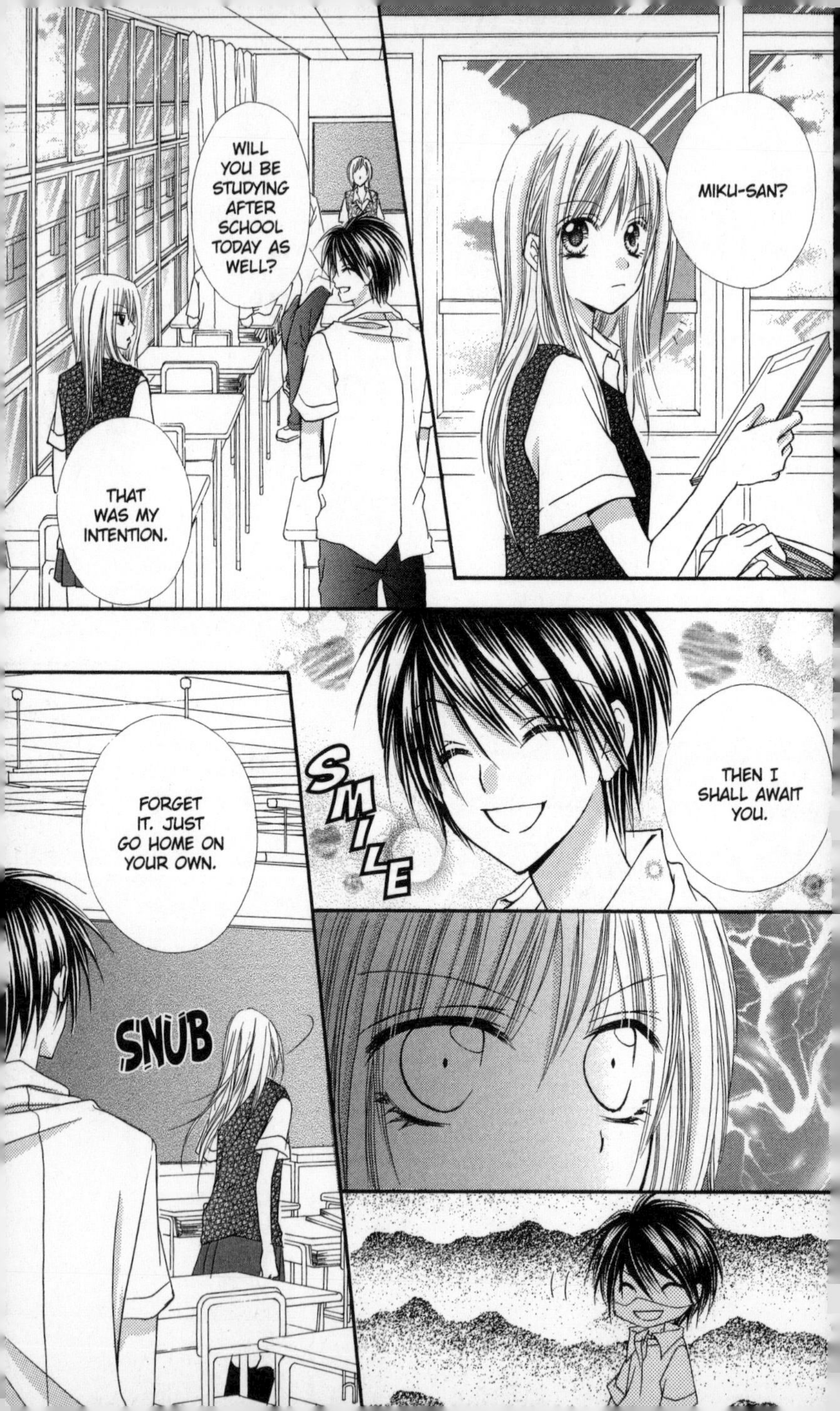
MIKU-SAN?
WILL YOU BE STUDYING AFTER SCHOOL TODAY AS WELL?
THAT WAS MY INTENTION.
SMILE
THEN I SHALL AWAIT YOU.
FORGET IT. JUST GO HOME ON YOUR OWN.
SNUB

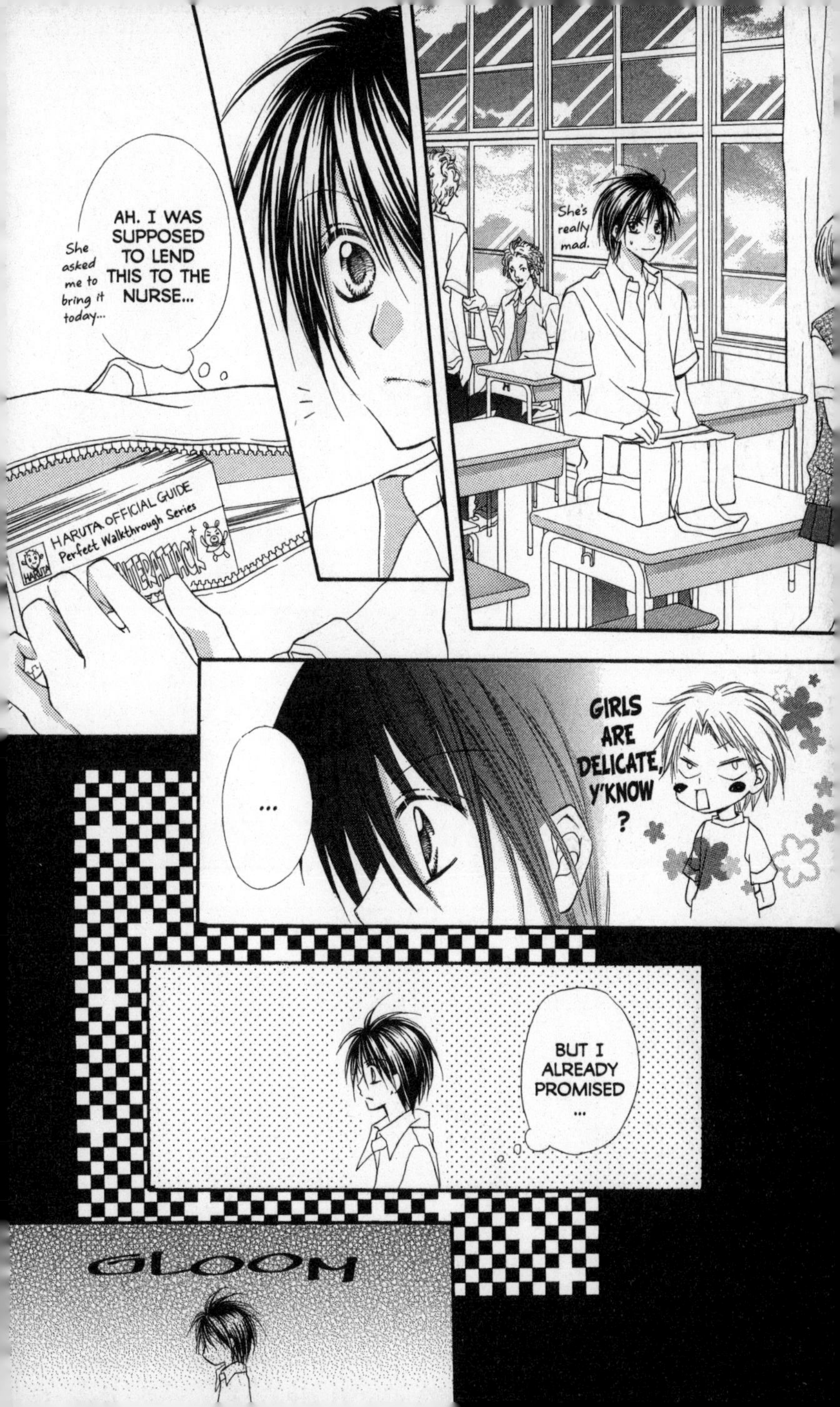
She's really mad.
She asked me to bring it today...
AH. I WAS SUPPOSED TO LEND THIS TO THE NURSE...
HARUTA OFFICIAL GUIDE
Perfect Walkthrough Series
HARUTA
GIRLS ARE DELICATE, Y'KNOW ?
...
BUT I ALREADY PROMISED ...
GLOOM

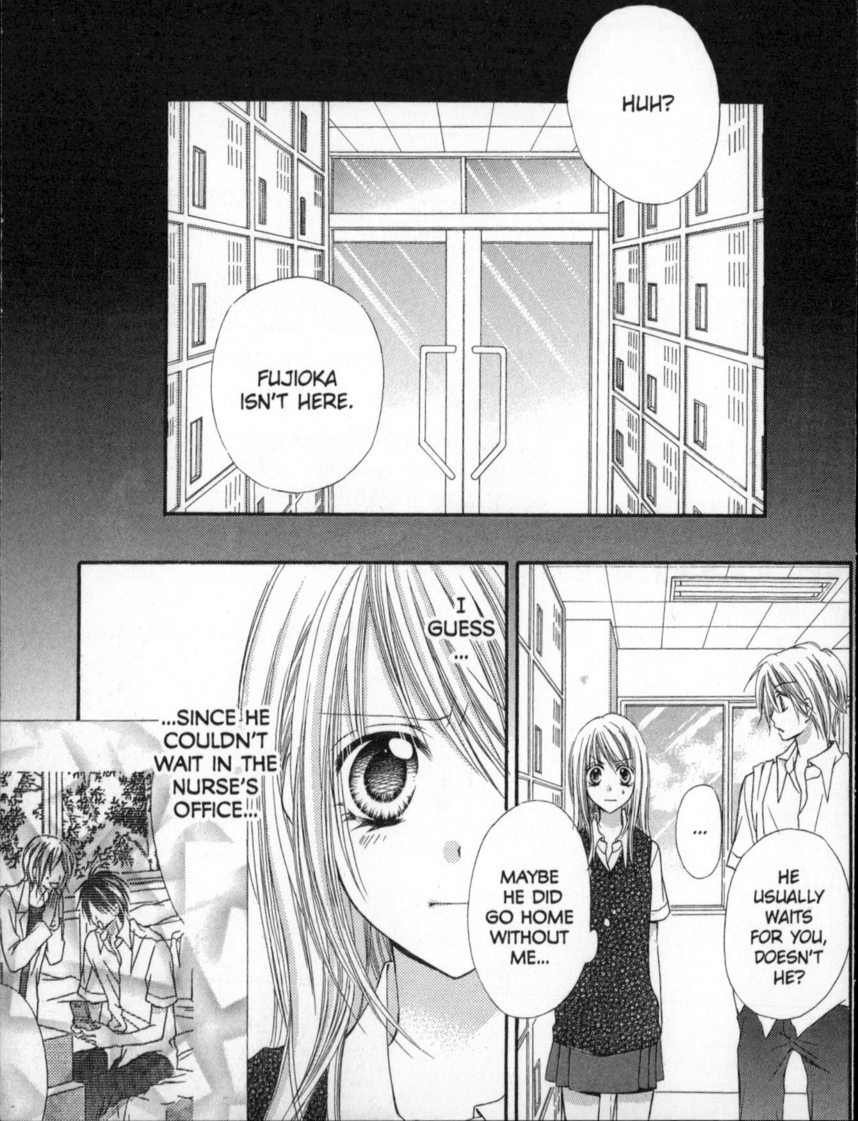
HUH?
FUJIOKA ISN'T HERE.
...
HE USUALLY WAITS FOR YOU, DOESN'T HE?
MAYBE HE DID GO HOME WITHOUT ME...
I GUESS...
...SINCE HE COULDN'T WAIT IN THE NURSE'S OFFICE...

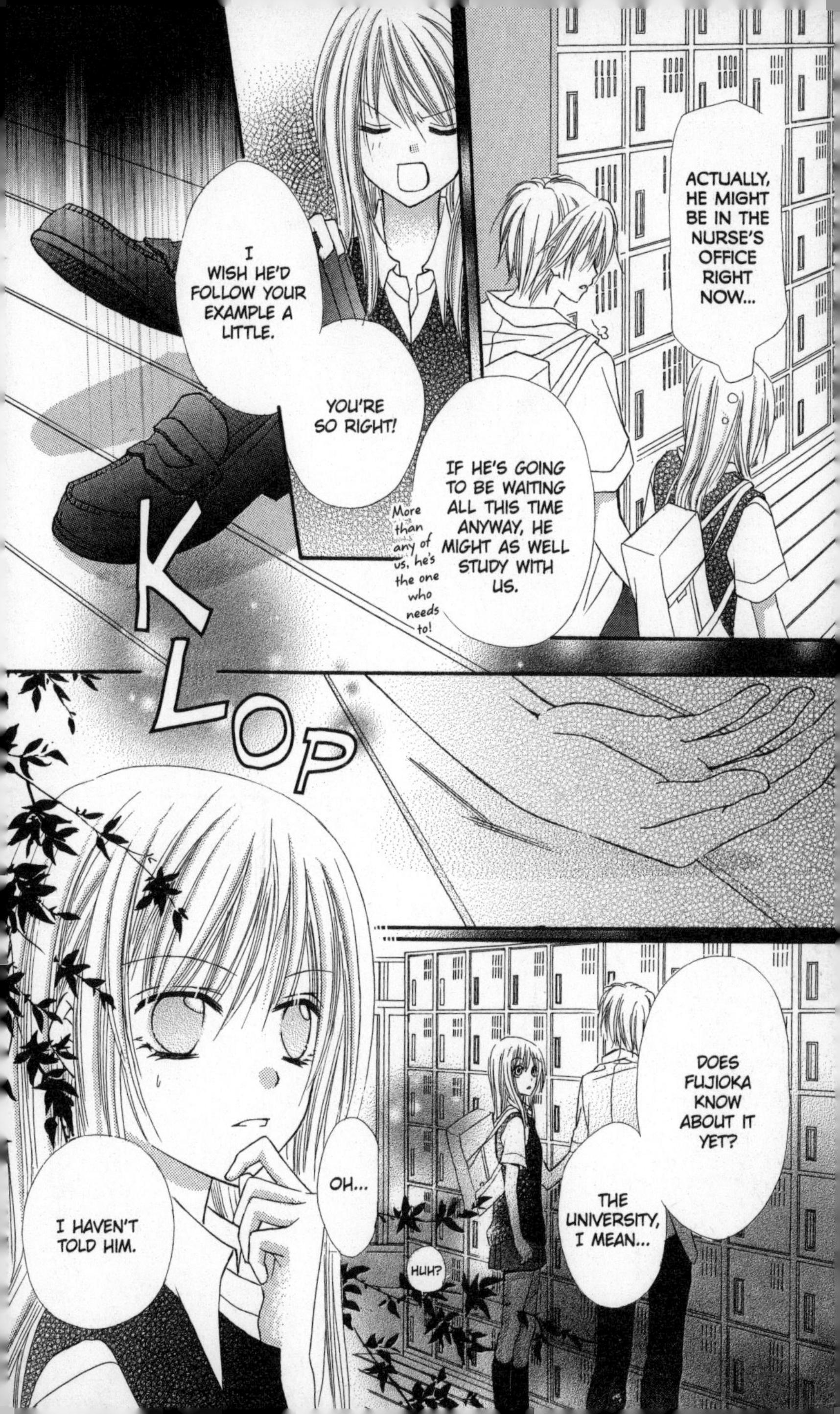
ACTUALLY, HE MIGHT BE IN THE NURSE'S OFFICE RIGHT NOW...
I WISH HE'D FOLLOW YOUR EXAMPLE A LITTLE.
YOU'RE SO RIGHT!
IF HE'S GOING TO BE WAITING ALL THIS TIME ANYWAY, HE MIGHT AS WELL STUDY WITH US.
More than any of us, he's the one who needs to!
KLOP
DOES FUJIOKA KNOW ABOUT IT YET?
THE UNIVERSITY, I MEAN...
HUH?
OH...
I HAVEN'T TOLD HIM.

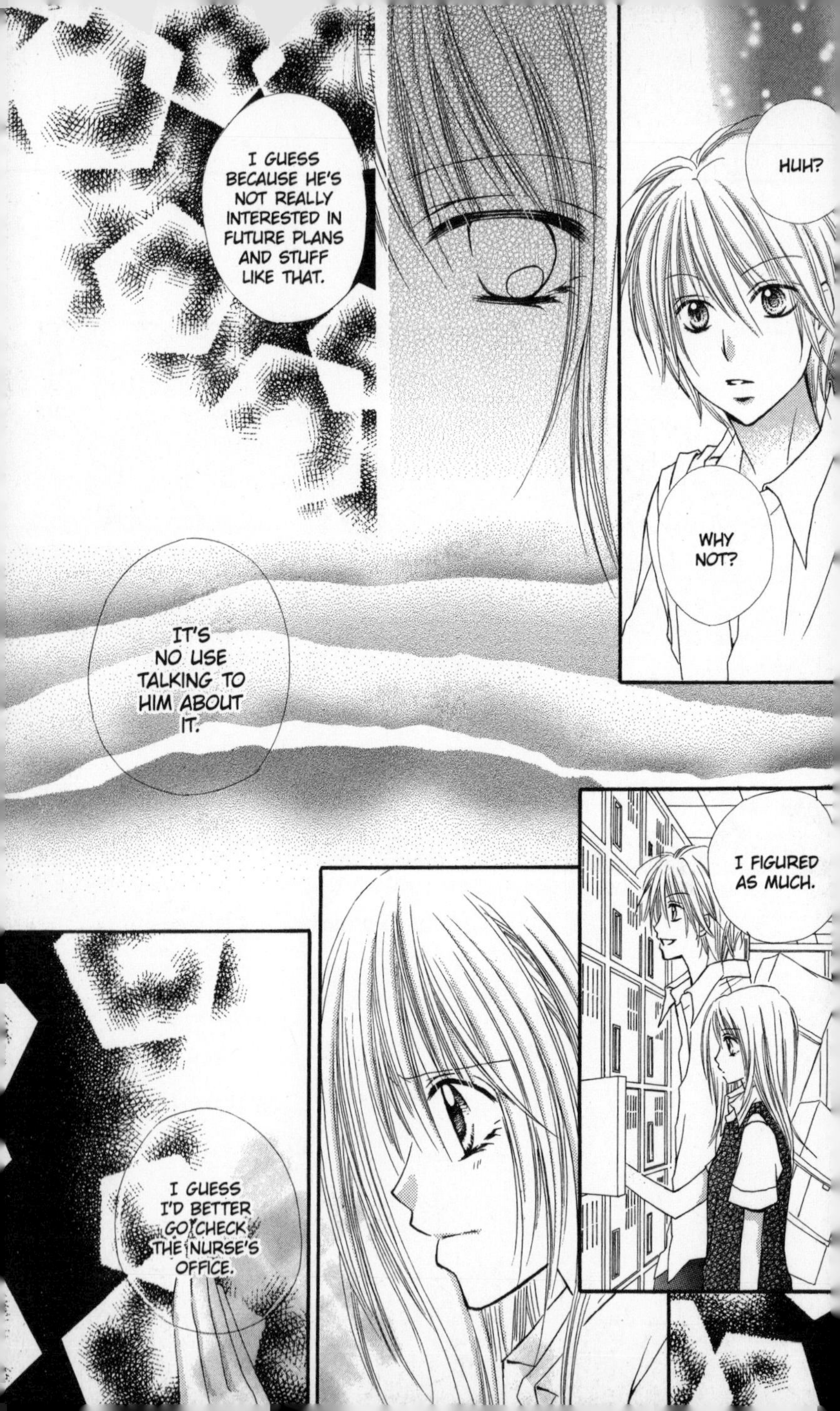
HUH?
WHY NOT?
I GUESS BECAUSE HE'S NOT REALLY INTERESTED IN FUTURE PLANS AND STUFF LIKE THAT.
IT'S NO USE TALKING TO HIM ABOUT IT.
I FIGURED AS MUCH.
I GUESS I'D BETTER GO CHECK THE NURSE'S OFFICE.

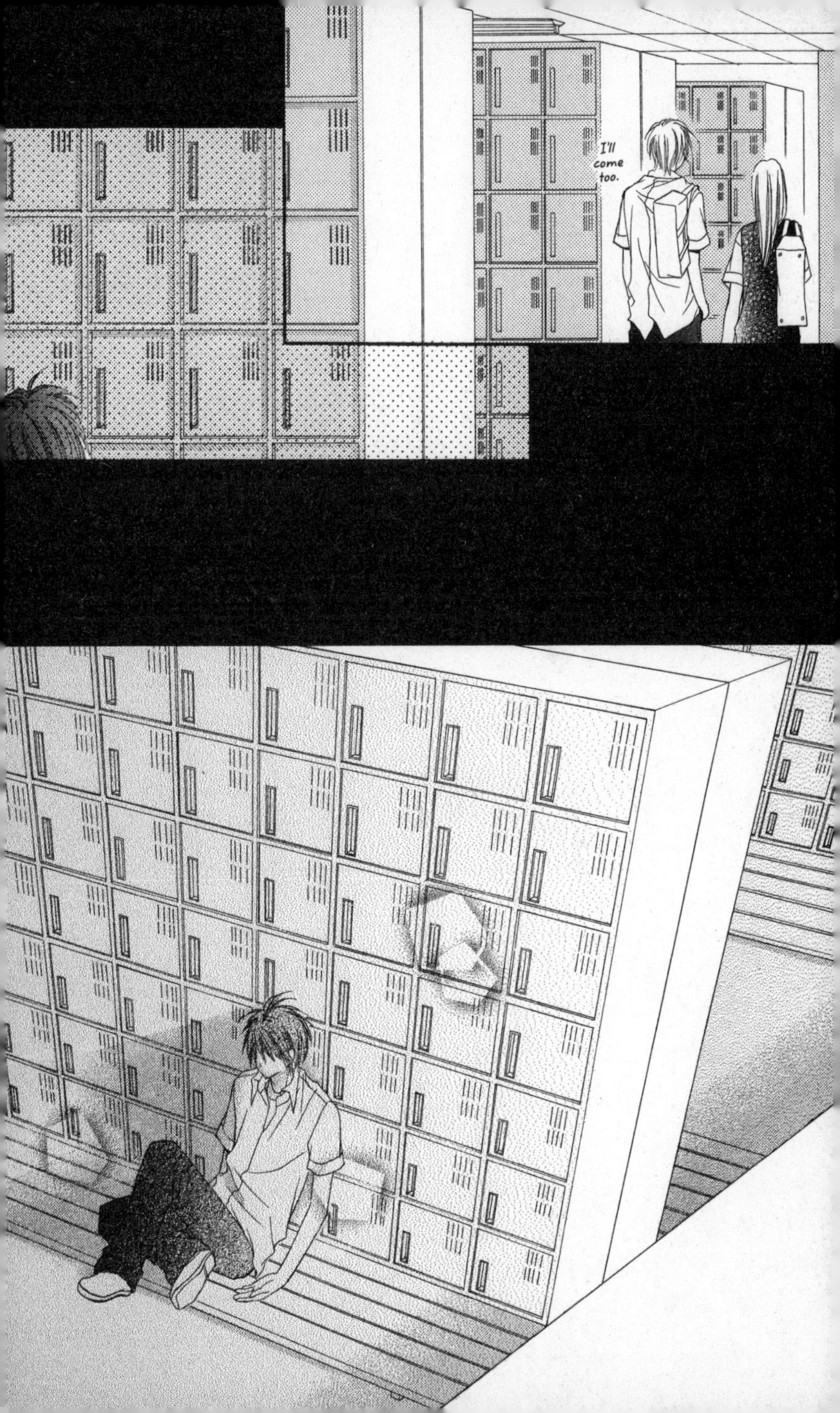
I'll come too.

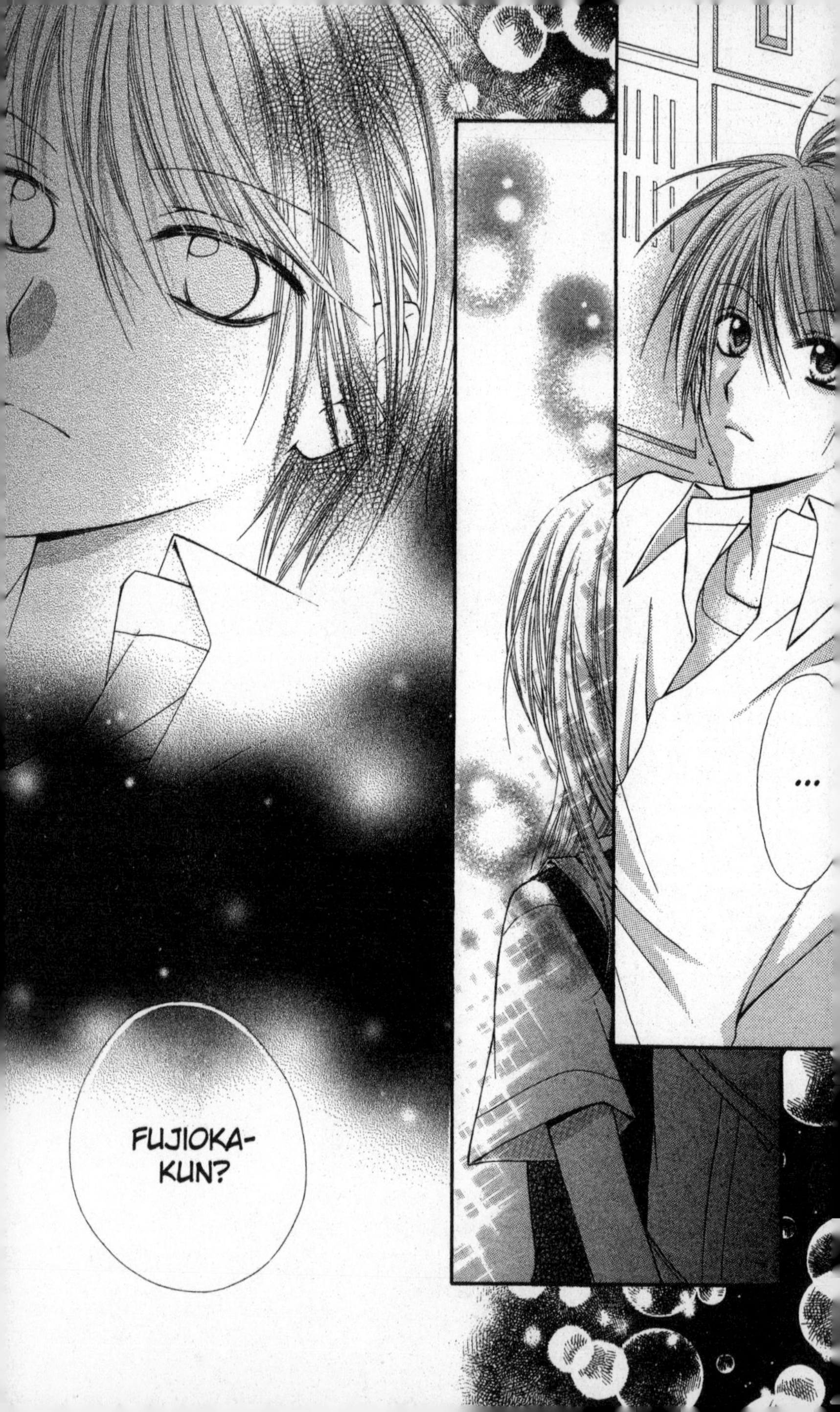
...
FUJIOKA-KUN?

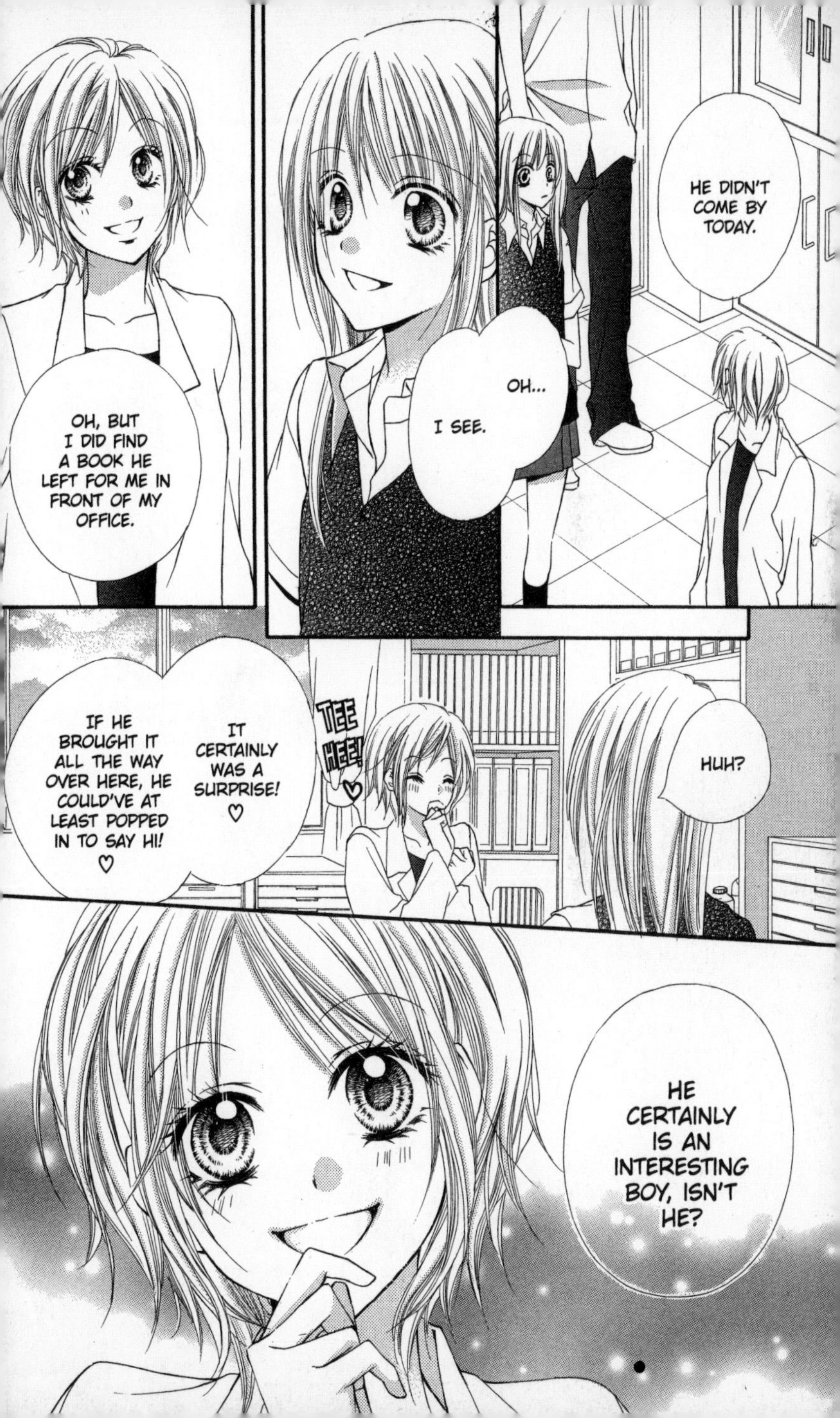
HE DIDN'T COME BY TODAY.
OH... I SEE.
OH, BUT I DID FIND A BOOK HE LEFT FOR ME IN FRONT OF MY OFFICE.
HUH?
TEE HEE! ♡
IT CERTAINLY WAS A SURPRISE! ♡
IF HE BROUGHT IT ALL THE WAY OVER HERE, HE COULD'VE AT LEAST POPPED IN TO SAY HI! ♡
HE CERTAINLY IS AN INTERESTING BOY, ISN'T HE?

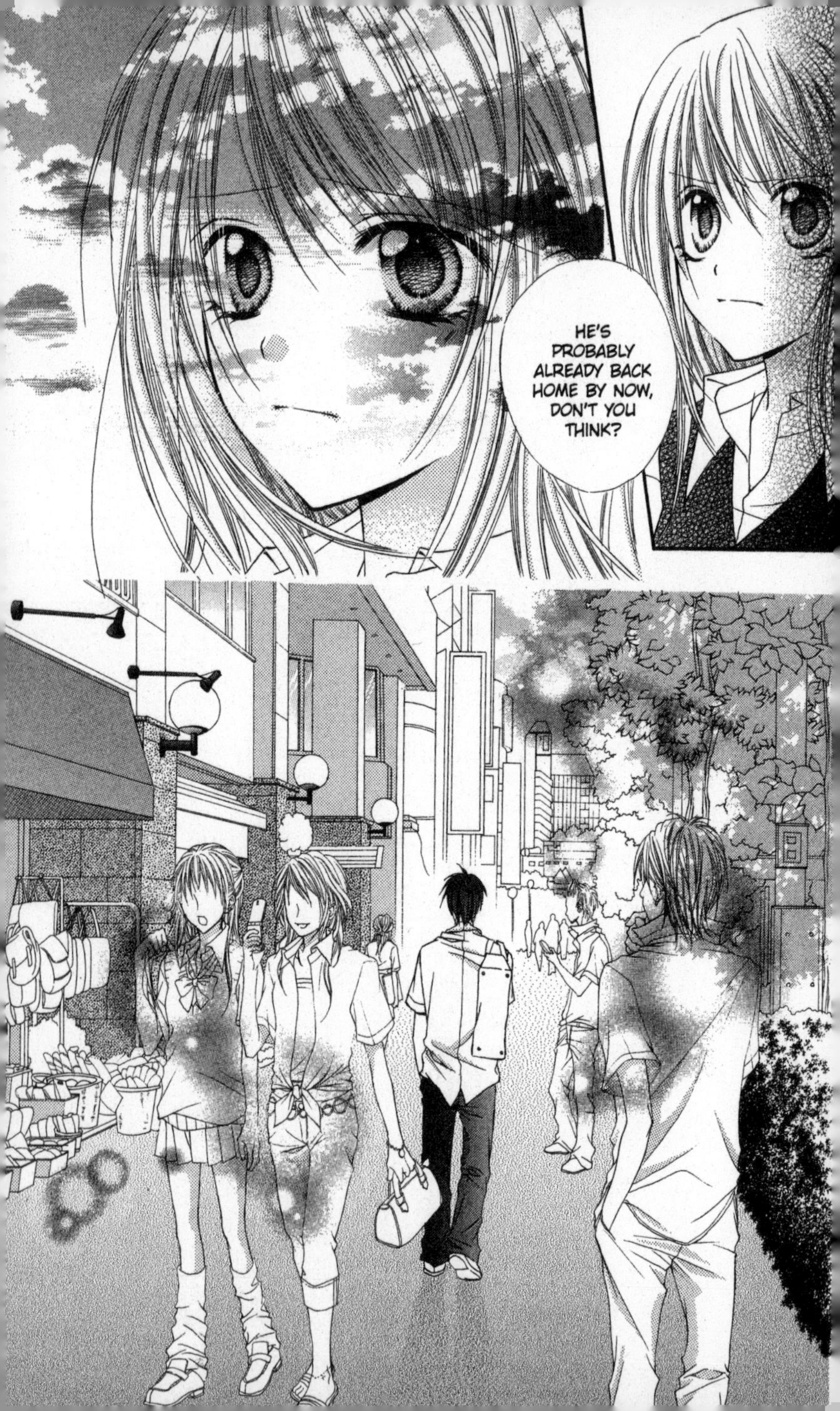
HE'S PROBABLY ALREADY BACK HOME BY NOW, DON'T YOU THINK?

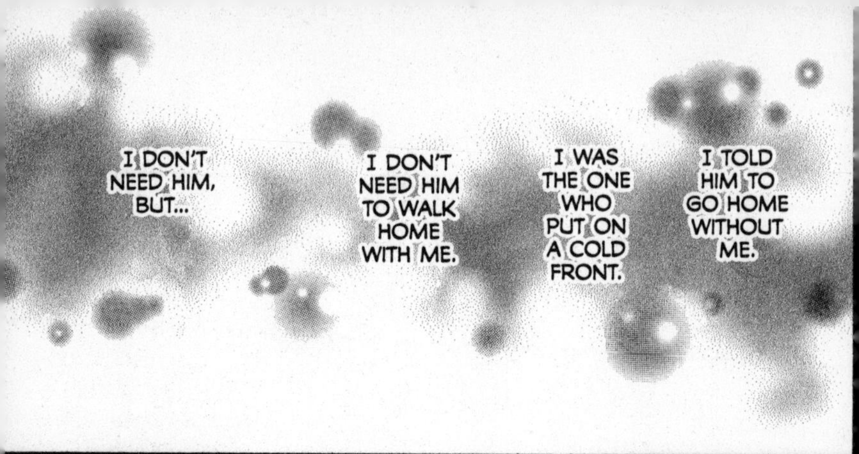
I TOLD HIM TO GO HOME WITHOUT ME.
I WAS THE ONE WHO PUT ON A COLD FRONT.
I DON'T NEED HIM TO WALK HOME WITH ME.
I DON'T NEED HIM, BUT...

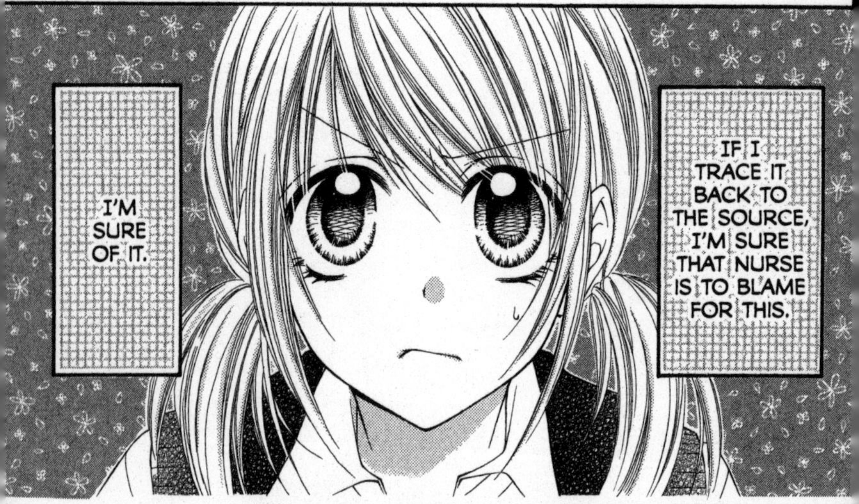
IF I TRACE IT BACK TO THE SOURCE, I'M SURE THAT NURSE IS TO BLAME FOR THIS.
I'M SURE OF IT.

SMALL TALK ②

Ah, Natsukawa-kun. He's utterly charming to the very end. Though he ended up being demoted to a mere gag character, I really enjoyed drawing him. My soul rejoices for these "charming type" characters.

I'm not sure where this came from, but my editor suddenly told me one day, "Natsukawa-kun is totally with Tomo-chan (the nurse), isn't he?"¿I was so surprised—it's quite a nice memory now. (laugh) But why?! Yet the idea really appealed to me. I wish I could've drawn that!

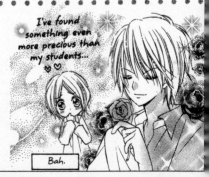

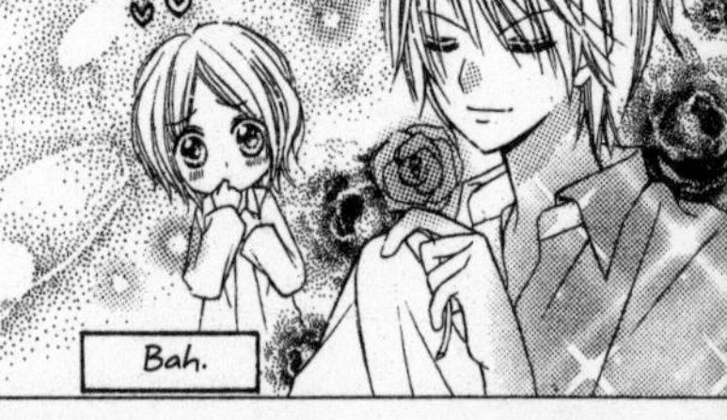
I've found something even more precious than my students... ♡♡
Bah.

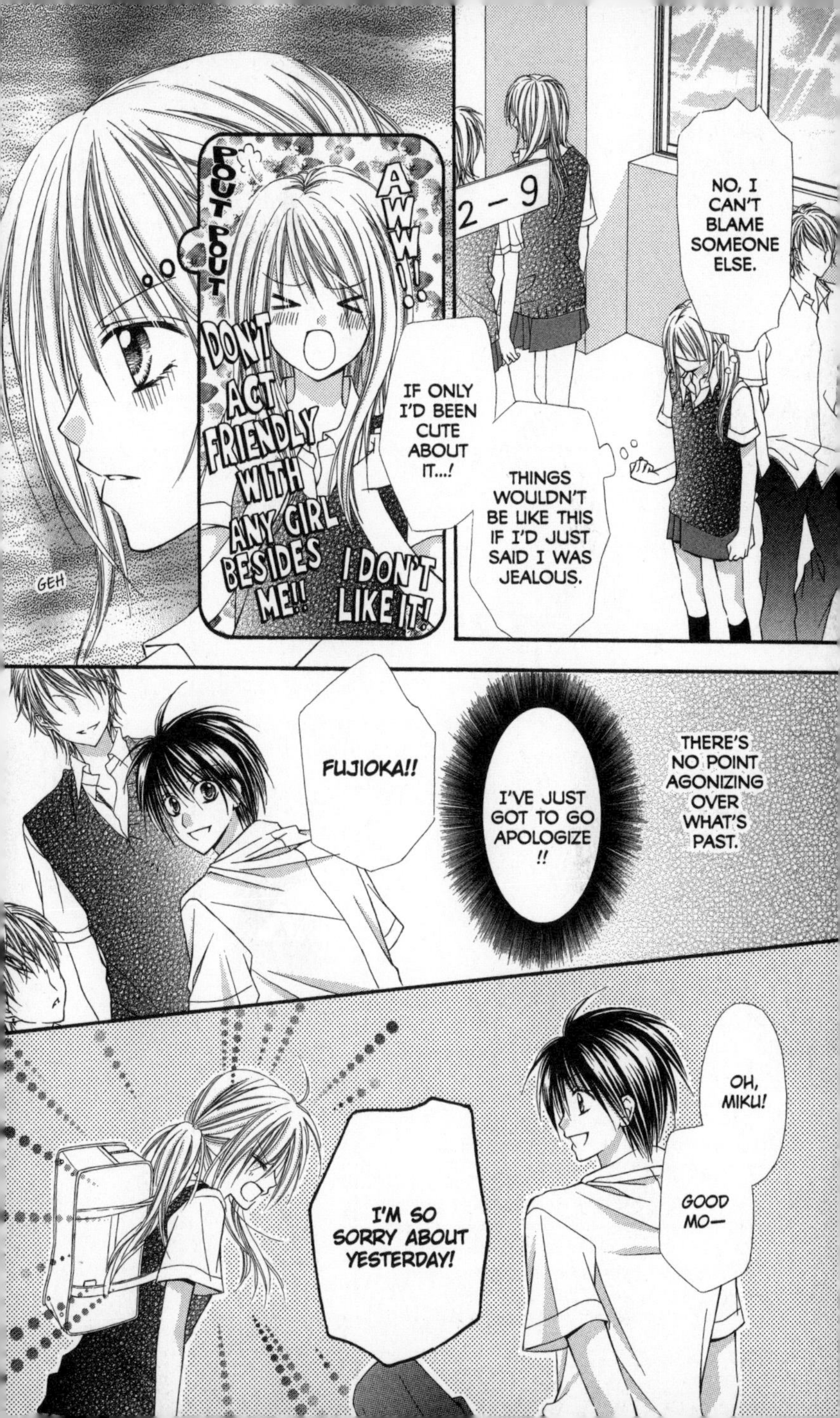
2-9
NO, I CAN'T BLAME SOMEONE ELSE.
THINGS WOULDN'T BE LIKE THIS IF I'D JUST SAID I WAS JEALOUS.
IF ONLY I'D BEEN CUTE ABOUT IT...!
AWW!!
POUT POUT
DON'T ACT FRIENDLY WITH ANY GIRL BESIDES ME!!
I DON'T LIKE IT!
GEH
THERE'S NO POINT AGONIZING OVER WHAT'S PAST.
I'VE JUST GOT TO GO APOLOGIZE!!
FUJIOKA!!
OH, MIKU!
GOOD MO—
I'M SO SORRY ABOUT YESTERDAY!

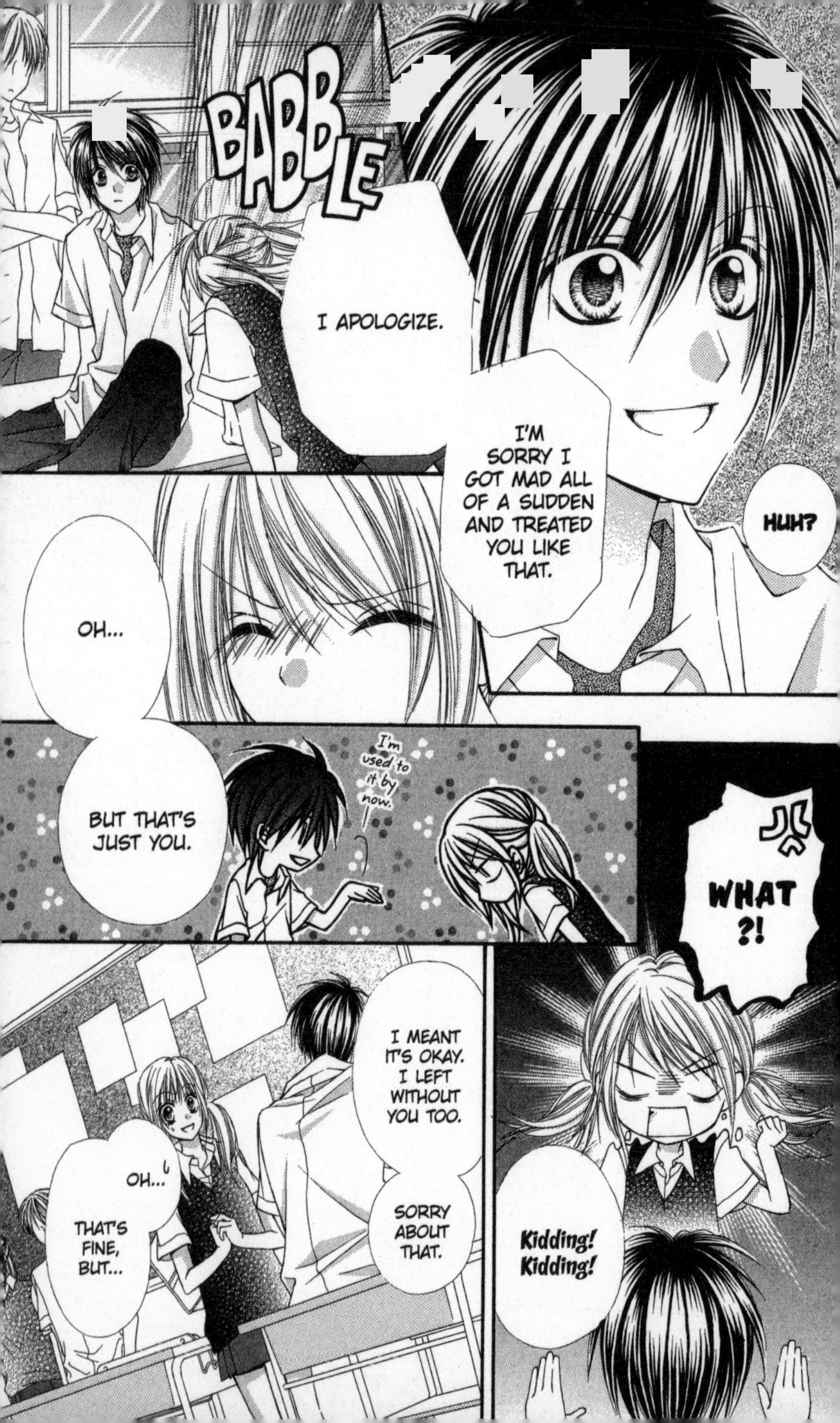

BABBLE
I APOLOGIZE.
I'M SORRY I GOT MAD ALL OF A SUDDEN AND TREATED YOU LIKE THAT.
HUH?
OH...
BUT THAT'S JUST YOU.
I'm used to it by now.
WHAT ?!
Kidding! Kidding!
I MEANT IT'S OKAY. I LEFT WITHOUT YOU TOO.
SORRY ABOUT THAT.
OH...
THAT'S FINE, BUT...

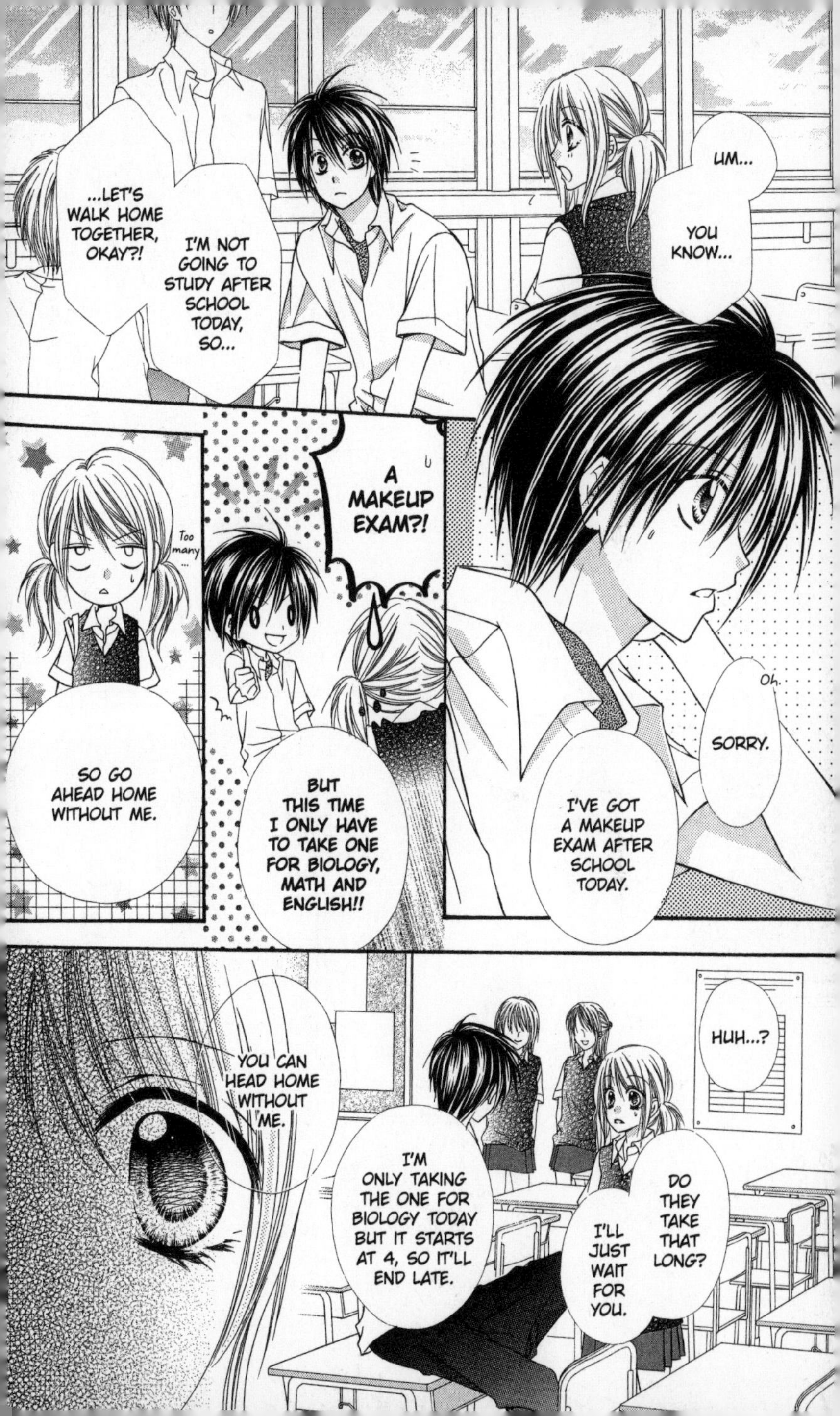
UM...
YOU KNOW...
I'M NOT GOING TO STUDY AFTER SCHOOL TODAY, SO...
...LET'S WALK HOME TOGETHER, OKAY?!
Oh.
SORRY.
I'VE GOT A MAKEUP EXAM AFTER SCHOOL TODAY.
A MAKEUP EXAM?!
BUT THIS TIME I ONLY HAVE TO TAKE ONE FOR BIOLOGY, MATH AND ENGLISH!!
Too many...
SO GO AHEAD HOME WITHOUT ME.
HUH...?
DO THEY TAKE THAT LONG?
I'LL JUST WAIT FOR YOU.
I'M ONLY TAKING THE ONE FOR BIOLOGY TODAY BUT IT STARTS AT 4, SO IT'LL END LATE.
YOU CAN HEAD HOME WITHOUT ME.

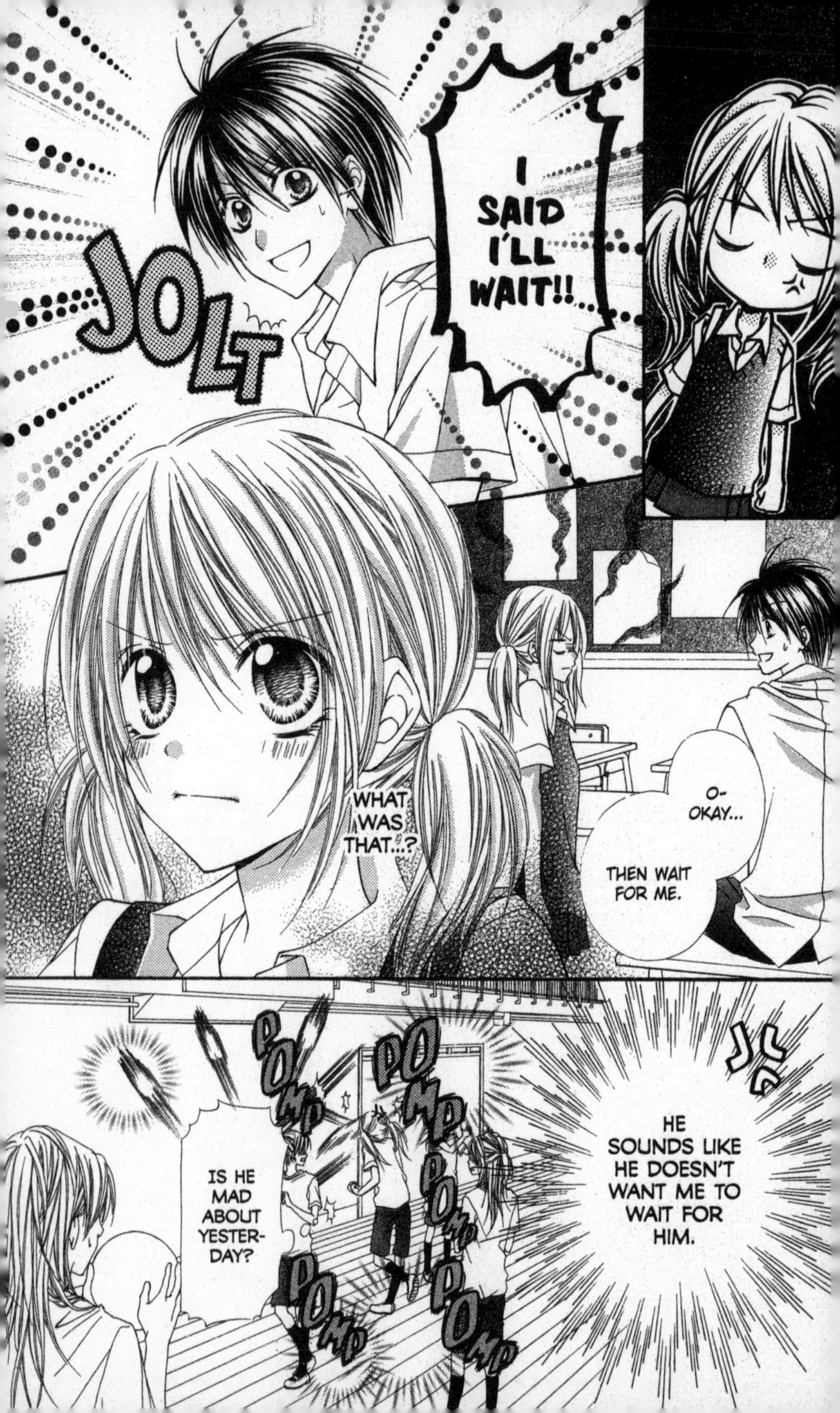
I SAID I'LL WAIT!!...
JOLT
O-OKAY...
THEN WAIT FOR ME.
WHAT WAS THAT...?
HE SOUNDS LIKE HE DOESN'T WANT ME TO WAIT FOR HIM.
POMP POMP POMP POMP
IS HE MAD ABOUT YESTER-DAY?

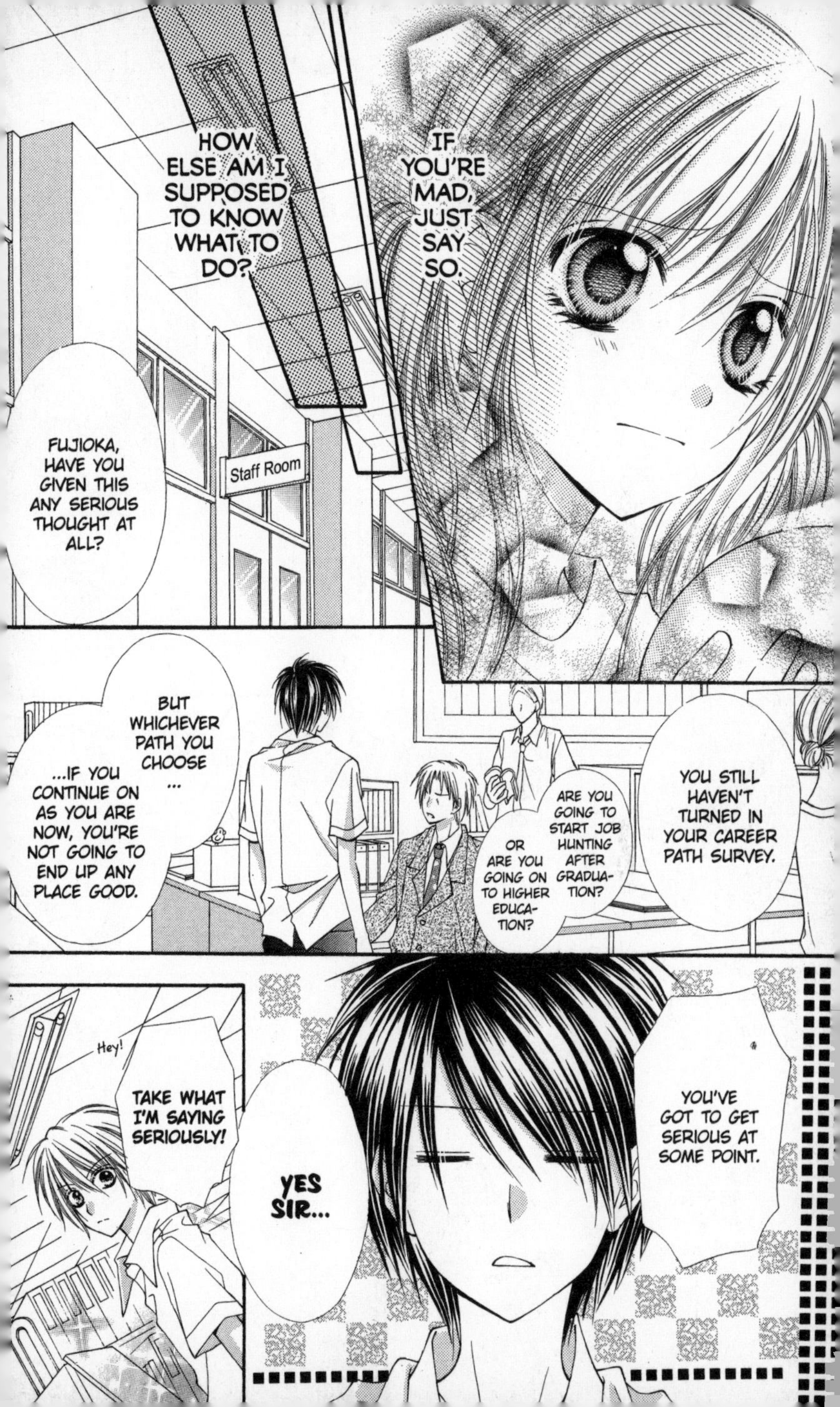
IF YOU'RE MAD, JUST SAY SO.
HOW ELSE AM I SUPPOSED TO KNOW WHAT TO DO?
Staff Room
FUJIOKA, HAVE YOU GIVEN THIS ANY SERIOUS THOUGHT AT ALL?
YOU STILL HAVEN'T TURNED IN YOUR CAREER PATH SURVEY.
ARE YOU GOING TO START JOB HUNTING AFTER GRADUATION?
OR ARE YOU GOING ON TO HIGHER EDUCATION?
BUT WHICHEVER PATH YOU CHOOSE...
...IF YOU CONTINUE ON AS YOU ARE NOW, YOU'RE NOT GOING TO END UP ANY PLACE GOOD.
YOU'VE GOT TO GET SERIOUS AT SOME POINT.
YES SIR...
TAKE WHAT I'M SAYING SERIOUSLY!
Hey!

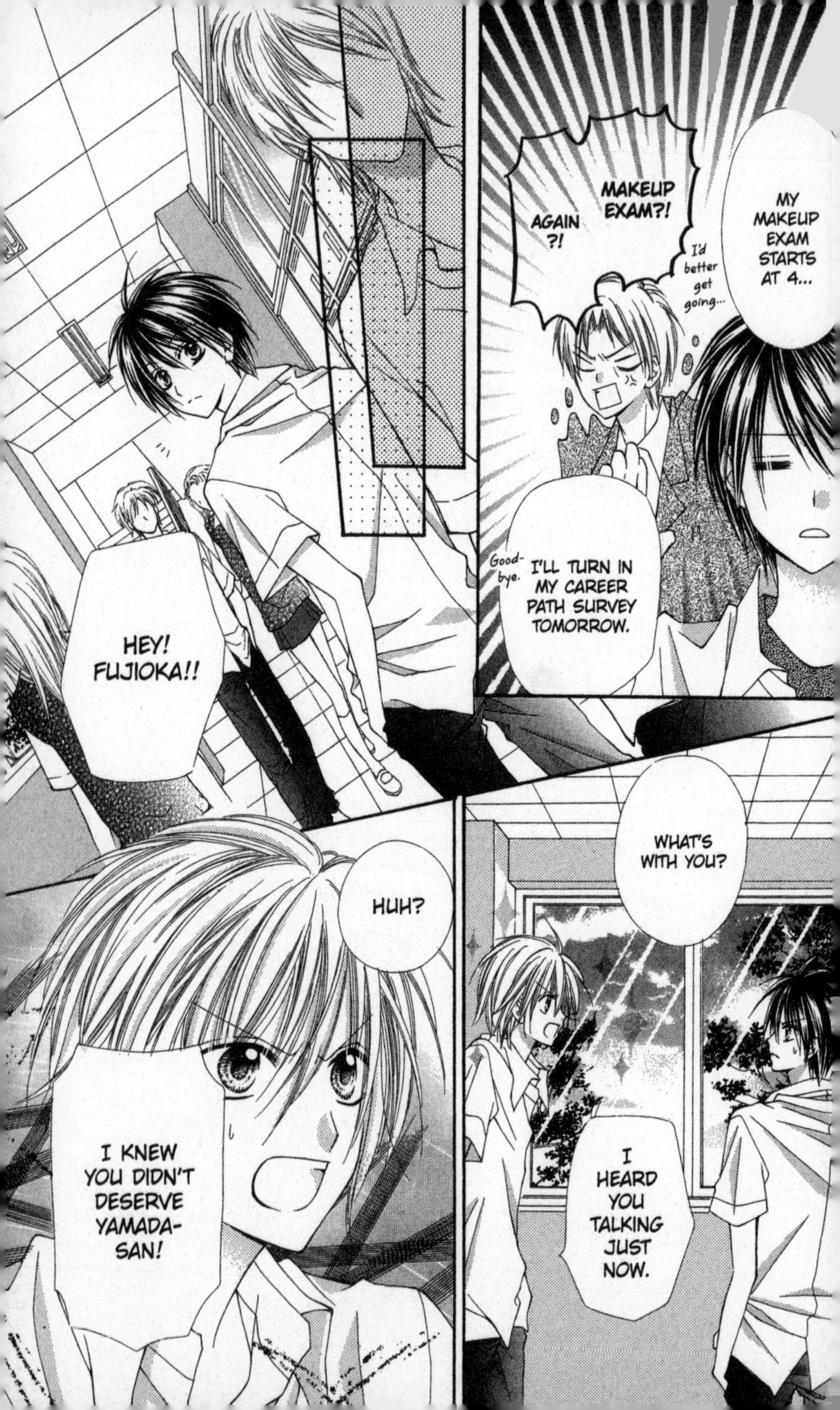
MY MAKEUP EXAM STARTS AT 4...
I'd better get going...
MAKEUP EXAM?!
AGAIN?!
I'LL TURN IN MY CAREER PATH SURVEY TOMORROW.
Good-bye.
HEY! FUJIOKA!!
WHAT'S WITH YOU?
I HEARD YOU TALKING JUST NOW.
HUH?
I KNEW YOU DIDN'T DESERVE YAMADA-SAN!

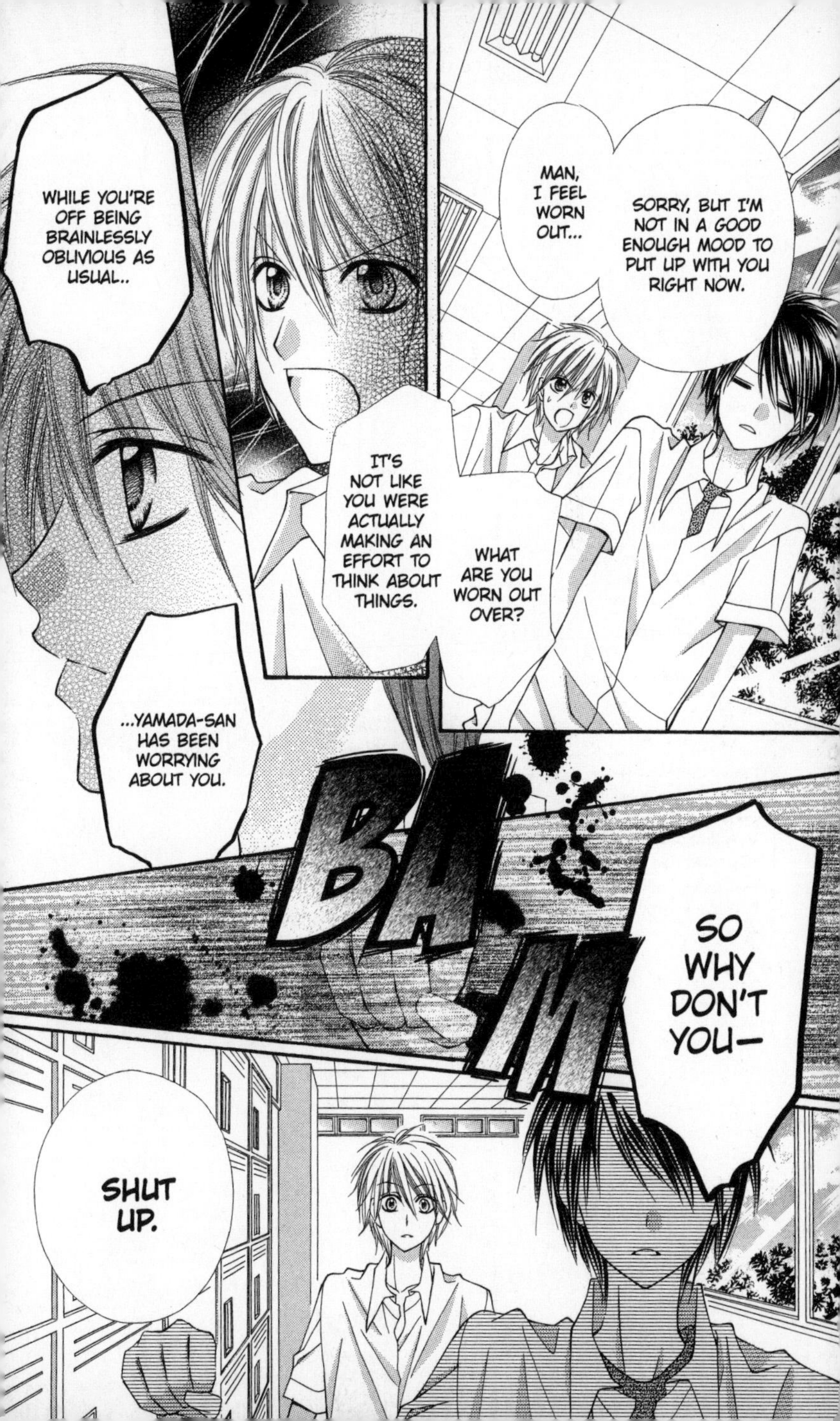
SORRY, BUT I'M NOT IN A GOOD ENOUGH MOOD TO PUT UP WITH YOU RIGHT NOW.
MAN, I FEEL WORN OUT...
WHAT ARE YOU WORN OUT OVER?
IT'S NOT LIKE YOU WERE ACTUALLY MAKING AN EFFORT TO THINK ABOUT THINGS.
WHILE YOU'RE OFF BEING BRAINLESSLY OBLIVIOUS AS USUAL..
...YAMADA-SAN HAS BEEN WORRYING ABOUT YOU.
SO WHY DON'T YOU—
BAM
SHUT UP.

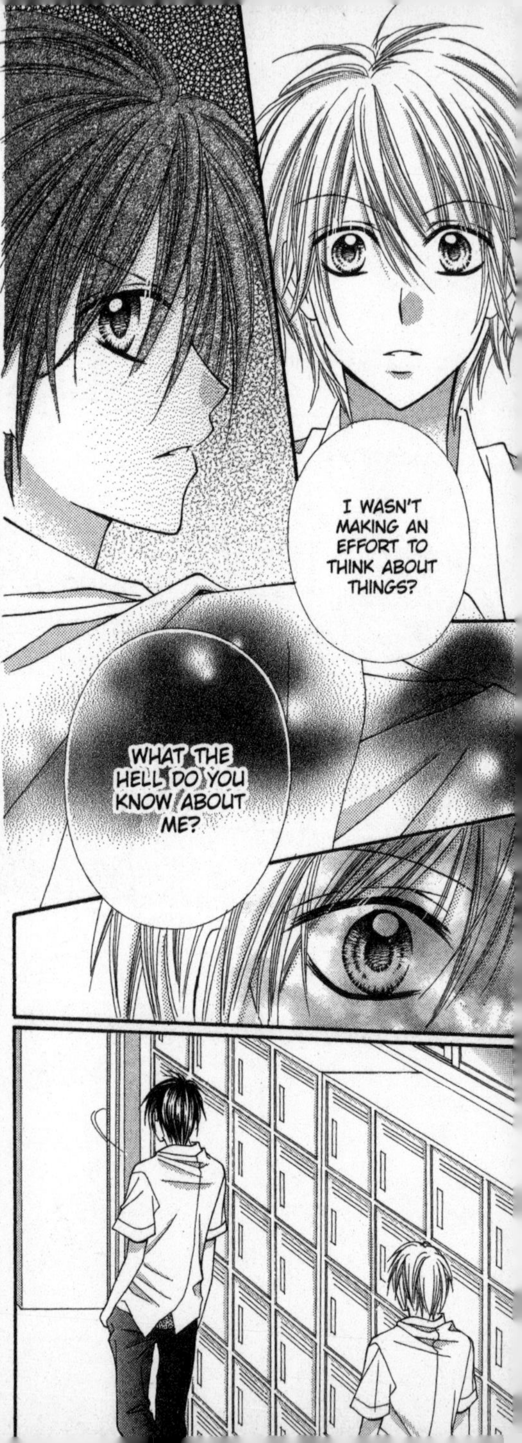
I WASN'T MAKING AN EFFORT TO THINK ABOUT THINGS?
WHAT THE HELL DO YOU KNOW ABOUT ME?

4
four

Continued from Author's Column 3 ←

Inside the time capsule there was this faux slam book that my friend from middle school and I used to write in. The things we wrote inside were so naïve, so embarrassing, so not cool that I couldn't read it with a straight face. I was such a little idiot back then! (I guess I still am.)

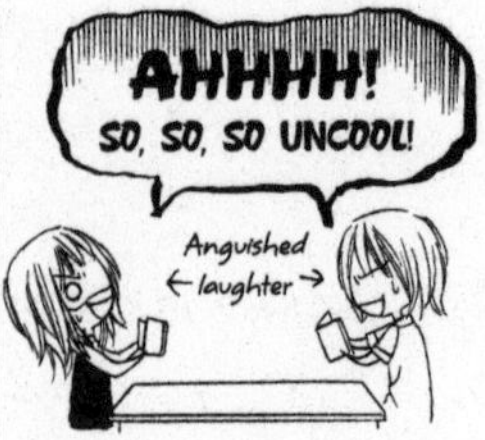
AHHHH!
SO, SO, SO UNCOOL!
Anguished ←laughter→

I swear it's an enchanted notebook or something that forces you to read it even though you really don't want to. Even though it's so awful that you slam it closed immediately, somehow you feel compelled to pick it up and open it again later! (laugh) Even though I say "third year middle school" like it was ancient history, it was only about five years ago. I guess I haven't grown up enough yet to just look back at it and laugh fondly... Joy...

Under the "My Happy Ending" section, we both wrote we wanted to "get married at the same time, have kids and then look back nostalgically at this notebook." I guess then I wasn't supposed to be re-reading it yet... Oh well, I can look forward to opening my "Pandora's Box" again next year!

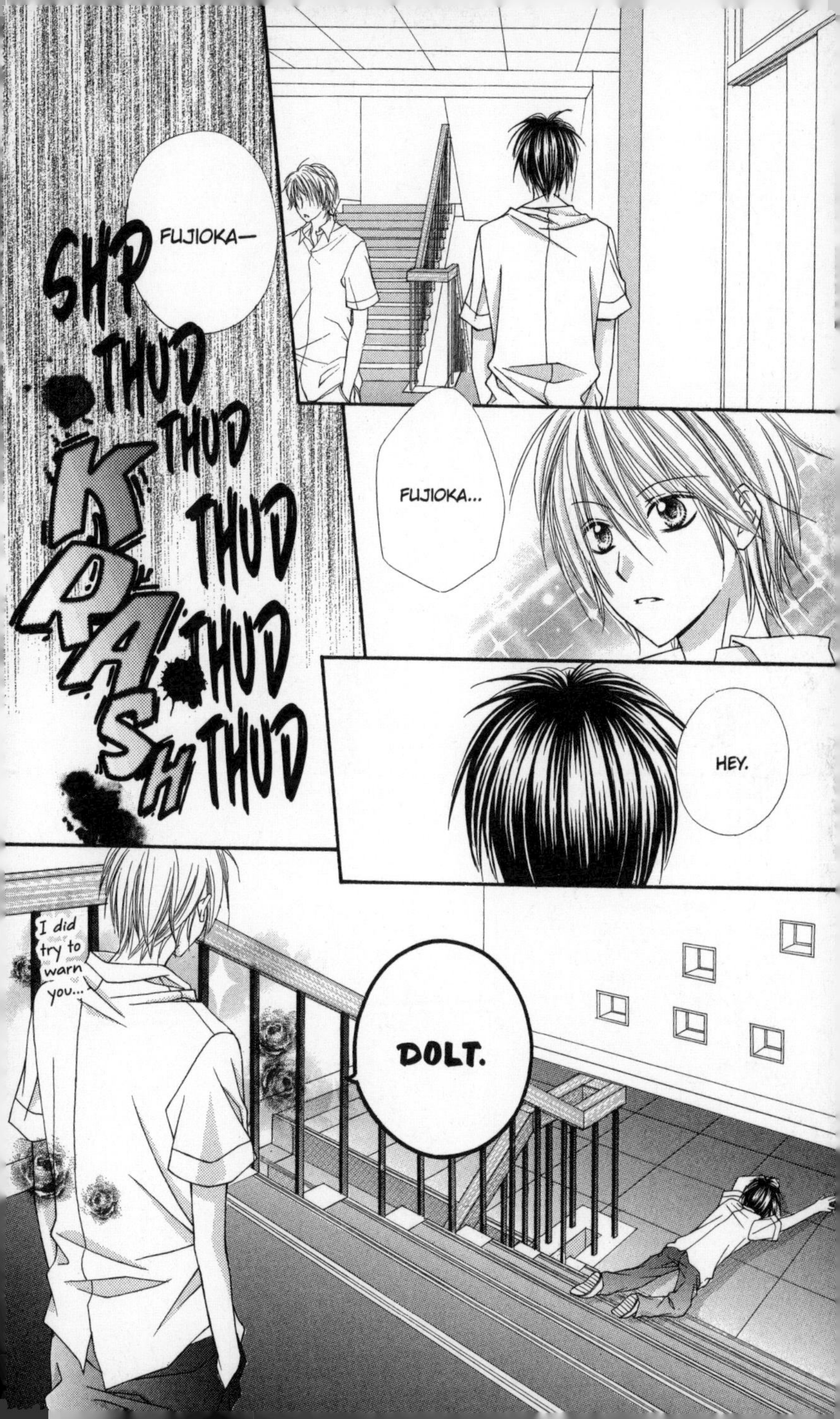
FUJIOKA—
FUJIOKA...
HEY.
SHP
THUD THUD THUD THUD THUD
KRASH
DOLT.
I did try to warn you...

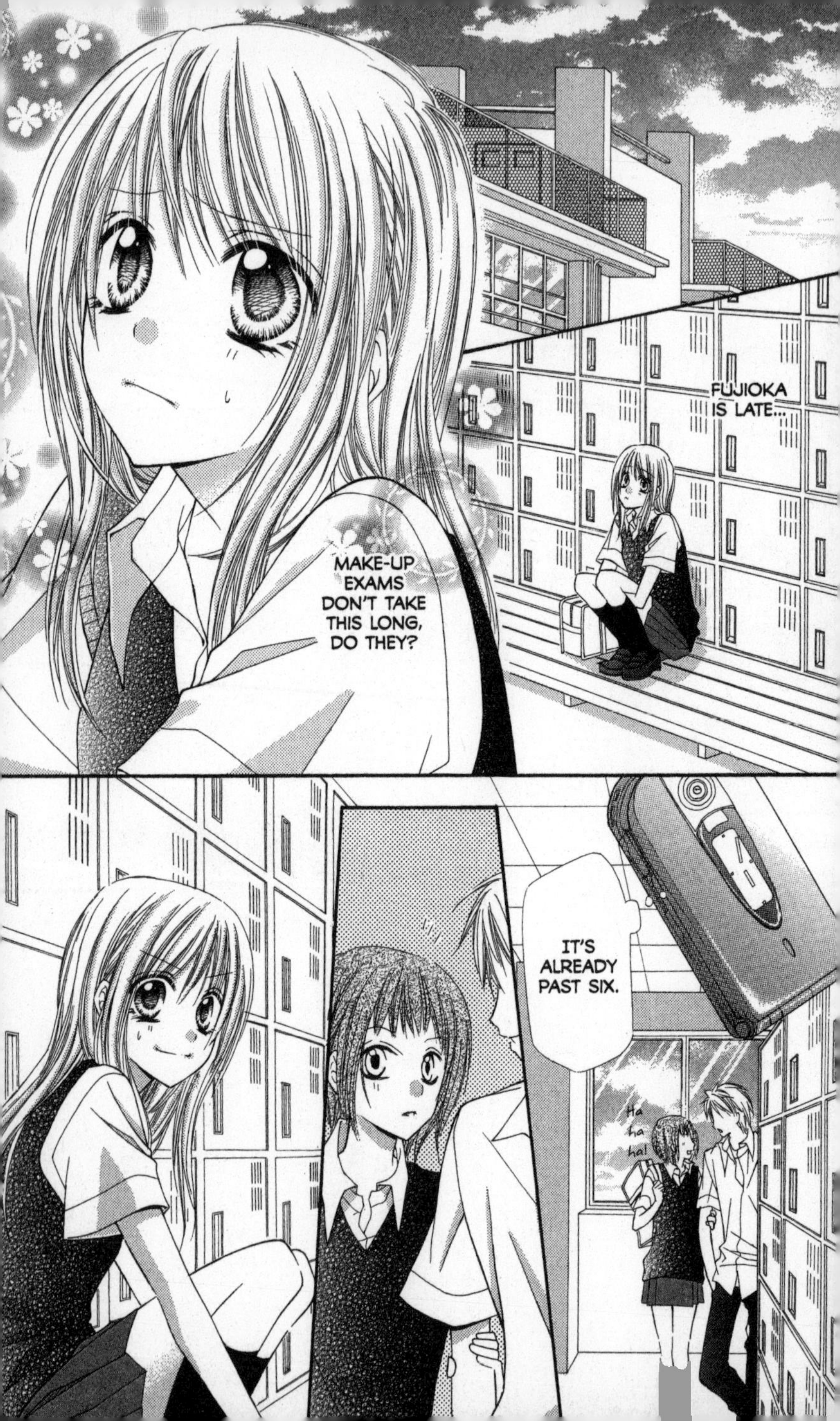
FUJIOKA IS LATE...
MAKE-UP EXAMS DON'T TAKE THIS LONG, DO THEY?
IT'S ALREADY PAST SIX.
Ha ha ha!

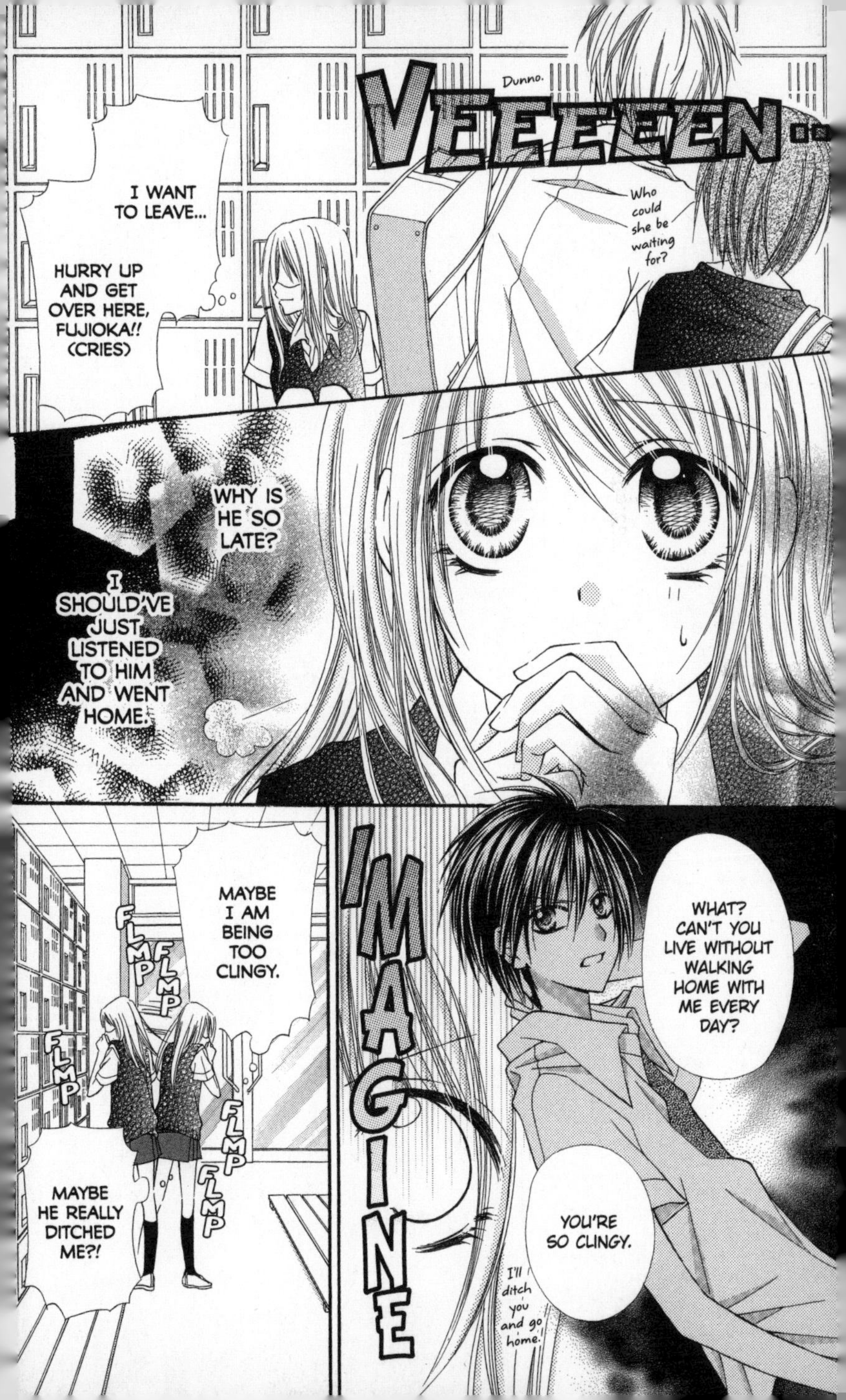
Dunno.
VEEEEEN..
Who could she be waiting for?
I WANT TO LEAVE...
HURRY UP AND GET OVER HERE, FUJIOKA!! (CRIES)
WHY IS HE SO LATE?
I SHOULD'VE JUST LISTENED TO HIM AND WENT HOME.
IMAGINE
WHAT? CAN'T YOU LIVE WITHOUT WALKING HOME WITH ME EVERY DAY?
YOU'RE SO CLINGY.
I'll ditch you and go home.
MAYBE I AM BEING TOO CLINGY.
FLMP FLMP FLMP
FLMP FLMP FLMP
MAYBE HE REALLY DITCHED ME?!

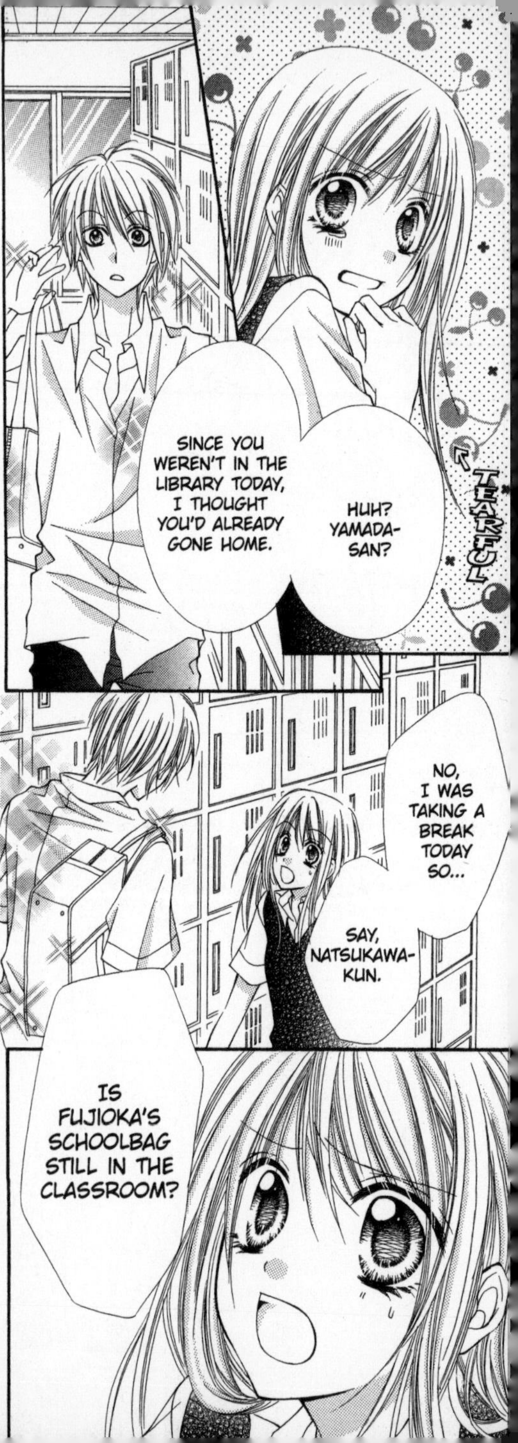
HUH? YAMADA-SAN?
TEARFUL
SINCE YOU WEREN'T IN THE LIBRARY TODAY, I THOUGHT YOU'D ALREADY GONE HOME.
NO, I WAS TAKING A BREAK TODAY SO...
SAY, NATSUKAWA-KUN.
IS FUJIOKA'S SCHOOLBAG STILL IN THE CLASSROOM?

5
five

4 Continued from Author's Column ←

I think I (much more than normal people) look back at my past self and think, "Man, was I stupid or what?" This started after I graduated from middle school when, all of a sudden, my personality got a lot colder (though not so much that it was jarringly out of character or anything).

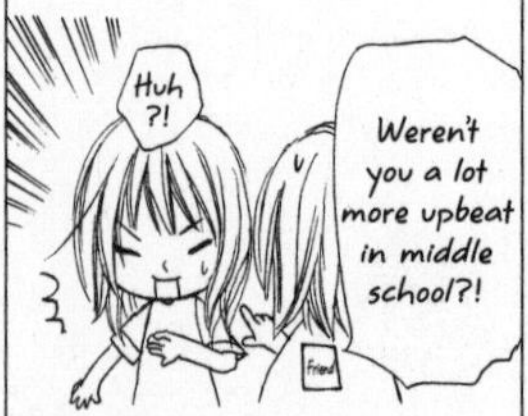
Huh ?!
Weren't you a lot more upbeat in middle school?!
Friend

↑ This was a scene repeated time and again with a variety of my childhood friends. (laugh) Doesn't everyone get more energetic when they're out having fun with their friends? But even at times when I was out with them and had been thinking to myself, "I'm so cheerful right now!" I'd get the above ↑ reaction. It's awful, isn't it?
Even when we were digging up our time capsule...

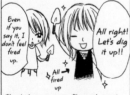

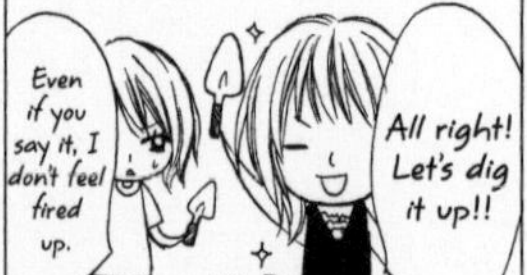
All right! Let's dig it up!!
Even if you say it, I don't feel fired up.
All fired up

That's how it was. Thus, the only person in this world who thinks I'm a driven, energetic individual is my editor Morii-sama. Though I won't tell you why.

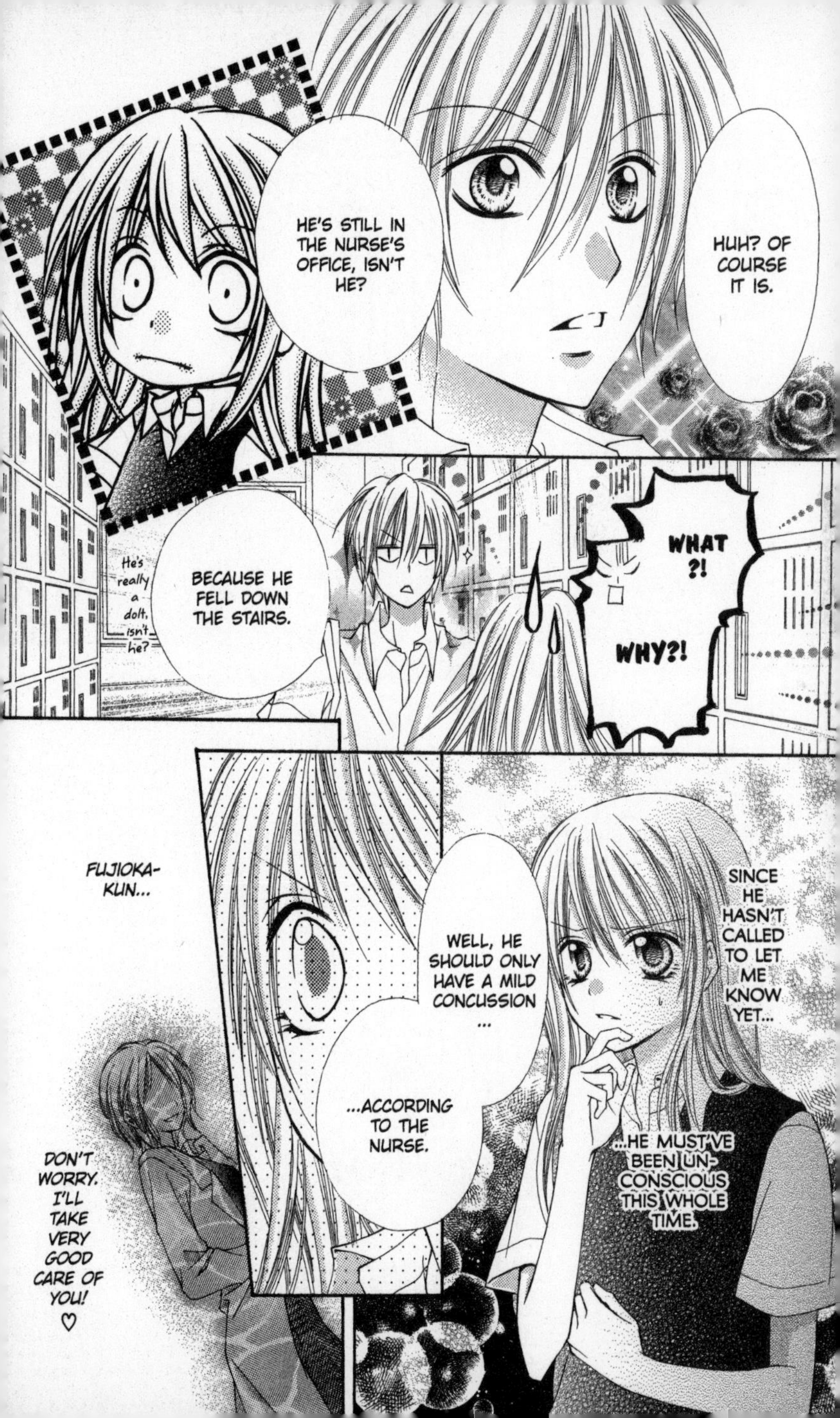
HUH? OF COURSE IT IS.
HE'S STILL IN THE NURSE'S OFFICE, ISN'T HE?
WHAT?!
WHY?!
BECAUSE HE FELL DOWN THE STAIRS.
He's really a dolt, isn't he?
SINCE HE HASN'T CALLED TO LET ME KNOW YET...
...HE MUST'VE BEEN UN-CONSCIOUS THIS WHOLE TIME.
WELL, HE SHOULD ONLY HAVE A MILD CONCUSSION ...
...ACCORDING TO THE NURSE.
FUJIOKA-KUN...
DON'T WORRY. I'LL TAKE VERY GOOD CARE OF YOU! ♡

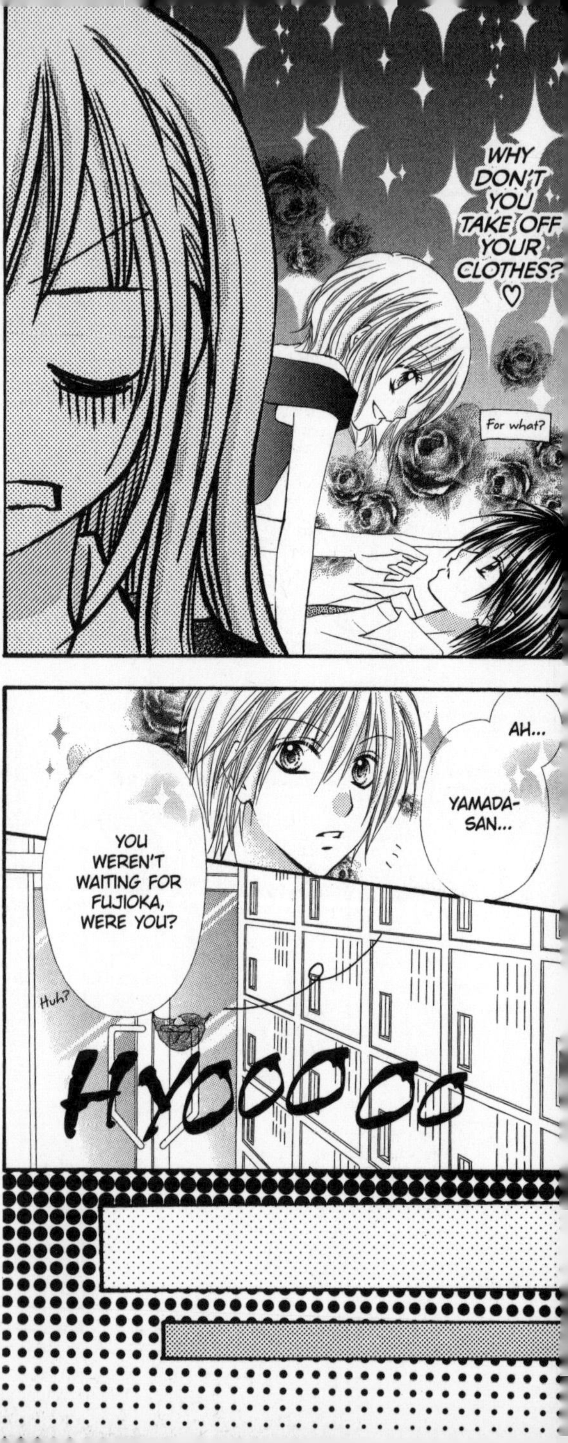
WHY DON'T YOU TAKE OFF YOUR CLOTHES? ♡
For what?
AH... YAMADA-SAN...
YOU WEREN'T WAITING FOR FUJIOKA, WERE YOU?
Huh?
HYOOOOO

6
six

Oh, yeah—in July, I went to another w-inds concert. Two of them, actually—both the Yokohama and Niigata concerts! The venue in Niigata was really small, so since I got a pretty good seat, I was three meters away from the band and could see everything super clearly!♢ But actually, people I see regularly on TV are just like manga characters to me—it's like they come from another world so there shouldn't actually be any possibility I could really meet them. So when I was sitting that close to them, I had this really surreal moment when I thought, "Wait, that's not really them, is it...?" ◊ It really didn't feel real for a moment there. I mean, they looked so cool they couldn't have been real.

Haruta's thoughts during the concert.

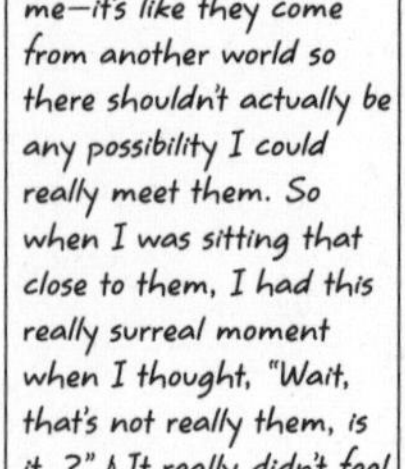
VEEN
Keita's arms are so hot... I wish I could draw guys' arms hot like that...
Pen light
Yeah... I should totally put a concert scene in my manga.
SHK SHK
Ack!
Concentrate on the concert, stupid!!
Thinking about work at a time like this?!
Endless.

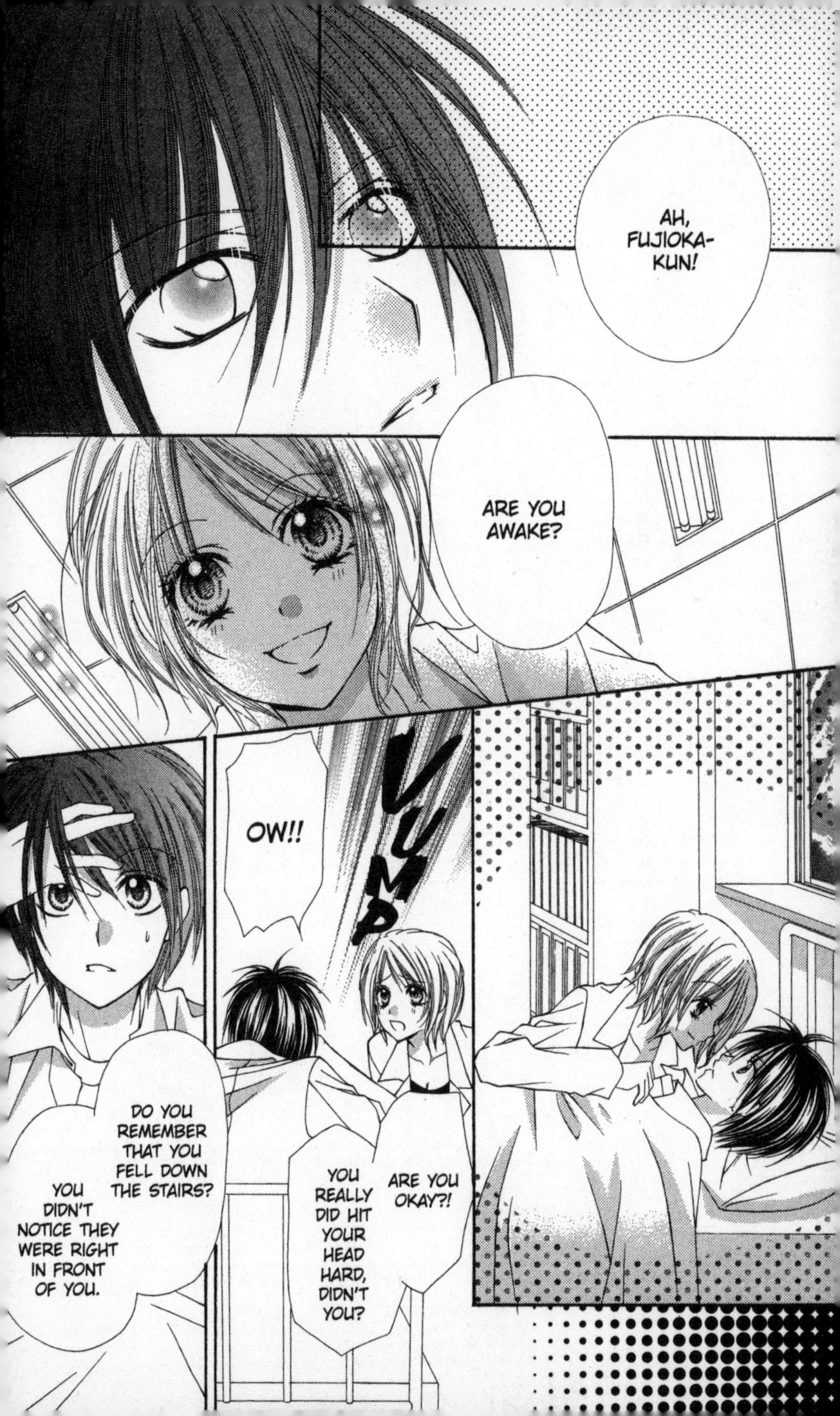
AH, FUJIOKA-KUN!
ARE YOU AWAKE?
OW!!
ARE YOU OKAY?!
YOU REALLY DID HIT YOUR HEAD HARD, DIDN'T YOU?
DO YOU REMEMBER THAT YOU FELL DOWN THE STAIRS?
YOU DIDN'T NOTICE THEY WERE RIGHT IN FRONT OF YOU.

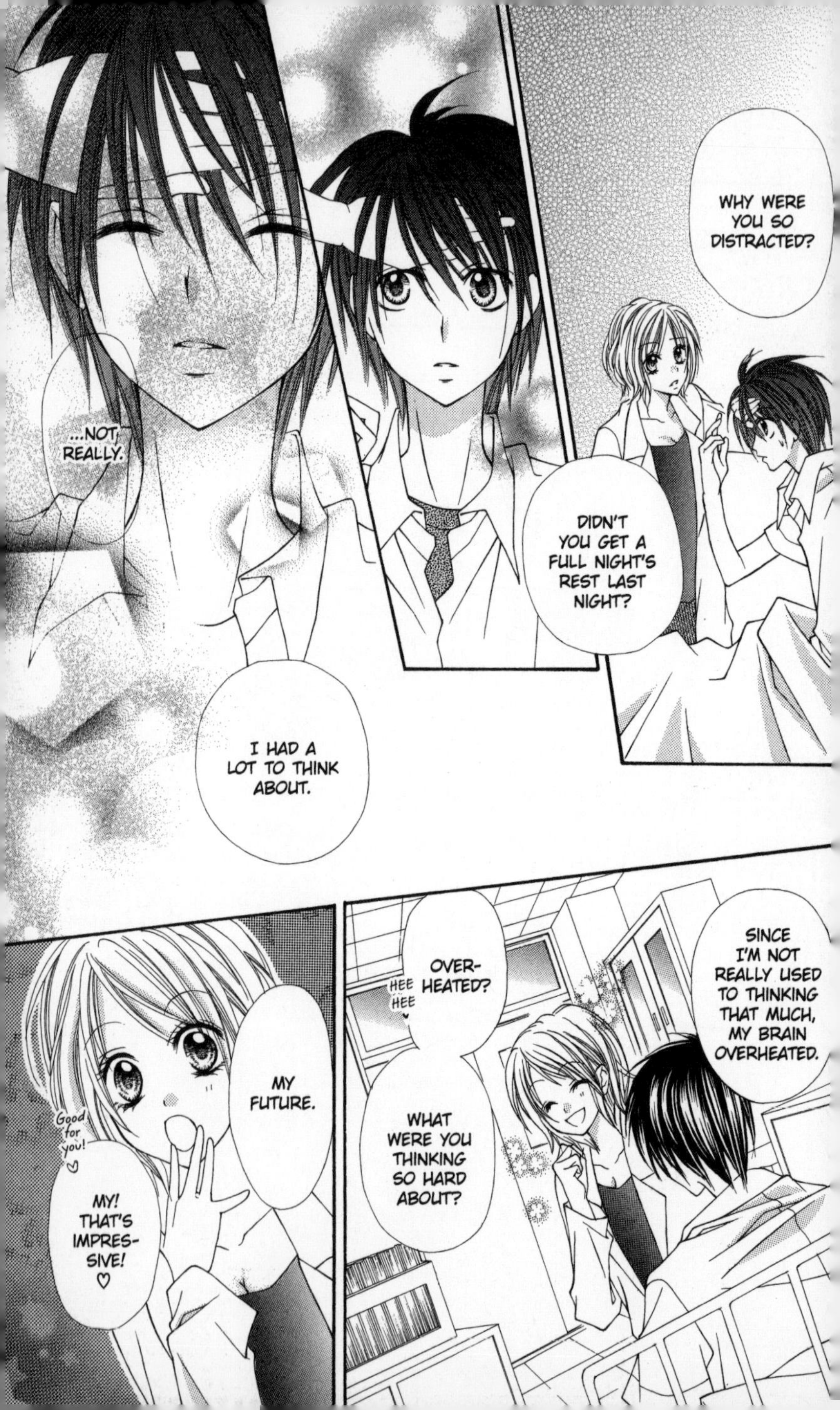
WHY WERE YOU SO DISTRACTED?
DIDN'T YOU GET A FULL NIGHT'S REST LAST NIGHT?
...NOT REALLY.
I HAD A LOT TO THINK ABOUT.
SINCE I'M NOT REALLY USED TO THINKING THAT MUCH, MY BRAIN OVERHEATED.
HEE HEE
OVER-HEATED?
WHAT WERE YOU THINKING SO HARD ABOUT?
MY FUTURE.
Good for you! ♡
MY! THAT'S IMPRESSIVE! ♡

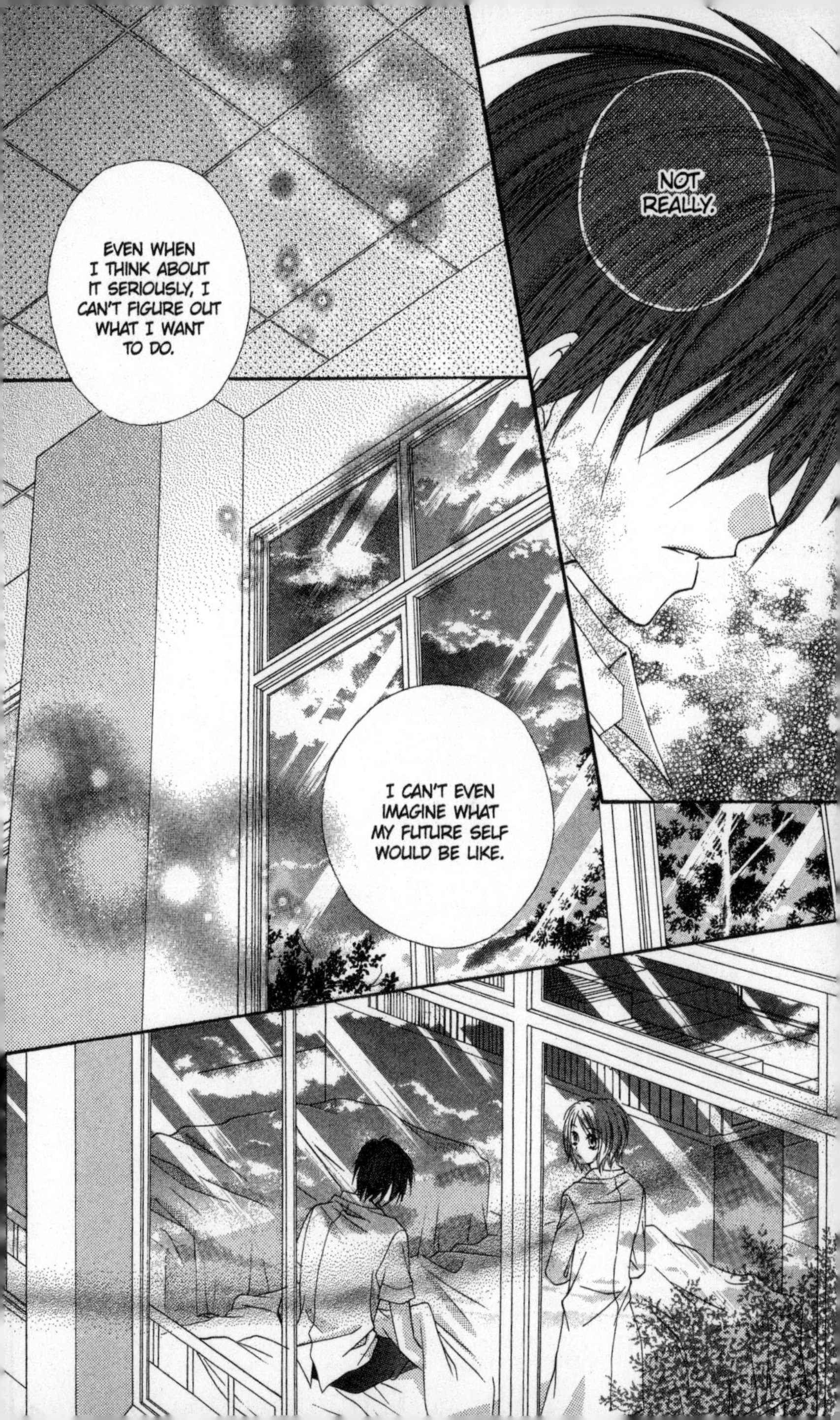
NOT REALLY.
EVEN WHEN I THINK ABOUT IT SERIOUSLY, I CAN'T FIGURE OUT WHAT I WANT TO DO.
I CAN'T EVEN IMAGINE WHAT MY FUTURE SELF WOULD BE LIKE.

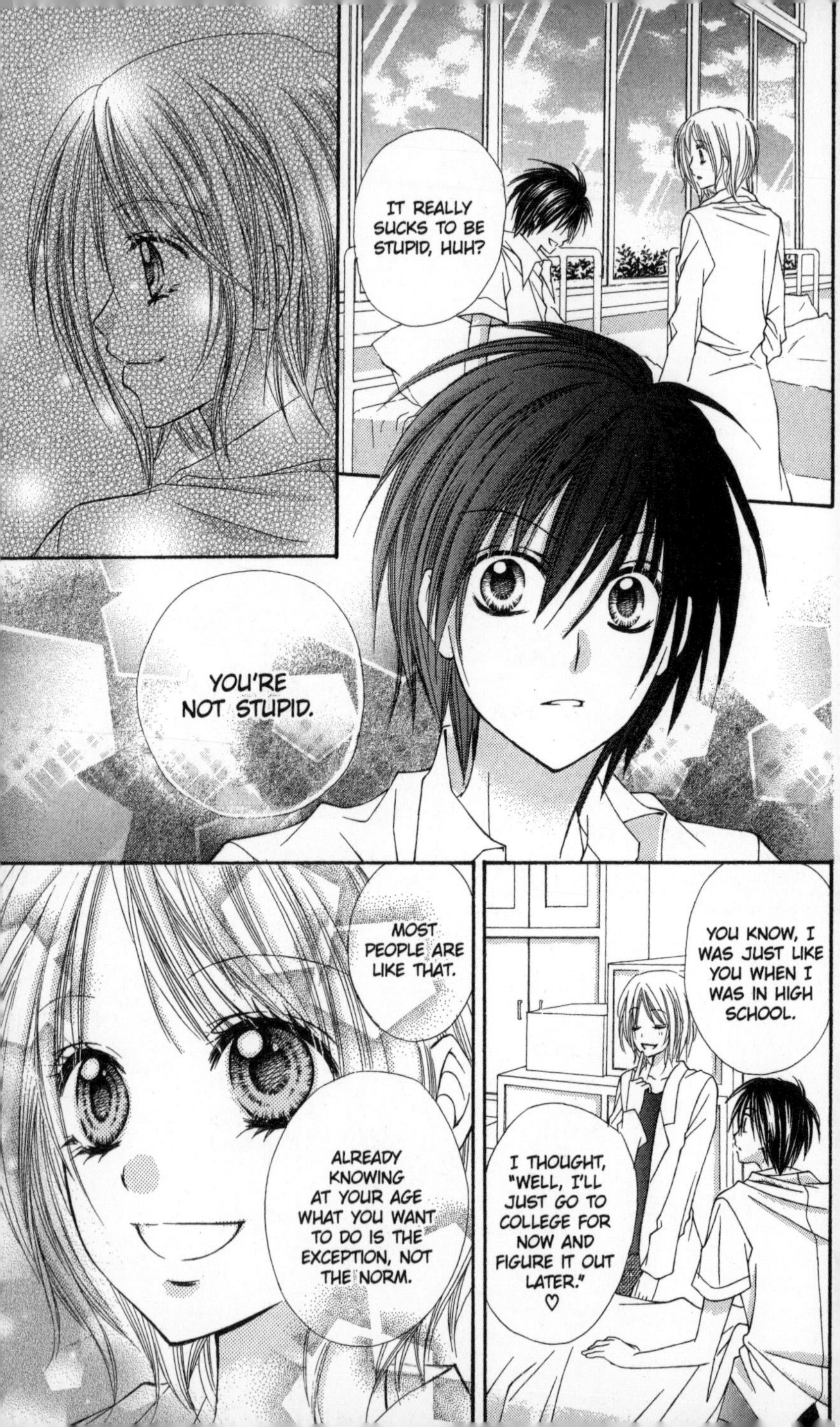
IT REALLY SUCKS TO BE STUPID, HUH?
YOU'RE NOT STUPID.
YOU KNOW, I WAS JUST LIKE YOU WHEN I WAS IN HIGH SCHOOL.
I THOUGHT, "WELL, I'LL JUST GO TO COLLEGE FOR NOW AND FIGURE IT OUT LATER." ♡
MOST PEOPLE ARE LIKE THAT.
ALREADY KNOWING AT YOUR AGE WHAT YOU WANT TO DO IS THE EXCEPTION, NOT THE NORM.

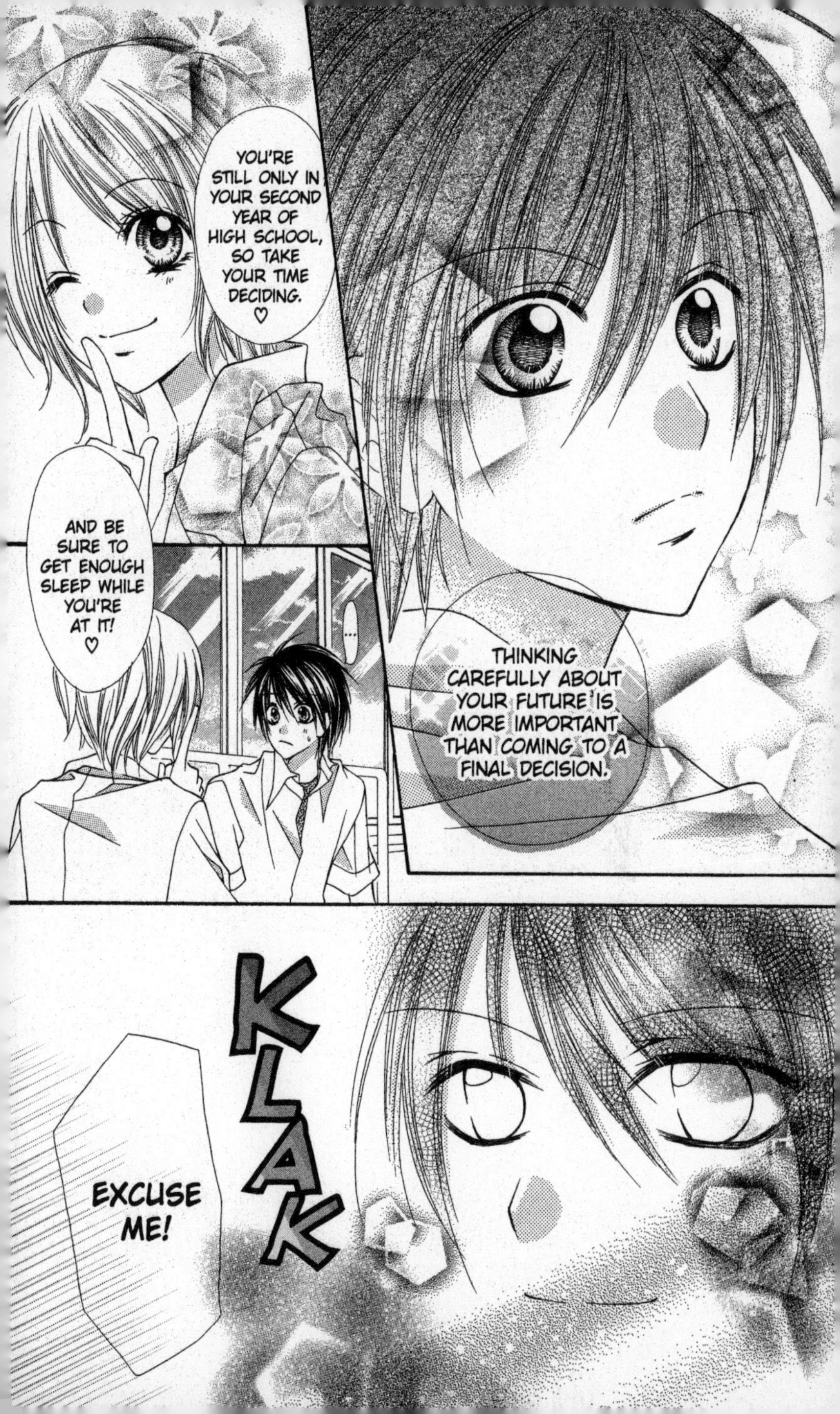
THINKING CAREFULLY ABOUT YOUR FUTURE IS MORE IMPORTANT THAN COMING TO A FINAL DECISION.
YOU'RE STILL ONLY IN YOUR SECOND YEAR OF HIGH SCHOOL, SO TAKE YOUR TIME DECIDING. ♡
AND BE SURE TO GET ENOUGH SLEEP WHILE YOU'RE AT IT! ♡
...
KLAK
EXCUSE ME!

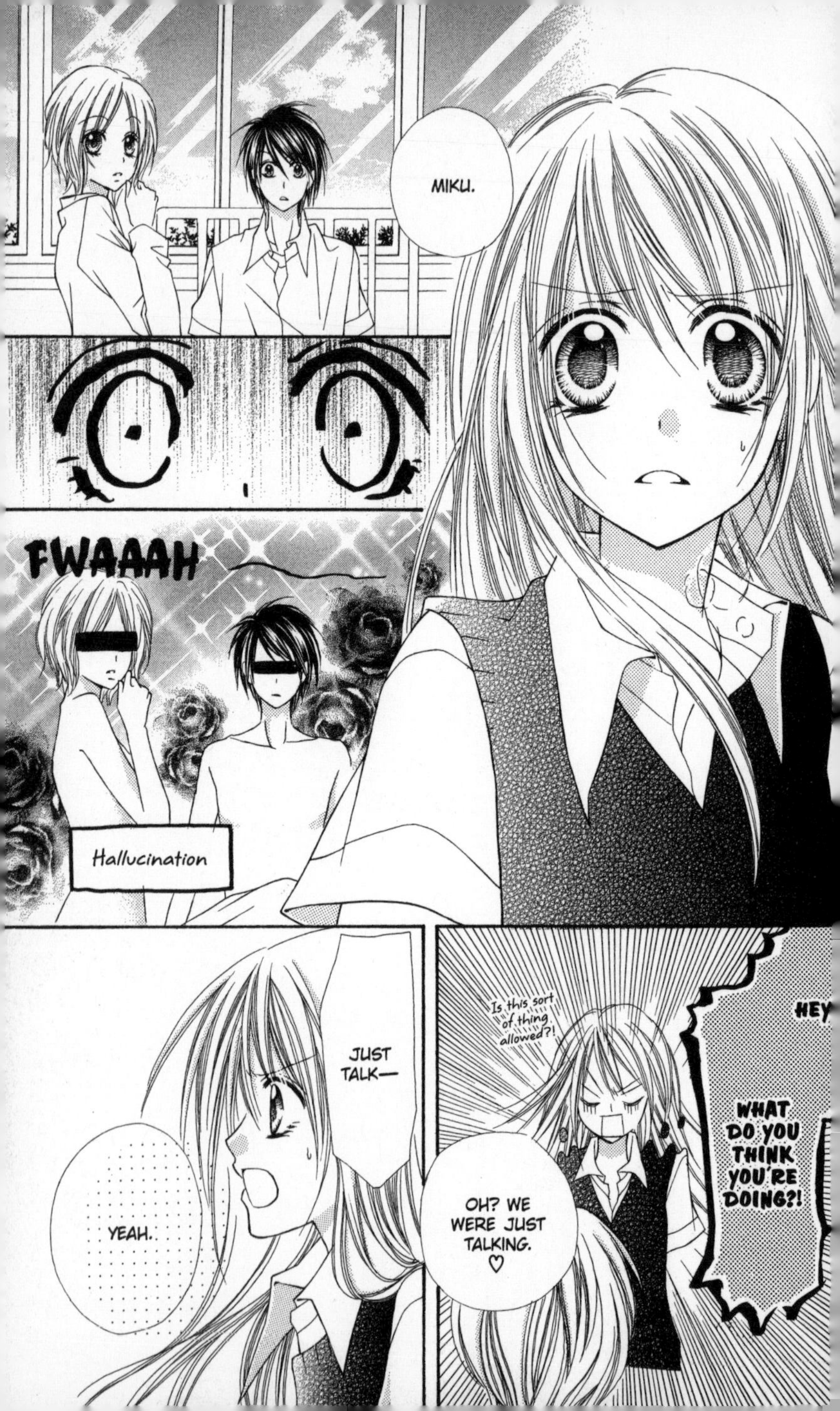
MIKU.
FWAAAH
Hallucination
HEY
WHAT DO YOU THINK YOU'RE DOING?!
Is this sort of thing allowed?!
OH? WE WERE JUST TALKING. ♡
JUST TALK—
YEAH.

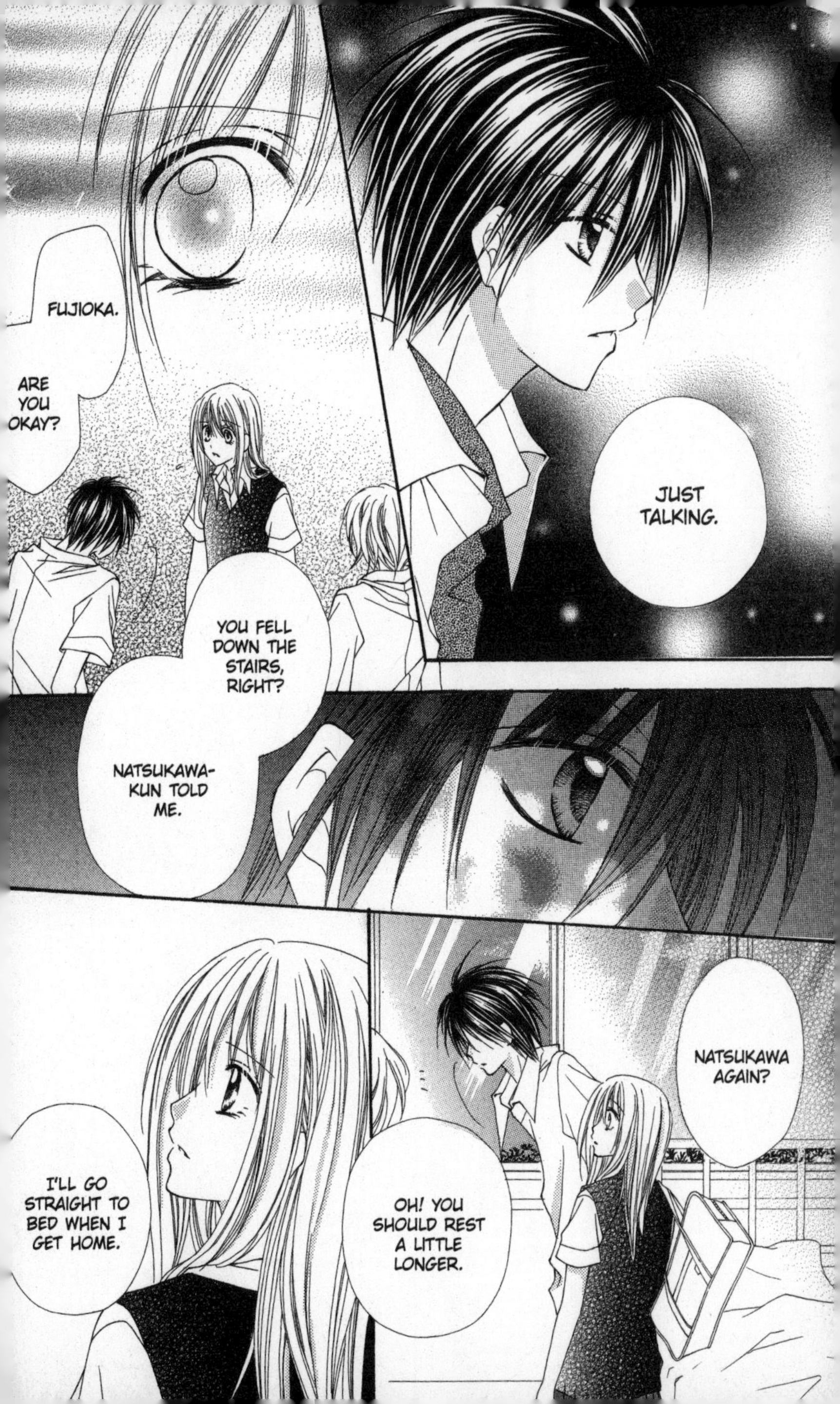
JUST TALKING.
FUJIOKA.
ARE YOU OKAY?
YOU FELL DOWN THE STAIRS, RIGHT?
NATSUKAWA-KUN TOLD ME.
NATSUKAWA AGAIN?
OH! YOU SHOULD REST A LITTLE LONGER.
I'LL GO STRAIGHT TO BED WHEN I GET HOME.

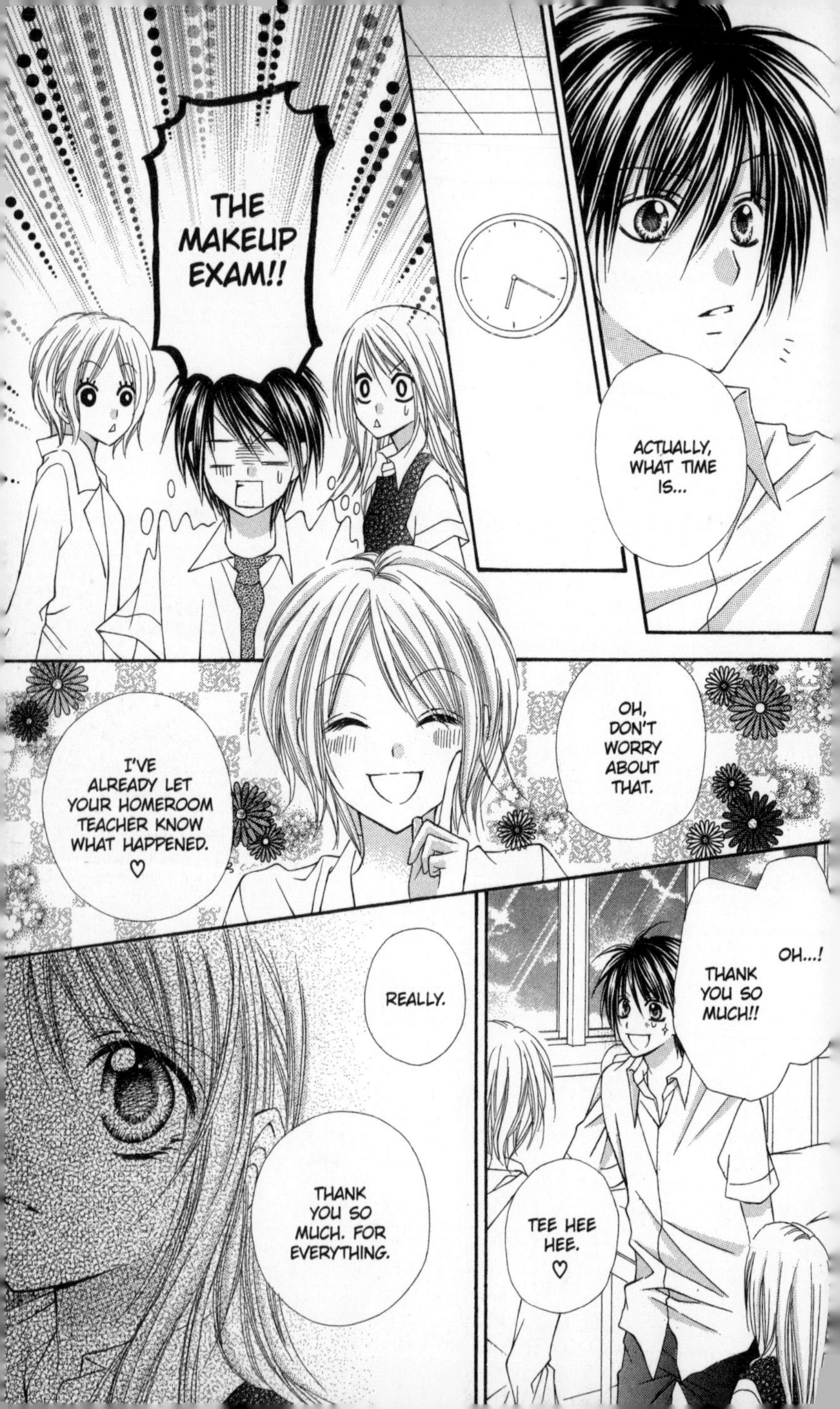
ACTUALLY, WHAT TIME IS...
THE MAKEUP EXAM!!
OH, DON'T WORRY ABOUT THAT.
I'VE ALREADY LET YOUR HOMEROOM TEACHER KNOW WHAT HAPPENED. ♡
OH...!
THANK YOU SO MUCH!!
TEE HEE HEE. ♡
REALLY.
THANK YOU SO MUCH. FOR EVERYTHING.

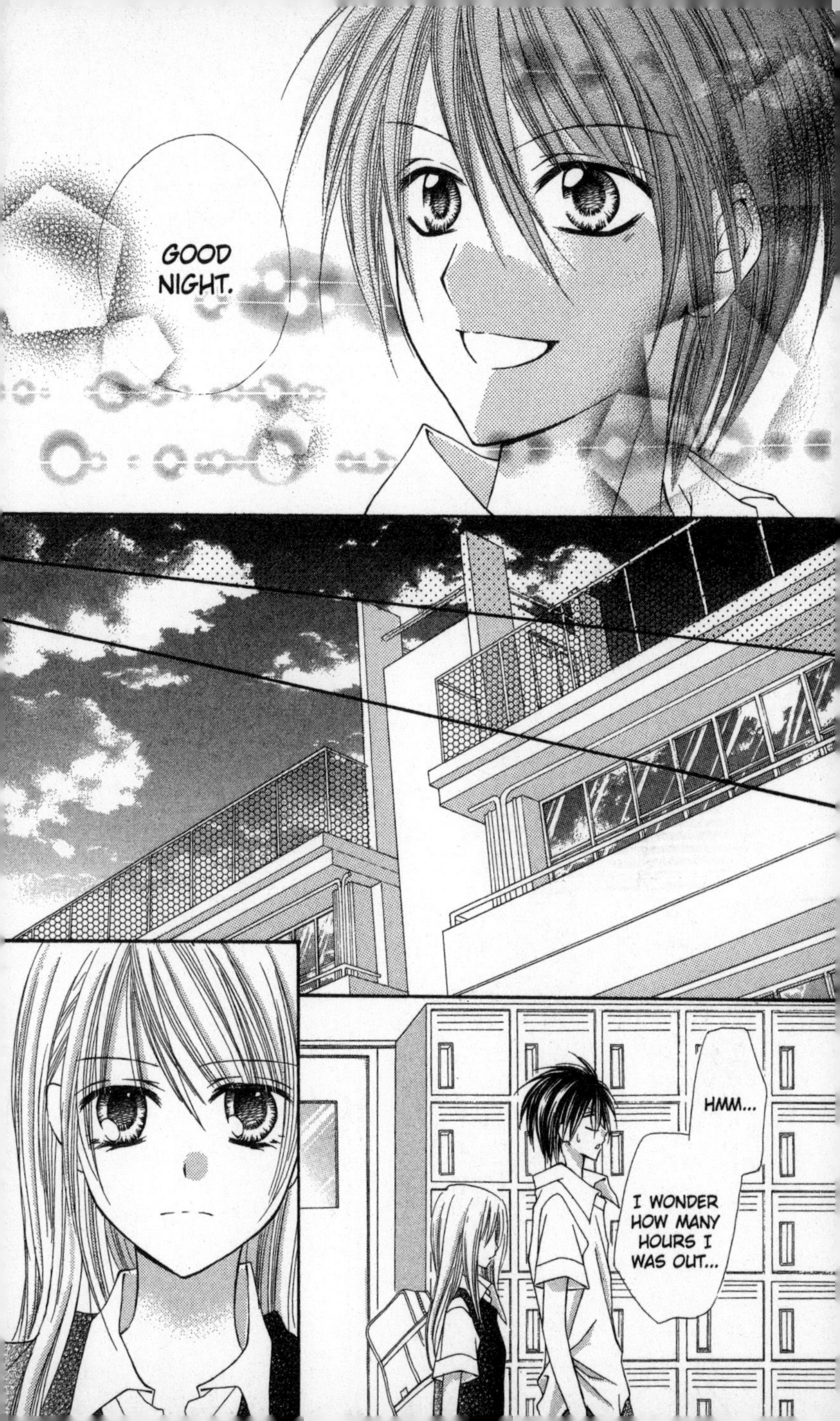
GOOD NIGHT.
HMM...
I WONDER HOW MANY HOURS I WAS OUT...

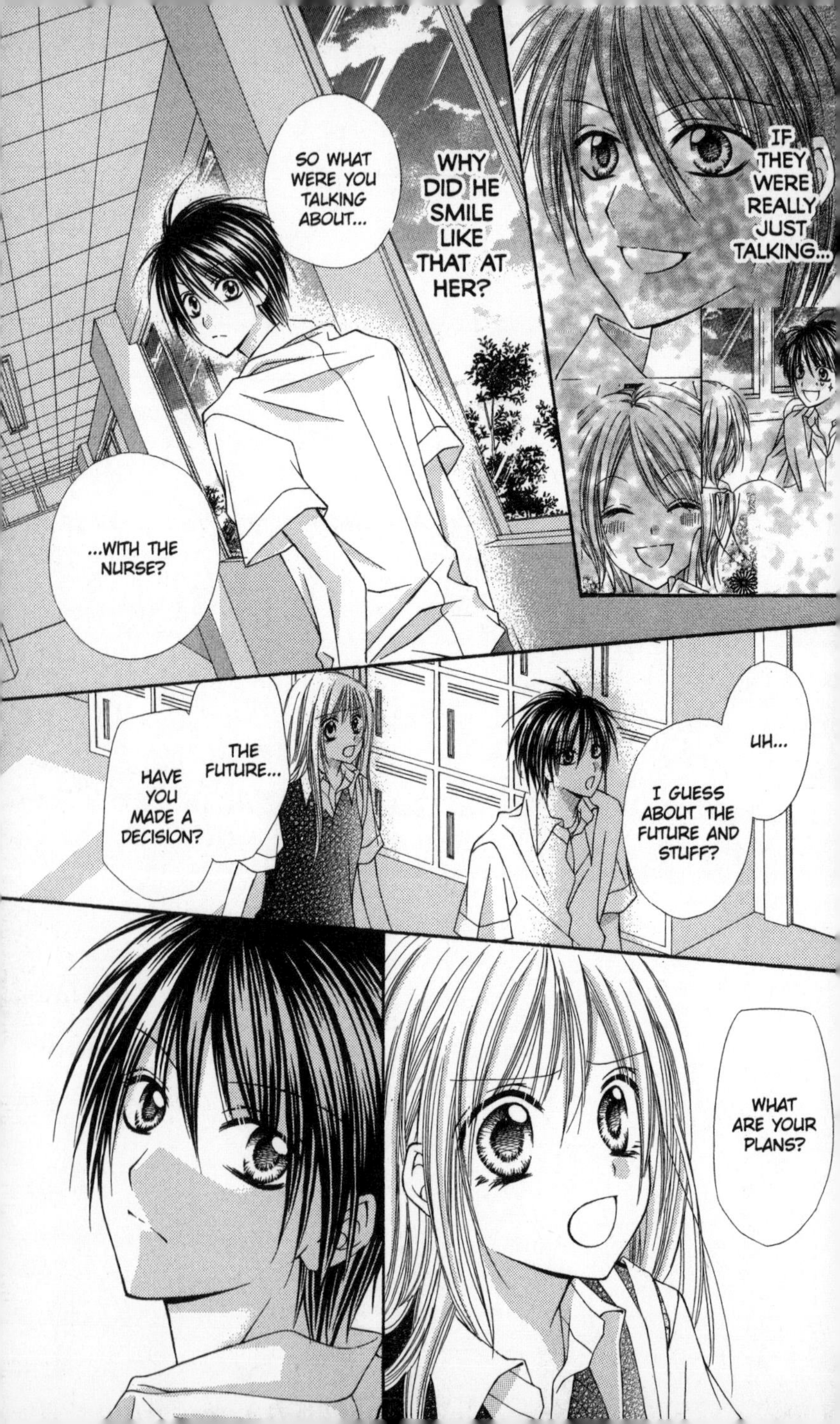
IF THEY WERE REALLY JUST TALKING...
WHY DID HE SMILE LIKE THAT AT HER?
SO WHAT WERE YOU TALKING ABOUT...
...WITH THE NURSE?
UH...
I GUESS ABOUT THE FUTURE AND STUFF?
THE FUTURE...
HAVE YOU MADE A DECISION?
WHAT ARE YOUR PLANS?

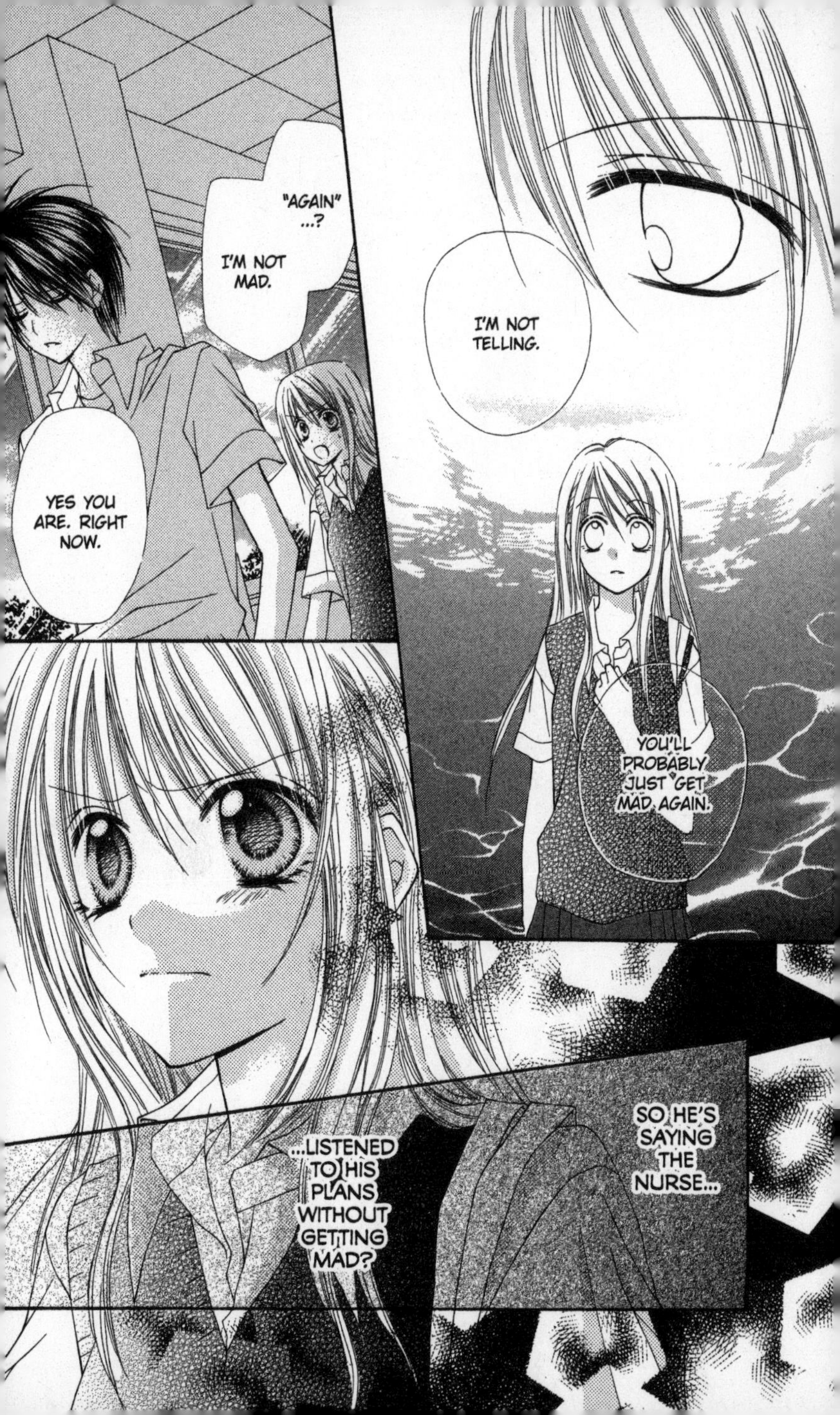
I'M NOT TELLING.
YOU'LL PROBABLY JUST GET MAD AGAIN.
"AGAIN" ...?
I'M NOT MAD.
YES YOU ARE. RIGHT NOW.
SO HE'S SAYING THE NURSE...
...LISTENED TO HIS PLANS WITHOUT GETTING MAD?

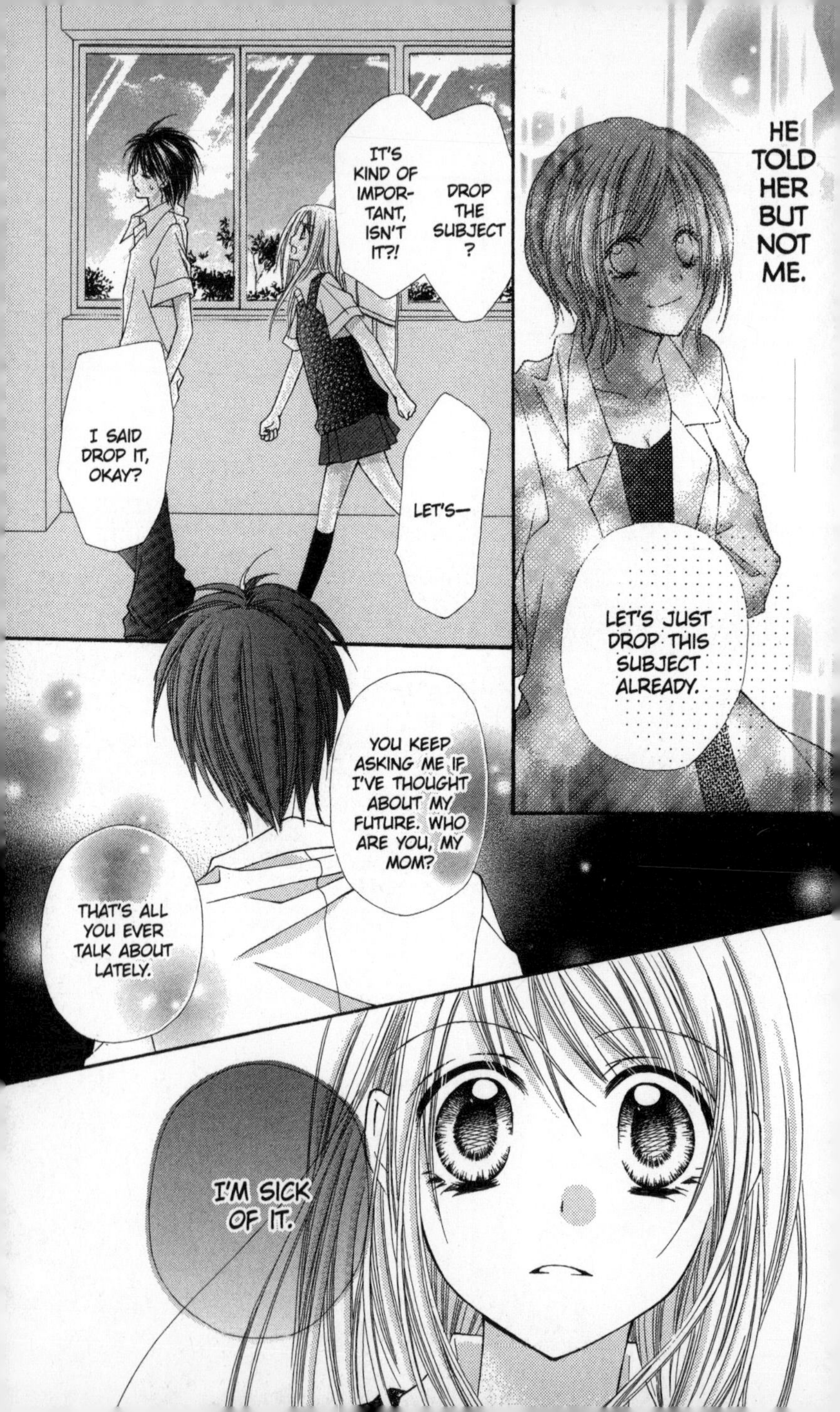
HE TOLD HER BUT NOT ME.
LET'S JUST DROP THIS SUBJECT ALREADY.
DROP THE SUBJECT?
IT'S KIND OF IMPORTANT, ISN'T IT?!
LET'S—
I SAID DROP IT, OKAY?
YOU KEEP ASKING ME IF I'VE THOUGHT ABOUT MY FUTURE. WHO ARE YOU, MY MOM?
THAT'S ALL YOU EVER TALK ABOUT LATELY.
I'M SICK OF IT.

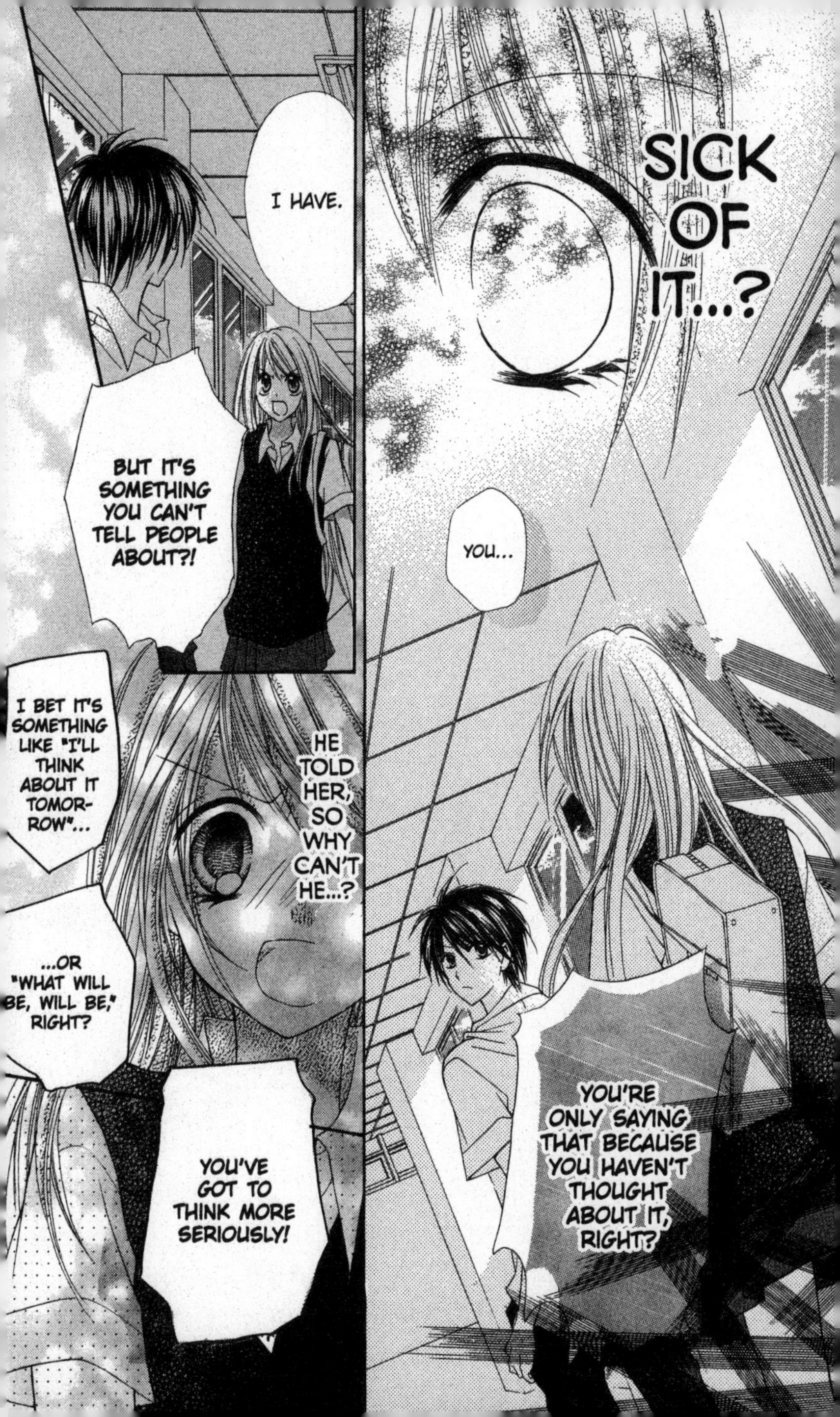
SICK OF IT...?
YOU...
YOU'RE ONLY SAYING THAT BECAUSE YOU HAVEN'T THOUGHT ABOUT IT, RIGHT?
I HAVE.
BUT IT'S SOMETHING YOU CAN'T TELL PEOPLE ABOUT?!
HE TOLD HER, SO WHY CAN'T HE...?
I BET IT'S SOMETHING LIKE "I'LL THINK ABOUT IT TOMORROW"...
...OR "WHAT WILL BE, WILL BE," RIGHT?
YOU'VE GOT TO THINK MORE SERIOUSLY!

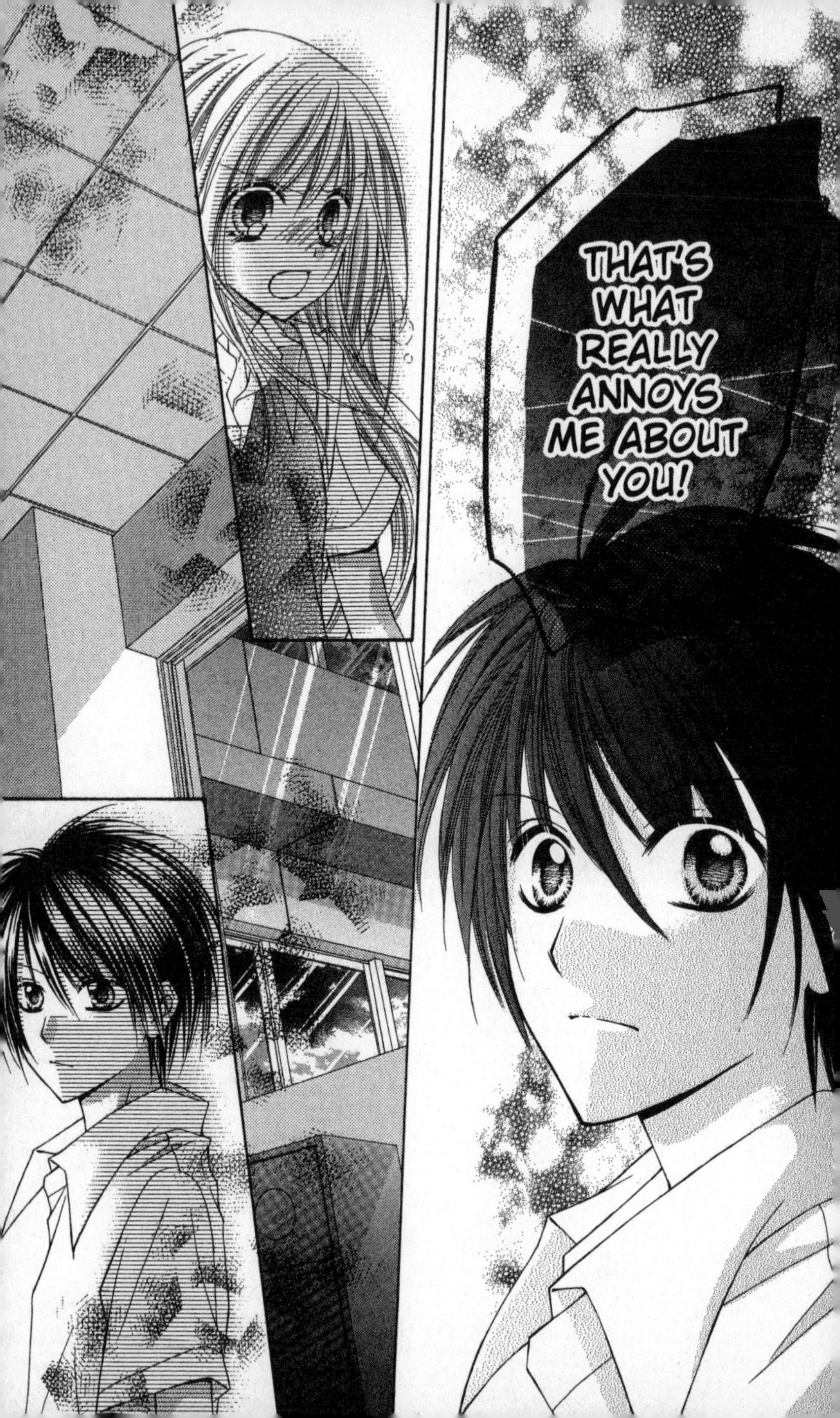
THAT'S WHAT REALLY ANNOYS ME ABOUT YOU!

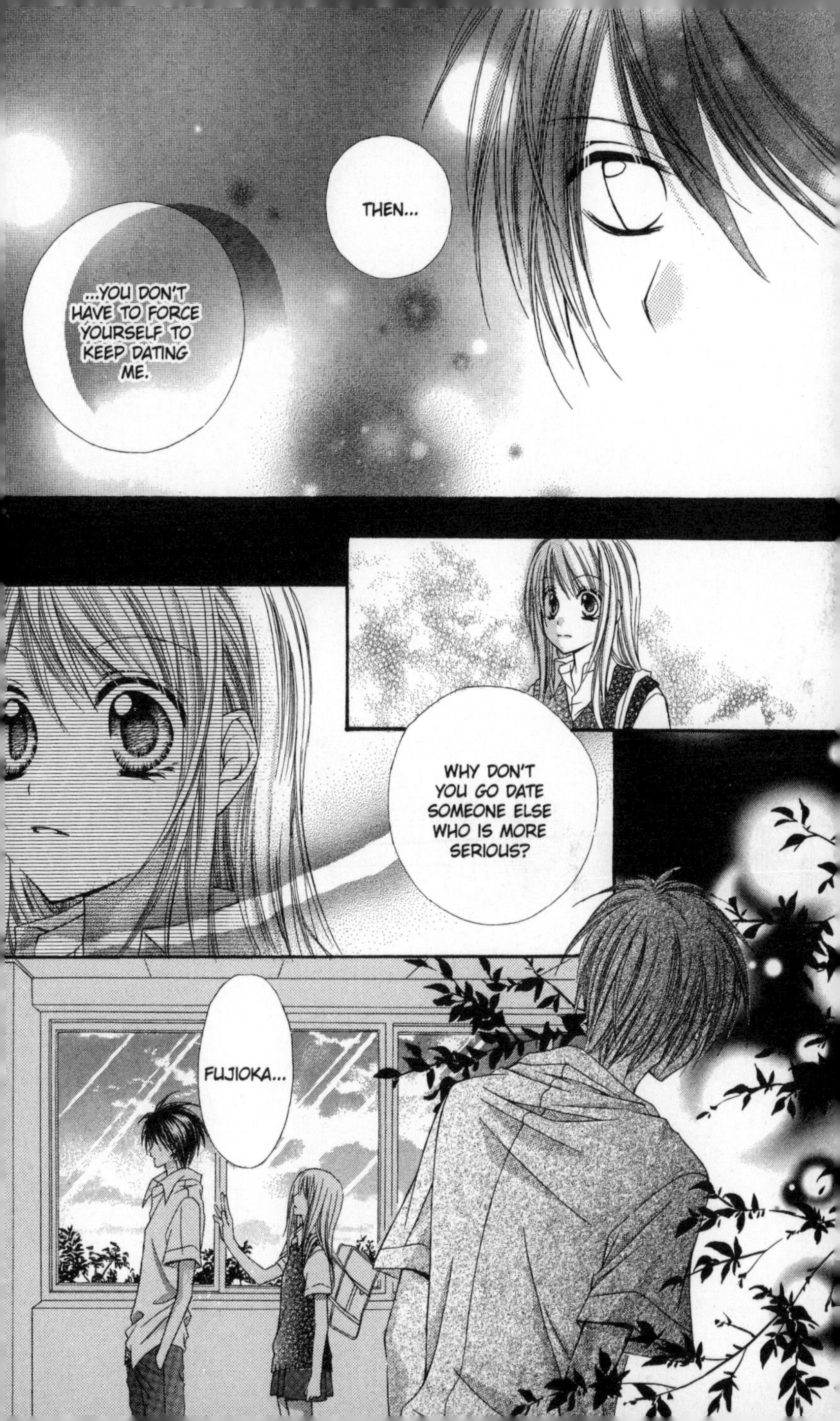
THEN...
...YOU DON'T HAVE TO FORCE YOURSELF TO KEEP DATING ME.
WHY DON'T YOU GO DATE SOMEONE ELSE WHO IS MORE SERIOUS?
FUJIOKA...

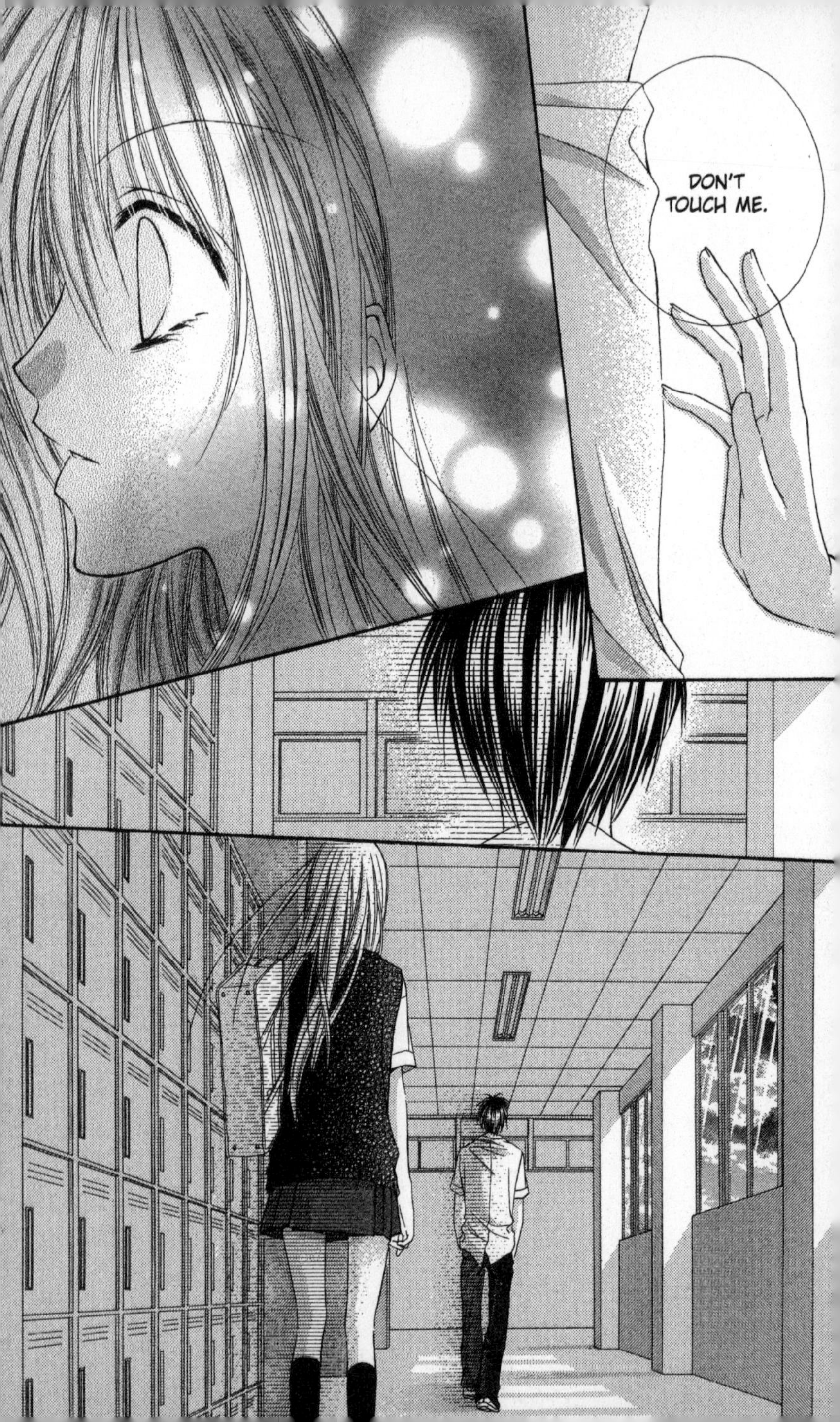
DON'T TOUCH ME.

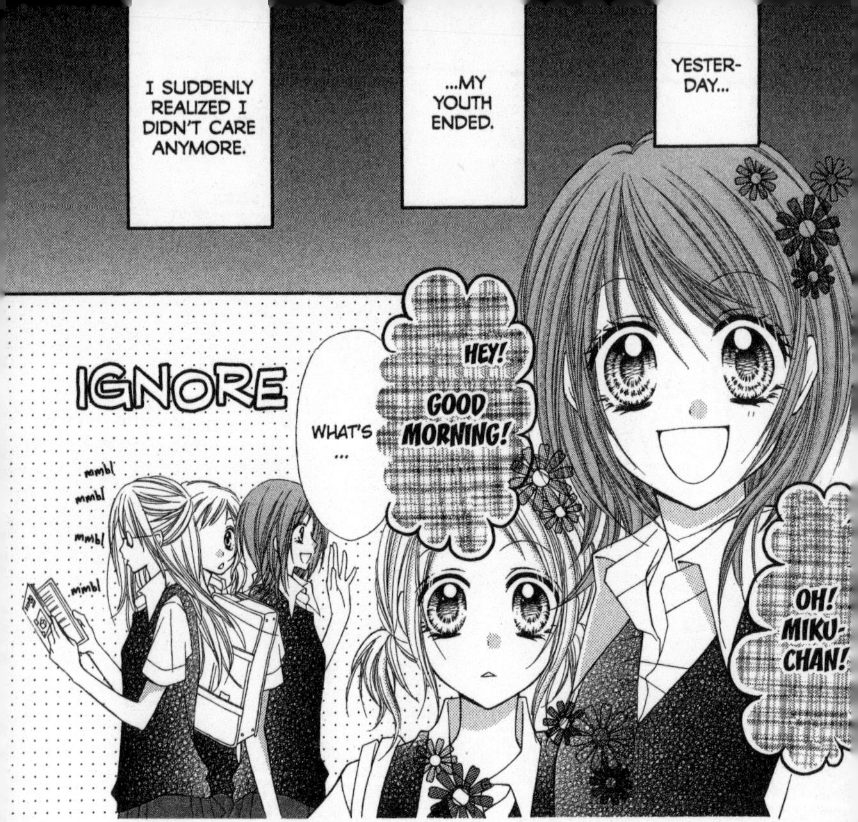
YESTER-DAY...
...MY YOUTH ENDED.
I SUDDENLY REALIZED I DIDN'T CARE ANYMORE.
OH! MIKU-CHAN!
HEY! GOOD MORNING!
WHAT'S ...
IGNORE
mmbl
mmbl
mmbl
mmbl

SMALL TALK 3

A lot of people (various friends, etc.) have said to me, "The ending was so ordinary." So can someone explain to me what a "not ordinary" ending is supposed to be like?! (←I've got a very limited imagination.)

My assistants had some fun inserting their own names into that scene where Miku is imagining Fujioka's future "prospects."

Apparently, my assistants are all perverts.

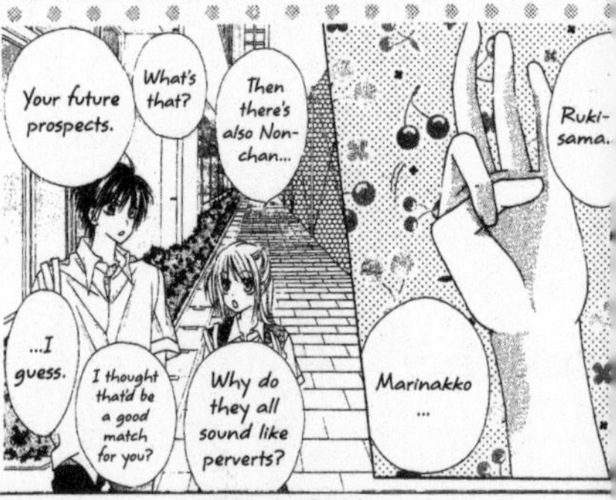
Ruki-sama...
Marinakko ...
Then there's also Non-chan...
What's that?
Your future prospects.
Why do they all sound like perverts?
I thought that'd be a good match for you?
...I guess.

↑ How could he say "...I guess?!" (laugh)

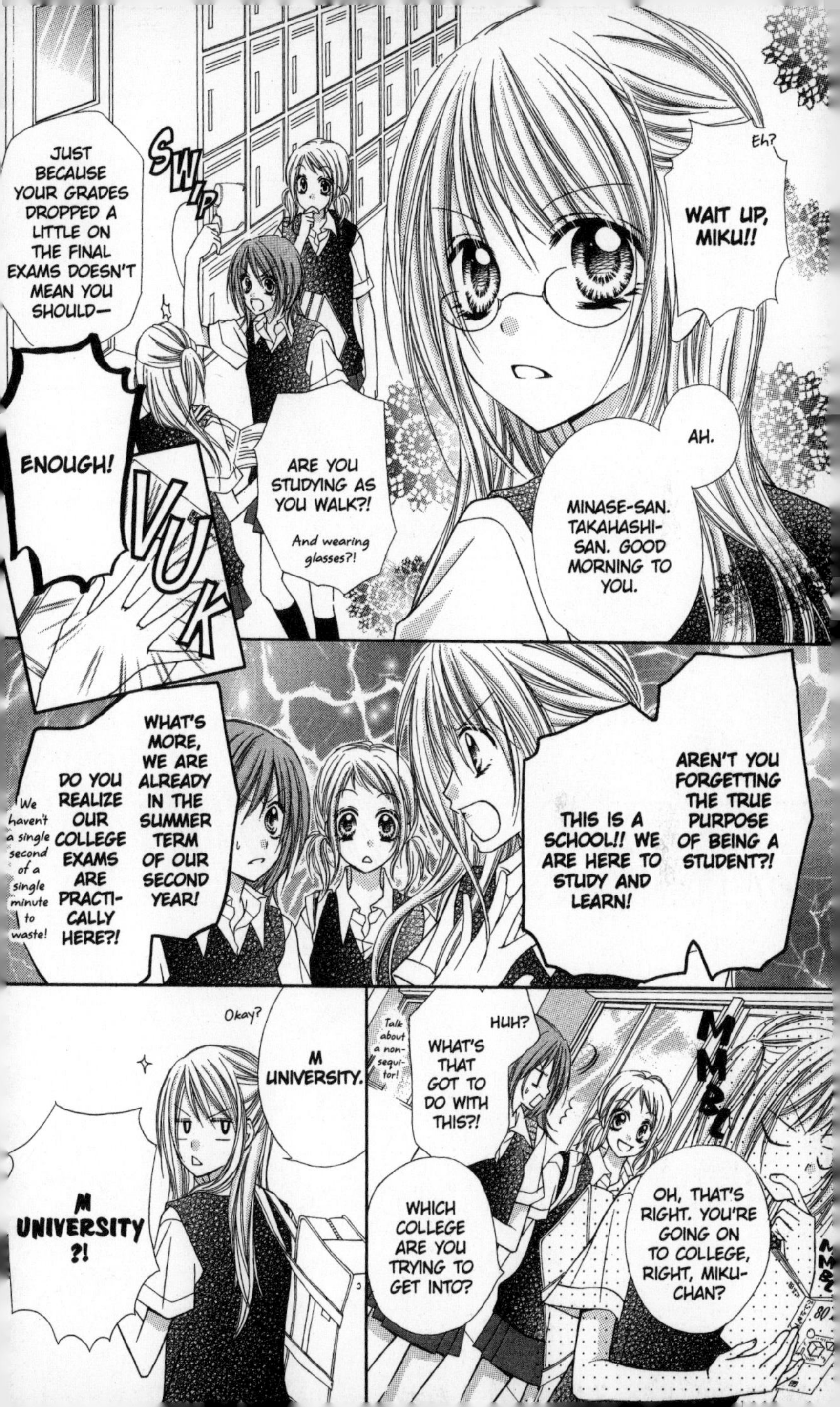
Eh?
WAIT UP, MIKU!!
AH.
MINASE-SAN. TAKAHASHI-SAN. GOOD MORNING TO YOU.
ARE YOU STUDYING AS YOU WALK?!
And wearing glasses?!
SWIP
JUST BECAUSE YOUR GRADES DROPPED A LITTLE ON THE FINAL EXAMS DOESN'T MEAN YOU SHOULD—
VUK
ENOUGH!
AREN'T YOU FORGETTING THE TRUE PURPOSE OF BEING A STUDENT?!
THIS IS A SCHOOL!! WE ARE HERE TO STUDY AND LEARN!
WHAT'S MORE, WE ARE ALREADY IN THE SUMMER TERM OF OUR SECOND YEAR!
DO YOU REALIZE OUR COLLEGE EXAMS ARE PRACTI-CALLY HERE?!
We haven't a single second of a single minute to waste!
MMBL
OH, THAT'S RIGHT. YOU'RE GOING ON TO COLLEGE, RIGHT, MIKU-CHAN?
MMBL
HUH? WHAT'S THAT GOT TO DO WITH THIS?!
Talk about a non-sequitor!
WHICH COLLEGE ARE YOU TRYING TO GET INTO?
Okay?
M UNIVERSITY.
M UNIVERSITY ?!

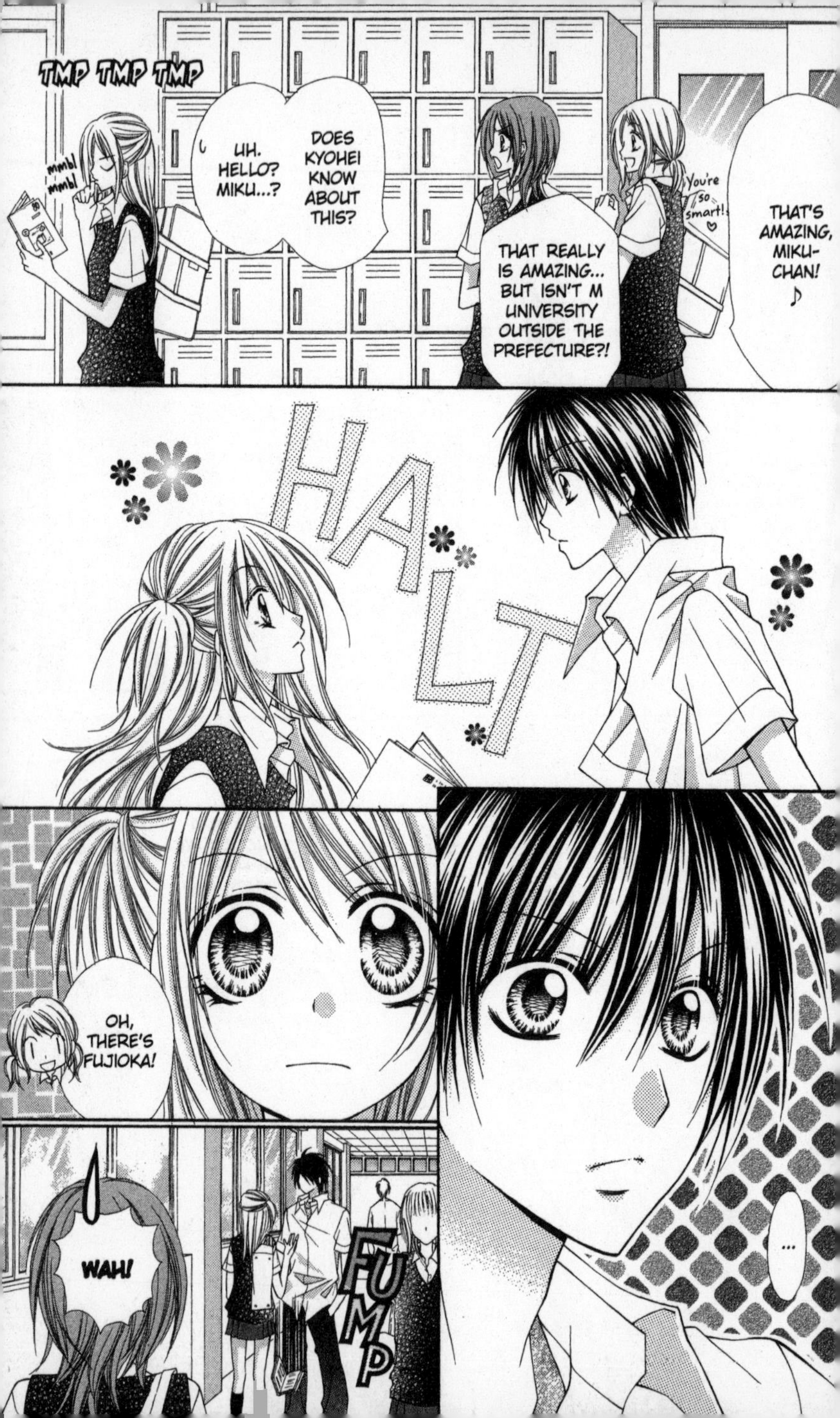

THAT'S AMAZING, MIKU-CHAN! ♪
You're so smart! ♡
THAT REALLY IS AMAZING... BUT ISN'T M UNIVERSITY OUTSIDE THE PREFECTURE?!
DOES KYOHEI KNOW ABOUT THIS?
UH. HELLO? MIKU...?
mmbl mmbl
TMP TMP TMP
HALT
...
OH, THERE'S FUJIOKA!
WAH!
FUMP

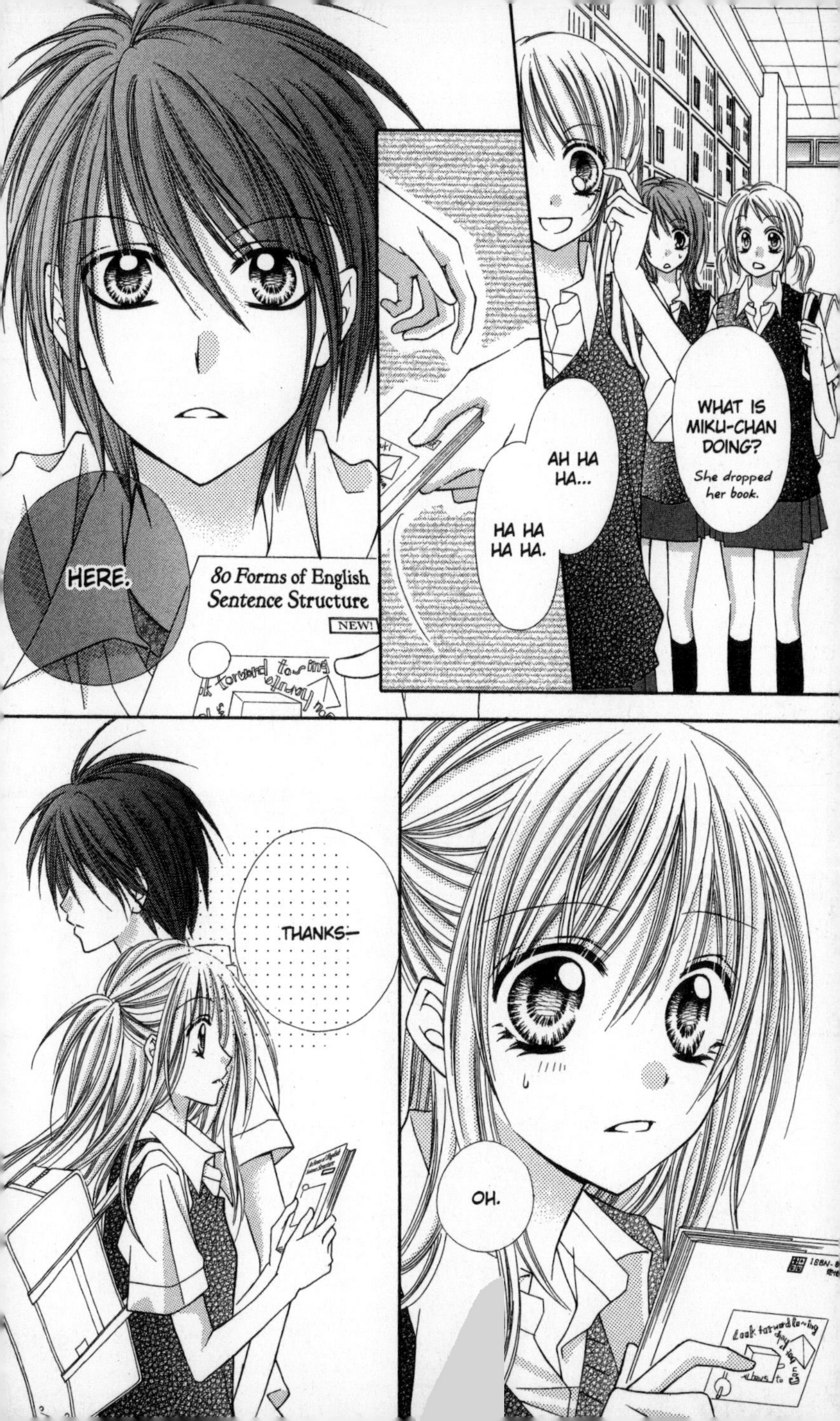
WHAT IS MIKU-CHAN DOING?
She dropped her book.
AH HA HA...
HA HA HA HA.
HERE.
80 Forms of English Sentence Structure
NEW!
OH.
THANKS—

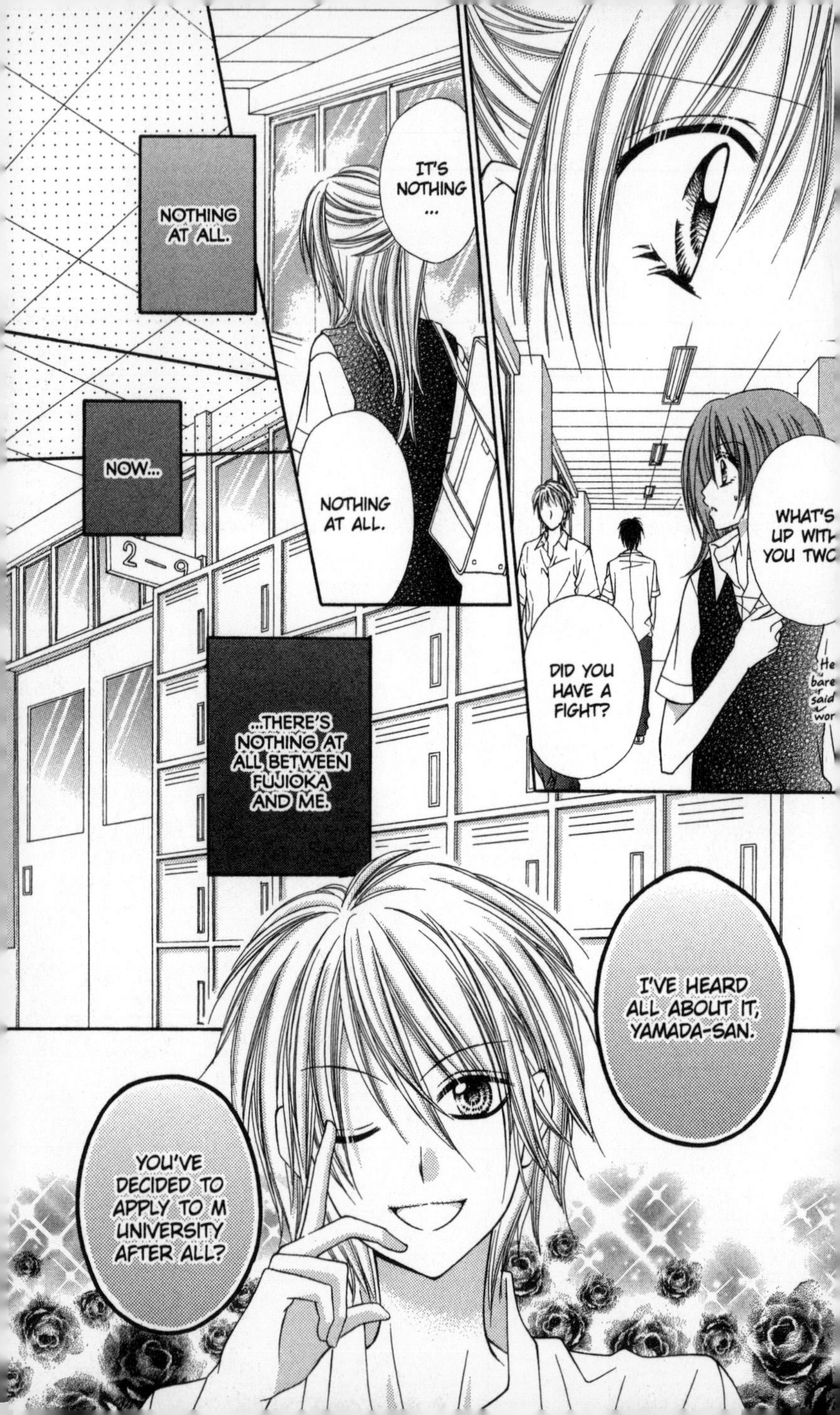

WHAT'S UP WITH YOU TWO
DID YOU HAVE A FIGHT?
IT'S NOTHING...
NOTHING AT ALL.
NOTHING AT ALL.
NOW...
...THERE'S NOTHING AT ALL BETWEEN FUJIOKA AND ME.
I'VE HEARD ALL ABOUT IT, YAMADA-SAN.
YOU'VE DECIDED TO APPLY TO M UNIVERSITY AFTER ALL?

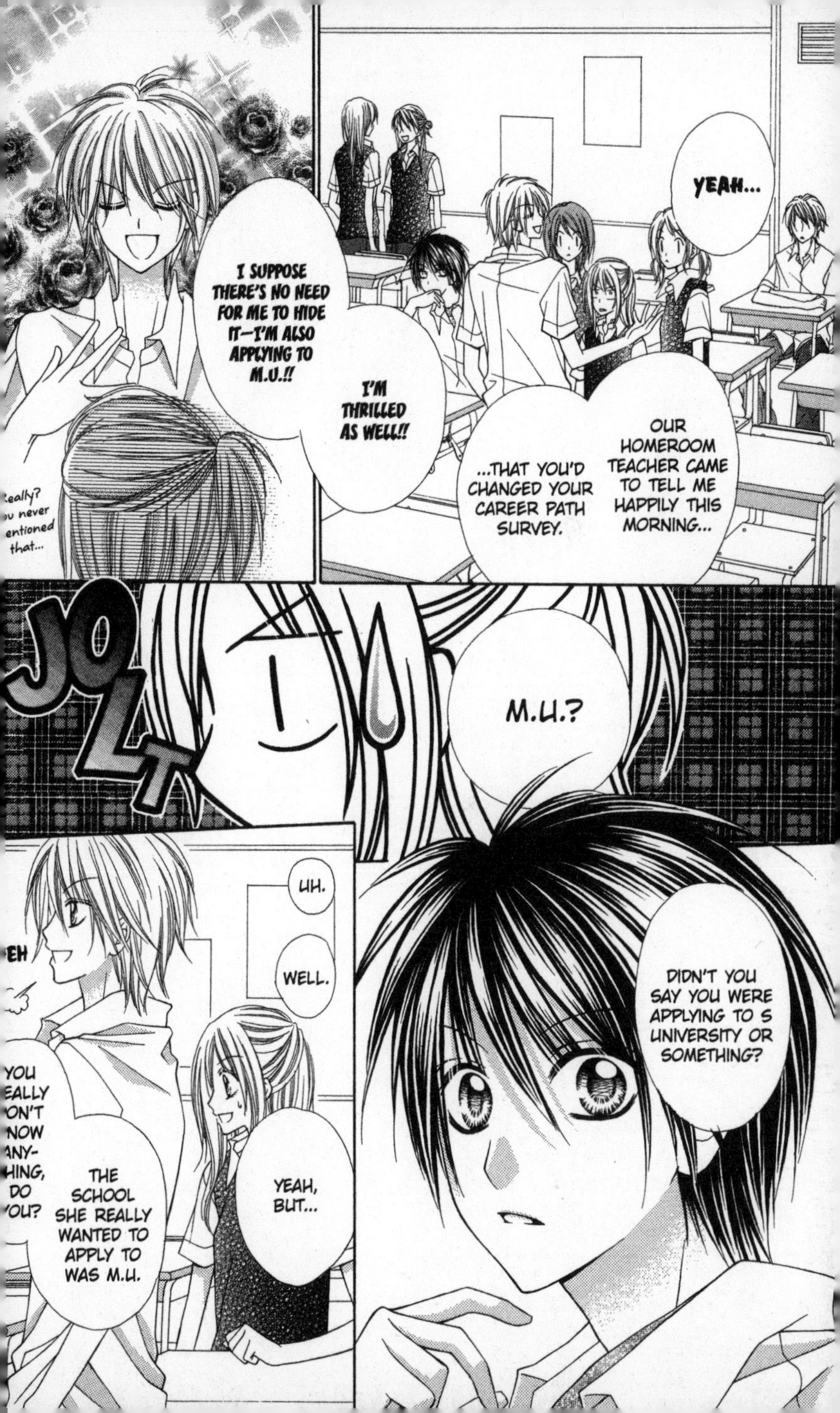
YEAH...
OUR HOMEROOM TEACHER CAME TO TELL ME HAPPILY THIS MORNING...
...THAT YOU'D CHANGED YOUR CAREER PATH SURVEY.
I'M THRILLED AS WELL!!
I SUPPOSE THERE'S NO NEED FOR ME TO HIDE IT—I'M ALSO APPLYING TO M.U.!!
eally? ou never entioned that...
JOLT
M.U.?
DIDN'T YOU SAY YOU WERE APPLYING TO S UNIVERSITY OR SOMETHING?
UH.
WELL.
YEAH, BUT...
THE SCHOOL SHE REALLY WANTED TO APPLY TO WAS M.U.
EH
YOU EALLY ON'T NOW ANY- HING, DO OU?

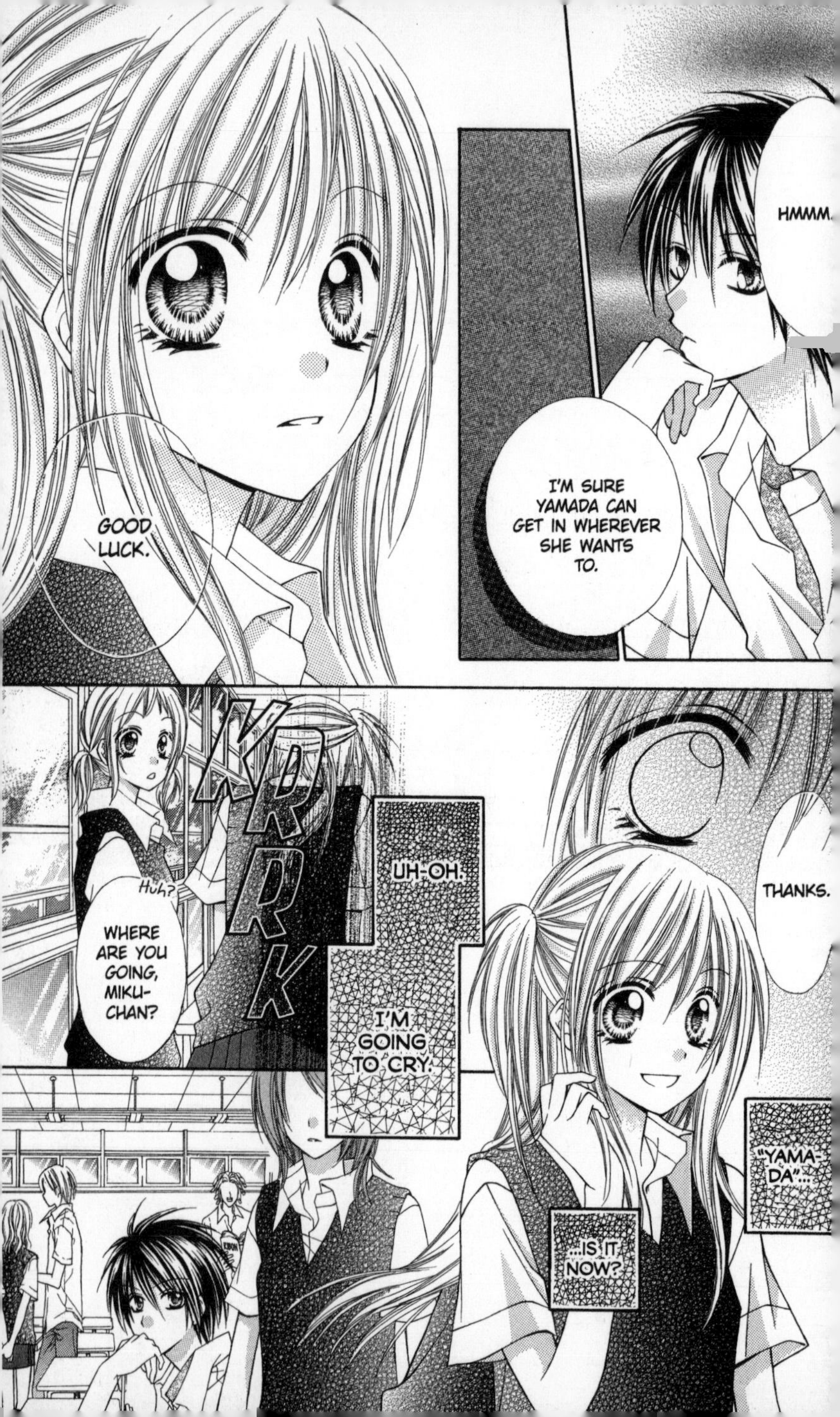
HMMM.
I'M SURE YAMADA CAN GET IN WHEREVER SHE WANTS TO.
GOOD LUCK.
THANKS.
"YAMA-DA"...
...IS IT NOW?
UH-OH.
I'M GOING TO CRY.
KRRK
Huh?
WHERE ARE YOU GOING, MIKU-CHAN?

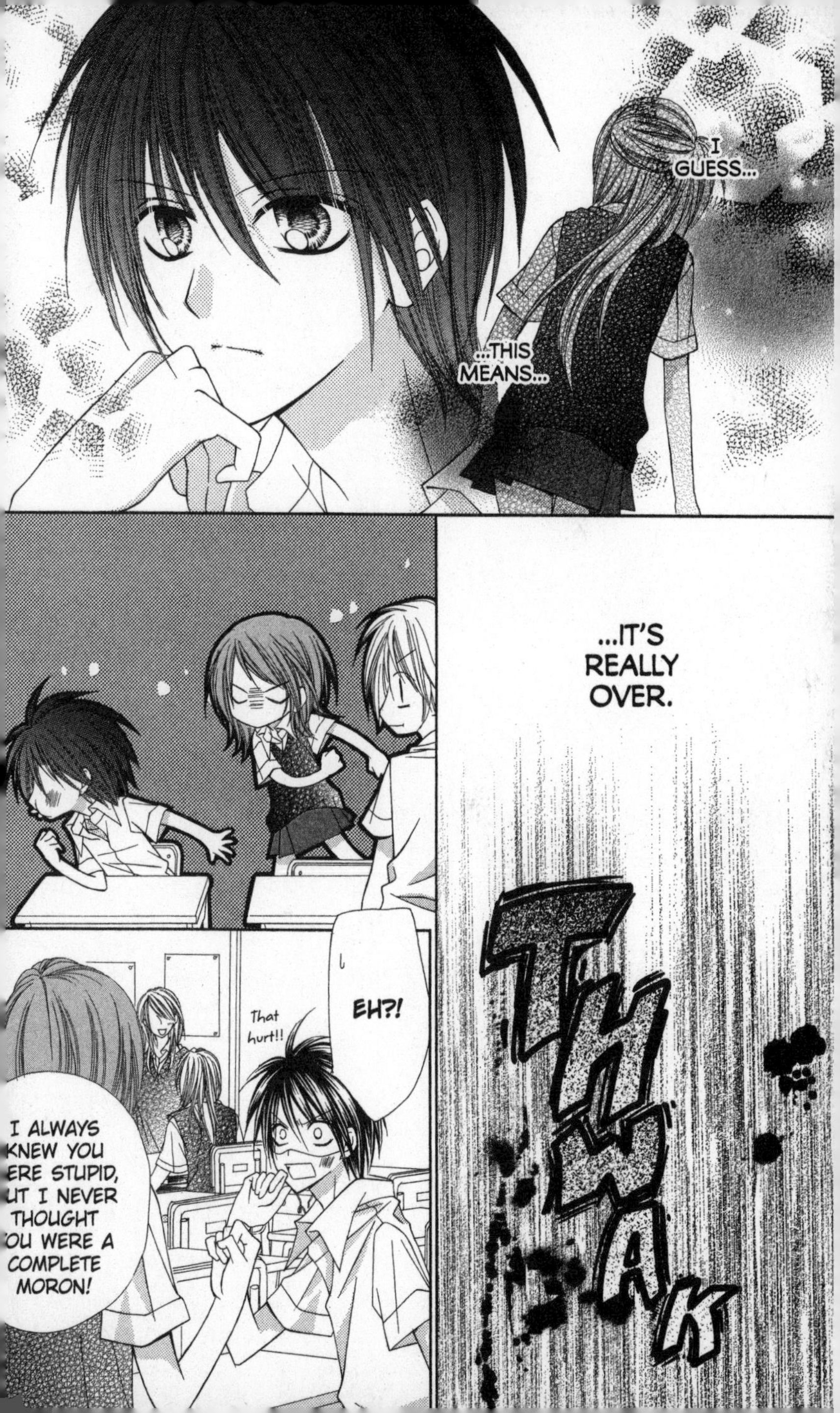
I GUESS...
...THIS MEANS...
...IT'S REALLY OVER.
THWAK
EH?!
That hurt!!
I ALWAYS KNEW YOU ERE STUPID, UT I NEVER THOUGHT OU WERE A COMPLETE MORON!

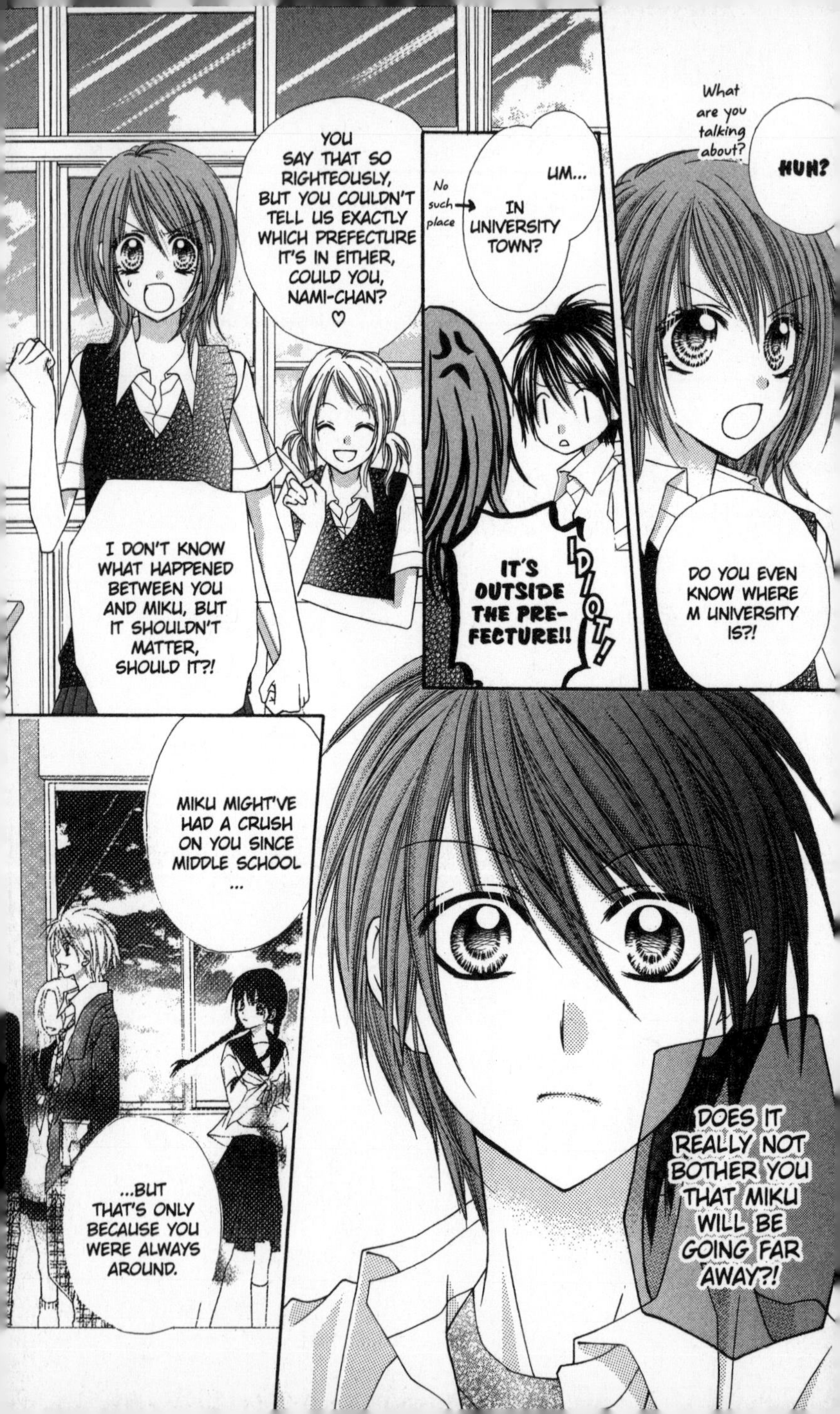
What are you talking about?
HUH?
DO YOU EVEN KNOW WHERE M UNIVERSITY IS?!
UM... IN UNIVERSITY TOWN?
No such place
IT'S OUTSIDE THE PRE-FECTURE!!
IDIOT!
YOU SAY THAT SO RIGHTEOUSLY, BUT YOU COULDN'T TELL US EXACTLY WHICH PREFECTURE IT'S IN EITHER, COULD YOU, NAMI-CHAN? ♡
I DON'T KNOW WHAT HAPPENED BETWEEN YOU AND MIKU, BUT IT SHOULDN'T MATTER, SHOULD IT?!
DOES IT REALLY NOT BOTHER YOU THAT MIKU WILL BE GOING FAR AWAY?!
MIKU MIGHT'VE HAD A CRUSH ON YOU SINCE MIDDLE SCHOOL ...
...BUT THAT'S ONLY BECAUSE YOU WERE ALWAYS AROUND.

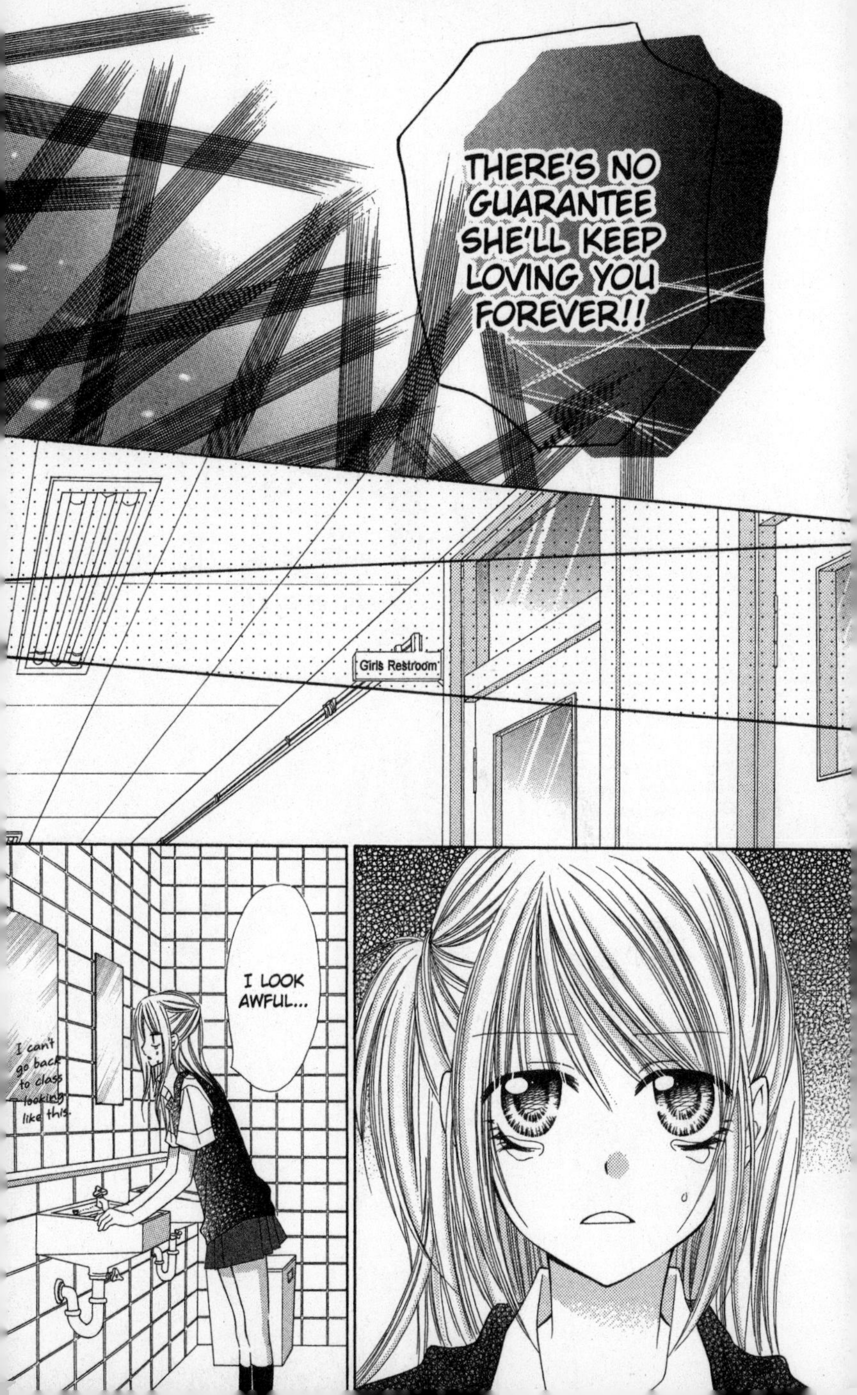
THERE'S NO GUARANTEE SHE'LL KEEP LOVING YOU FOREVER!!
Girls Restroom
I LOOK AWFUL...
I can't go back to class looking like this.

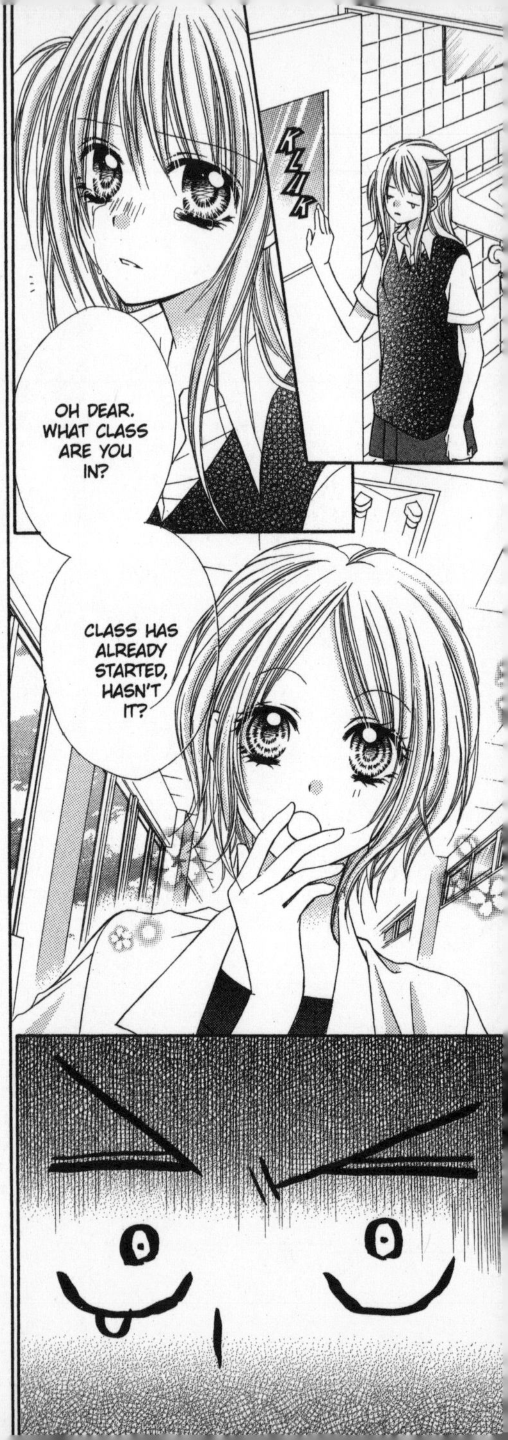
KLIK
OH DEAR. WHAT CLASS ARE YOU IN?
CLASS HAS ALREADY STARTED, HASN'T IT?

7
seven

That's right! Speaking of people on TV, recently (by which I mean back in June) I saw Gou Morita-sama and Ken Miyake-sama from V6* at Tokyo Station! I was so surprised!

I'd been scheduled for an autograph session in Sendai that day and had been staring blankly out the window while waiting for the Shinkansen to depart when I saw them. I thought, "Hey, that person looks just like Gou Morita, and the guy next to him looks a lot like Ken Miyake... Wait, is that really them?!"

In any case, I wanted to tell someone and squee over it together, but at the time I was with my editor and our Chief Editor—two respectable, proper adults—so I had to keep my great discovery to myself... Or so I thought, when my editor spotted them herself and jumped to her feet! She totally surprised me! (laugh)

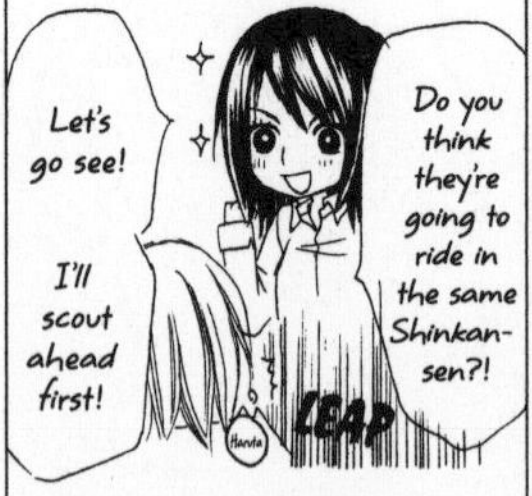
Do you think they're going to ride in the same Shinkansen?!
Let's go see!
I'll scout ahead first!
LEAP

Well, her scouting didn't turn up much since we were stuck inside the train. Our Chief Editor's reaction was, "Ah, that's nice," without a shred of interest. I knew it!!

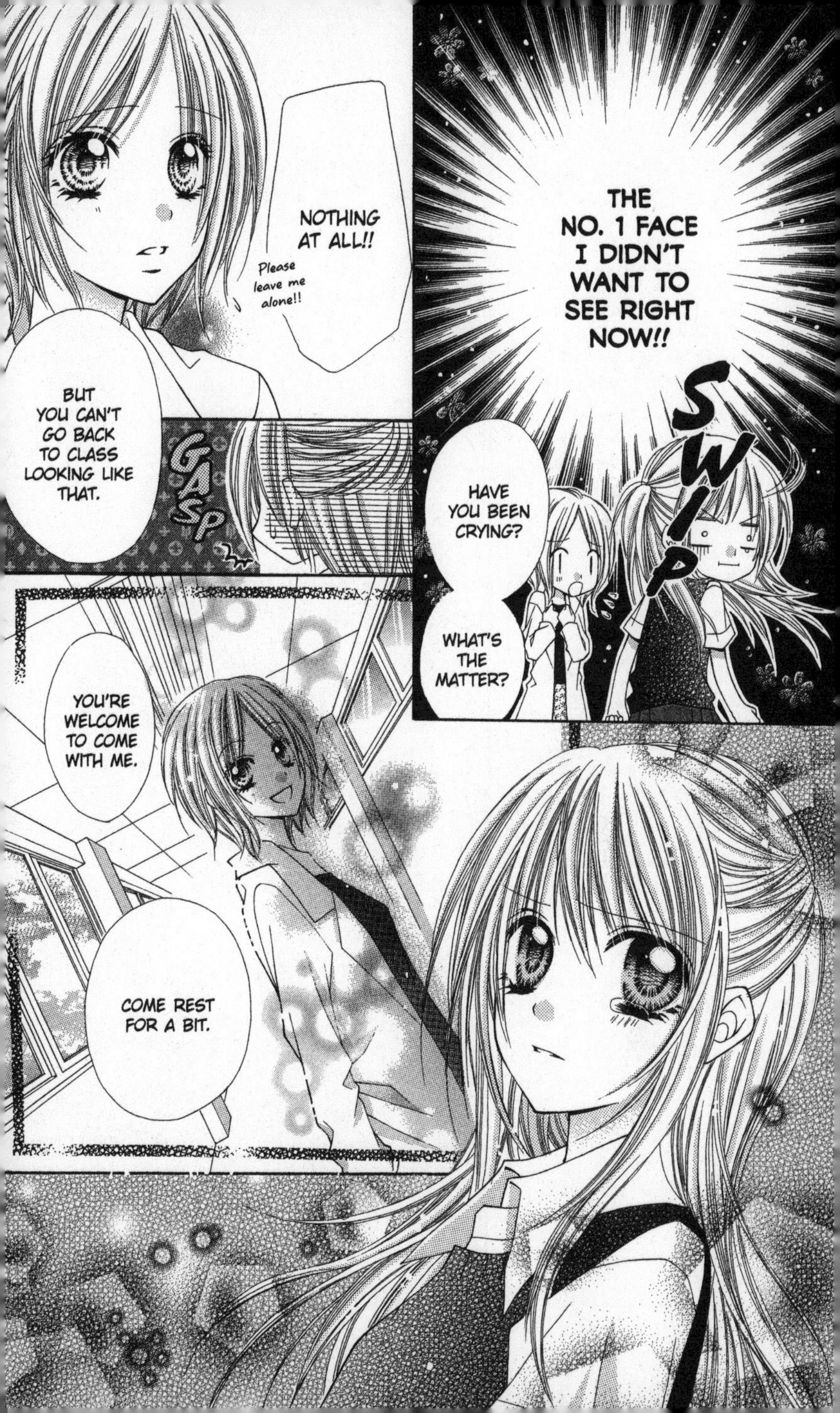
THE NO. 1 FACE I DIDN'T WANT TO SEE RIGHT NOW!!
SWIP
HAVE YOU BEEN CRYING?
WHAT'S THE MATTER?
NOTHING AT ALL!!
Please leave me alone!!
BUT YOU CAN'T GO BACK TO CLASS LOOKING LIKE THAT.
GASP
YOU'RE WELCOME TO COME WITH ME.
COME REST FOR A BIT.

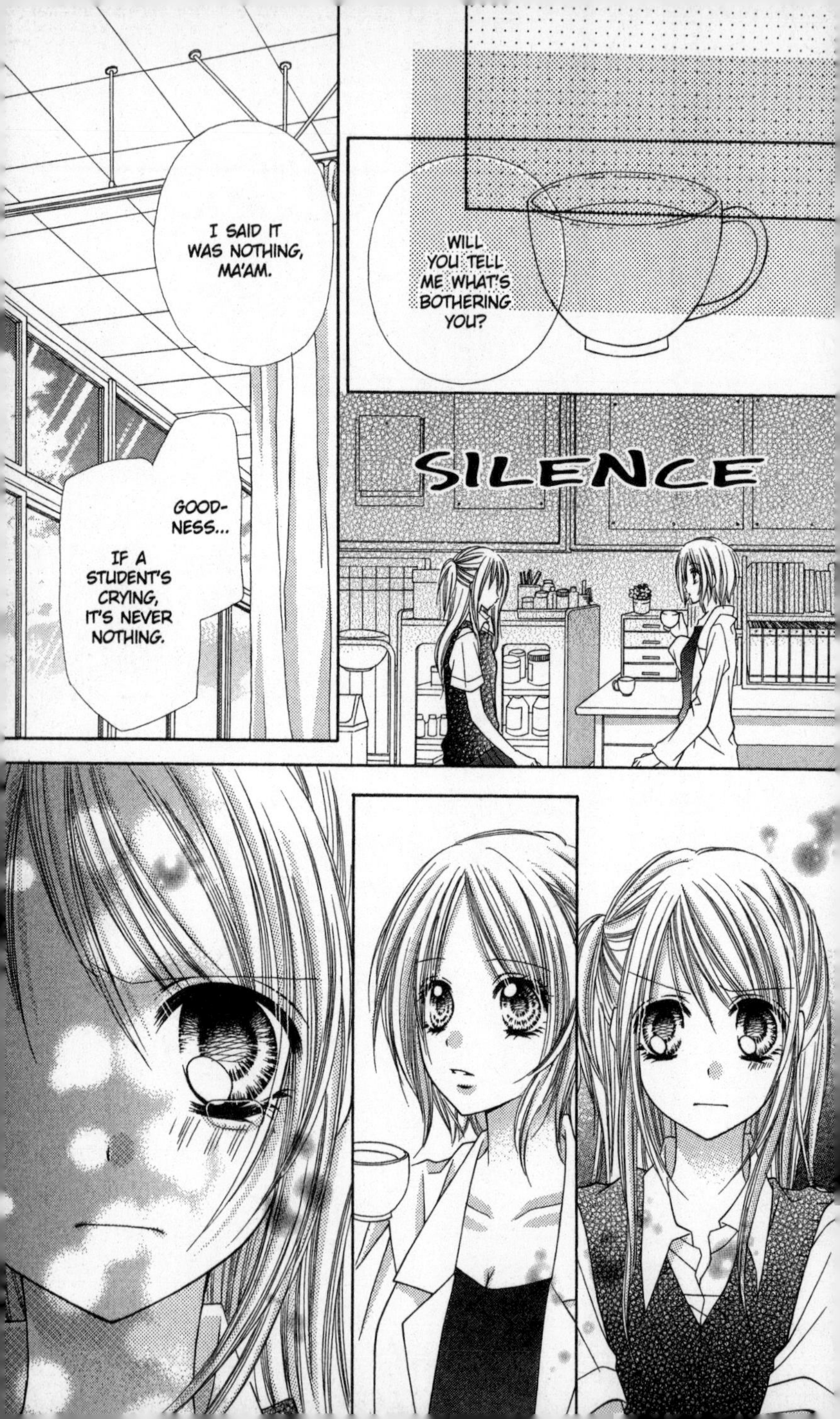
WILL YOU TELL ME WHAT'S BOTHERING YOU?
SILENCE
I SAID IT WAS NOTHING, MA'AM.
GOODNESS...
IF A STUDENT'S CRYING, IT'S NEVER NOTHING.

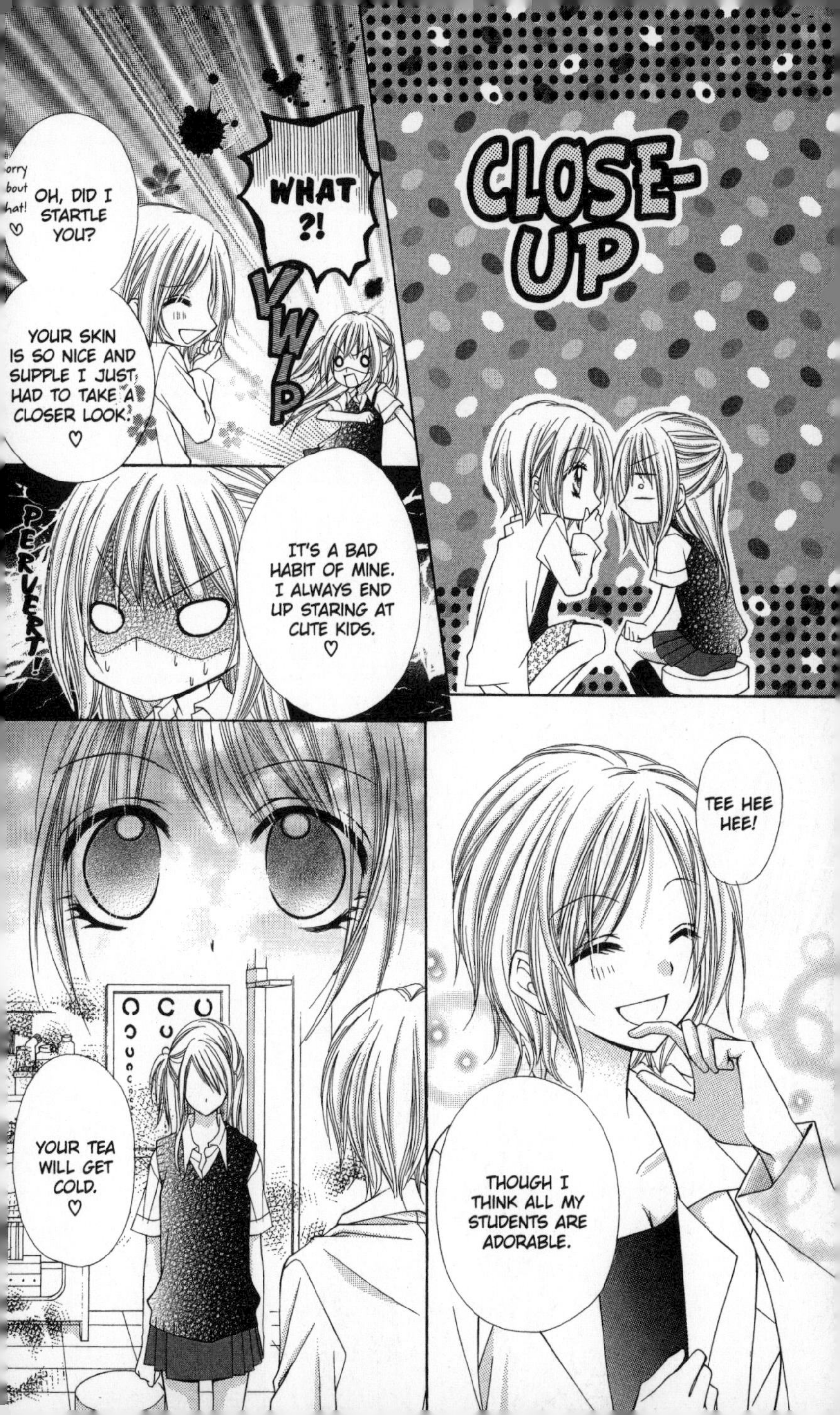
CLOSE-UP
WHAT?!
VWIP
orry bout hat! ♡
OH, DID I STARTLE YOU?
YOUR SKIN IS SO NICE AND SUPPLE I JUST HAD TO TAKE A CLOSER LOOK. ♡
IT'S A BAD HABIT OF MINE. I ALWAYS END UP STARING AT CUTE KIDS. ♡
PERVERT!
TEE HEE HEE!
THOUGH I THINK ALL MY STUDENTS ARE ADORABLE.
YOUR TEA WILL GET COLD. ♡

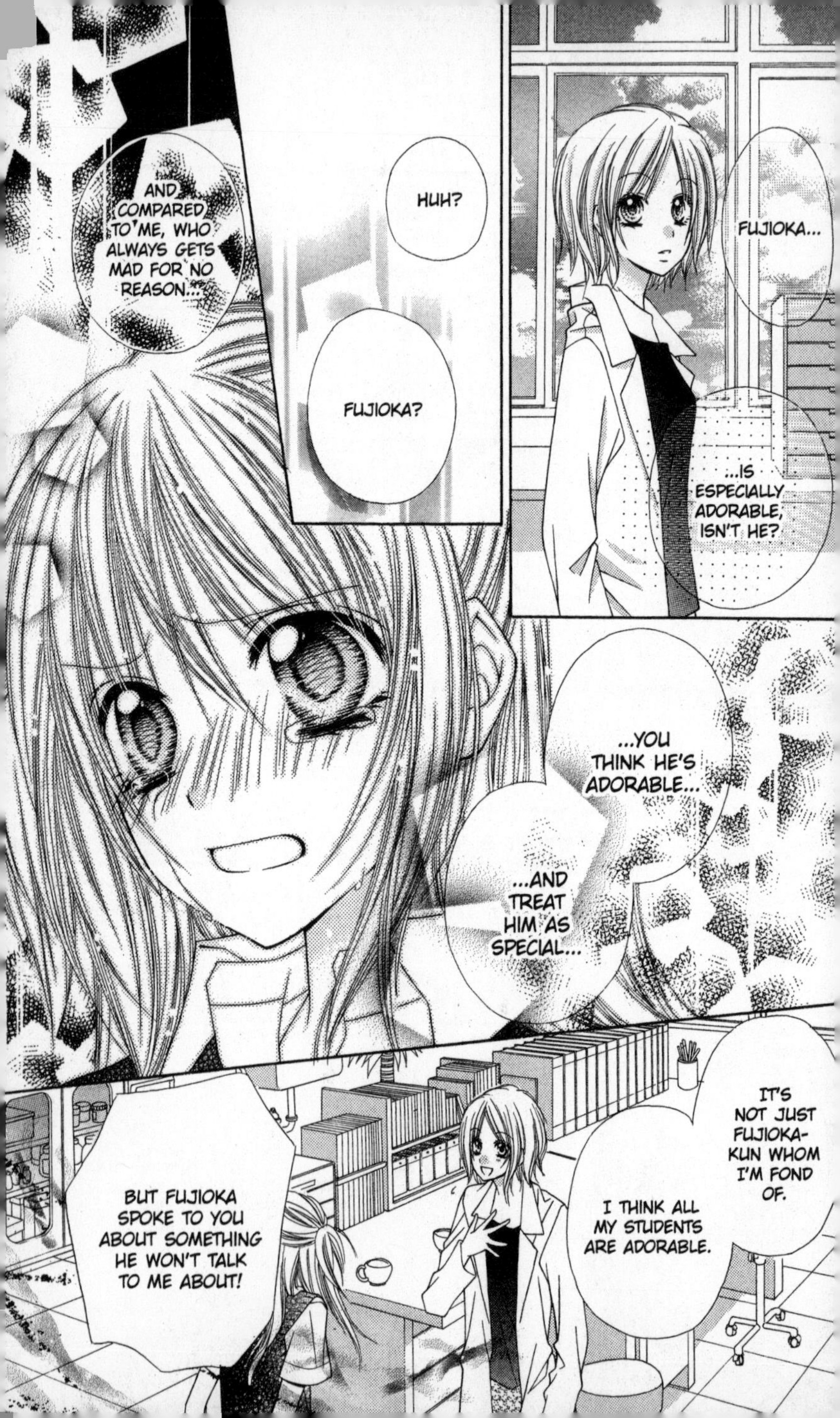
FUJIOKA...
...IS ESPECIALLY ADORABLE, ISN'T HE?
HUH?
FUJIOKA?
AND COMPARED TO ME, WHO ALWAYS GETS MAD FOR NO REASON...
...YOU THINK HE'S ADORABLE...
...AND TREAT HIM AS SPECIAL...
IT'S NOT JUST FUJIOKA-KUN WHOM I'M FOND OF.
I THINK ALL MY STUDENTS ARE ADORABLE.
BUT FUJIOKA SPOKE TO YOU ABOUT SOMETHING HE WON'T TALK TO ME ABOUT!

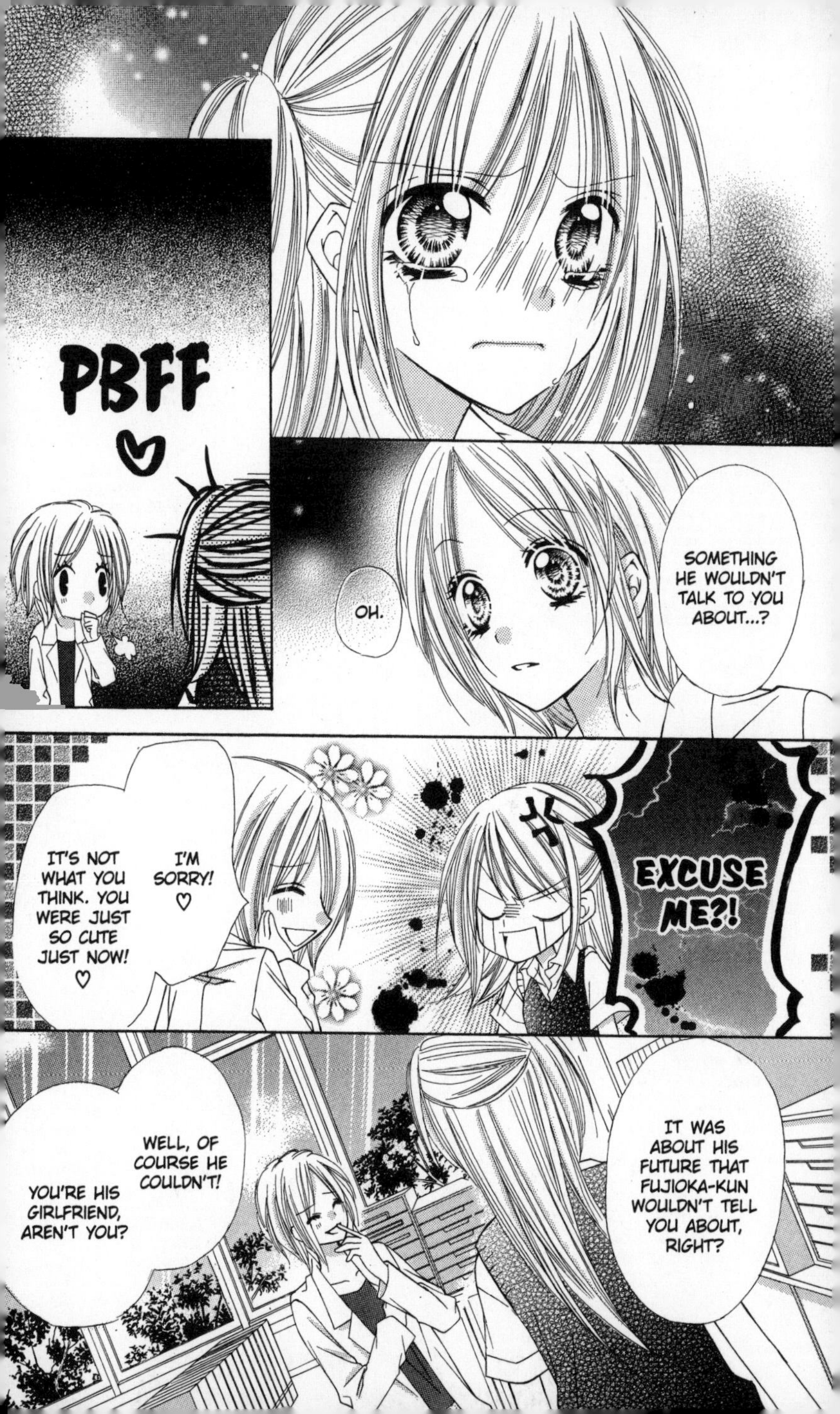
SOMETHING HE WOULDN'T TALK TO YOU ABOUT...?
OH.
PBFF ♡
EXCUSE ME?!
I'M SORRY! ♡
IT'S NOT WHAT YOU THINK. YOU WERE JUST SO CUTE JUST NOW! ♡
IT WAS ABOUT HIS FUTURE THAT FUJIOKA-KUN WOULDN'T TELL YOU ABOUT, RIGHT?
WELL, OF COURSE HE COULDN'T!
YOU'RE HIS GIRLFRIEND, AREN'T YOU?

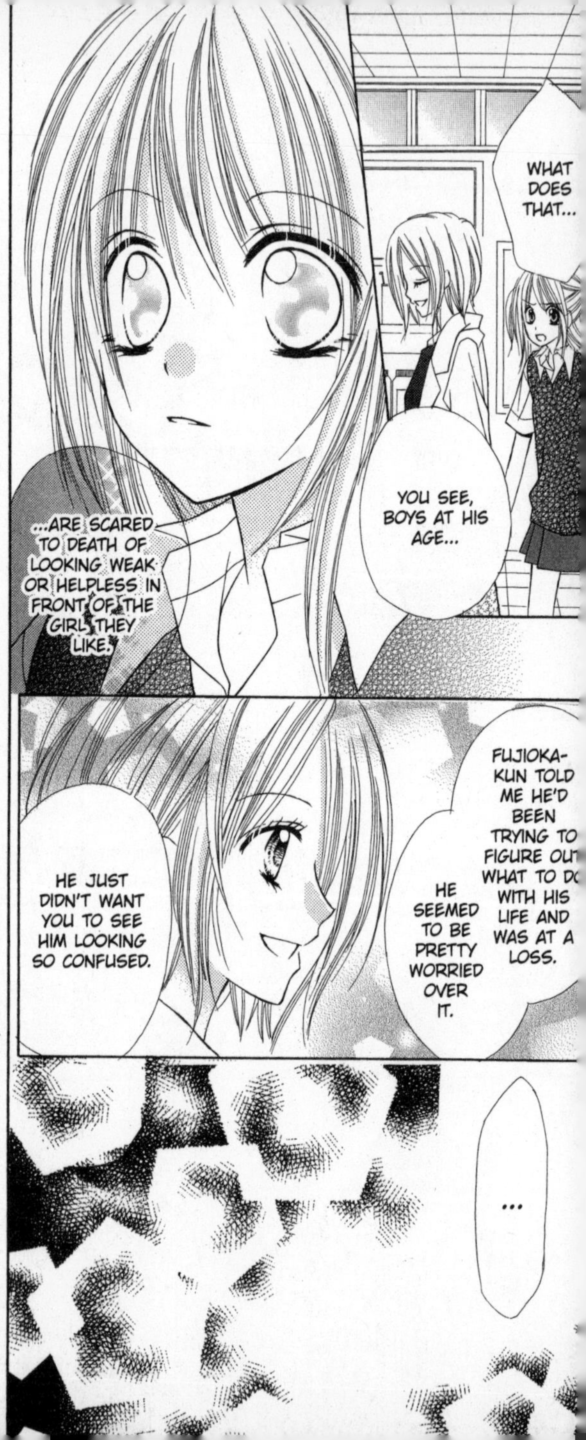
WHAT DOES THAT...
YOU SEE, BOYS AT HIS AGE...
...ARE SCARED TO DEATH OF LOOKING WEAK OR HELPLESS IN FRONT OF THE GIRL THEY LIKE.
FUJIOKA-KUN TOLD ME HE'D BEEN TRYING TO FIGURE OUT WHAT TO DO WITH HIS LIFE AND WAS AT A LOSS.
HE SEEMED TO BE PRETTY WORRIED OVER IT.
HE JUST DIDN'T WANT YOU TO SEE HIM LOOKING SO CONFUSED.
...

8
eight

As I touched on in [7], I got to have an autograph session in Sendai in celebration of the release of Cactus volume 3! ✧

It was the first time I've had an autograph session solely for me so I was full of nerves and extremely worried that no one would show up. But a lot of people actually came! It was such a relief. Phew!

When I get really nervous, I start shaking, so the first few autographs I signed were so wiggly that you'd think I was randomly doodling or something... I'm so sorry about that. Even though the session took place in Sendai, there were a few people who came from as far as Fukushima and Yamagata—I was truly thrilled and grateful. I feel really disappointed in myself for being such an idiot I couldn't even say anything interesting or meaningful to my fans during this extremely rare chance to talk with them face-to-face. Despite that, I still had so much fun at the event! Thank you so much to everyone who came and participated!

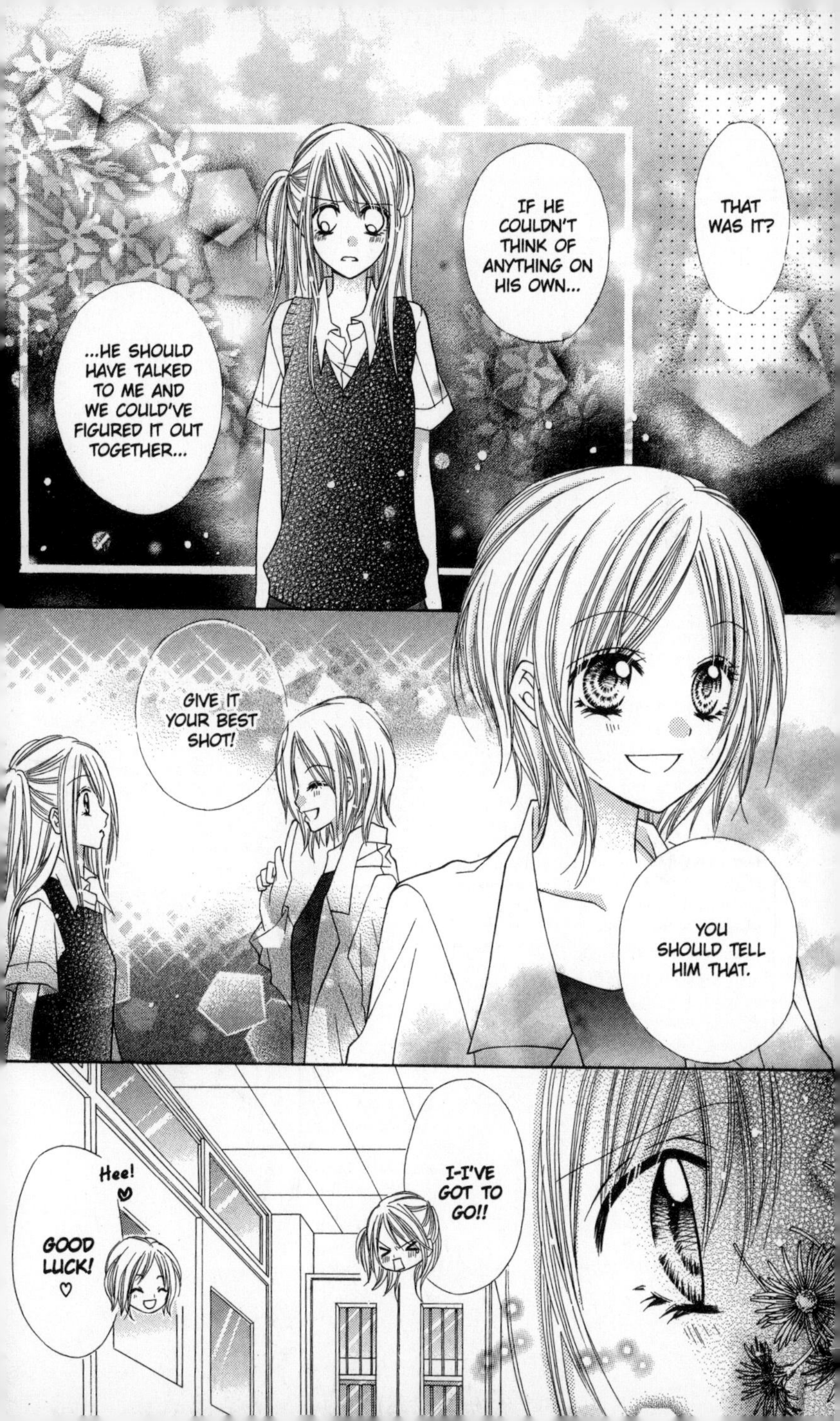
THAT WAS IT?
IF HE COULDN'T THINK OF ANYTHING ON HIS OWN...
...HE SHOULD HAVE TALKED TO ME AND WE COULD'VE FIGURED IT OUT TOGETHER...
YOU SHOULD TELL HIM THAT.
GIVE IT YOUR BEST SHOT!
I-I'VE GOT TO GO!!
Hee! ♥
GOOD LUCK! ♥

9
nine

This is the last column! There were only 9 this time, so I've had it a little easier than usual. Oh, but I'm not being lazy and skimping on columns or anything—there's really only nine!

So with this, my work on *Cactus* will officially be over. I know in the first column I mentioned there were a few things I was "hesitant" about with this series, but honestly, it is my own creation after all, and that alone makes it dear to me. Miku-tsun and Fujioka, may you find happiness together! That's how I feel about this series now.

And with those warm, fuzzy feelings, I'm ending my columns here. Please enjoy the bonus pages at the end of the book too. ☆

See you!

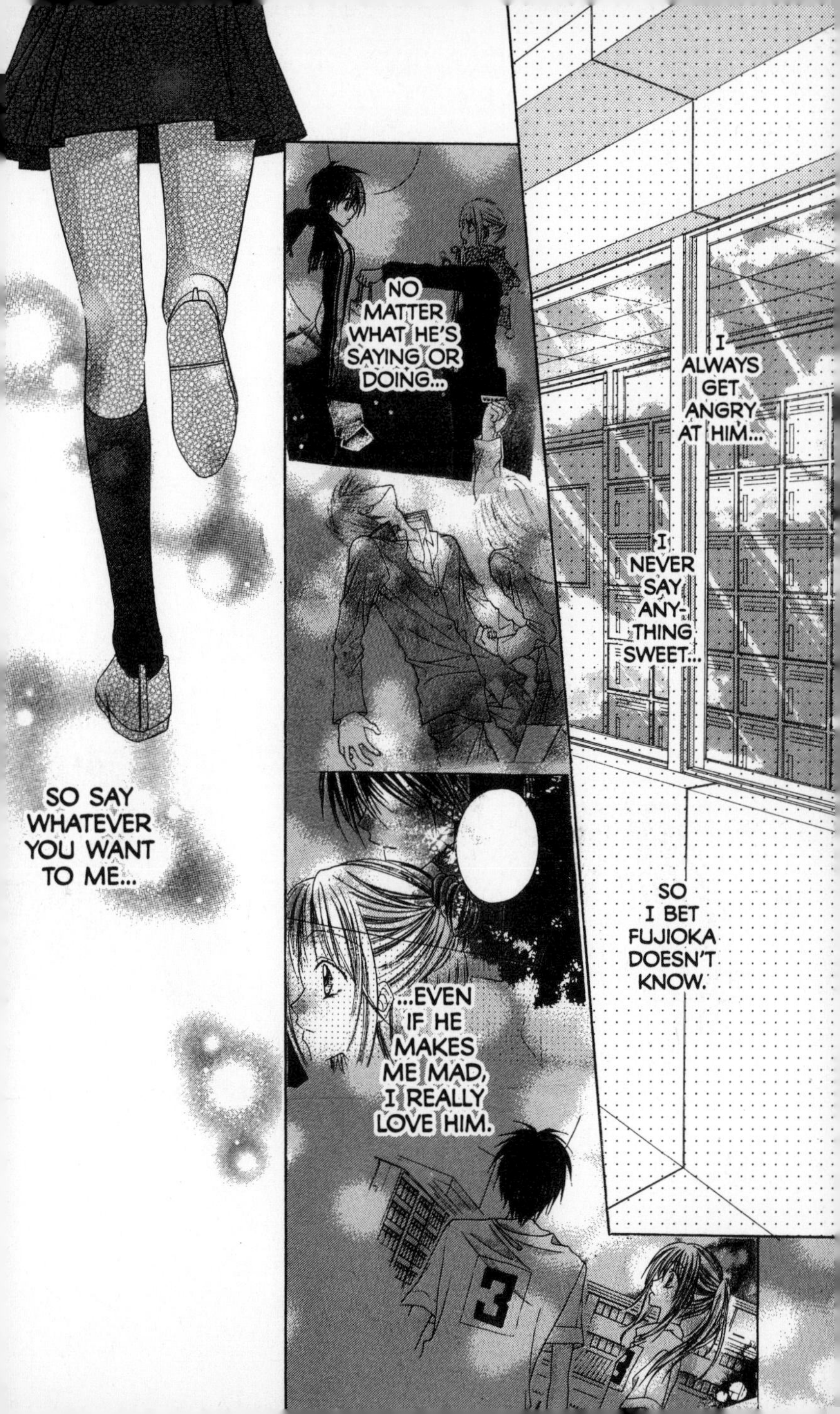
I ALWAYS GET ANGRY AT HIM...
I NEVER SAY ANY-THING SWEET...
SO I BET FUJIOKA DOESN'T KNOW.
NO MATTER WHAT HE'S SAYING OR DOING...
...EVEN IF HE MAKES ME MAD, I REALLY LOVE HIM.
SO SAY WHATEVER YOU WANT TO ME...

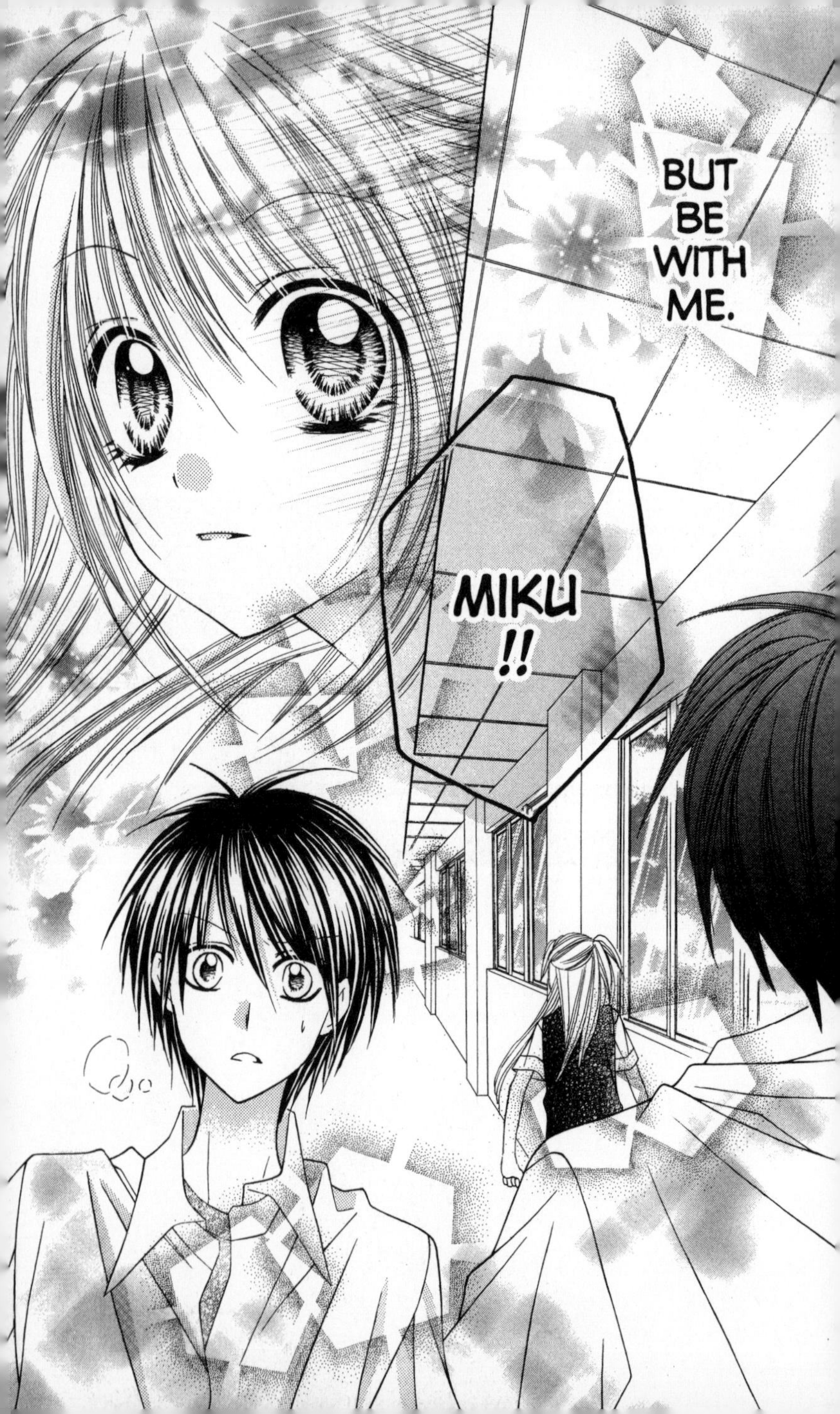
BUT BE WITH ME.
MIKU !!

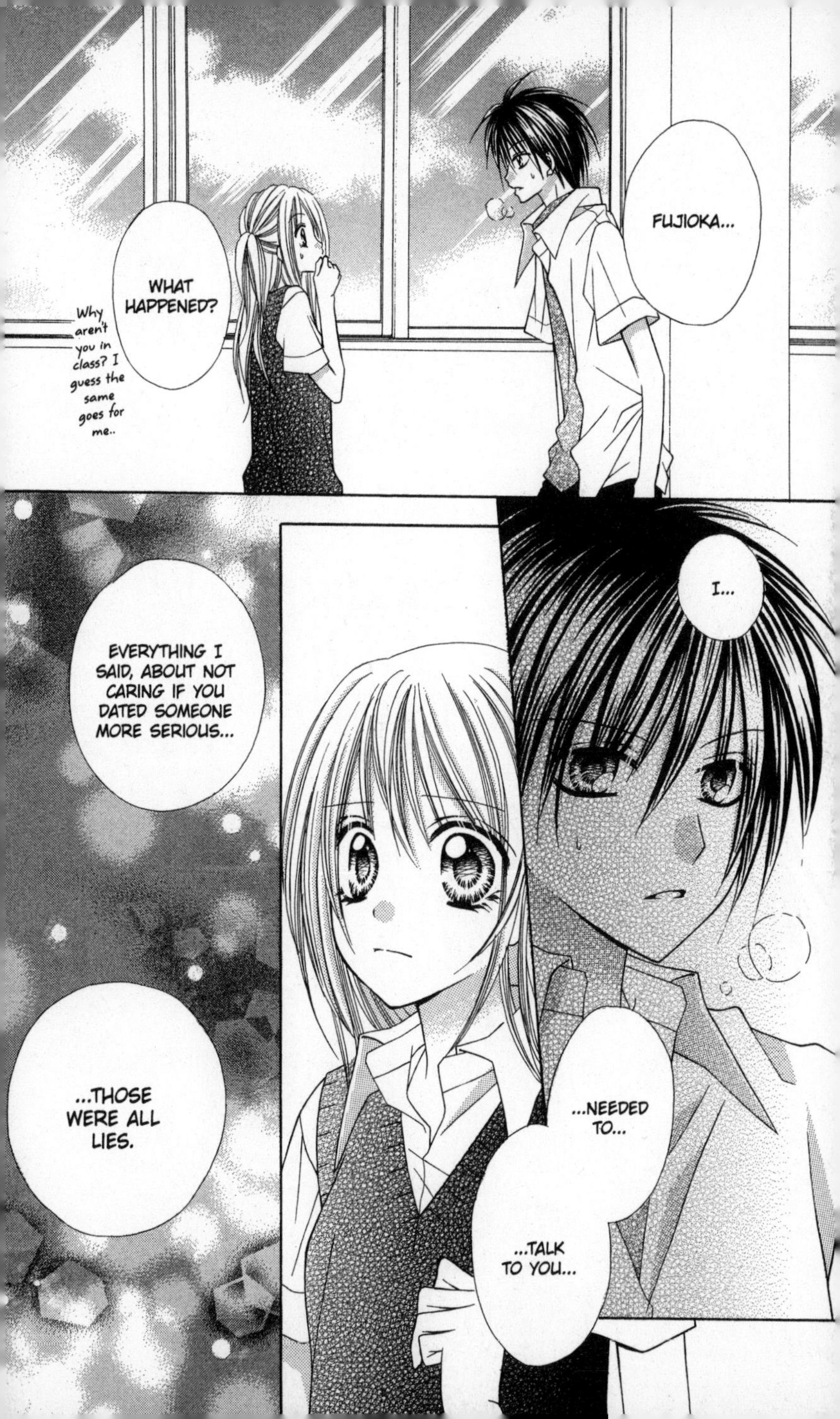
FUJIOKA...
WHAT HAPPENED?
Why aren't you in class? I guess the same goes for me..
I...
...NEEDED TO...
...TALK TO YOU...
EVERYTHING I SAID, ABOUT NOT CARING IF YOU DATED SOMEONE MORE SERIOUS...
...THOSE WERE ALL LIES.

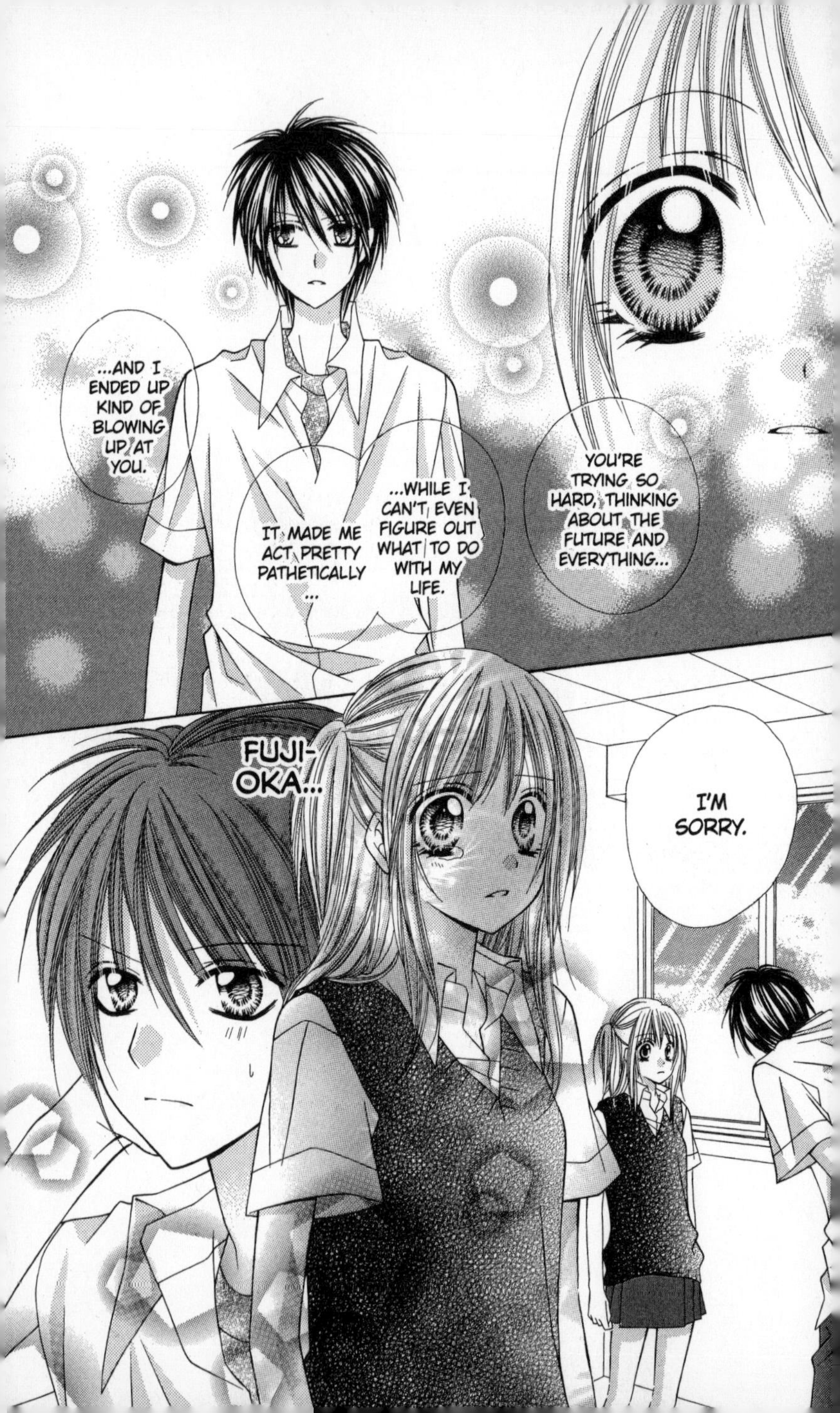
YOU'RE TRYING SO HARD, THINKING ABOUT THE FUTURE AND EVERYTHING...
...WHILE I CAN'T EVEN FIGURE OUT WHAT TO DO WITH MY LIFE.
IT MADE ME ACT PRETTY PATHETICALLY ...
...AND I ENDED UP KIND OF BLOWING UP AT YOU.
I'M SORRY.
FUJI-OKA...

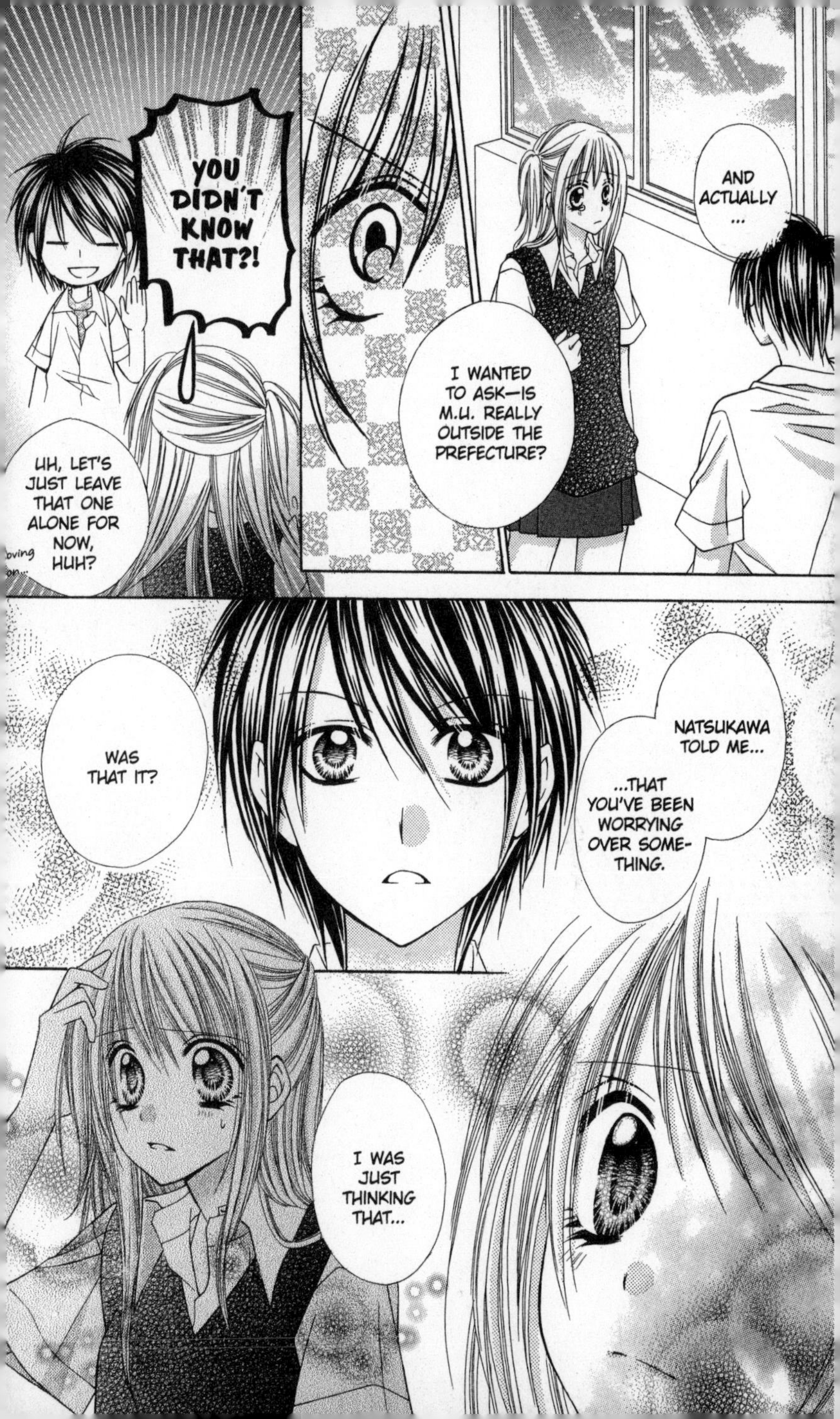
AND ACTUALLY ...
I WANTED TO ASK—IS M.U. REALLY OUTSIDE THE PREFECTURE?
YOU DIDN'T KNOW THAT?!
UH, LET'S JUST LEAVE THAT ONE ALONE FOR NOW, HUH?
NATSUKAWA TOLD ME...
...THAT YOU'VE BEEN WORRYING OVER SOME-THING.
WAS THAT IT?
I WAS JUST THINKING THAT...

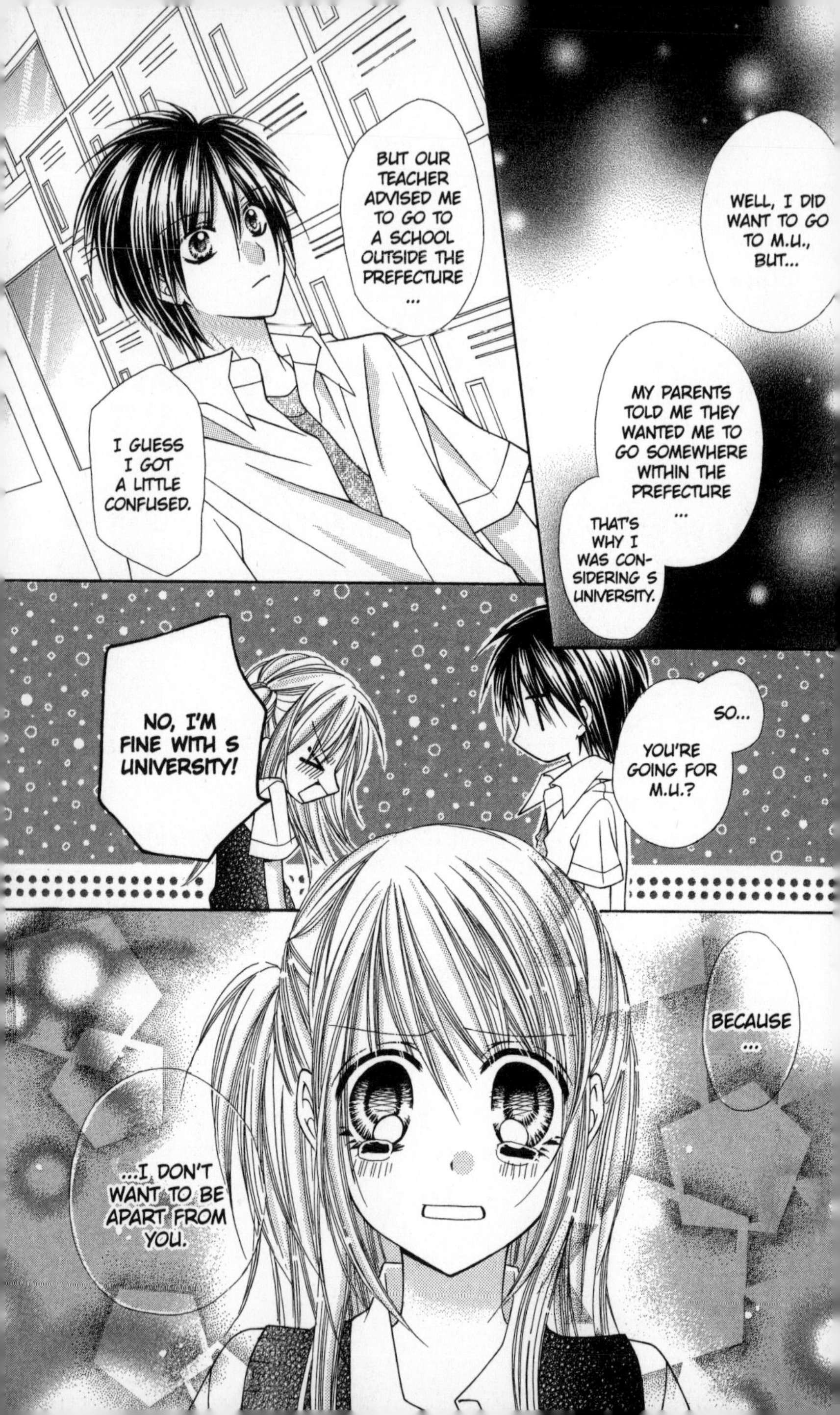
WELL, I DID WANT TO GO TO M.U., BUT...
MY PARENTS TOLD ME THEY WANTED ME TO GO SOMEWHERE WITHIN THE PREFECTURE ...
THAT'S WHY I WAS CONSIDERING S UNIVERSITY.
BUT OUR TEACHER ADVISED ME TO GO TO A SCHOOL OUTSIDE THE PREFECTURE ...
I GUESS I GOT A LITTLE CONFUSED.
SO...
YOU'RE GOING FOR M.U.?
NO, I'M FINE WITH S UNIVERSITY!
BECAUSE ...
...I DON'T WANT TO BE APART FROM YOU.

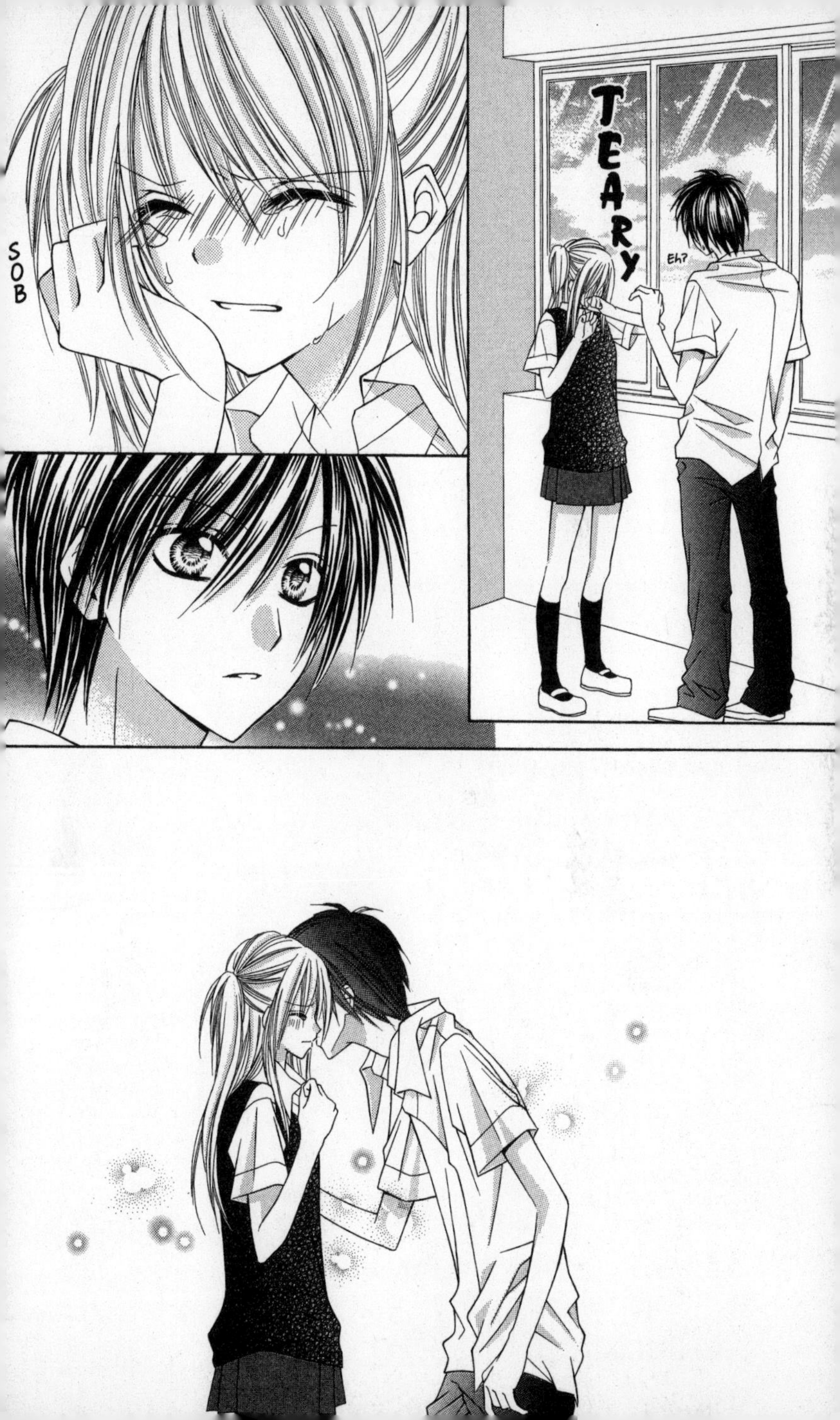
TEARY
Eh?
SOB

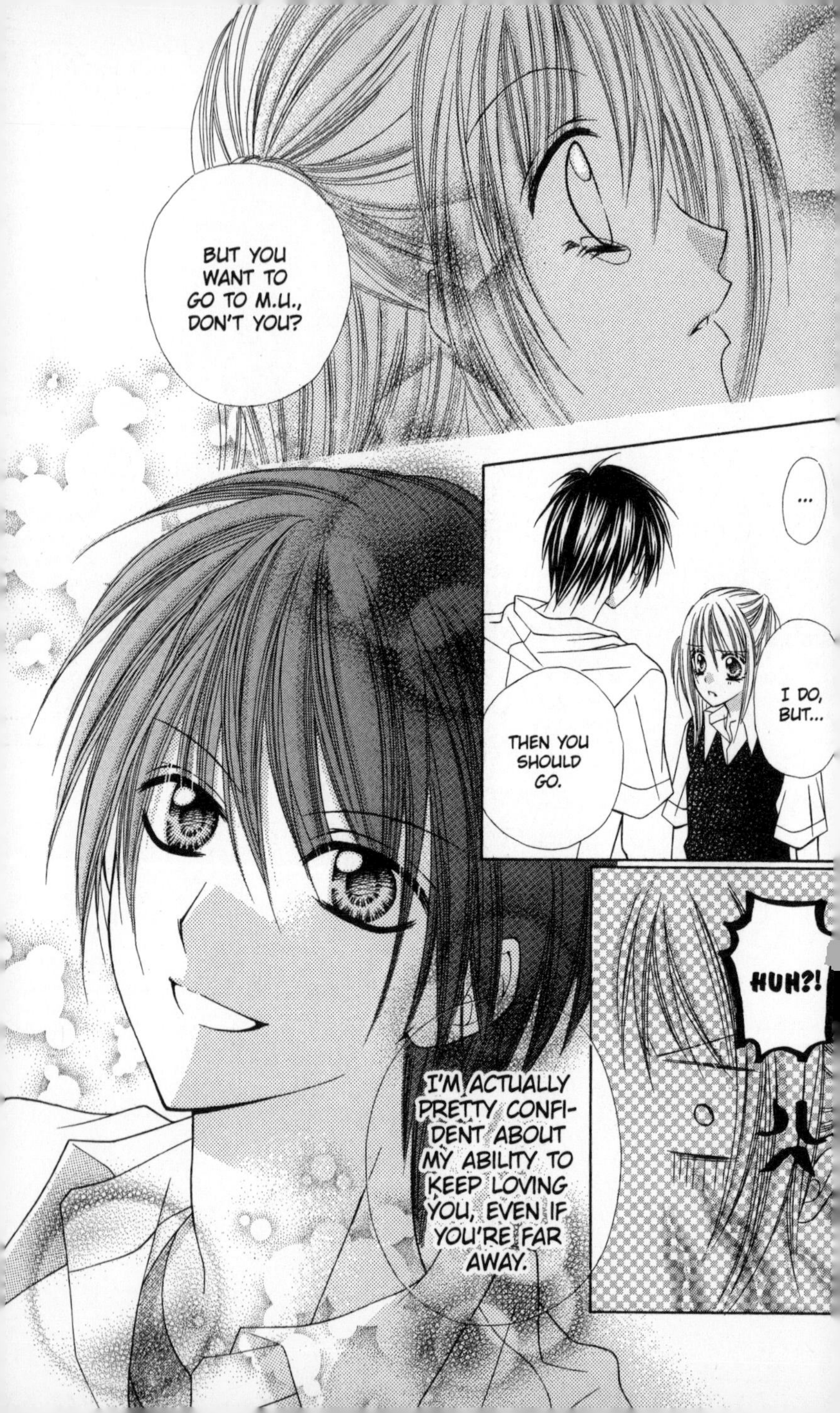
BUT YOU WANT TO GO TO M.U., DON'T YOU?
...
I DO, BUT...
THEN YOU SHOULD GO.
HUH?!
I'M ACTUALLY PRETTY CONFI-DENT ABOUT MY ABILITY TO KEEP LOVING YOU, EVEN IF YOU'RE FAR AWAY.

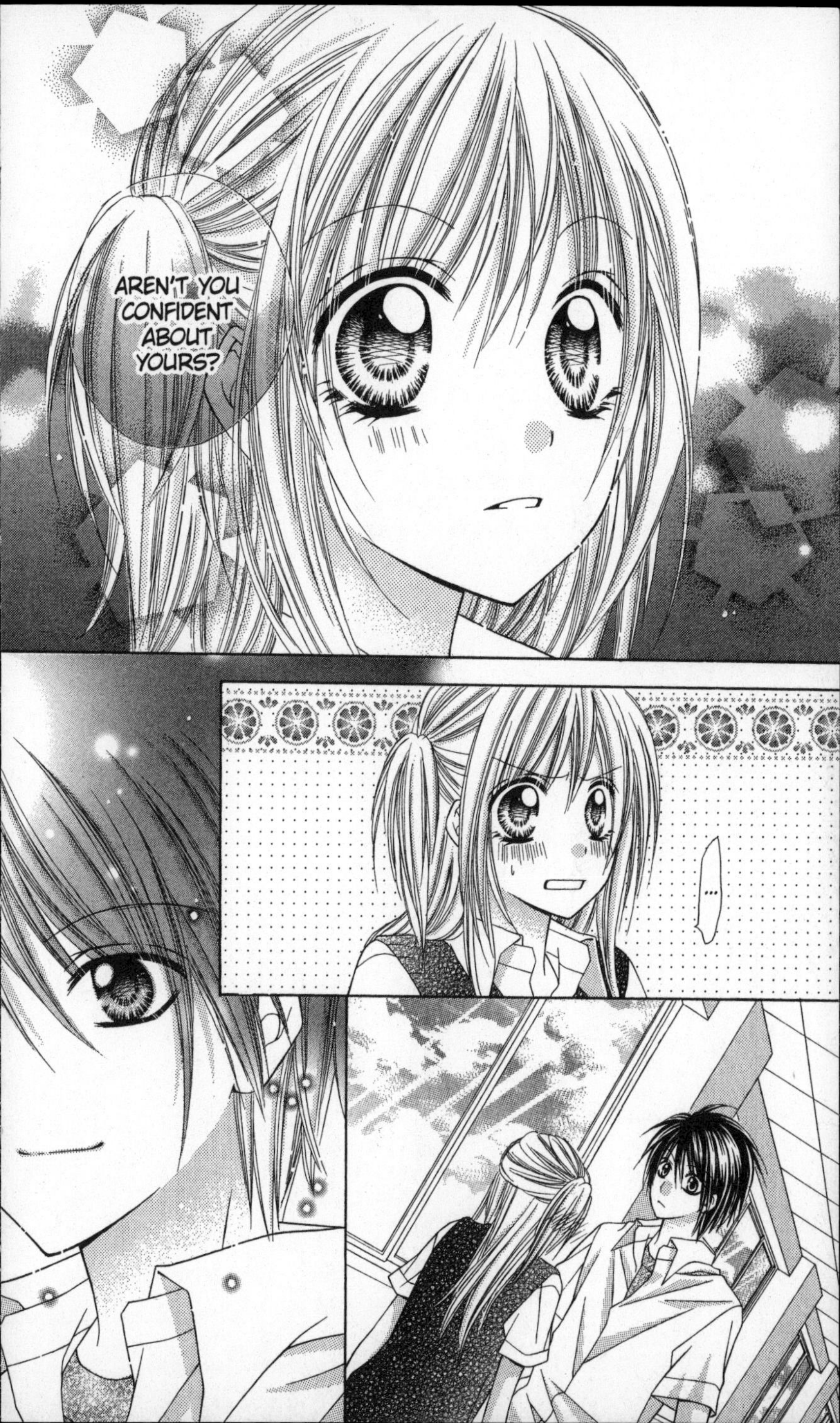
AREN'T YOU CONFIDENT ABOUT YOURS?
...

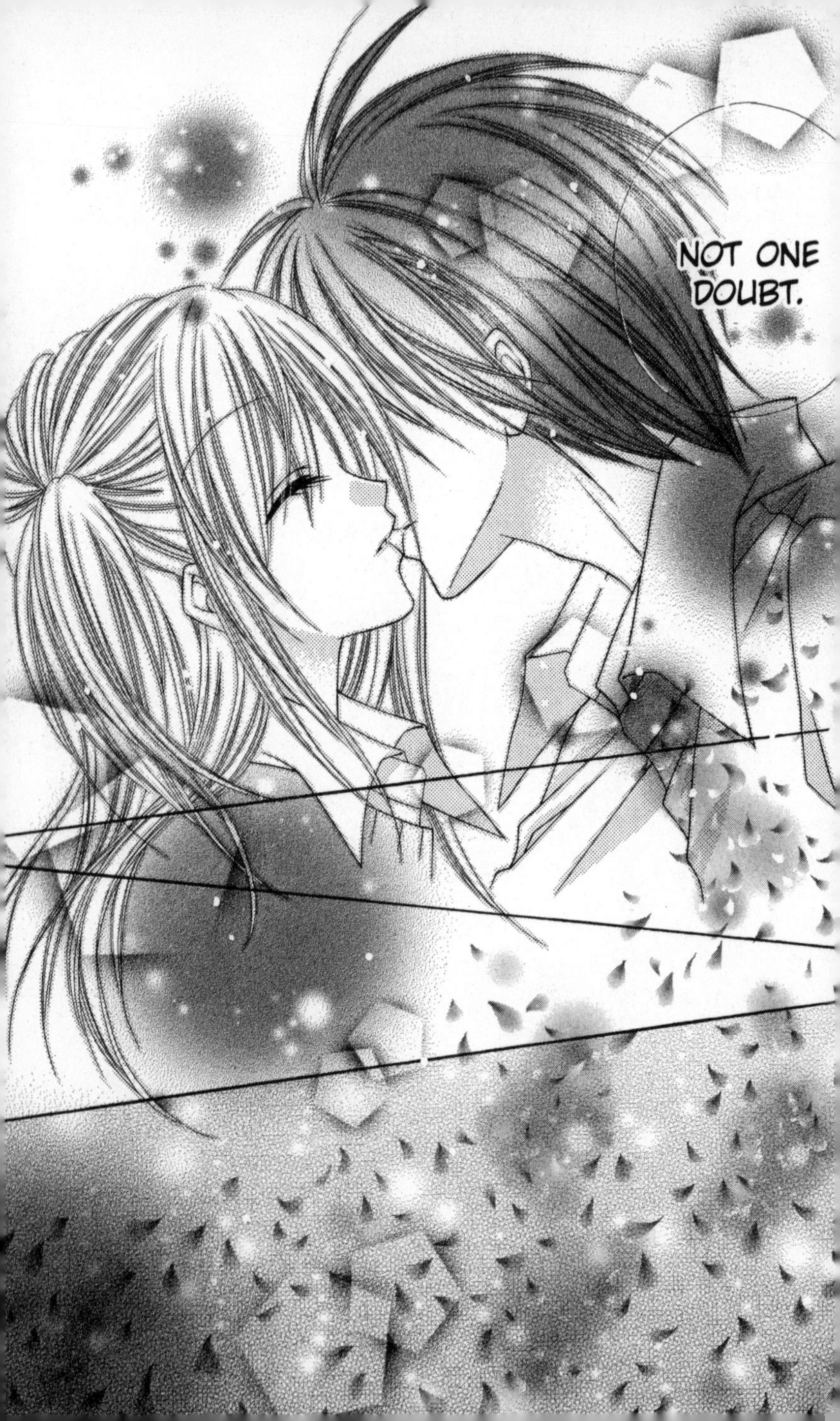
NOT ONE DOUBT.

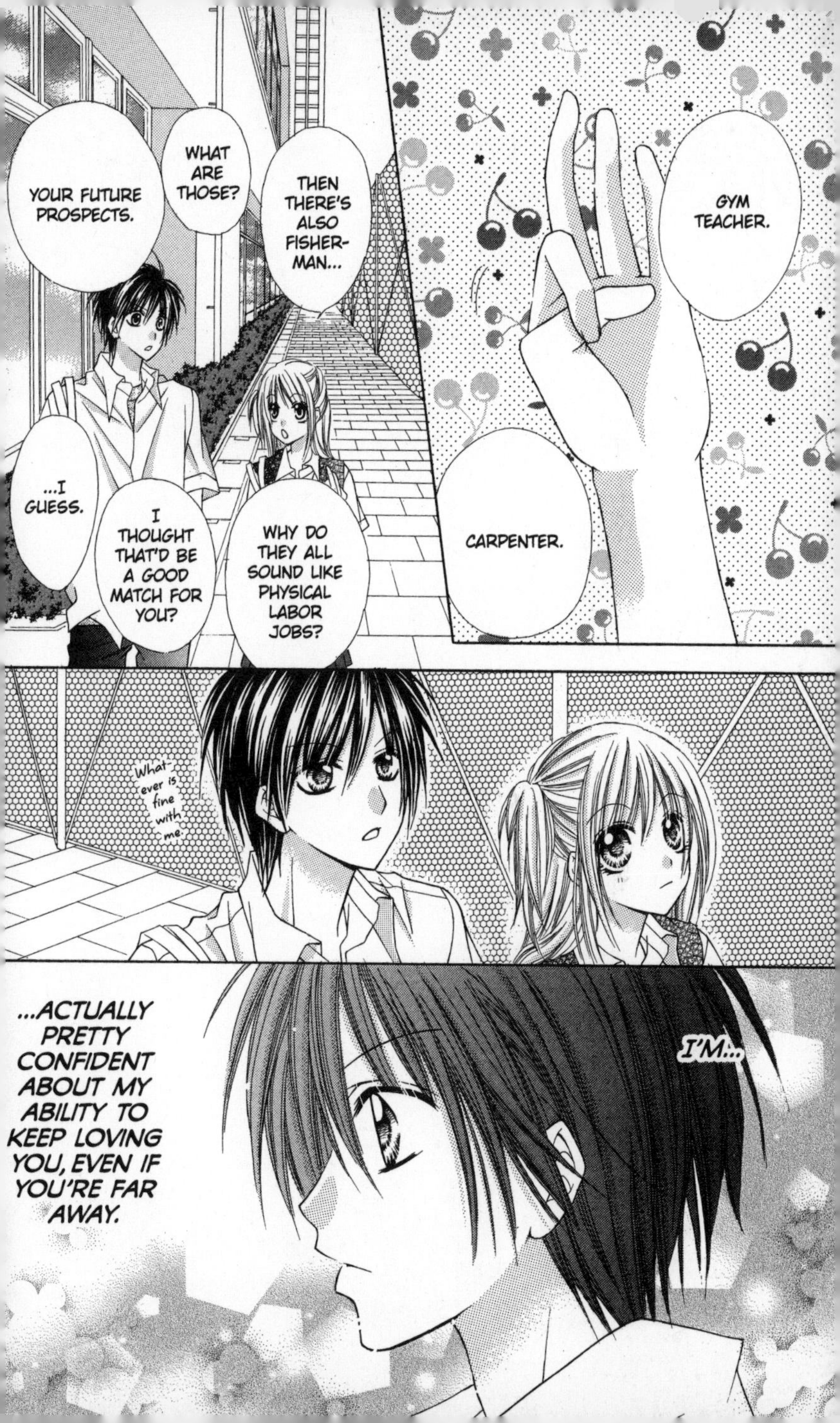
GYM TEACHER.
CARPENTER.
THEN THERE'S ALSO FISHER-MAN...
WHAT ARE THOSE?
YOUR FUTURE PROSPECTS.
WHY DO THEY ALL SOUND LIKE PHYSICAL LABOR JOBS?
I THOUGHT THAT'D BE A GOOD MATCH FOR YOU?
...I GUESS.
Whatever is fine with me.
I'M...
...ACTUALLY PRETTY CONFIDENT ABOUT MY ABILITY TO KEEP LOVING YOU, EVEN IF YOU'RE FAR AWAY.

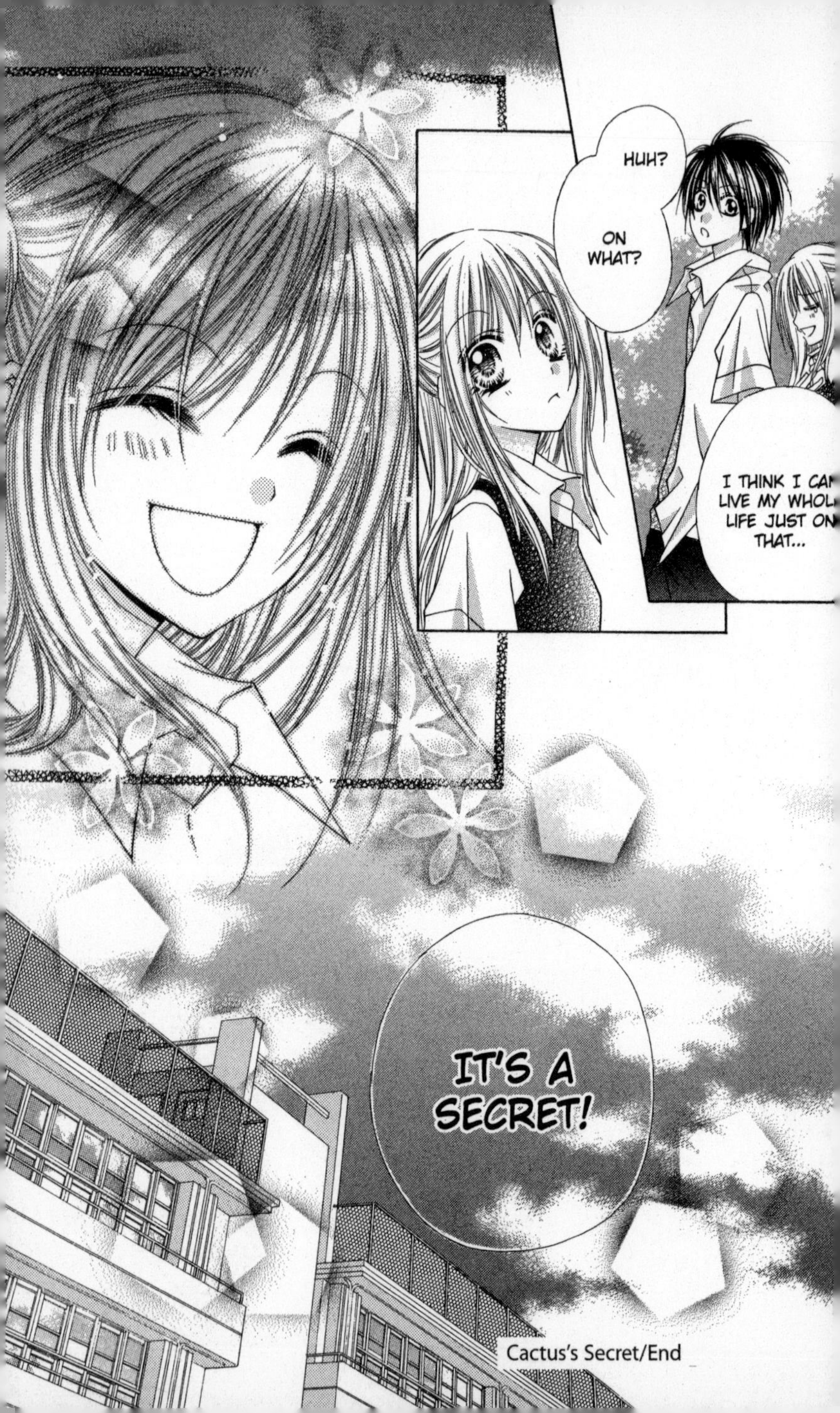
I THINK I CA
LIVE MY WHOL
LIFE JUST ON
THAT...
HUH?
ON WHAT?
IT'S A SECRET!
Cactus's Secret/End

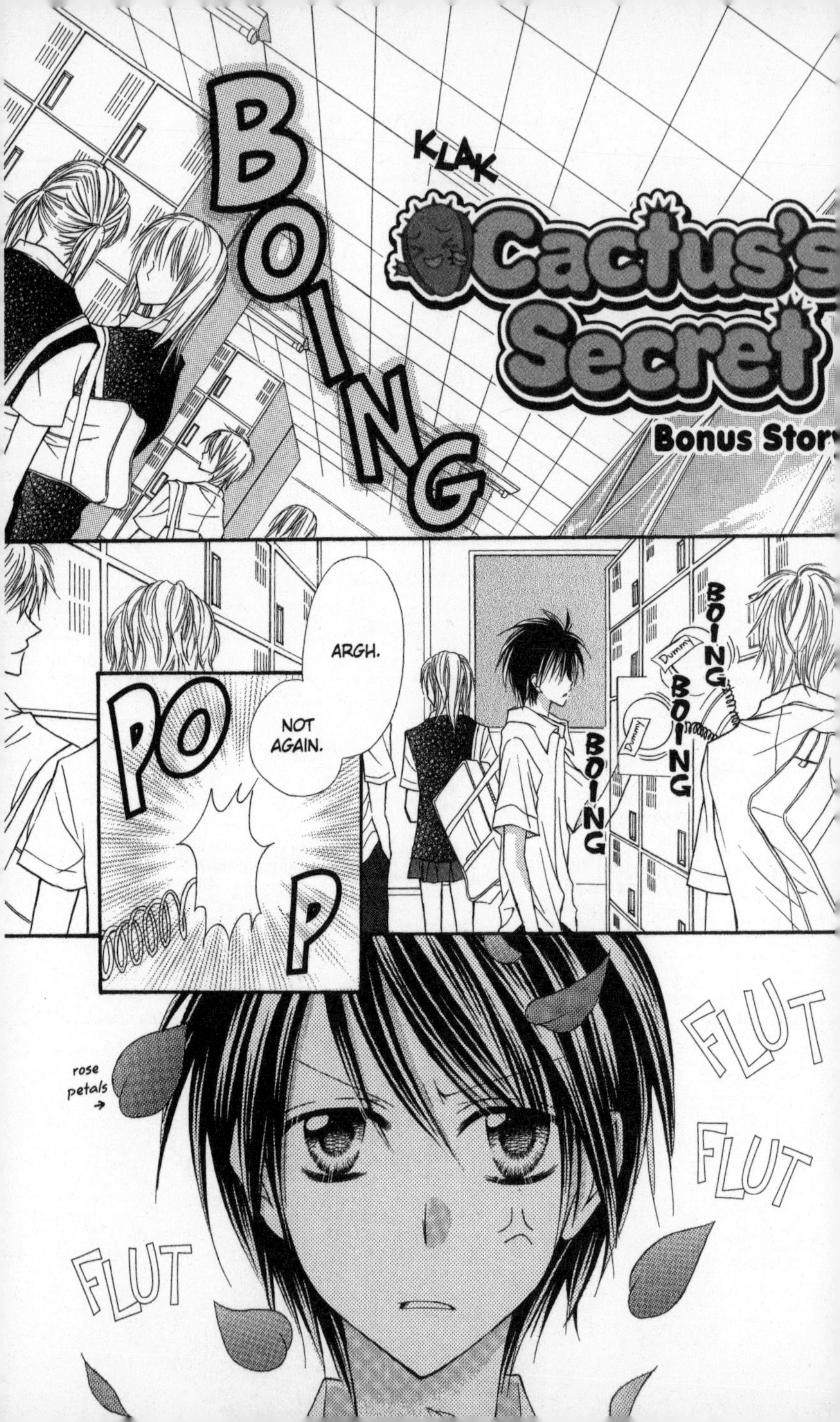
Cactus's Secret
Bonus Stor
KLAK
BOING
BOING
Dummy
BOING
Dummy
BOING
ARGH.
NOT AGAIN.
POP
FLUT
FLUT
rose petals →
FLUT

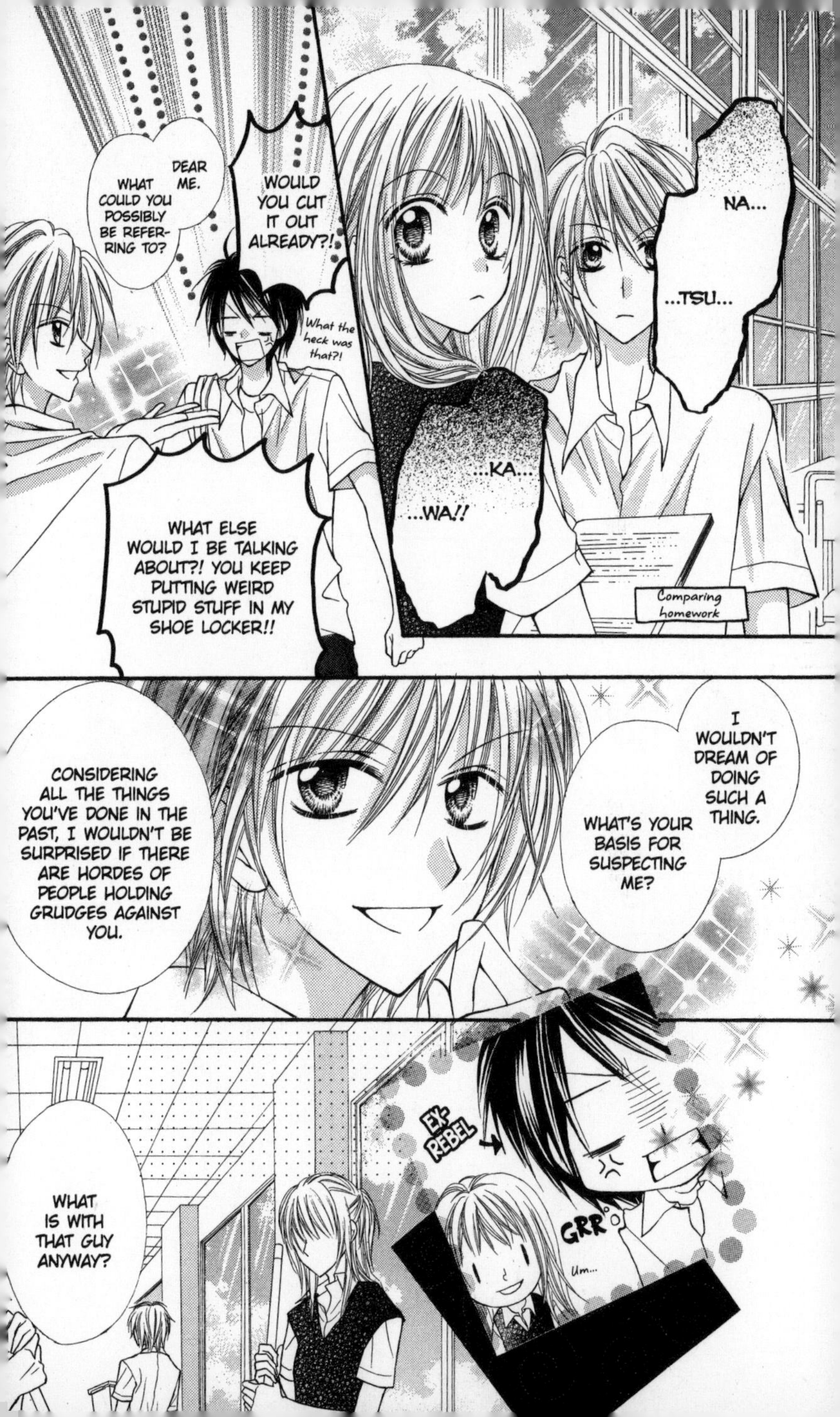
NA...
...TSU...
...KA...
...WA!!
Comparing homework
WOULD YOU CUT IT OUT ALREADY?!
What the heck was that?!
DEAR ME. WHAT COULD YOU POSSIBLY BE REFERRING TO?
WHAT ELSE WOULD I BE TALKING ABOUT?! YOU KEEP PUTTING WEIRD STUPID STUFF IN MY SHOE LOCKER!!
I WOULDN'T DREAM OF DOING SUCH A THING.
WHAT'S YOUR BASIS FOR SUSPECTING ME?
CONSIDERING ALL THE THINGS YOU'VE DONE IN THE PAST, I WOULDN'T BE SURPRISED IF THERE ARE HORDES OF PEOPLE HOLDING GRUDGES AGAINST YOU.
EX-REBEL
GRR
Um...
WHAT IS WITH THAT GUY ANYWAY?

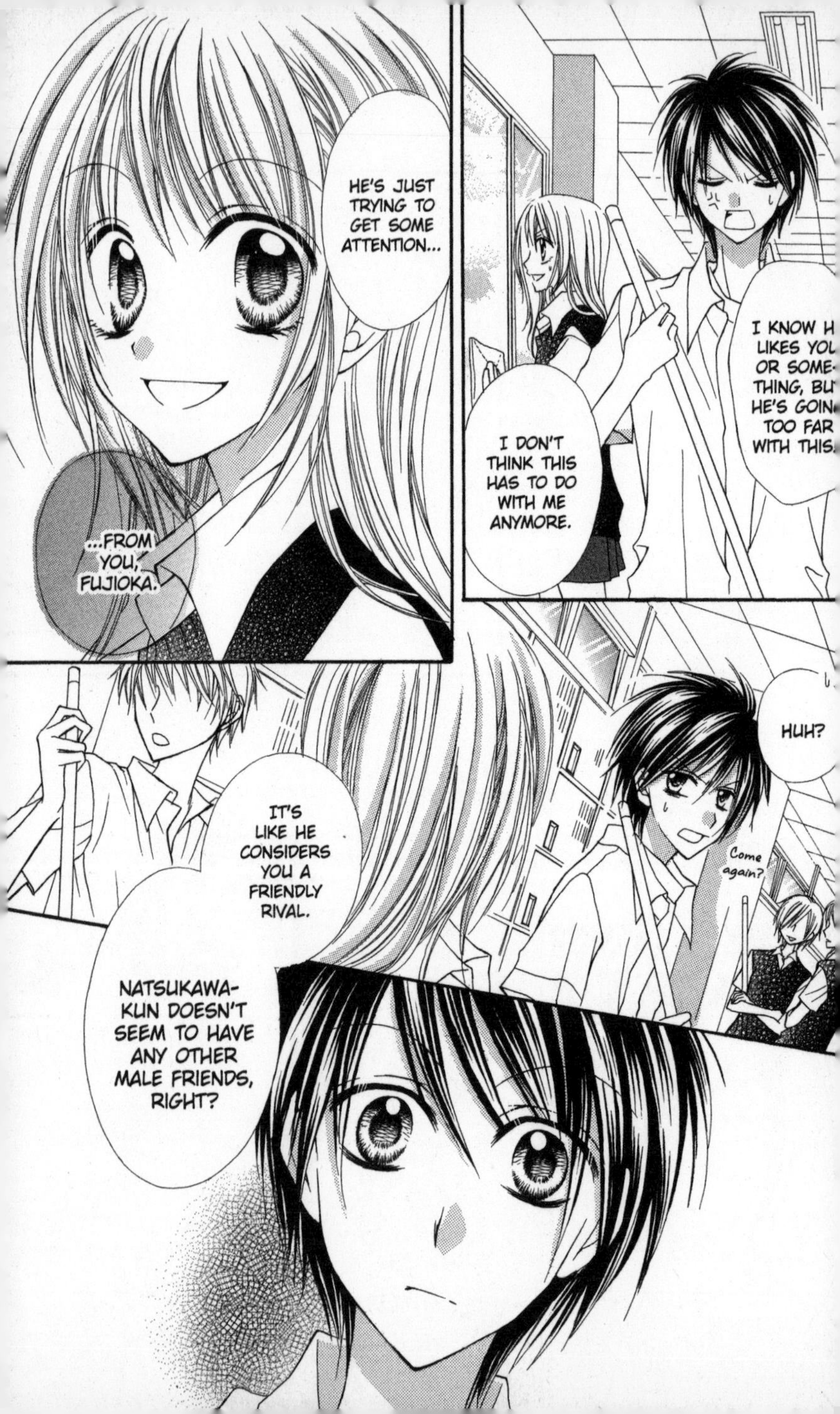
I KNOW H LIKES YOU OR SOME-THING, BU HE'S GOIN TOO FAR WITH THIS.
I DON'T THINK THIS HAS TO DO WITH ME ANYMORE.
HE'S JUST TRYING TO GET SOME ATTENTION...
...FROM YOU, FUJIOKA.
HUH?
Come again?
IT'S LIKE HE CONSIDERS YOU A FRIENDLY RIVAL.
NATSUKAWA-KUN DOESN'T SEEM TO HAVE ANY OTHER MALE FRIENDS, RIGHT?

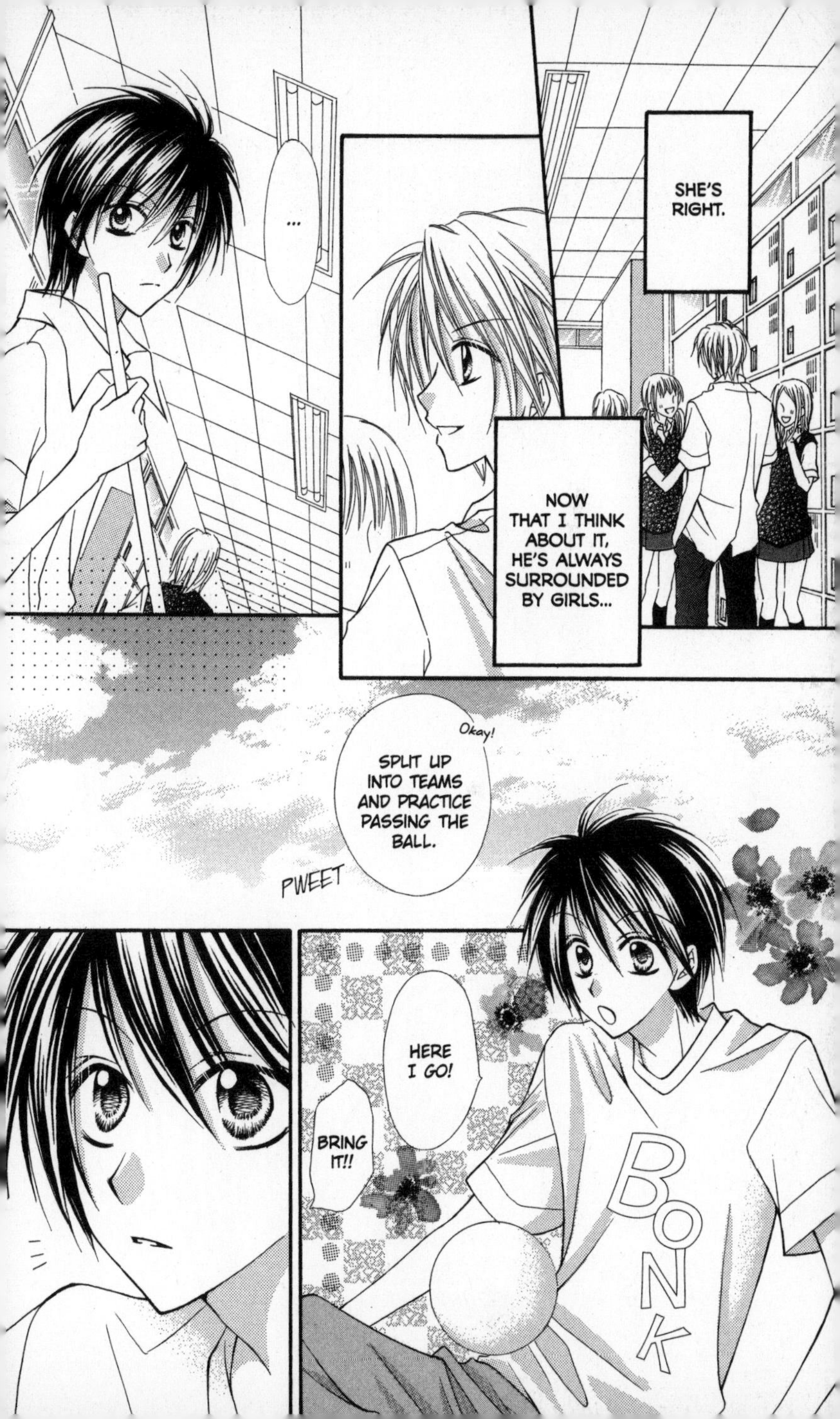
SHE'S RIGHT.
NOW THAT I THINK ABOUT IT, HE'S ALWAYS SURROUNDED BY GIRLS...
...
Okay!
SPLIT UP INTO TEAMS AND PRACTICE PASSING THE BALL.
PWEET
HERE I GO!
BRING IT!!
BONK

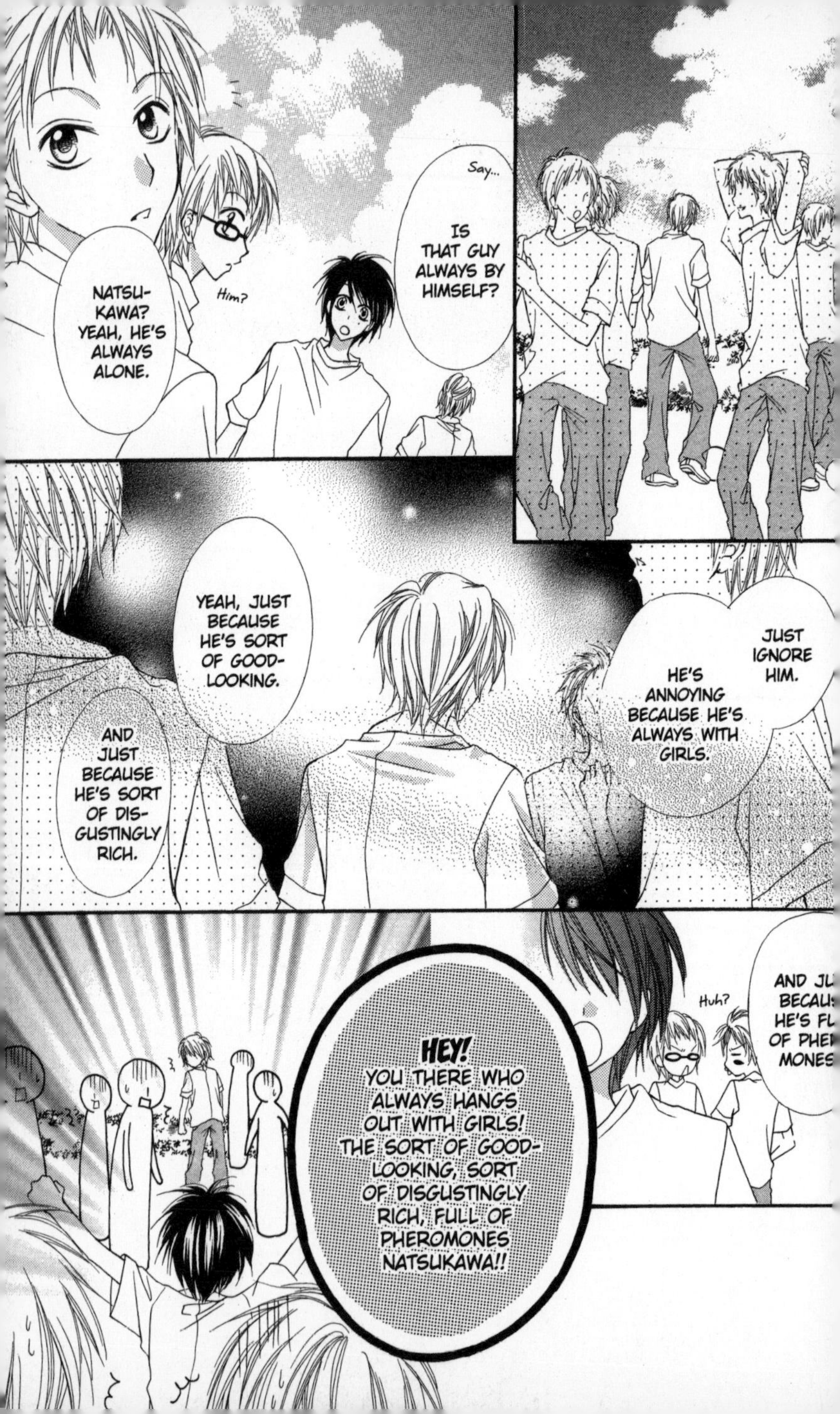
Say...
IS THAT GUY ALWAYS BY HIMSELF?
Him?
NATSU-KAWA? YEAH, HE'S ALWAYS ALONE.
JUST IGNORE HIM.
HE'S ANNOYING BECAUSE HE'S ALWAYS WITH GIRLS.
YEAH, JUST BECAUSE HE'S SORT OF GOOD-LOOKING.
AND JUST BECAUSE HE'S SORT OF DIS-GUSTINGLY RICH.
AND JU BECAU HE'S FU OF PHE MONES
Huh?
HEY! YOU THERE WHO ALWAYS HANGS OUT WITH GIRLS! THE SORT OF GOOD-LOOKING, SORT OF DISGUSTINGLY RICH, FULL OF PHEROMONES NATSUKAWA!!

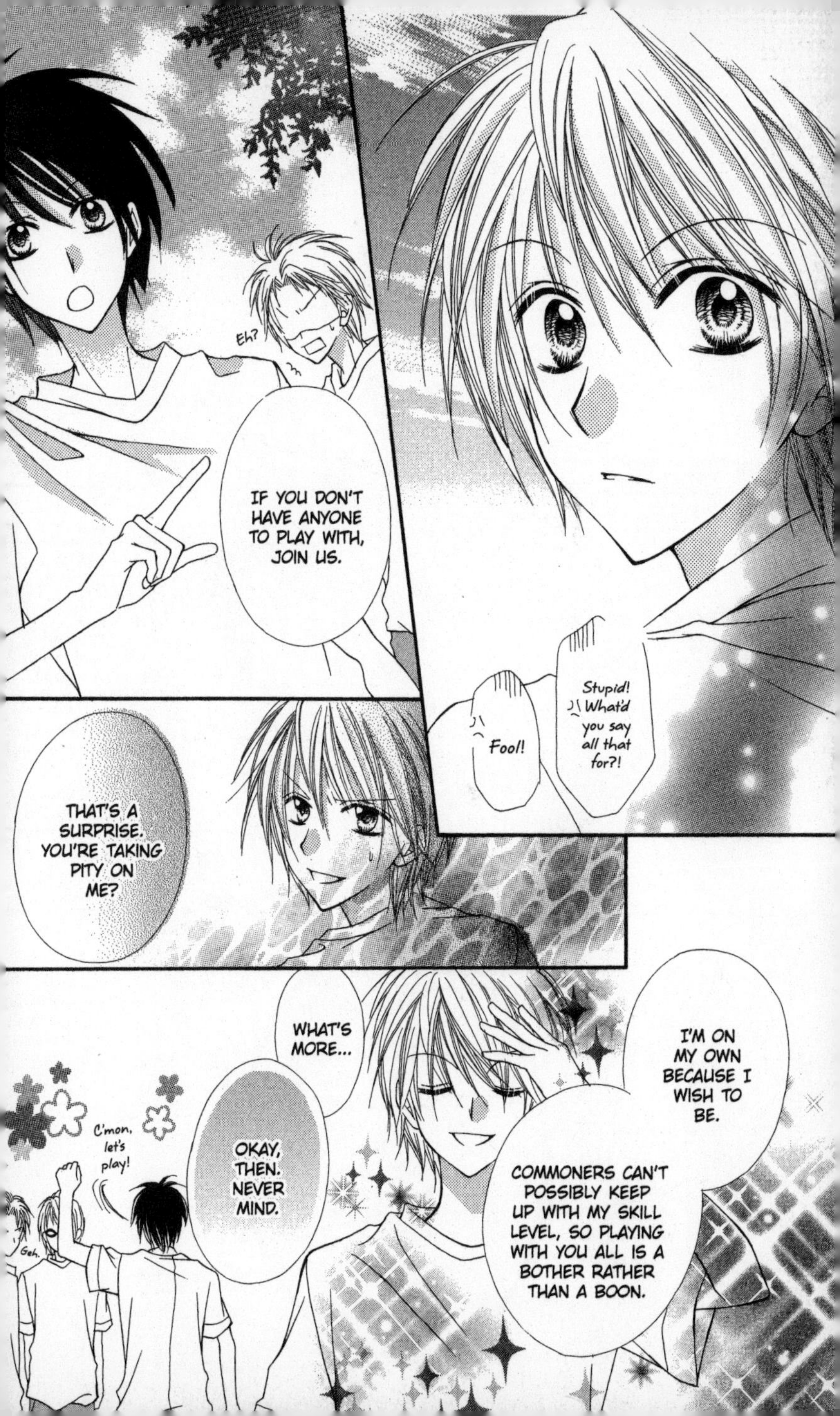
Stupid! What'd you say all that for?!
Fool!
IF YOU DON'T HAVE ANYONE TO PLAY WITH, JOIN US.
Eh?
THAT'S A SURPRISE. YOU'RE TAKING PITY ON ME?
I'M ON MY OWN BECAUSE I WISH TO BE.
WHAT'S MORE...
COMMONERS CAN'T POSSIBLY KEEP UP WITH MY SKILL LEVEL, SO PLAYING WITH YOU ALL IS A BOTHER RATHER THAN A BOON.
OKAY, THEN. NEVER MIND.
C'mon, let's play!
Geh.

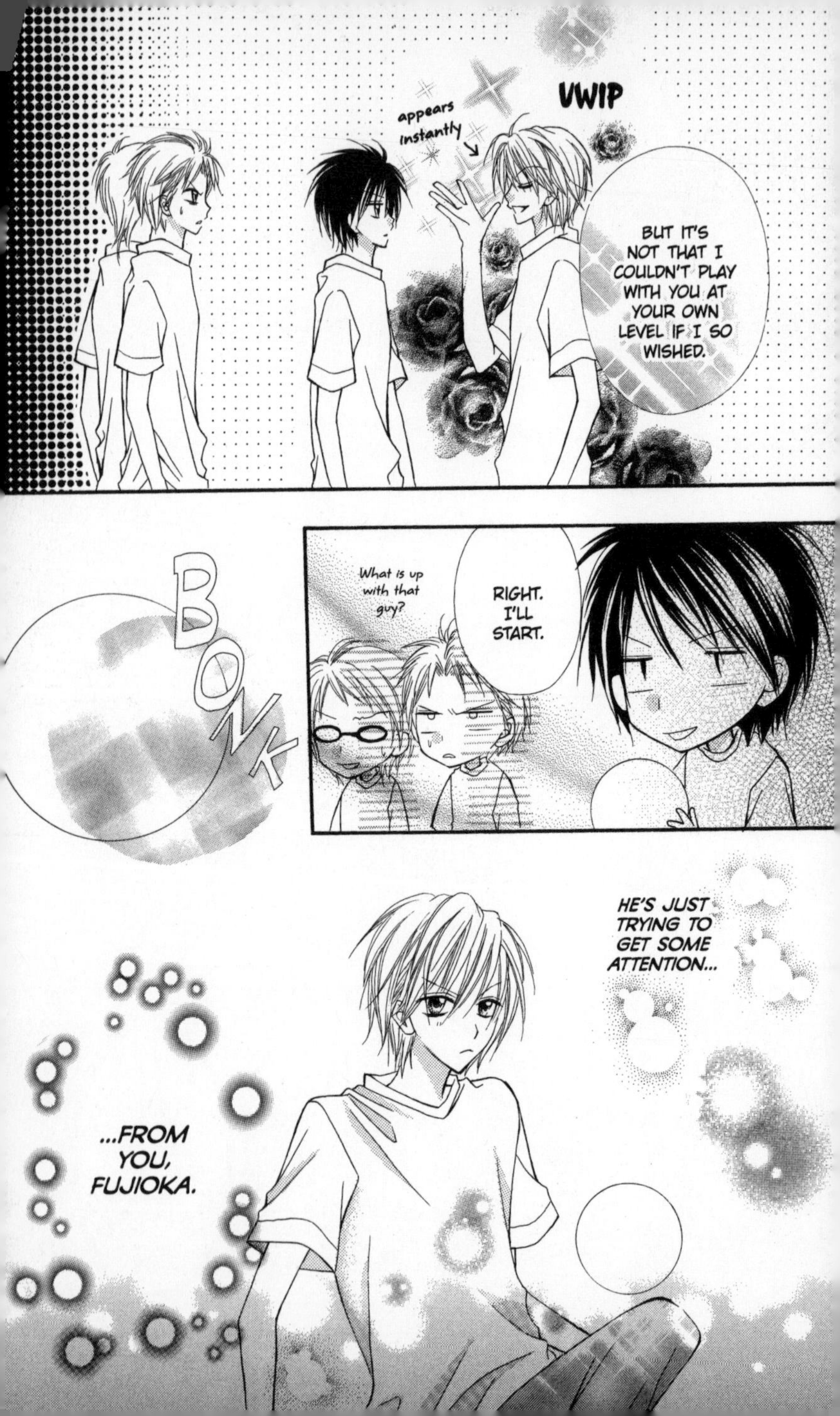
UWIP
appears instantly
BUT IT'S NOT THAT I COULDN'T PLAY WITH YOU AT YOUR OWN LEVEL IF I SO WISHED.
RIGHT. I'LL START.
What is up with that guy?
BONK
HE'S JUST TRYING TO GET SOME ATTENTION...
...FROM YOU, FUJIOKA.

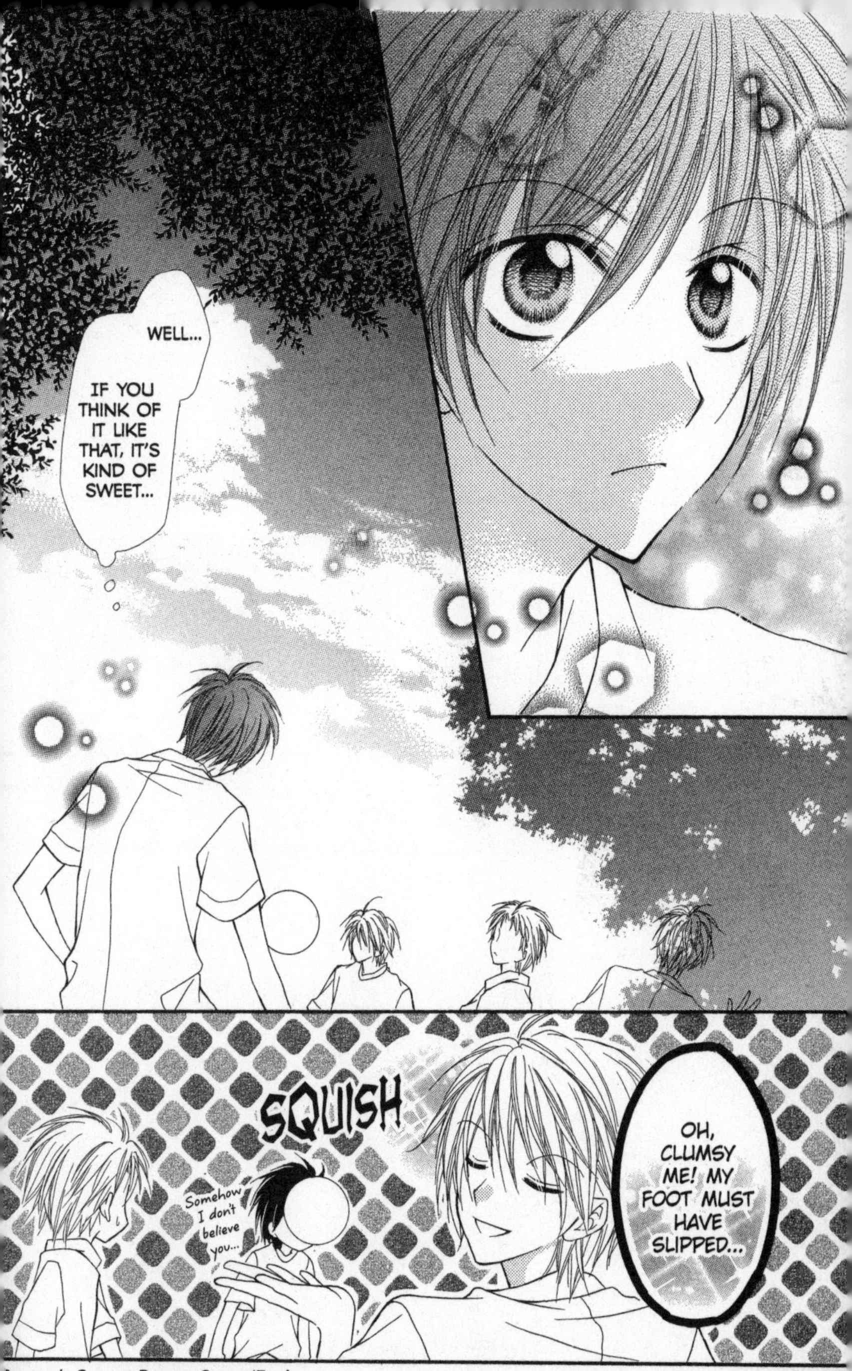
WELL...
IF YOU THINK OF IT LIKE THAT, IT'S KIND OF SWEET...
SQUISH
OH, CLUMSY ME! MY FOOT MUST HAVE SLIPPED...
Somehow I don't believe you...

Cactus's Secret Bonus Story/End

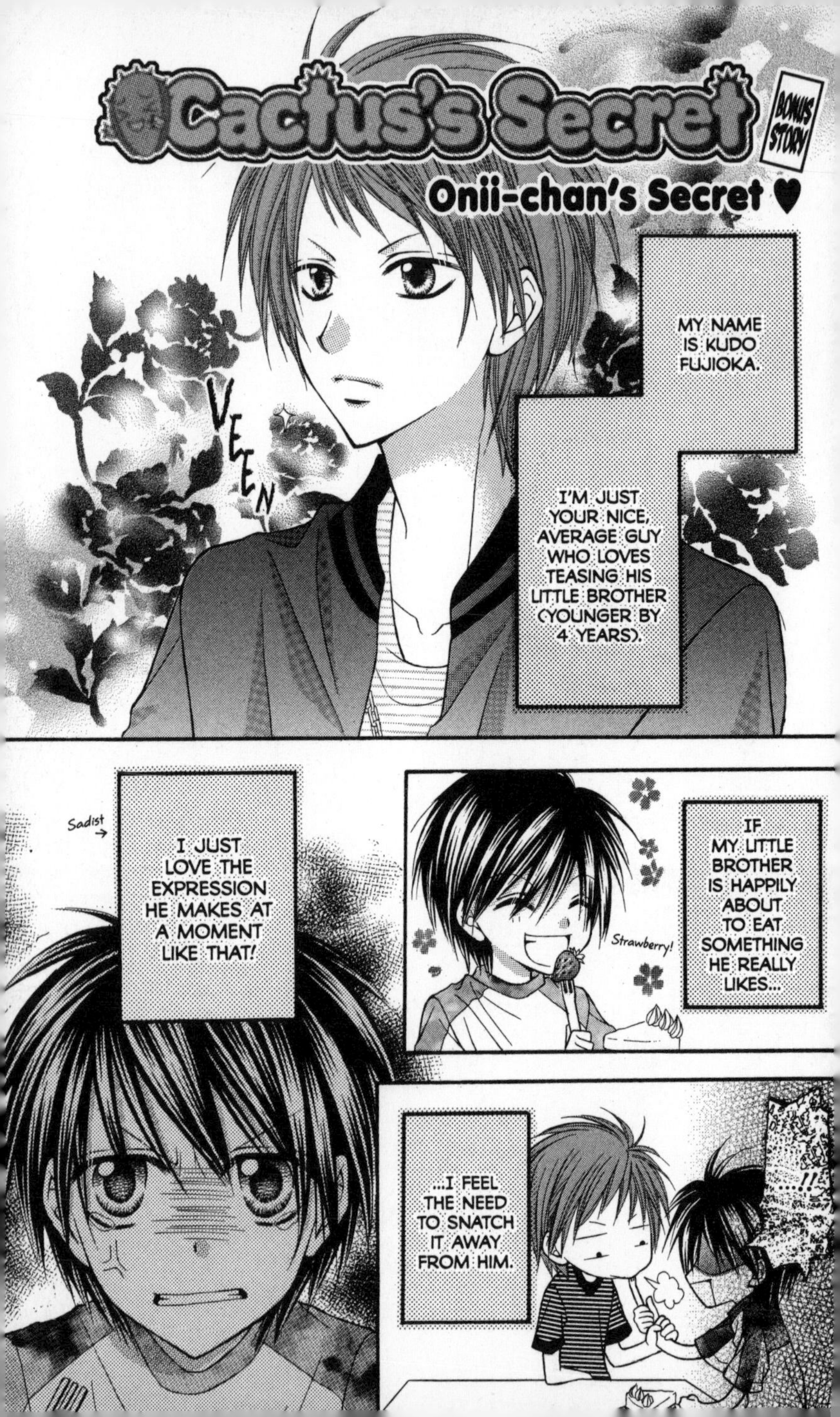
Cactus's Secret
BONUS STORY
Onii-chan's Secret ♥
MY NAME IS KUDO FUJIOKA.
VEEEN
I'M JUST YOUR NICE, AVERAGE GUY WHO LOVES TEASING HIS LITTLE BROTHER (YOUNGER BY 4 YEARS).
IF MY LITTLE BROTHER IS HAPPILY ABOUT TO EAT SOMETHING HE REALLY LIKES...
Strawberry!
...I FEEL THE NEED TO SNATCH IT AWAY FROM HIM.
...!!
Sadist →
I JUST LOVE THE EXPRESSION HE MAKES AT A MOMENT LIKE THAT!

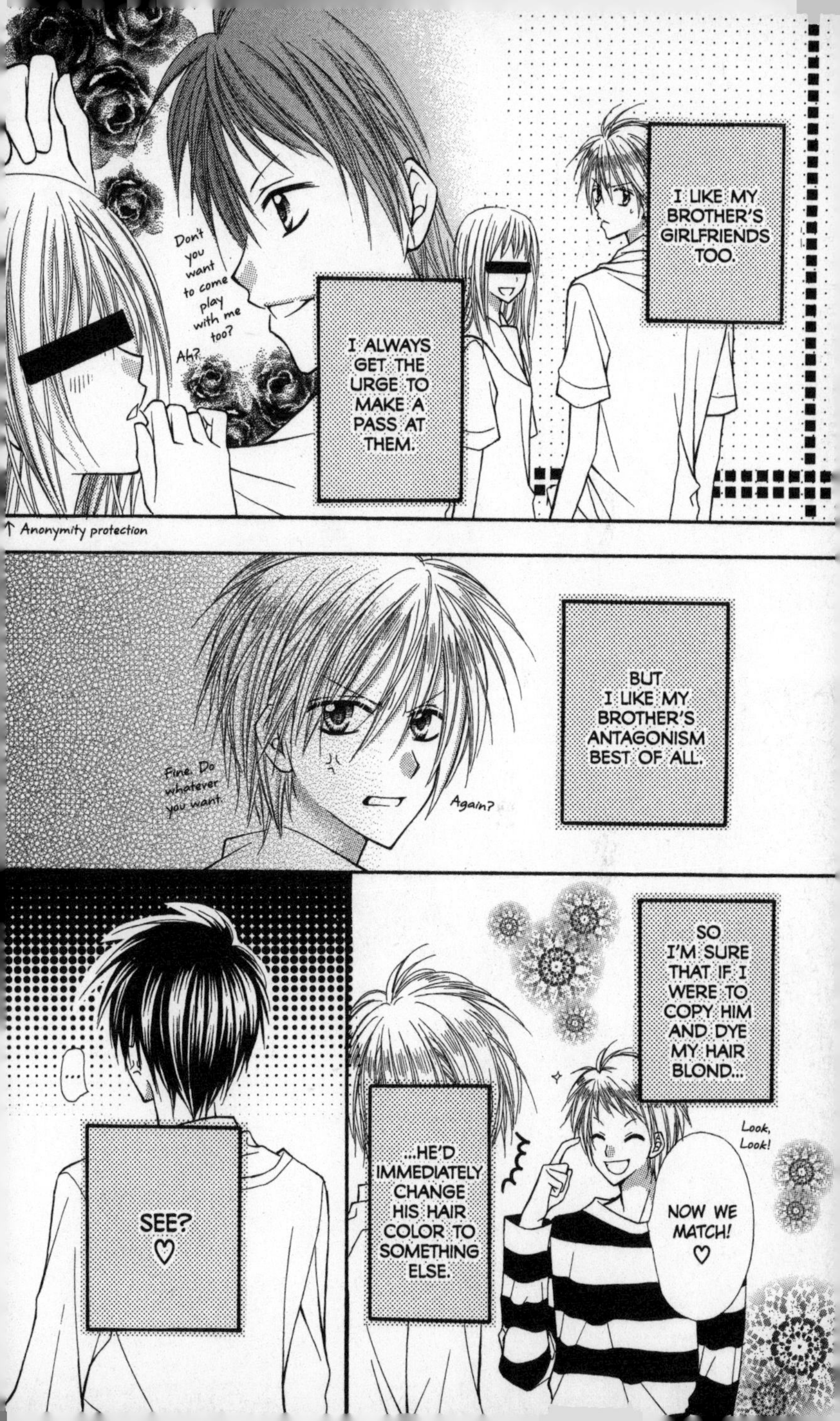
I LIKE MY BROTHER'S GIRLFRIENDS TOO.
I ALWAYS GET THE URGE TO MAKE A PASS AT THEM.
Don't you want to come play with me too?
Ah?
↑ Anonymity protection
BUT I LIKE MY BROTHER'S ANTAGONISM BEST OF ALL.
Again?
Fine. Do whatever you want.
SO I'M SURE THAT IF I WERE TO COPY HIM AND DYE MY HAIR BLOND...
Look, Look!
NOW WE MATCH! ♡
...HE'D IMMEDIATELY CHANGE HIS HAIR COLOR TO SOMETHING ELSE.
...
SEE? ♡

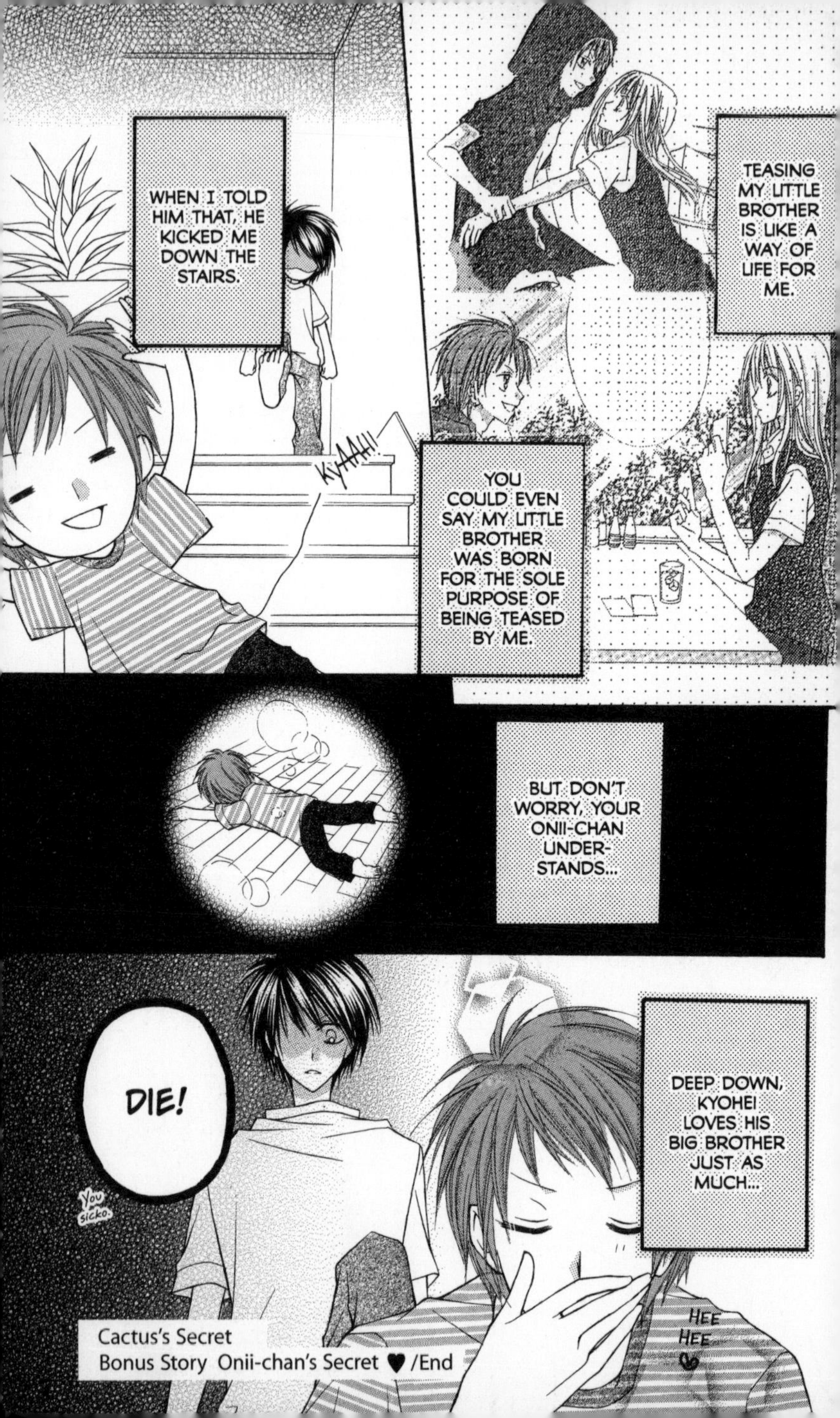
TEASING MY LITTLE BROTHER IS LIKE A WAY OF LIFE FOR ME.
YOU COULD EVEN SAY MY LITTLE BROTHER WAS BORN FOR THE SOLE PURPOSE OF BEING TEASED BY ME.
WHEN I TOLD HIM THAT, HE KICKED ME DOWN THE STAIRS.
KYAAH!!
BUT DON'T WORRY, YOUR ONII-CHAN UNDER-STANDS...
DEEP DOWN, KYOHEI LOVES HIS BIG BROTHER JUST AS MUCH...
HEE HEE
DIE!
You sicko.
Cactus's Secret
Bonus Story Onii-chan's Secret ♥ /End

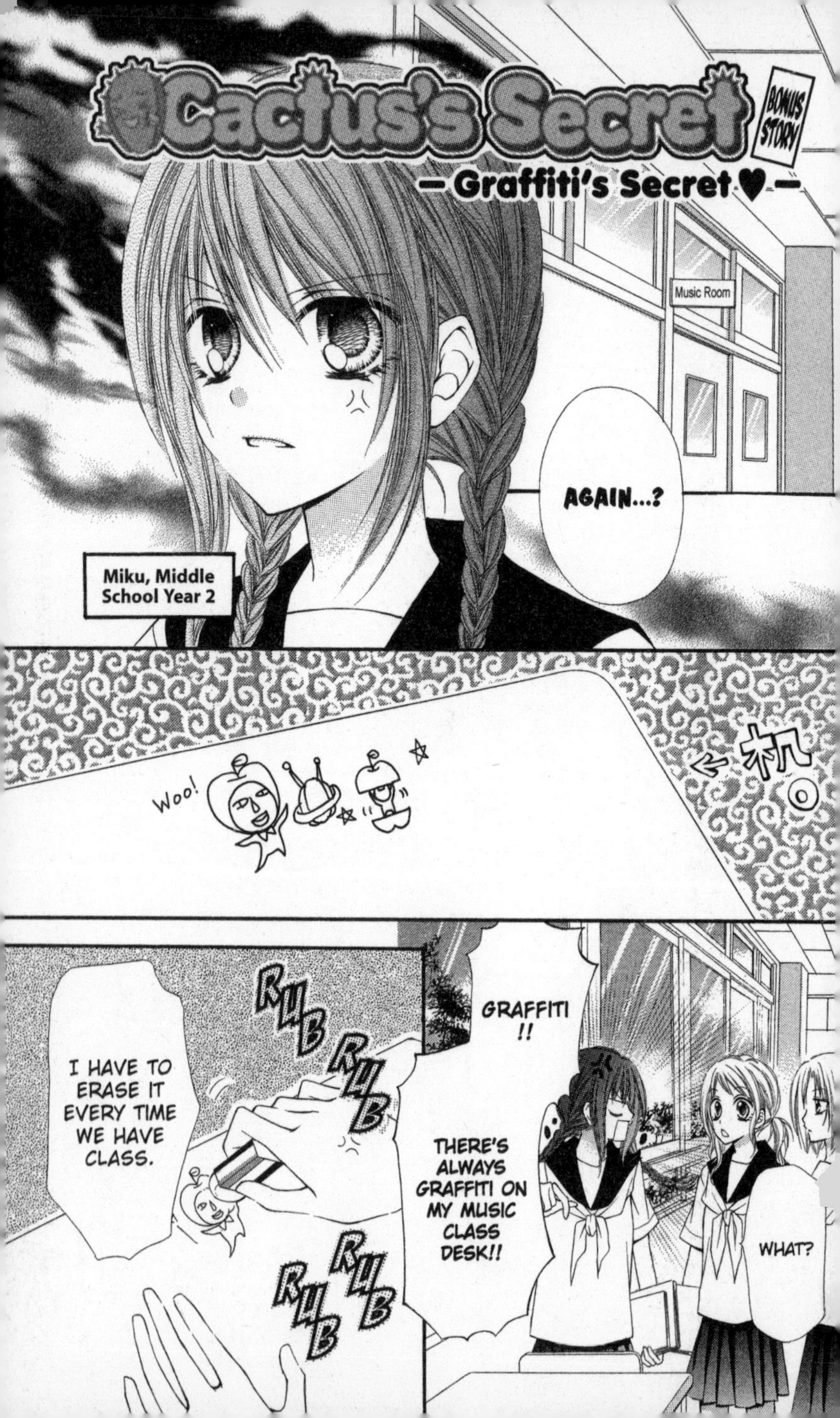
Cactus's Secret
BONUS STORY
—Graffiti's Secret♥—
Music Room
AGAIN...?
Miku, Middle School Year 2
机
Woo!
GRAFFITI!!
WHAT?
THERE'S ALWAYS GRAFFITI ON MY MUSIC CLASS DESK!!
RUB
RUB
I HAVE TO ERASE IT EVERY TIME WE HAVE CLASS.
RUB
RUB

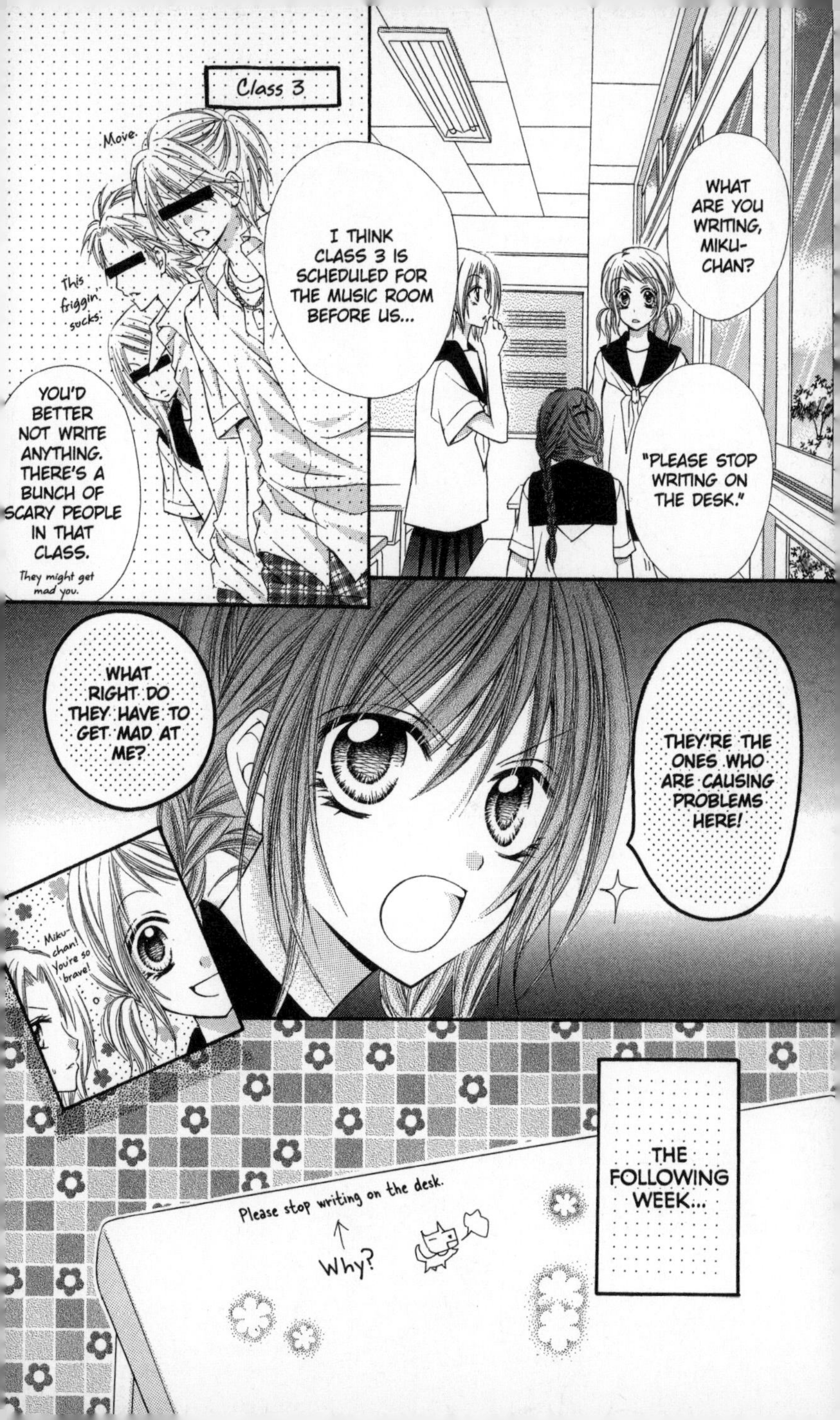
WHAT ARE YOU WRITING, MIKU-CHAN?
"PLEASE STOP WRITING ON THE DESK."
I THINK CLASS 3 IS SCHEDULED FOR THE MUSIC ROOM BEFORE US...
Class 3
Move.
This friggin' sucks.
YOU'D BETTER NOT WRITE ANYTHING. THERE'S A BUNCH OF SCARY PEOPLE IN THAT CLASS.
They might get mad you.
WHAT RIGHT DO THEY HAVE TO GET MAD AT ME?
THEY'RE THE ONES WHO ARE CAUSING PROBLEMS HERE!
Miku-chan! You're so brave!
THE FOLLOWING WEEK...
Please stop writing on the desk.
Why?

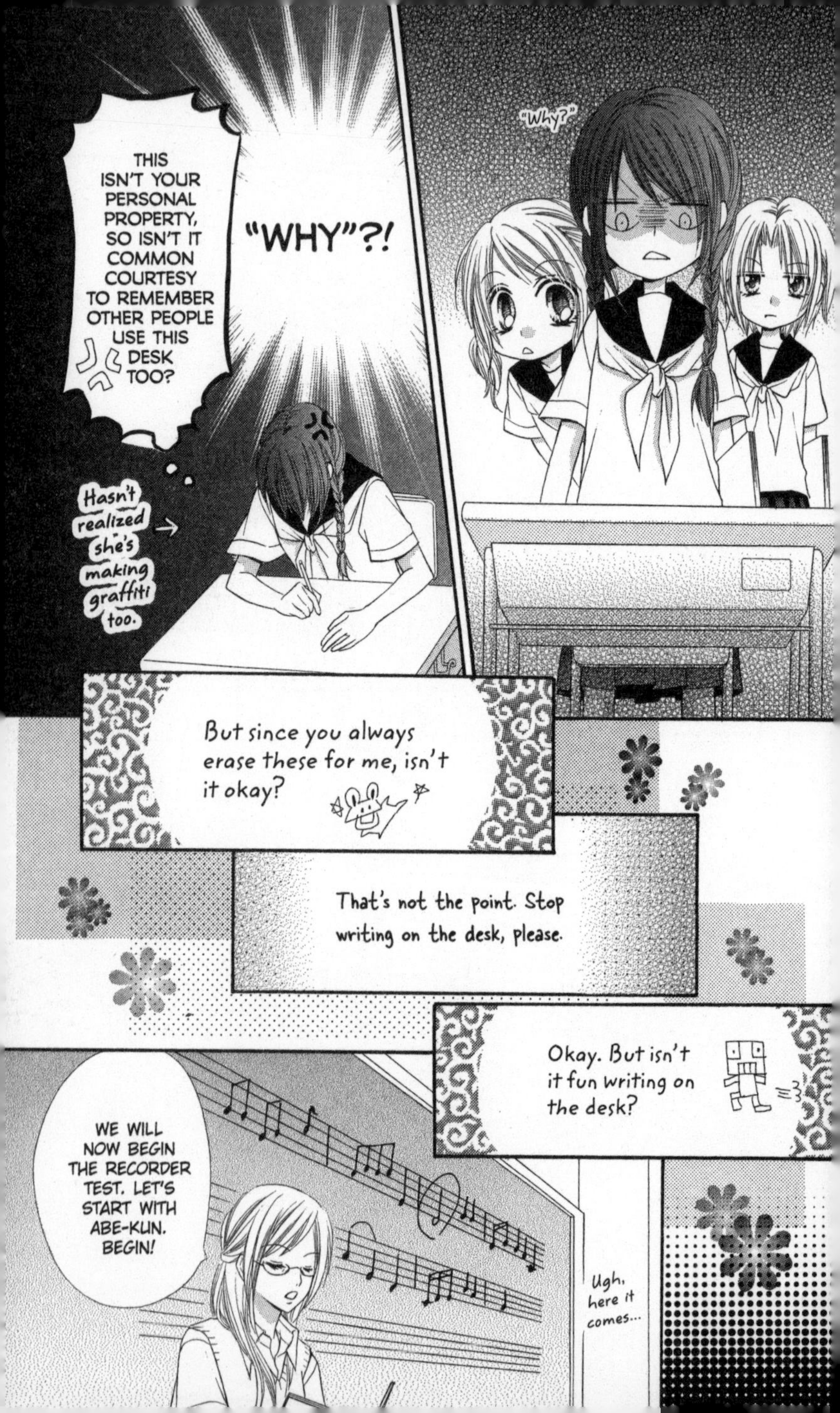
"Why?"
"WHY"?!
THIS ISN'T YOUR PERSONAL PROPERTY, SO ISN'T IT COMMON COURTESY TO REMEMBER OTHER PEOPLE USE THIS DESK TOO?
Hasn't realized she's making graffiti too.
But since you always erase these for me, isn't it okay?
That's not the point. Stop writing on the desk, please.
Okay. But isn't it fun writing on the desk?
WE WILL NOW BEGIN THE RECORDER TEST. LET'S START WITH ABE-KUN. BEGIN!
Ugh, here it comes...

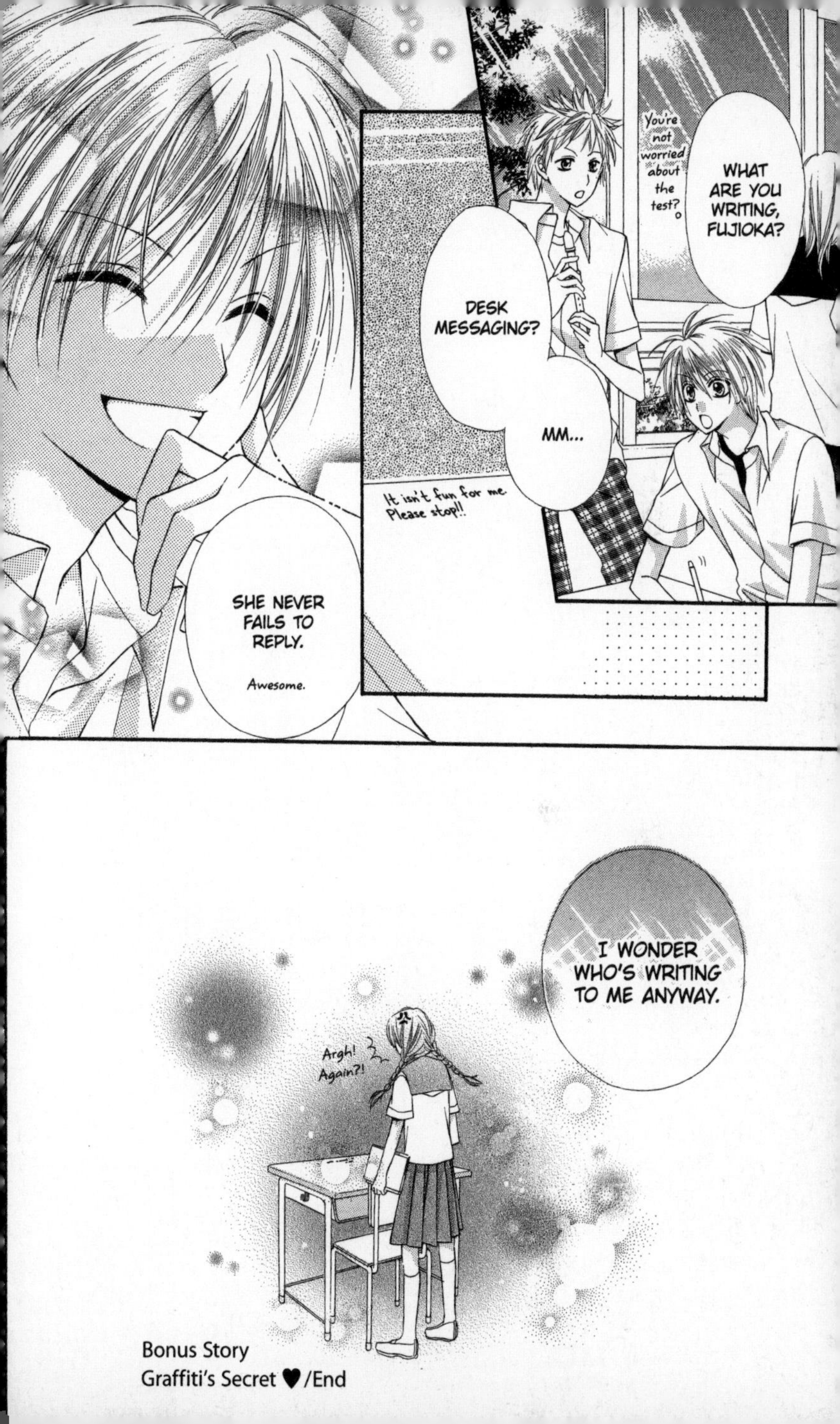
WHAT ARE YOU WRITING, FUJIOKA?
You're not worried about the test?
DESK MESSAGING?
MM...
It isn't fun for me. Please stop!!
SHE NEVER FAILS TO REPLY.
Awesome.
I WONDER WHO'S WRITING TO ME ANYWAY.
Argh! Again?!
Bonus Story
Graffiti's Secret ♥/End

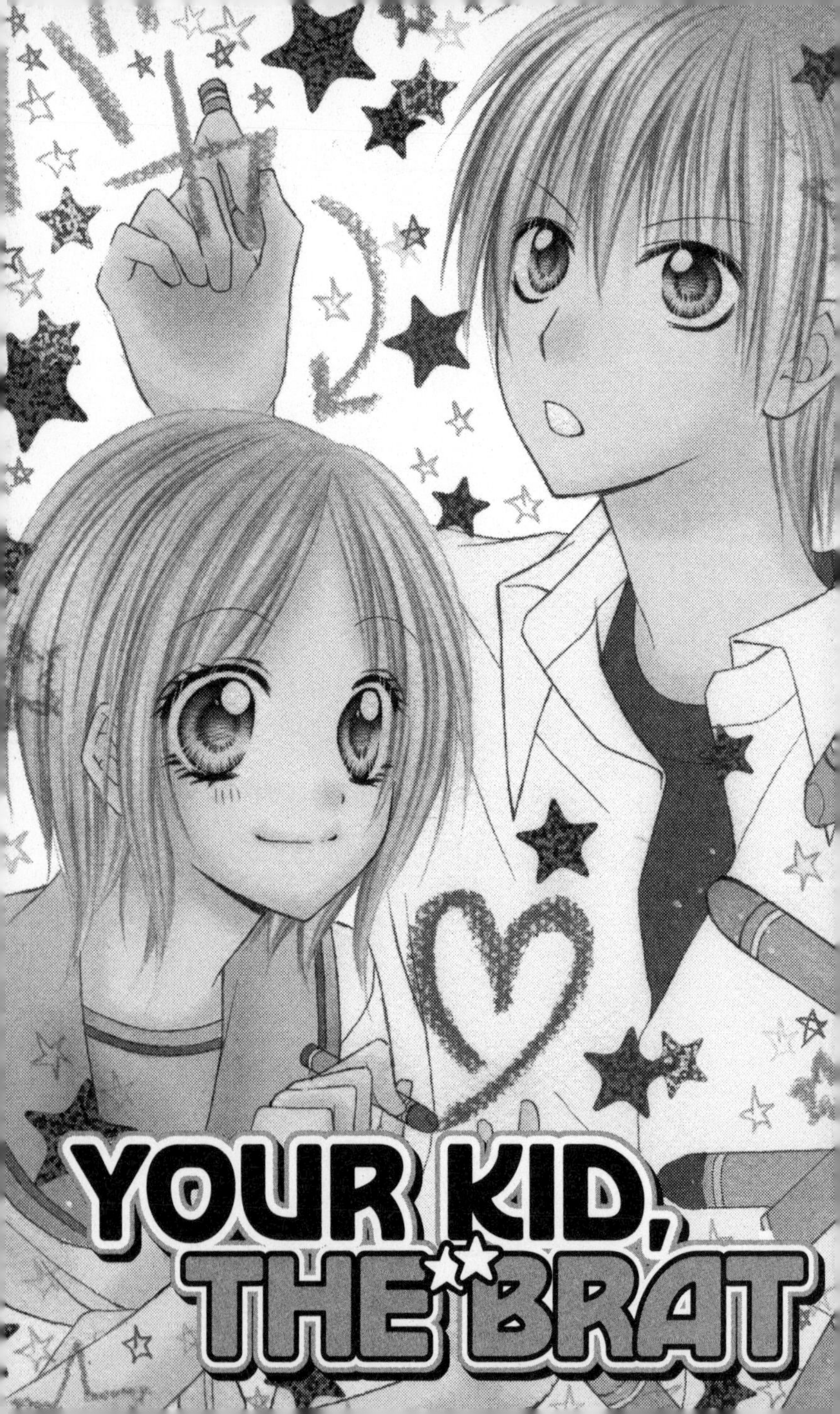
YOUR KID, THE BRAT

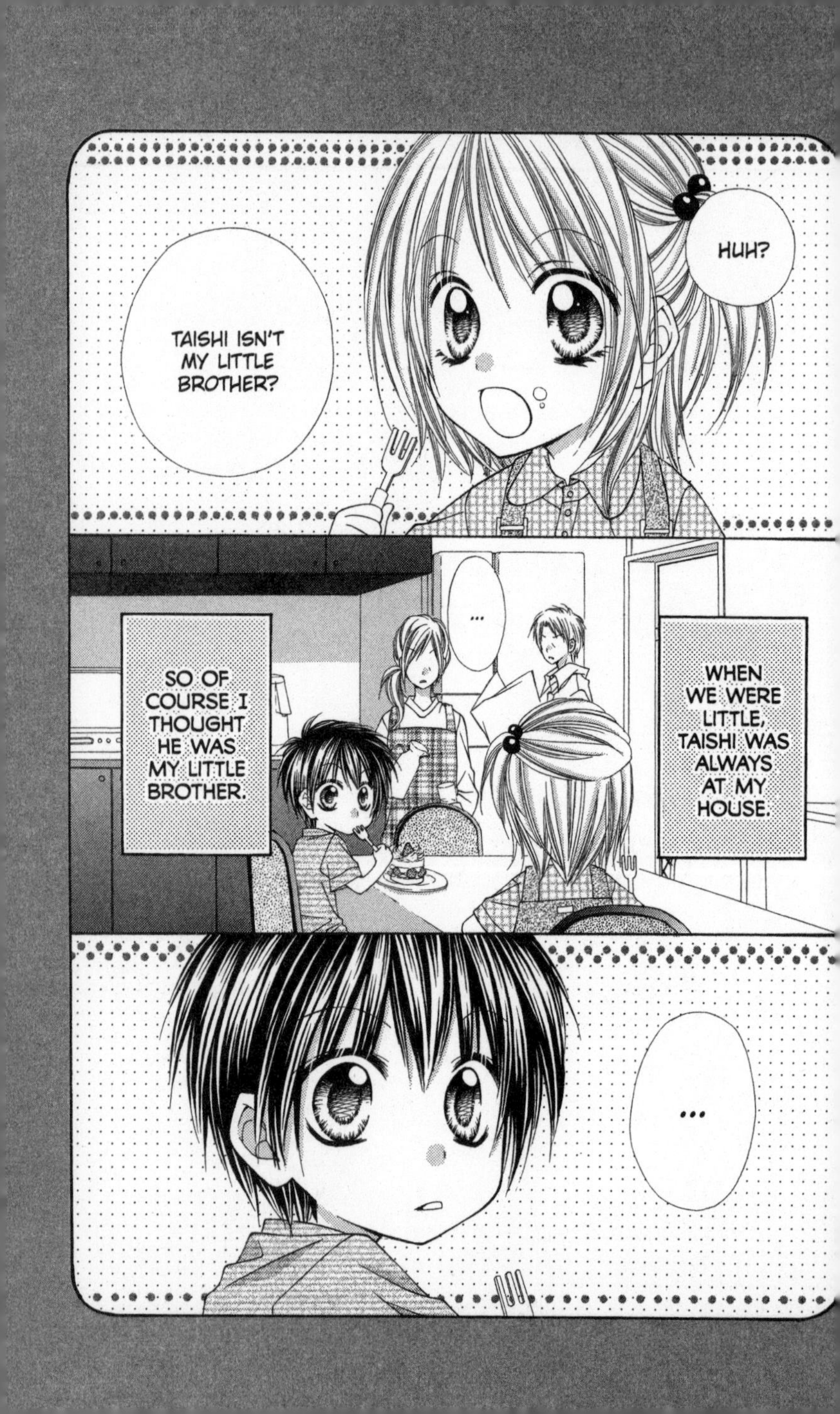
HUH?
TAISHI ISN'T MY LITTLE BROTHER?
WHEN WE WERE LITTLE, TAISHI WAS ALWAYS AT MY HOUSE.
...
SO OF COURSE I THOUGHT HE WAS MY LITTLE BROTHER.
...

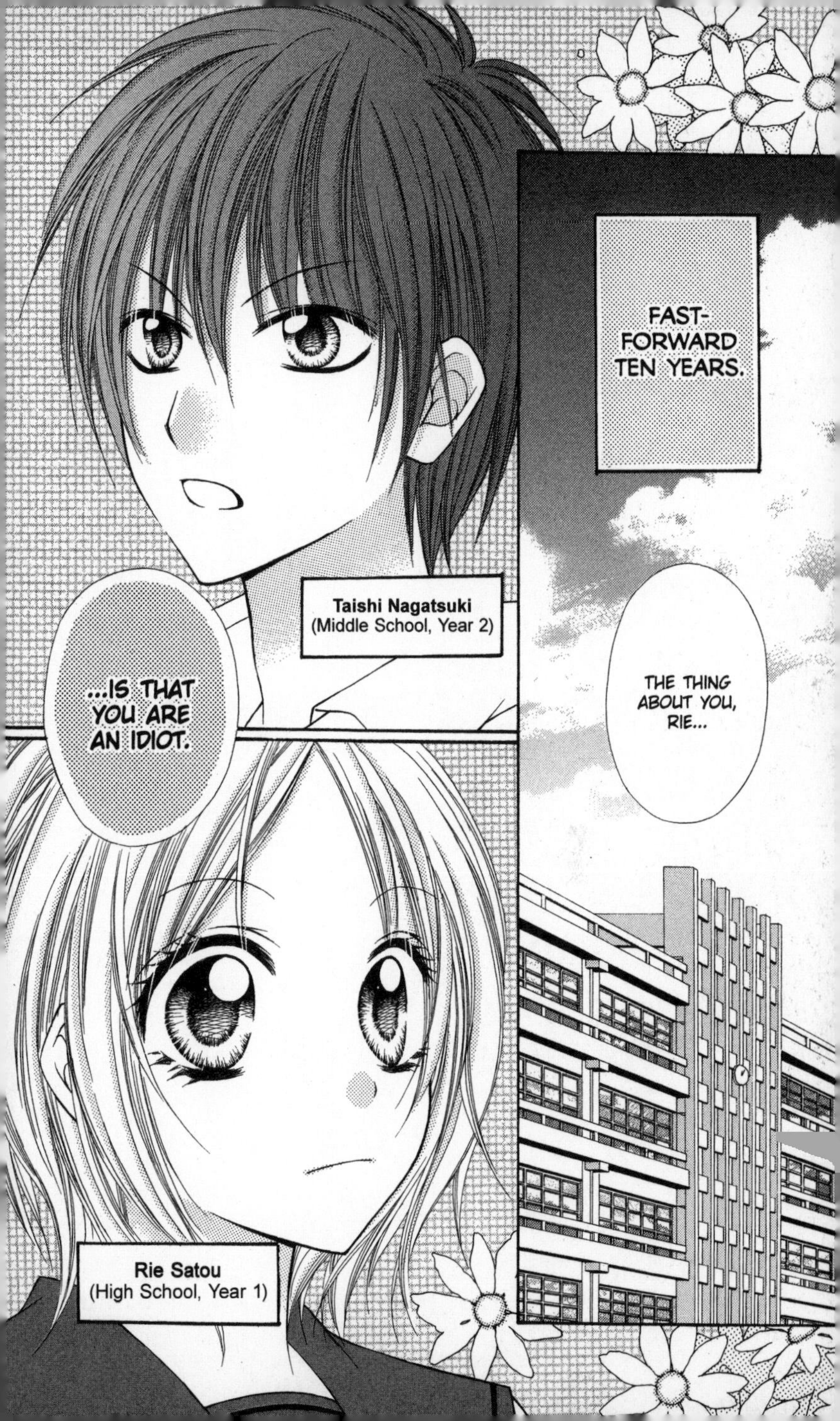
FAST-FORWARD TEN YEARS.
THE THING ABOUT YOU, RIE...
Taishi Nagatsuki (Middle School, Year 2)
...IS THAT YOU ARE AN IDIOT.
Rie Satou (High School, Year 1)

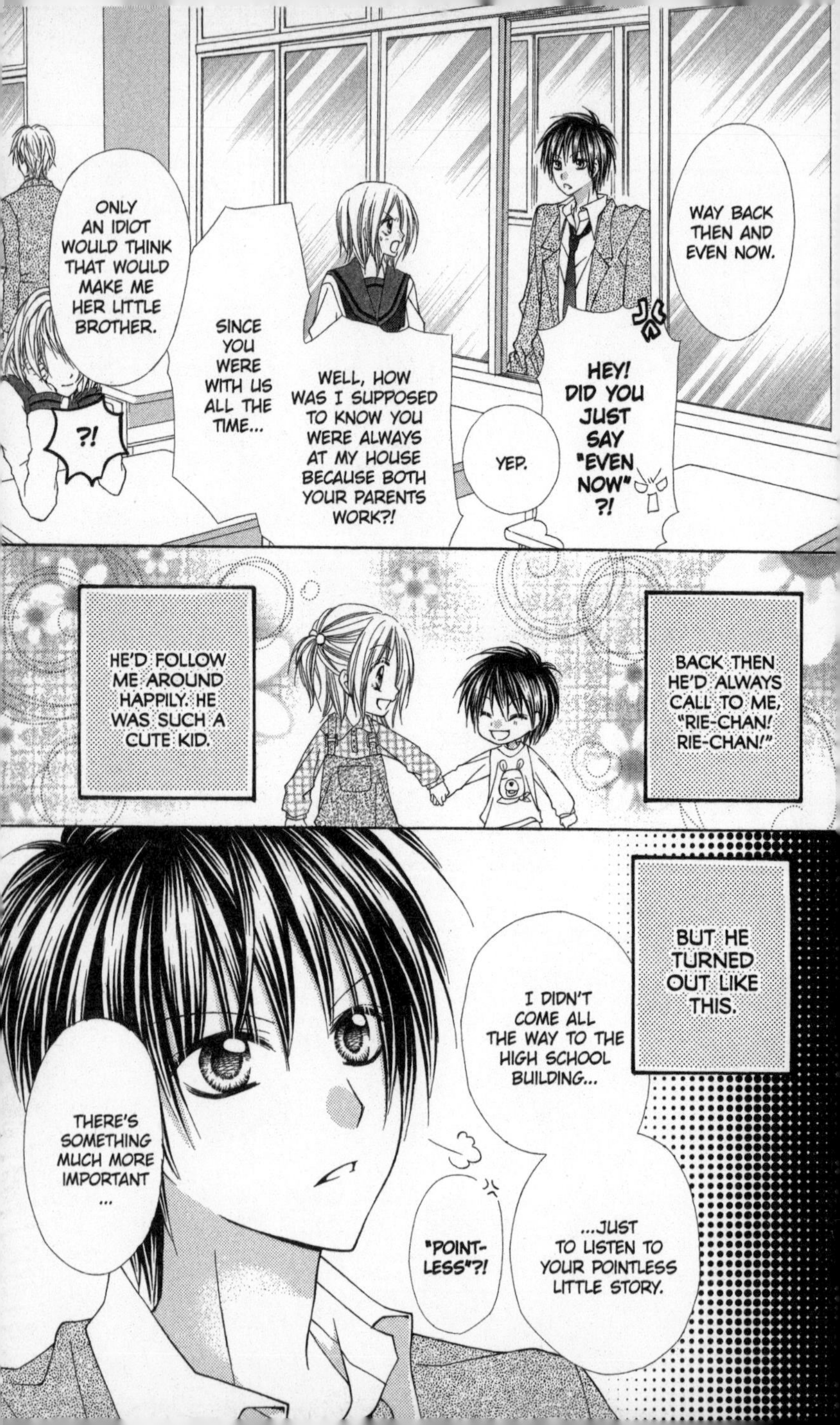
WAY BACK THEN AND EVEN NOW.
HEY! DID YOU JUST SAY "EVEN NOW"?!
YEP.
WELL, HOW WAS I SUPPOSED TO KNOW YOU WERE ALWAYS AT MY HOUSE BECAUSE BOTH YOUR PARENTS WORK?!
SINCE YOU WERE WITH US ALL THE TIME...
ONLY AN IDIOT WOULD THINK THAT WOULD MAKE ME HER LITTLE BROTHER.
?!
BACK THEN HE'D ALWAYS CALL TO ME, "RIE-CHAN! RIE-CHAN!"
HE'D FOLLOW ME AROUND HAPPILY. HE WAS SUCH A CUTE KID.
BUT HE TURNED OUT LIKE THIS.
I DIDN'T COME ALL THE WAY TO THE HIGH SCHOOL BUILDING...
...JUST TO LISTEN TO YOUR POINTLESS LITTLE STORY.
"POINT-LESS"?!
THERE'S SOMETHING MUCH MORE IMPORTANT ...

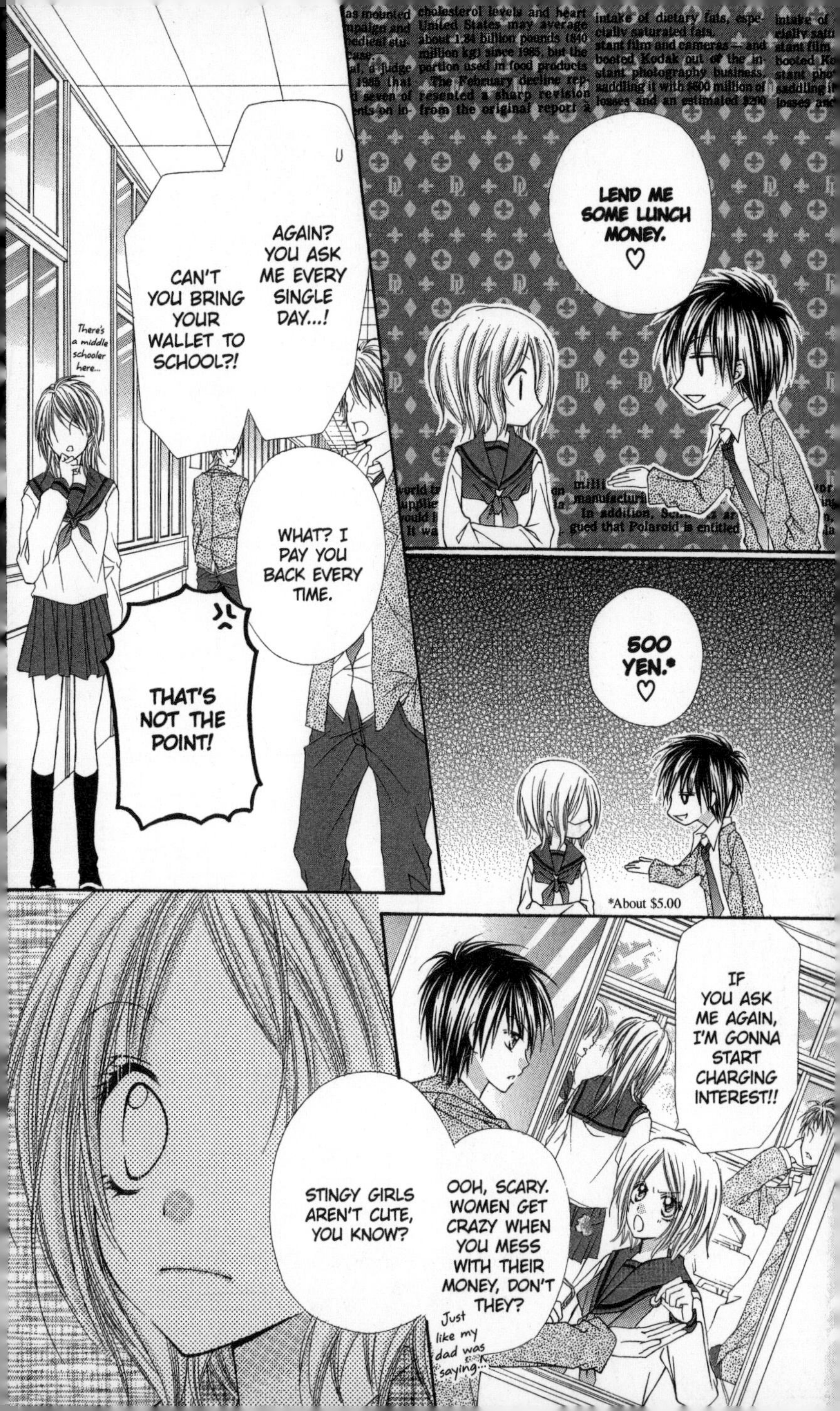

LEND ME SOME LUNCH MONEY. ♡
500 YEN.* ♡
AGAIN? YOU ASK ME EVERY SINGLE DAY...!
CAN'T YOU BRING YOUR WALLET TO SCHOOL?!
There's a middle schooler here...
WHAT? I PAY YOU BACK EVERY TIME.
THAT'S NOT THE POINT!
IF YOU ASK ME AGAIN, I'M GONNA START CHARGING INTEREST!!
OOH, SCARY. WOMEN GET CRAZY WHEN YOU MESS WITH THEIR MONEY, DON'T THEY?
Just like my dad was saying...
STINGY GIRLS AREN'T CUTE, YOU KNOW?

*About $5.00

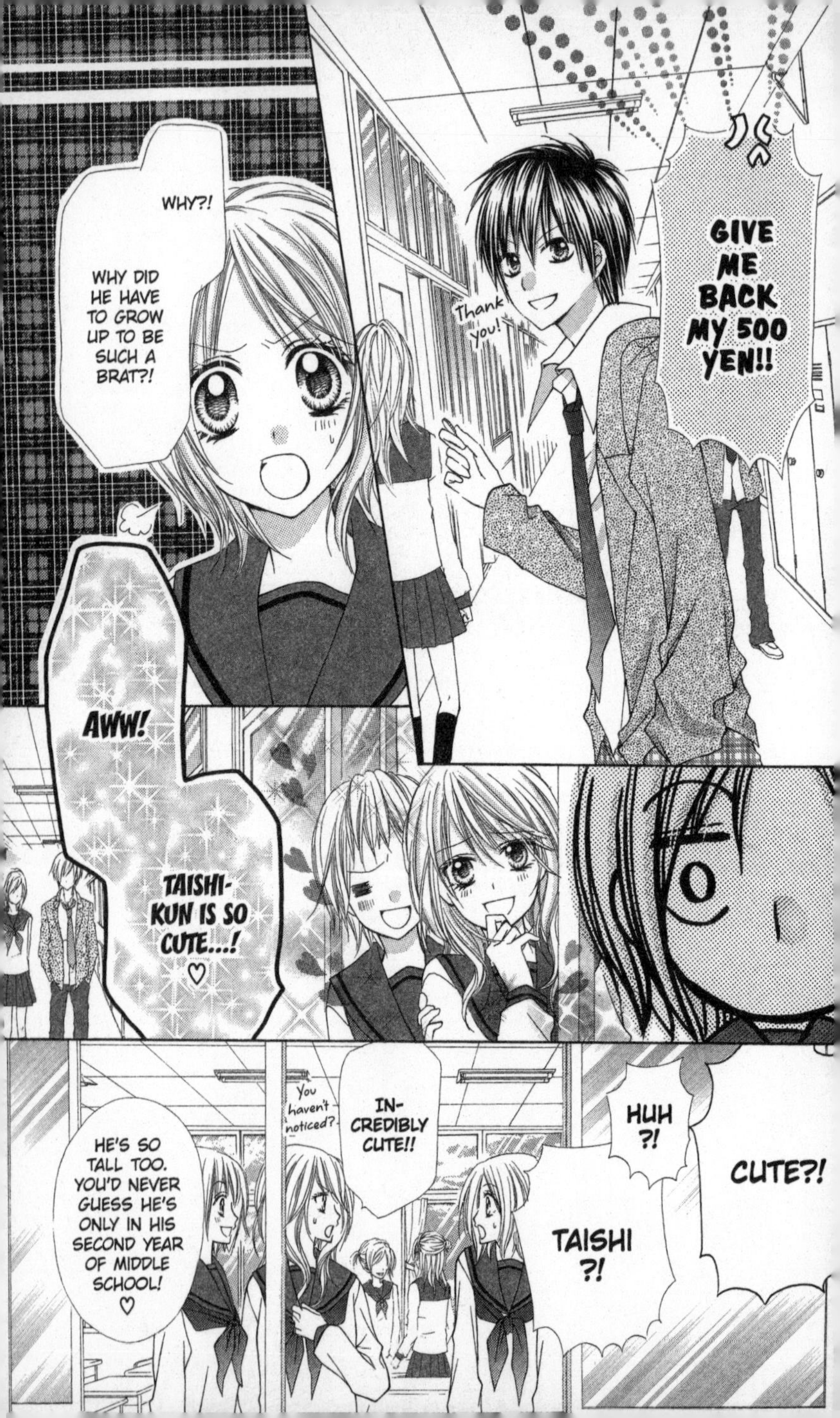
GIVE ME BACK MY 500 YEN!!
Thank you!
WHY?!
WHY DID HE HAVE TO GROW UP TO BE SUCH A BRAT?!
AWW!
TAISHI-KUN IS SO CUTE...! ♡
CUTE?!
HUH?!
TAISHI?!
IN-CREDIBLY CUTE!!
You haven't noticed?
HE'S SO TALL TOO. YOU'D NEVER GUESS HE'S ONLY IN HIS SECOND YEAR OF MIDDLE SCHOOL! ♡

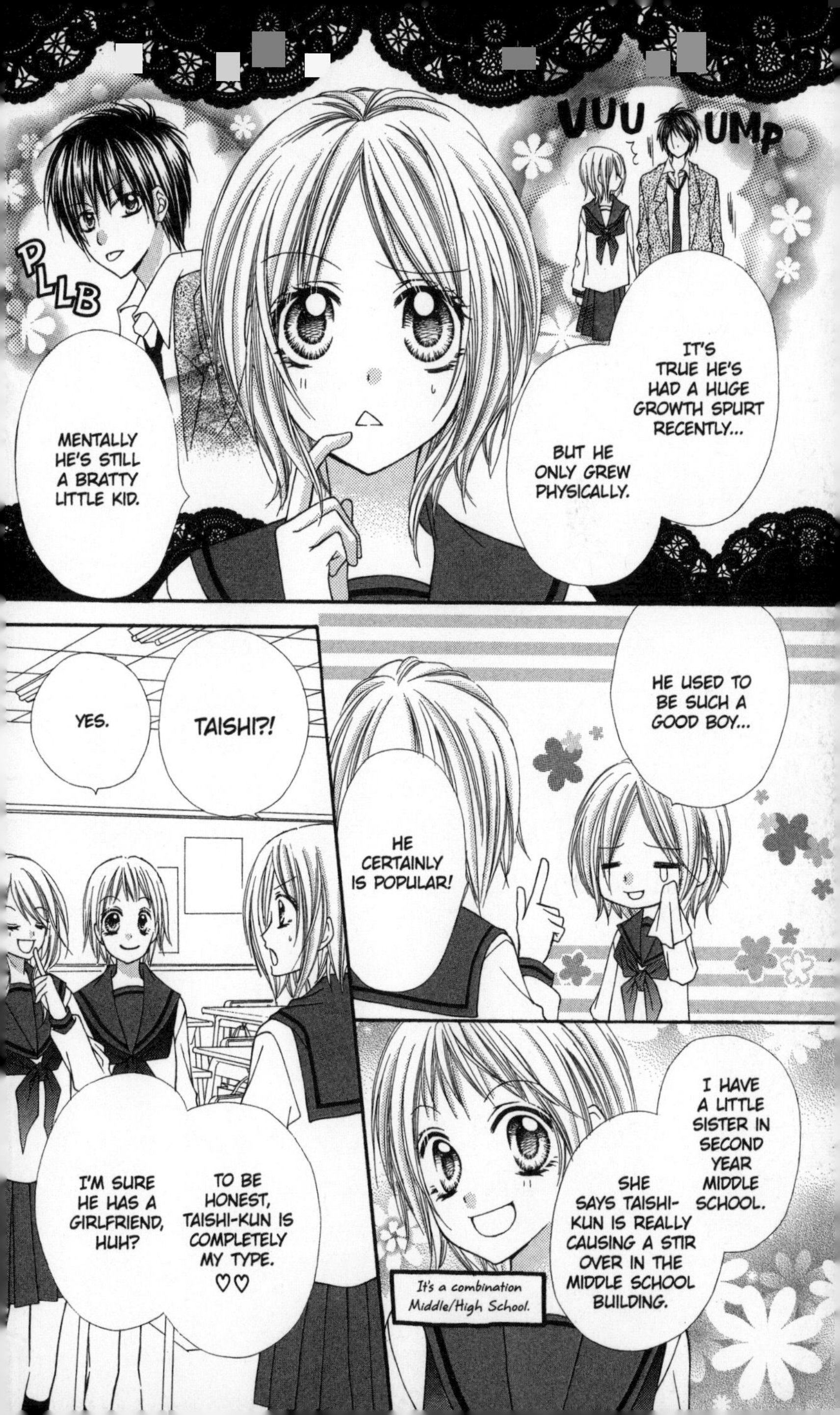
VUUUMP
IT'S TRUE HE'S HAD A HUGE GROWTH SPURT RECENTLY...
BUT HE ONLY GREW PHYSICALLY.
PLLB
MENTALLY HE'S STILL A BRATTY LITTLE KID.
HE USED TO BE SUCH A GOOD BOY...
HE CERTAINLY IS POPULAR!
I HAVE A LITTLE SISTER IN SECOND YEAR MIDDLE SCHOOL.
SHE SAYS TAISHI-KUN IS REALLY CAUSING A STIR OVER IN THE MIDDLE SCHOOL BUILDING.
It's a combination Middle/High School.
TAISHI?!
YES.
TO BE HONEST, TAISHI-KUN IS COMPLETELY MY TYPE. ♡♡
I'M SURE HE HAS A GIRLFRIEND, HUH?

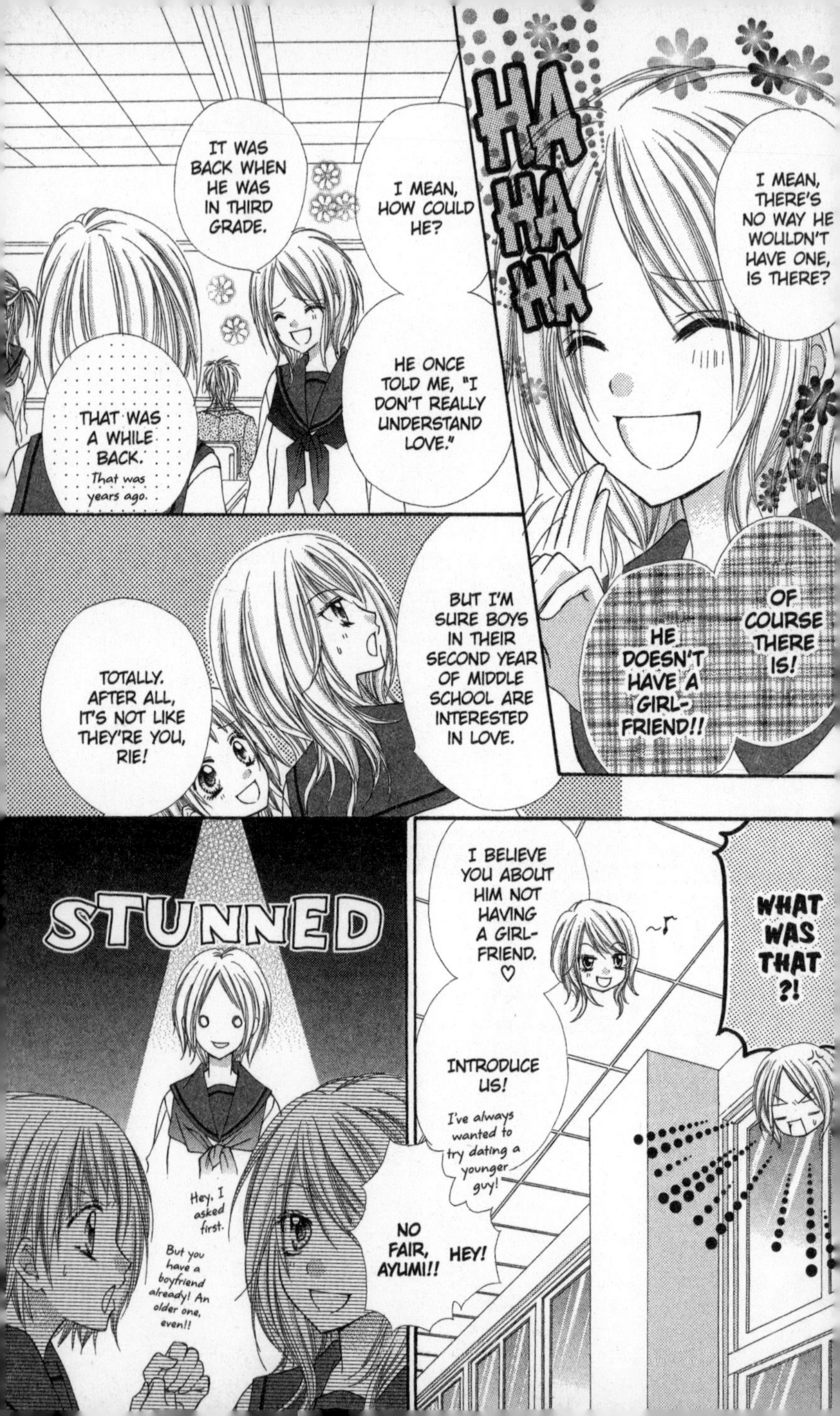
HA HA HA HA
I MEAN, THERE'S NO WAY HE WOULDN'T HAVE ONE, IS THERE?
OF COURSE THERE IS!
HE DOESN'T HAVE A GIRL-FRIEND!!
I MEAN, HOW COULD HE?
HE ONCE TOLD ME, "I DON'T REALLY UNDERSTAND LOVE."
IT WAS BACK WHEN HE WAS IN THIRD GRADE.
THAT WAS A WHILE BACK. That was years ago.
BUT I'M SURE BOYS IN THEIR SECOND YEAR OF MIDDLE SCHOOL ARE INTERESTED IN LOVE.
TOTALLY. AFTER ALL, IT'S NOT LIKE THEY'RE YOU, RIE!
WHAT WAS THAT?!
I BELIEVE YOU ABOUT HIM NOT HAVING A GIRL-FRIEND. ♡
INTRODUCE US! I've always wanted to try dating a younger guy!
STUNNED
HEY!
NO FAIR, AYUMI!!
Hey, I asked first.
But you have a boyfriend already! An older one, even!!

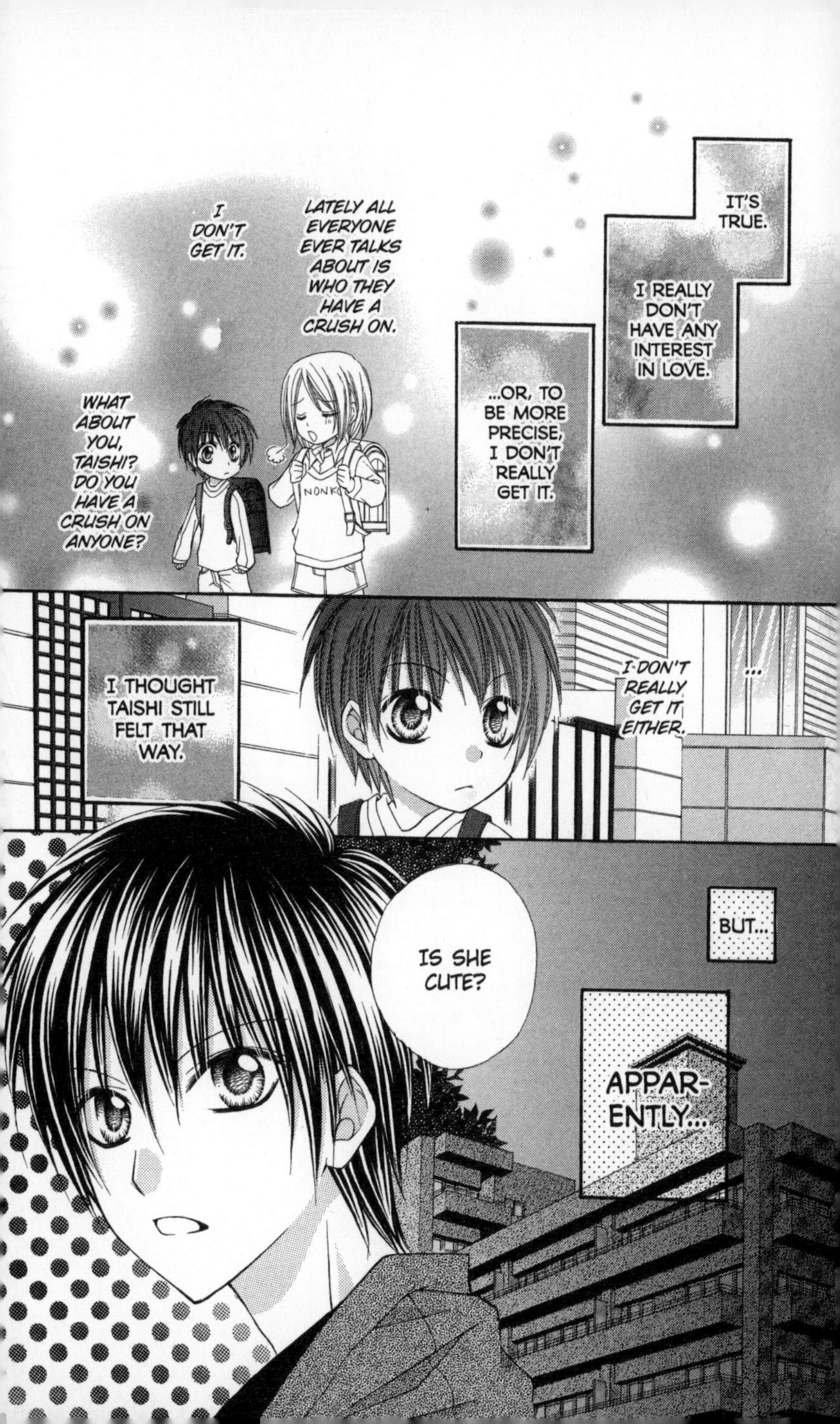
IT'S TRUE.
I REALLY DON'T HAVE ANY INTEREST IN LOVE.
...OR, TO BE MORE PRECISE, I DON'T REALLY GET IT.
LATELY ALL EVERYONE EVER TALKS ABOUT IS WHO THEY HAVE A CRUSH ON.
I DON'T GET IT.
NONKO
WHAT ABOUT YOU, TAISHI? DO YOU HAVE A CRUSH ON ANYONE?
...
I DON'T REALLY GET IT EITHER.
I THOUGHT TAISHI STILL FELT THAT WAY.
BUT...
APPAR-
ENTLY...
IS SHE CUTE?

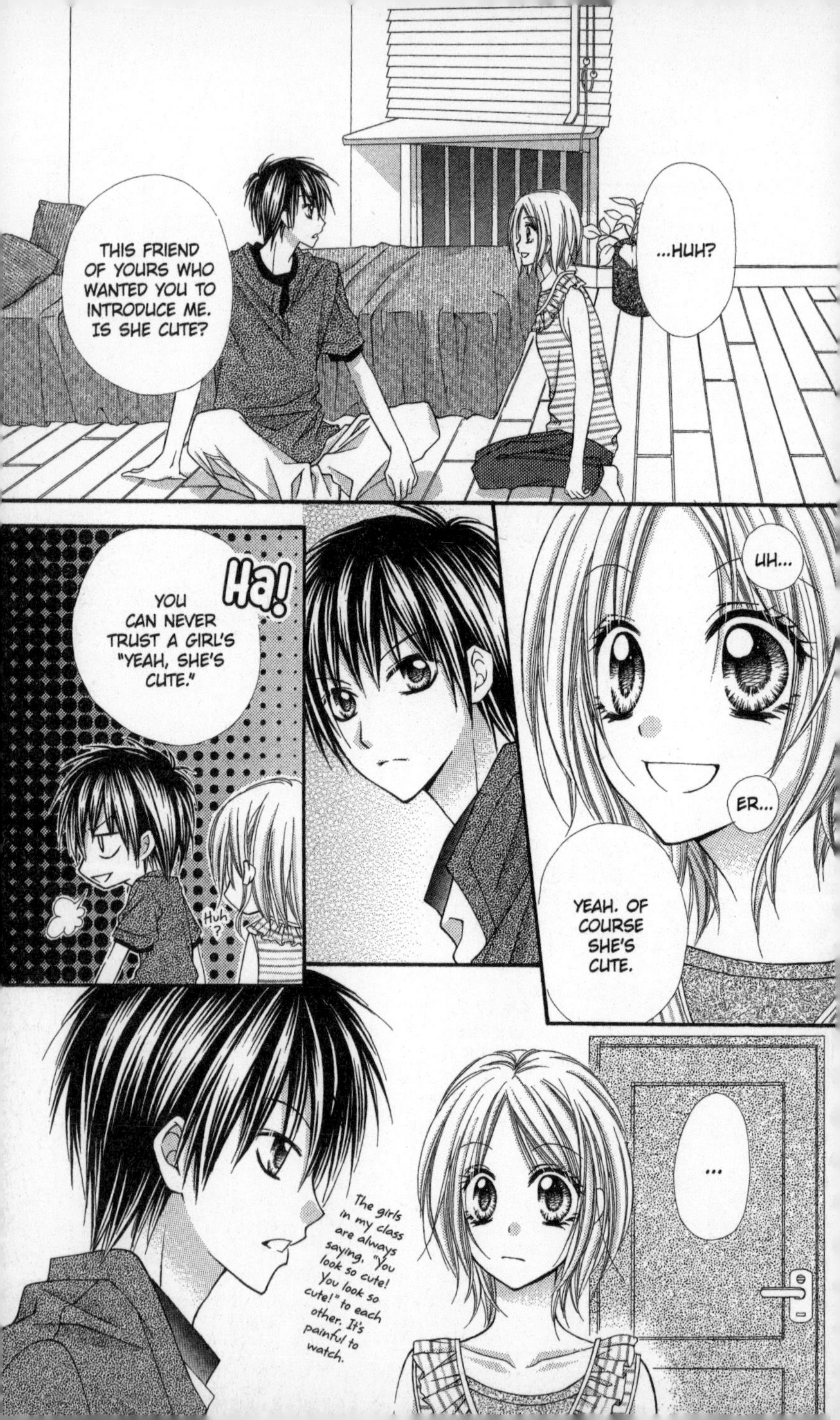
THIS FRIEND OF YOURS WHO WANTED YOU TO INTRODUCE ME. IS SHE CUTE?
...HUH?
UH...
ER...
YEAH. OF COURSE SHE'S CUTE.
Ha!
YOU CAN NEVER TRUST A GIRL'S "YEAH, SHE'S CUTE."
Huh?
...
The girls in my class are always saying, "You look so cute! You look so cute!" to each other. It's painful to watch.

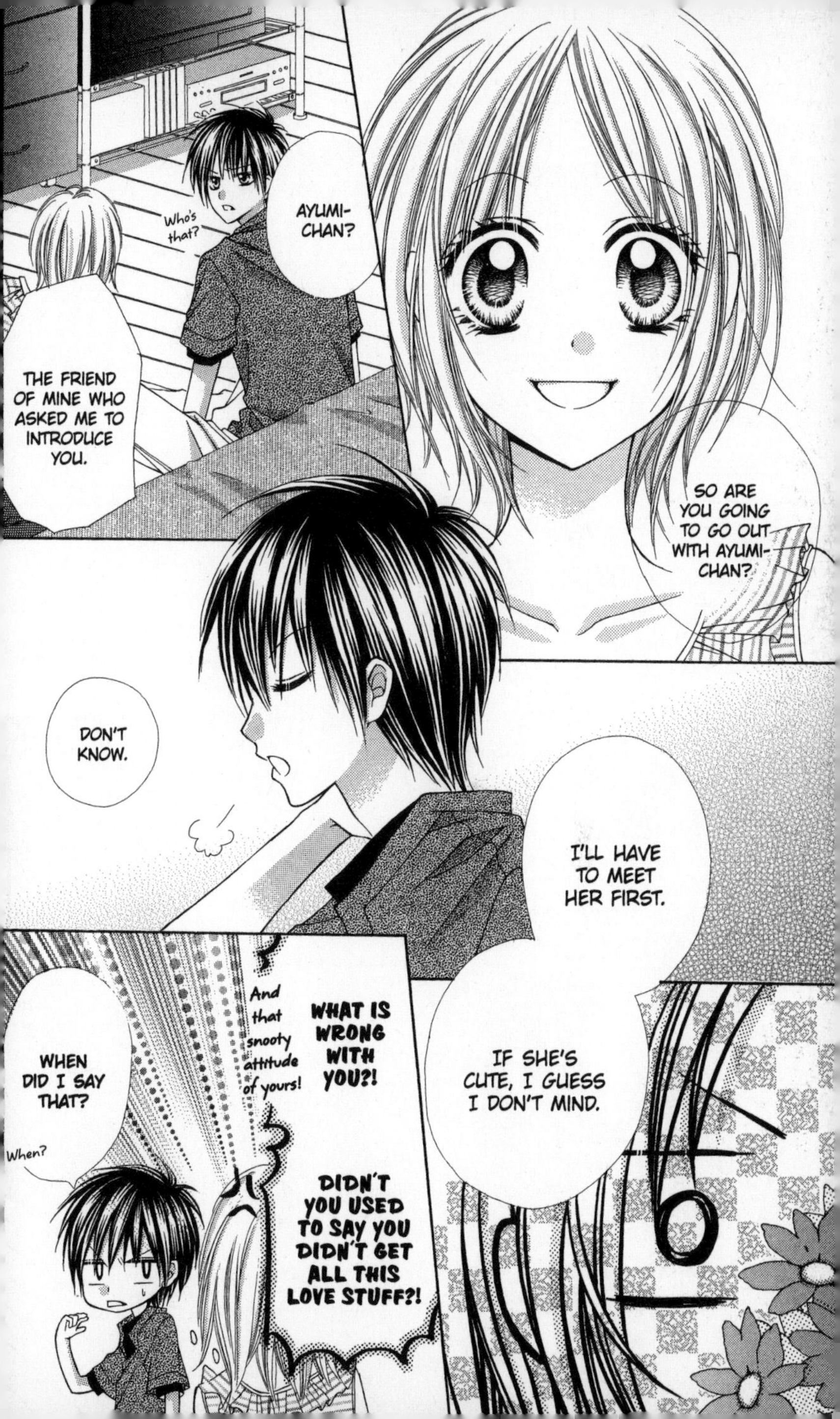
AYUMI-CHAN?
Who's that?
THE FRIEND OF MINE WHO ASKED ME TO INTRODUCE YOU.
SO ARE YOU GOING TO GO OUT WITH AYUMI-CHAN?
DON'T KNOW.
I'LL HAVE TO MEET HER FIRST.
IF SHE'S CUTE, I GUESS I DON'T MIND.
WHAT IS WRONG WITH YOU?!
And that snooty attitude of yours!
DIDN'T YOU USED TO SAY YOU DIDN'T GET ALL THIS LOVE STUFF?!
WHEN DID I SAY THAT?
When?

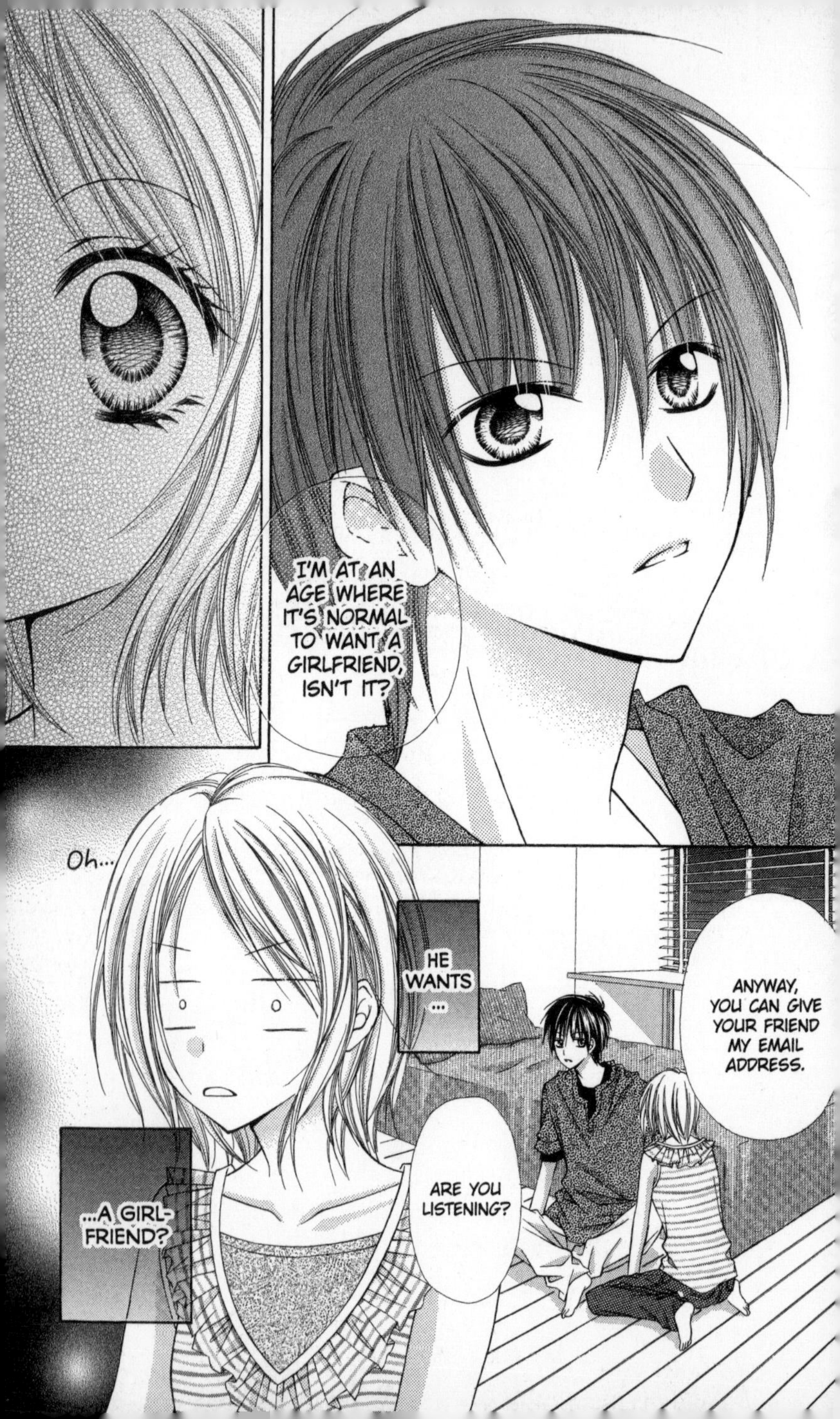
I'M AT AN AGE WHERE IT'S NORMAL TO WANT A GIRLFRIEND, ISN'T IT?
ANYWAY, YOU CAN GIVE YOUR FRIEND MY EMAIL ADDRESS.
ARE YOU LISTENING?
HE WANTS...
Oh...
...A GIRL-FRIEND?

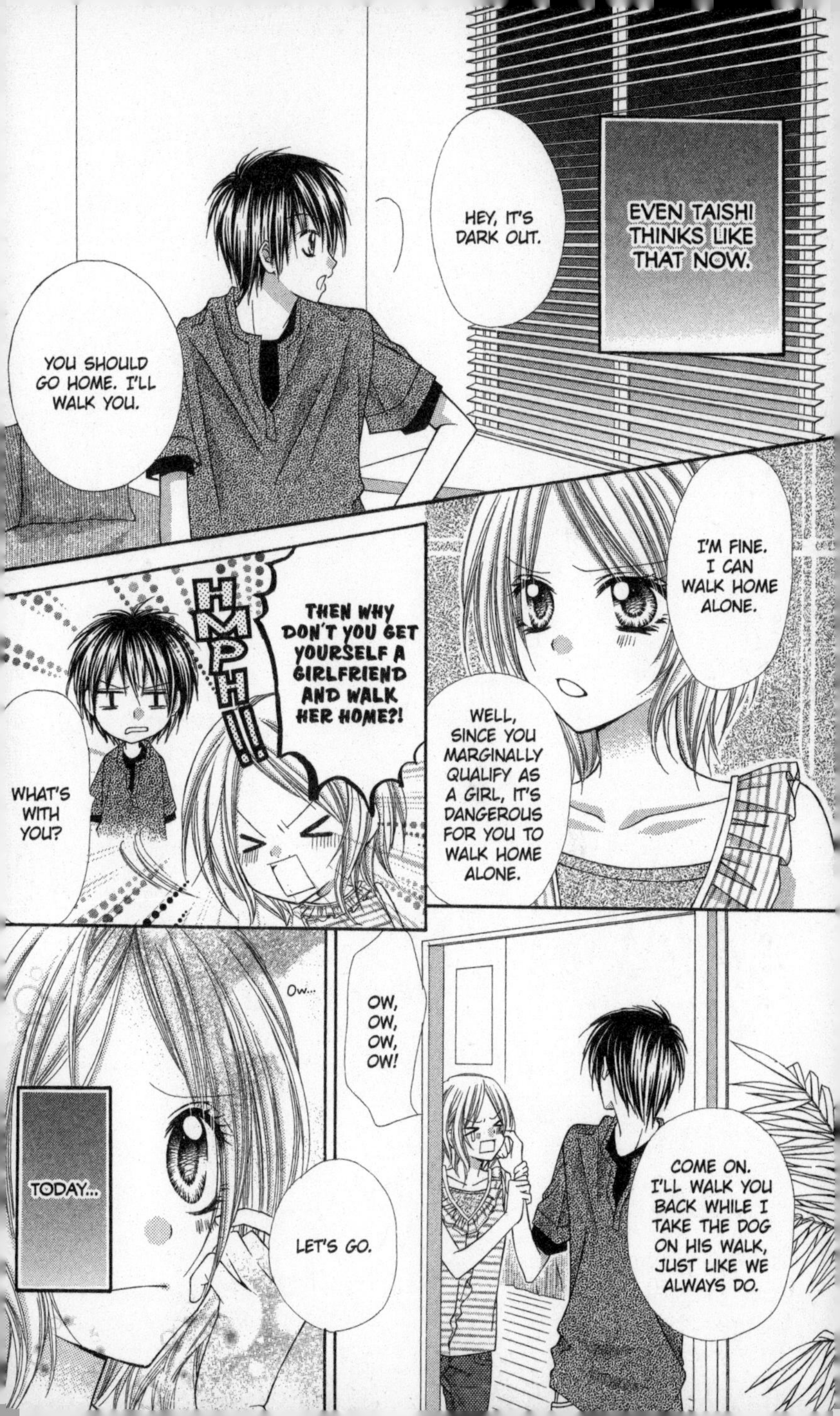
EVEN TAISHI THINKS LIKE THAT NOW.
HEY, IT'S DARK OUT.
YOU SHOULD GO HOME. I'LL WALK YOU.
I'M FINE. I CAN WALK HOME ALONE.
WELL, SINCE YOU MARGINALLY QUALIFY AS A GIRL, IT'S DANGEROUS FOR YOU TO WALK HOME ALONE.
HMPH!!
THEN WHY DON'T YOU GET YOURSELF A GIRLFRIEND AND WALK HER HOME?!
WHAT'S WITH YOU?
OW, OW, OW, OW!
Ow...
COME ON. I'LL WALK YOU BACK WHILE I TAKE THE DOG ON HIS WALK, JUST LIKE WE ALWAYS DO.
LET'S GO.
TODAY...

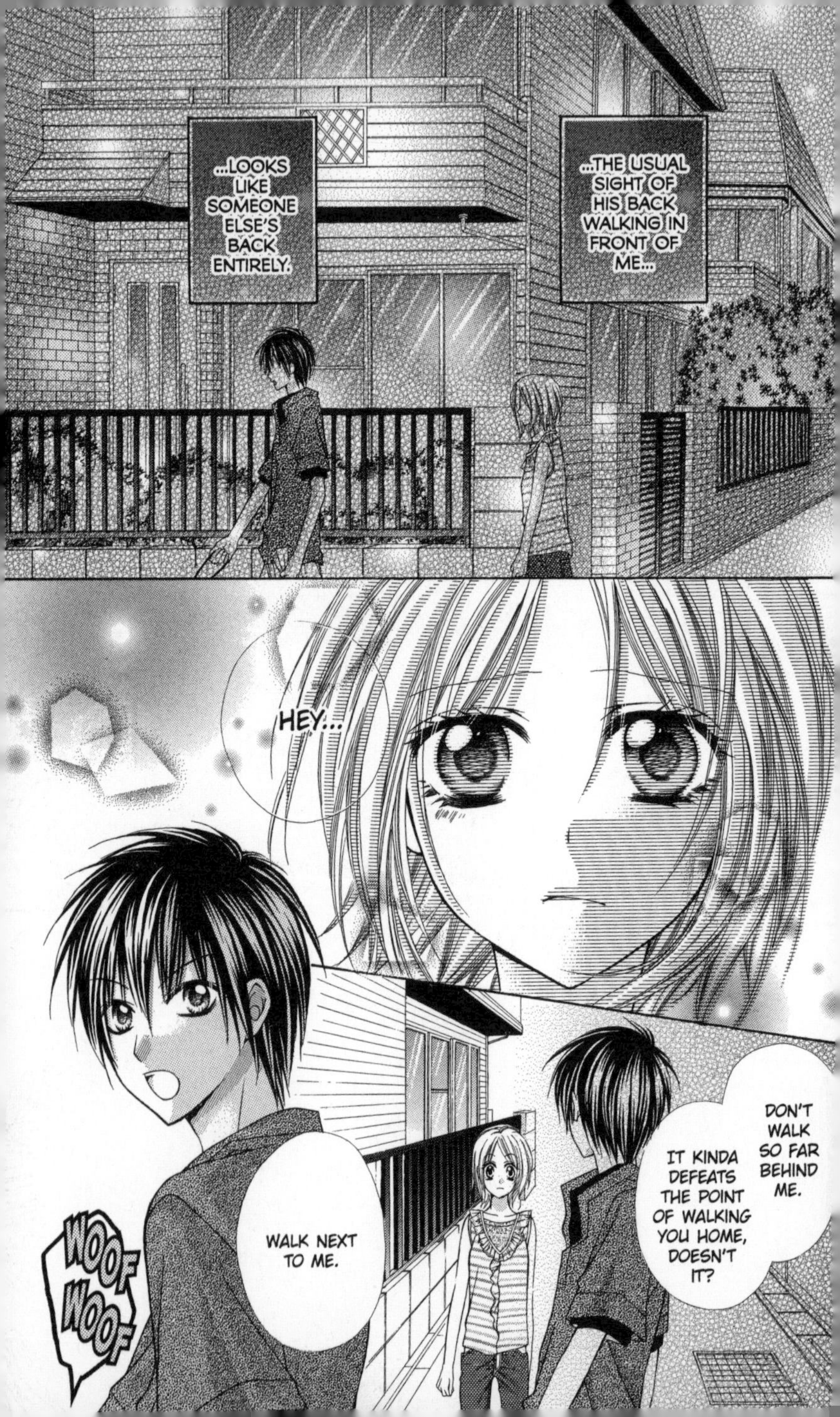
...THE USUAL SIGHT OF HIS BACK WALKING IN FRONT OF ME...
...LOOKS LIKE SOMEONE ELSE'S BACK ENTIRELY.
HEY...
DON'T WALK SO FAR BEHIND ME.
IT KINDA DEFEATS THE POINT OF WALKING YOU HOME, DOESN'T IT?
WALK NEXT TO ME.
WOOF WOOF

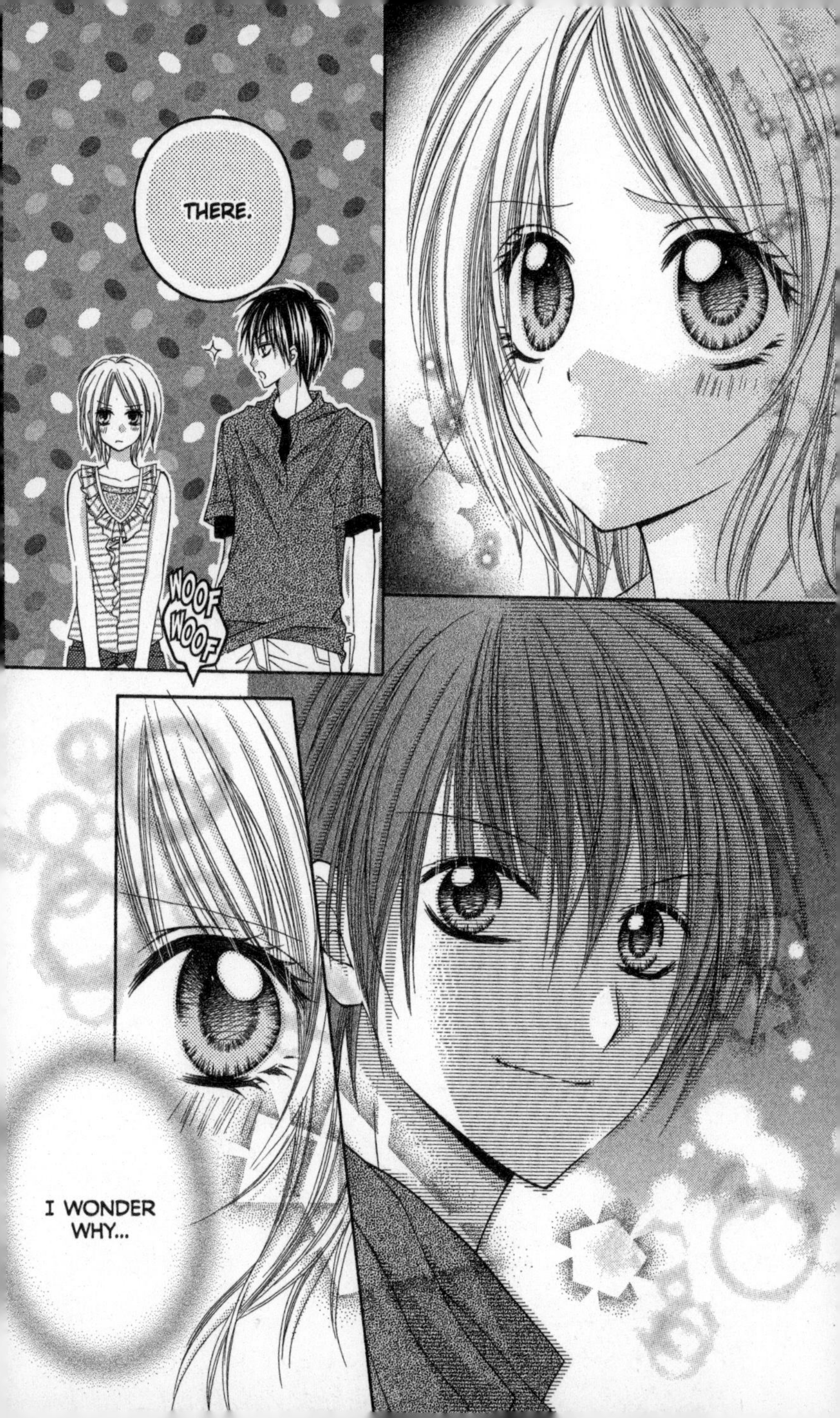
THERE.
WOOF WOOF
I WONDER WHY...

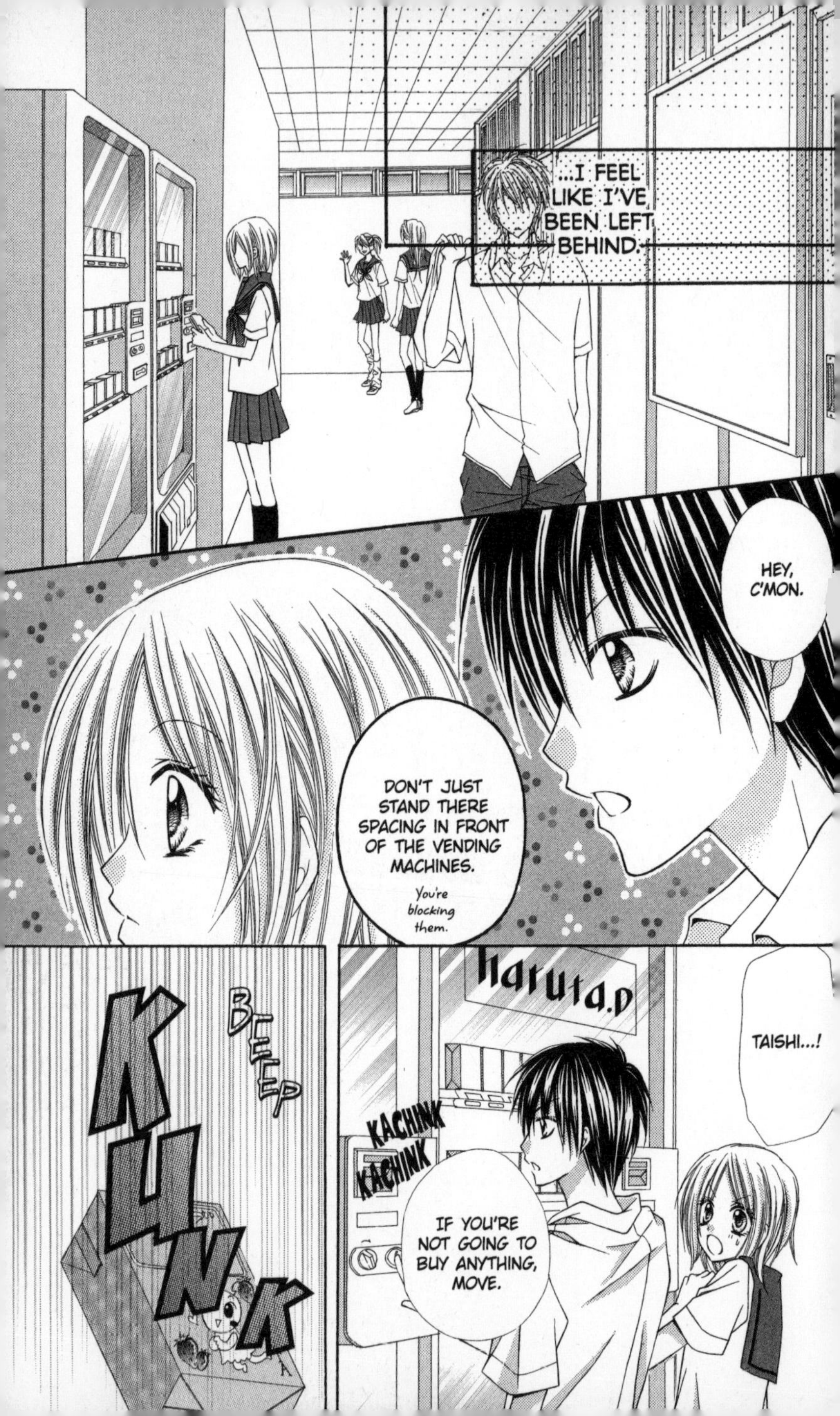
...I FEEL LIKE I'VE BEEN LEFT BEHIND.
HEY, C'MON.
DON'T JUST STAND THERE SPACING IN FRONT OF THE VENDING MACHINES.
You're blocking them.
TAISHI...!
KACHINK
KACHINK
IF YOU'RE NOT GOING TO BUY ANYTHING, MOVE.
KUNK
BEEEP

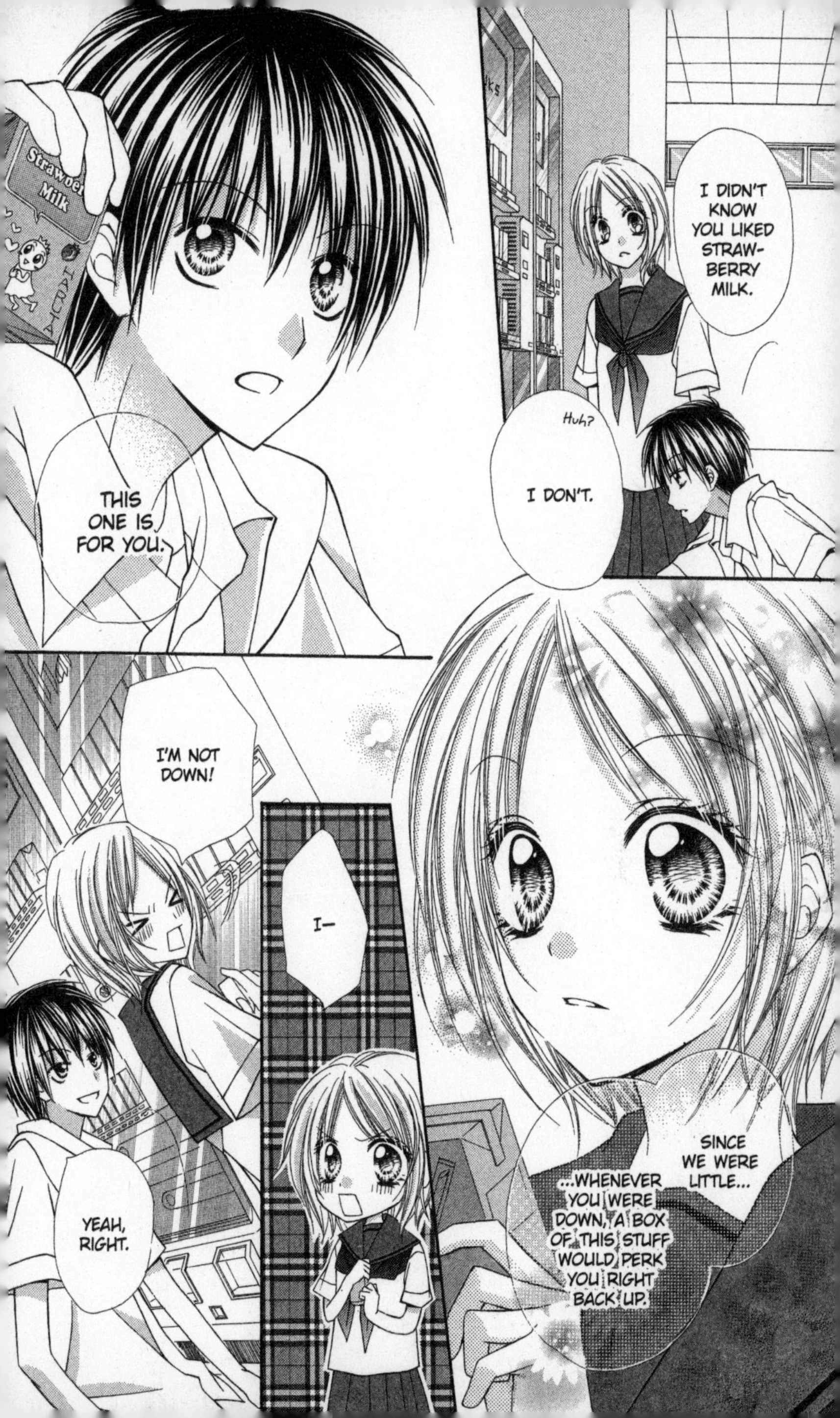
I DIDN'T KNOW YOU LIKED STRAW-BERRY MILK.
Huh?
I DON'T.
THIS ONE IS FOR YOU.
SINCE WE WERE LITTLE...
...WHENEVER YOU WERE DOWN, A BOX OF THIS STUFF WOULD PERK YOU RIGHT BACK UP.
I—
I'M NOT DOWN!
YEAH, RIGHT.

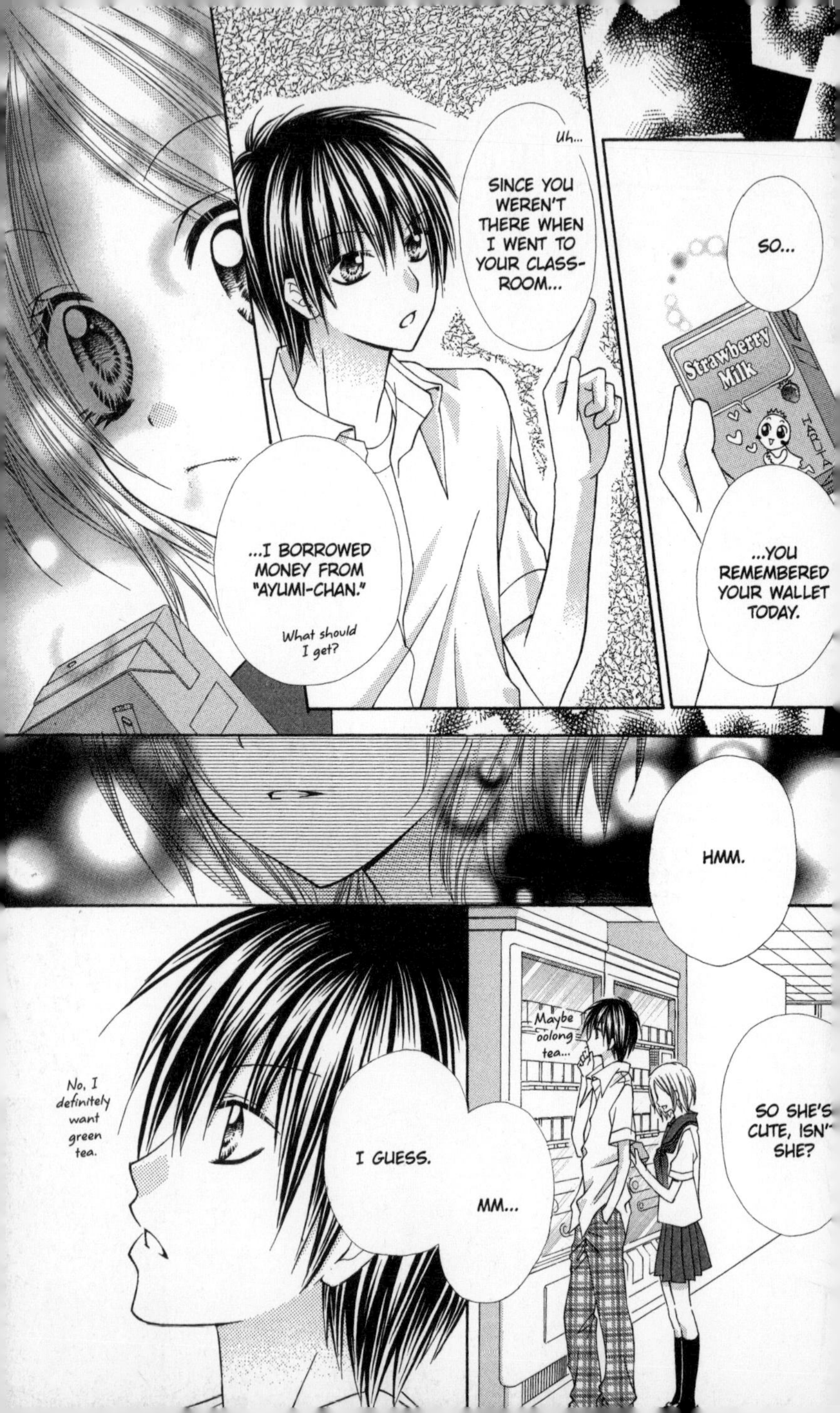
SO...
Strawberry Milk
...YOU REMEMBERED YOUR WALLET TODAY.
Uh...
SINCE YOU WEREN'T THERE WHEN I WENT TO YOUR CLASS-ROOM...
...I BORROWED MONEY FROM "AYUMI-CHAN."
What should I get?
HMM.
SO SHE'S CUTE, ISN' SHE?
Maybe oolong tea...
I GUESS.
MM...
No, I definitely want green tea.

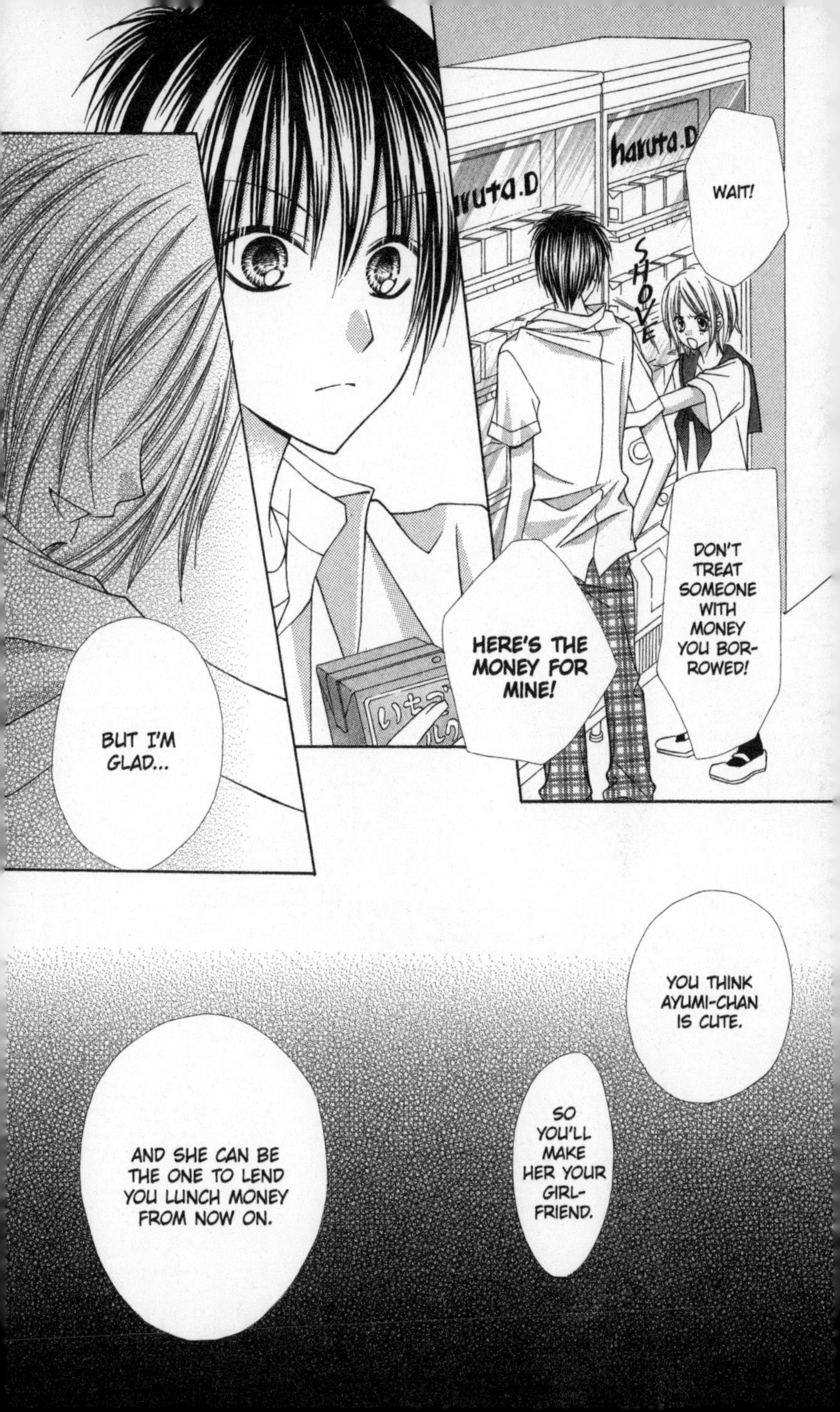
haruta.D
WAIT!
SHOVE
DON'T TREAT SOMEONE WITH MONEY YOU BORROWED!
HERE'S THE MONEY FOR MINE!
BUT I'M GLAD...
YOU THINK AYUMI-CHAN IS CUTE.
SO YOU'LL MAKE HER YOUR GIRLFRIEND.
AND SHE CAN BE THE ONE TO LEND YOU LUNCH MONEY FROM NOW ON.

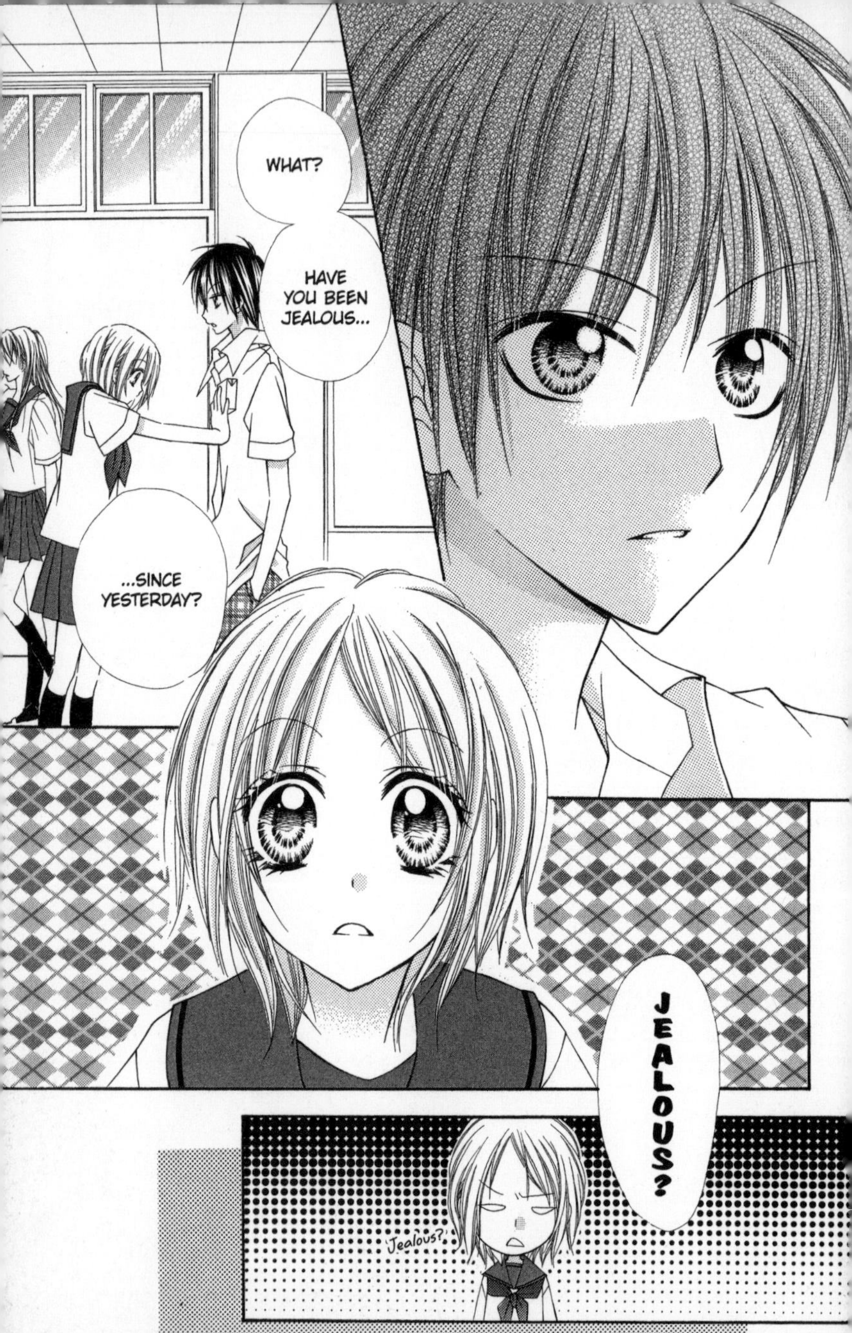
WHAT?
HAVE YOU BEEN JEALOUS...
...SINCE YESTERDAY?
JEALOUS?
Jealous?

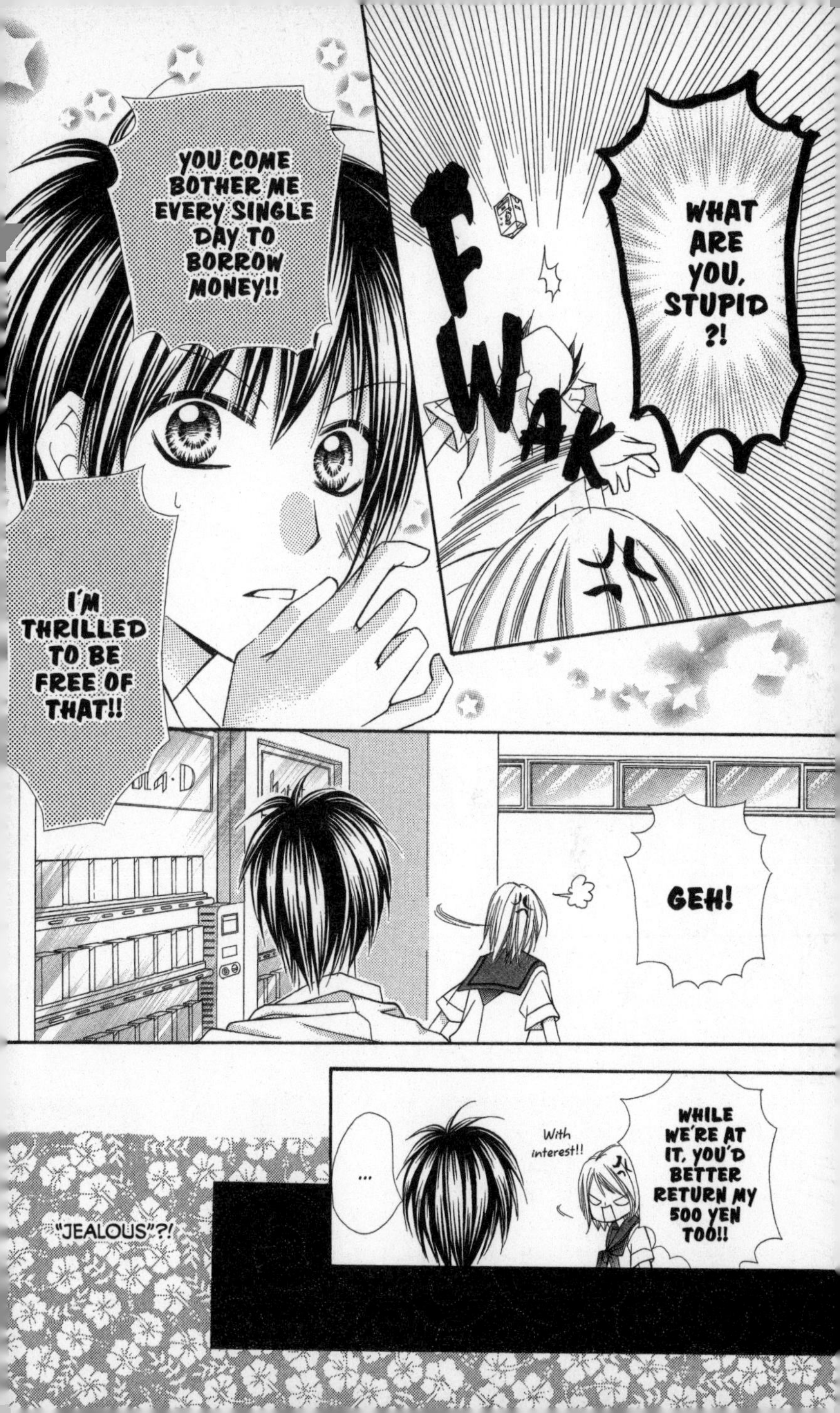
WHAT ARE YOU, STUPID?!
FWAK
YOU COME BOTHER ME EVERY SINGLE DAY TO BORROW MONEY!!
I'M THRILLED TO BE FREE OF THAT!!
GEH!
WHILE WE'RE AT IT, YOU'D BETTER RETURN MY 500 YEN TOO!!
With interest!!
...
"JEALOUS"?!

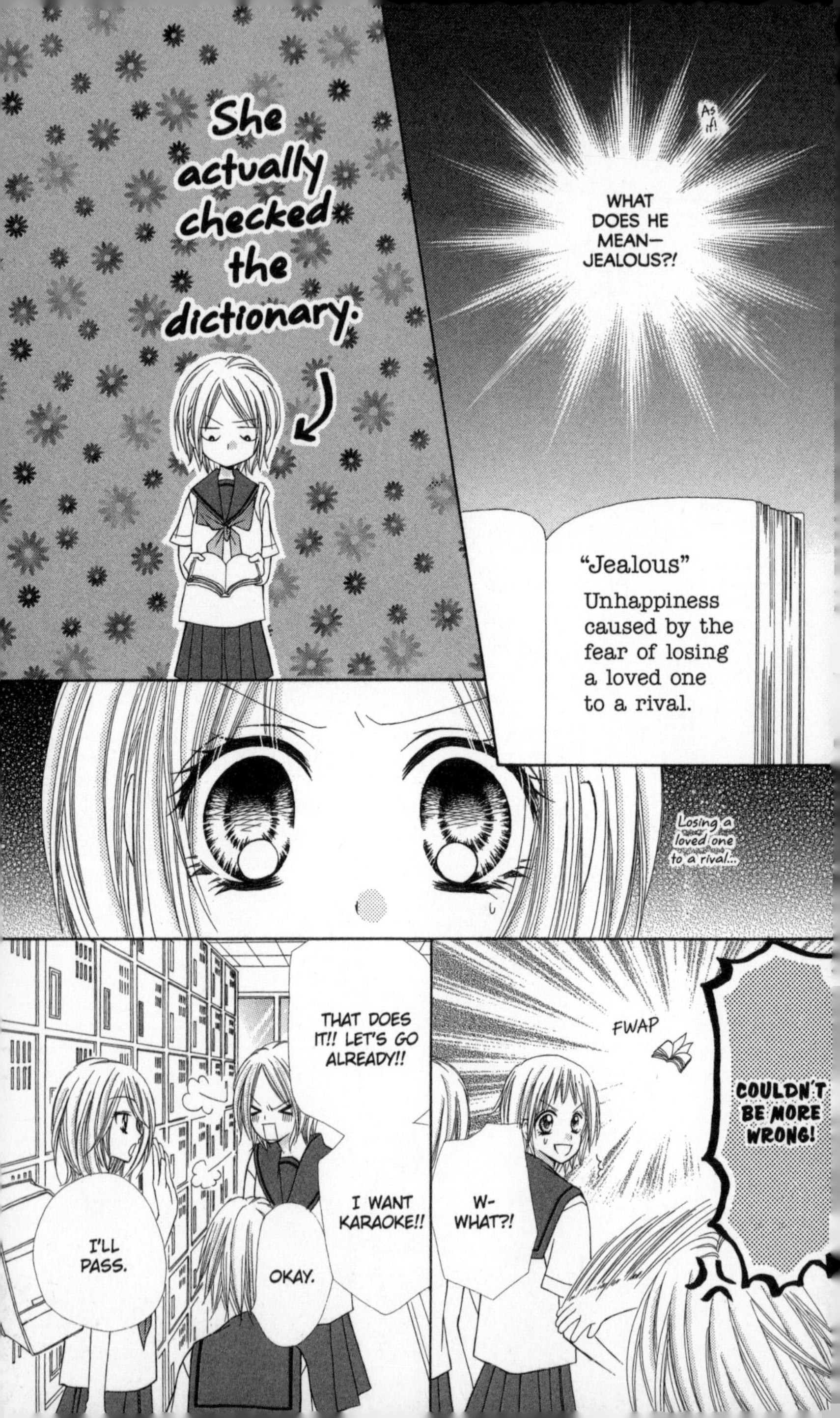
WHAT DOES HE MEAN—JEALOUS?!
As if!
"Jealous"
Unhappiness caused by the fear of losing a loved one to a rival.
She actually checked the dictionary.
Losing a loved one to a rival...
COULDN'T BE MORE WRONG!
FWAP
W-WHAT?!
THAT DOES IT!! LET'S GO ALREADY!!
I WANT KARAOKE!!
OKAY.
I'LL PASS.

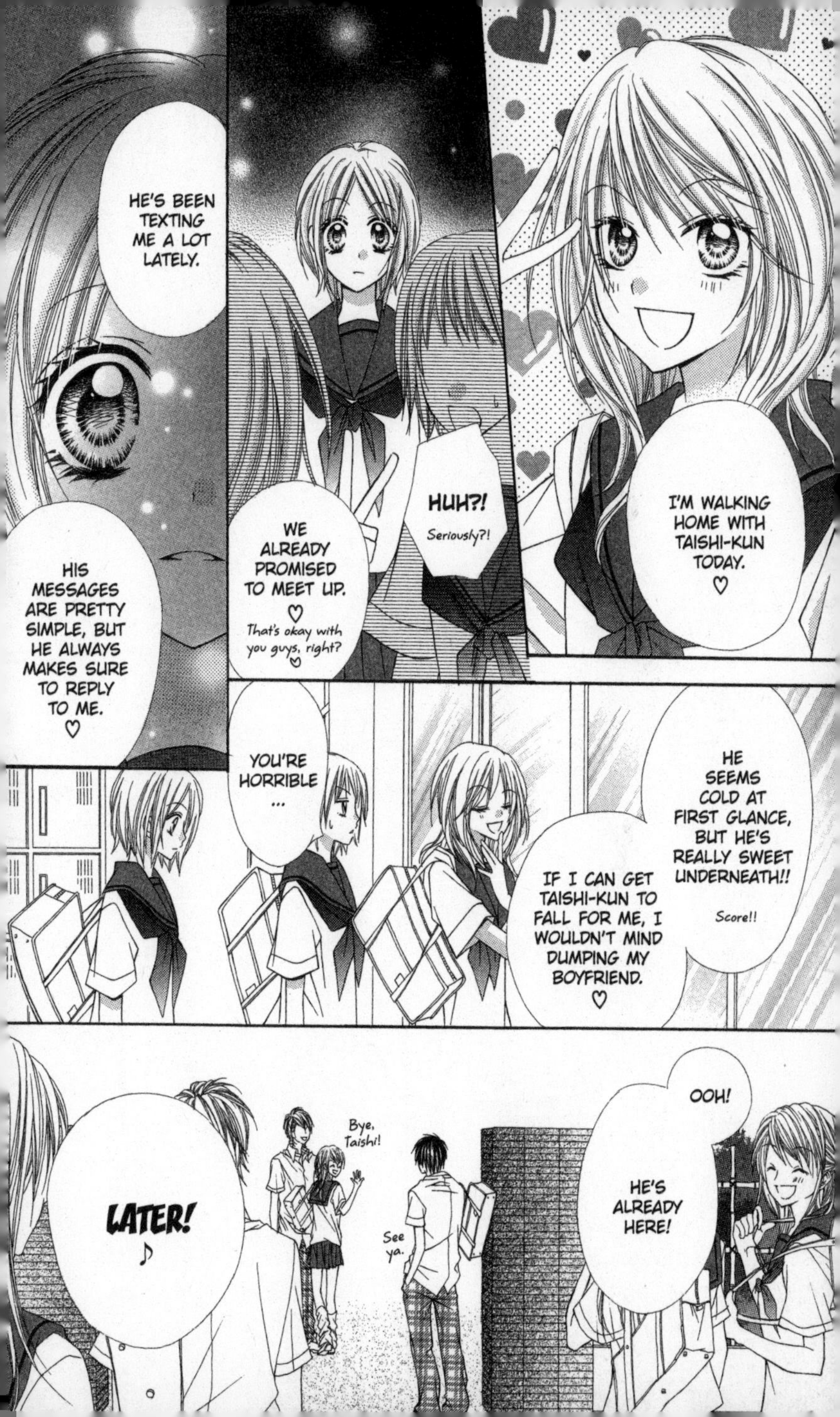
I'M WALKING HOME WITH TAISHI-KUN TODAY. ♡
HUH?!
Seriously?!
WE ALREADY PROMISED TO MEET UP. ♡
That's okay with you guys, right? ♡
HE'S BEEN TEXTING ME A LOT LATELY.
HIS MESSAGES ARE PRETTY SIMPLE, BUT HE ALWAYS MAKES SURE TO REPLY TO ME. ♡
HE SEEMS COLD AT FIRST GLANCE, BUT HE'S REALLY SWEET UNDERNEATH!!
Score!!
IF I CAN GET TAISHI-KUN TO FALL FOR ME, I WOULDN'T MIND DUMPING MY BOYFRIEND. ♡
YOU'RE HORRIBLE...
OOH!
HE'S ALREADY HERE!
See ya.
Bye, Taishi!
LATER! ♪

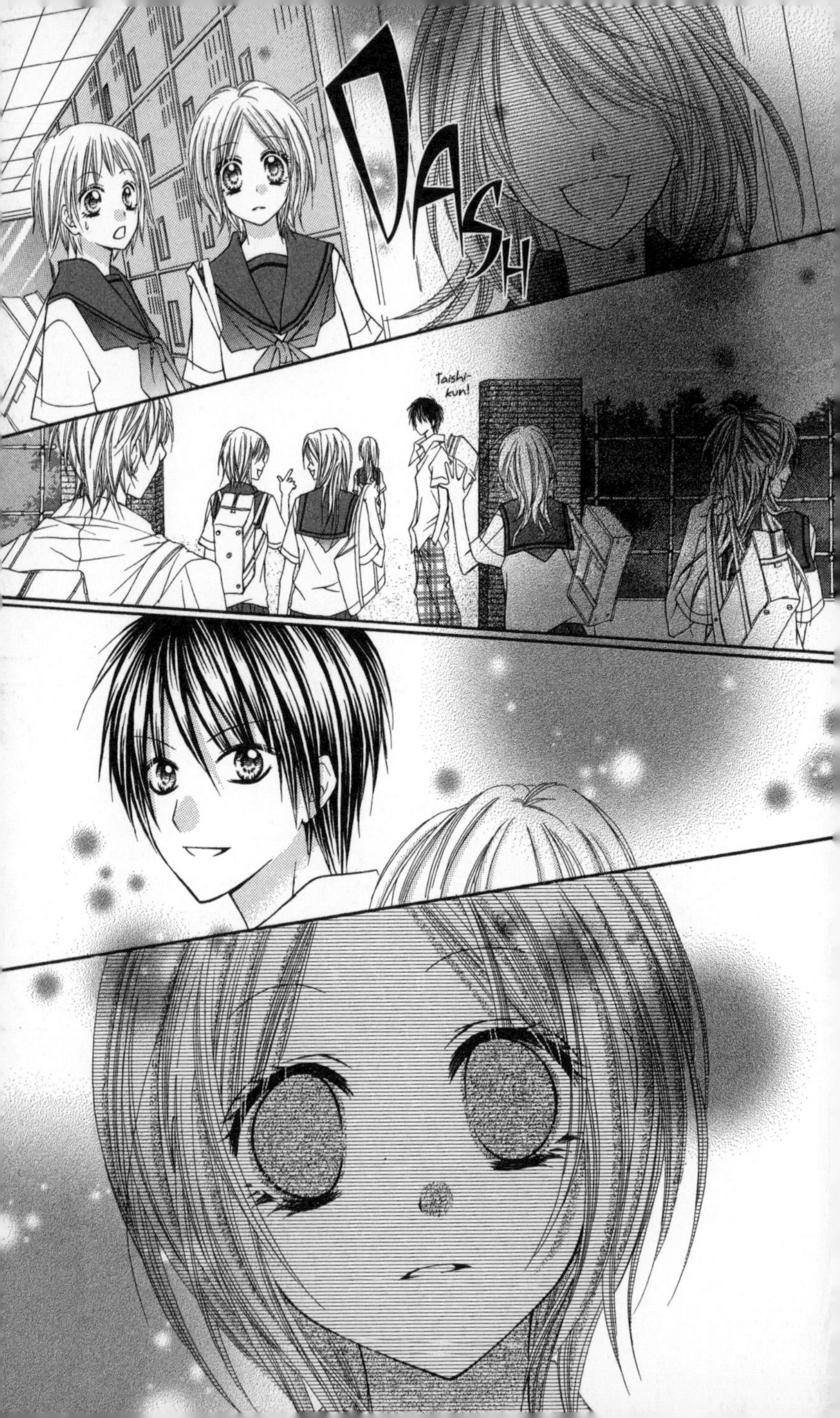
DASH
Taishi-kun!

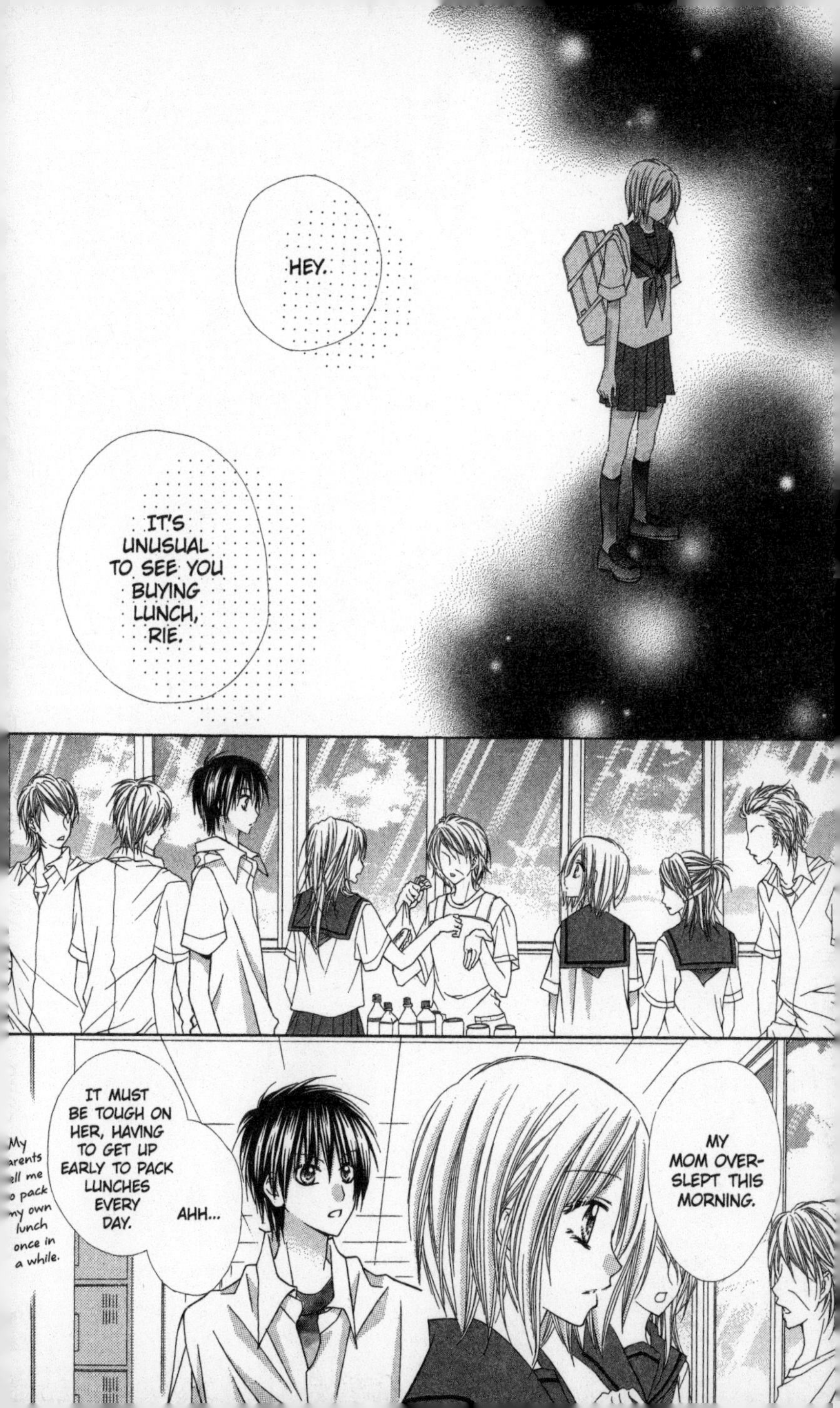
HEY.
IT'S UNUSUAL TO SEE YOU BUYING LUNCH, RIE.
MY MOM OVER-SLEPT THIS MORNING.
AHH...
IT MUST BE TOUGH ON HER, HAVING TO GET UP EARLY TO PACK LUNCHES EVERY DAY.
My arents ell me o pack my own lunch once in a while.

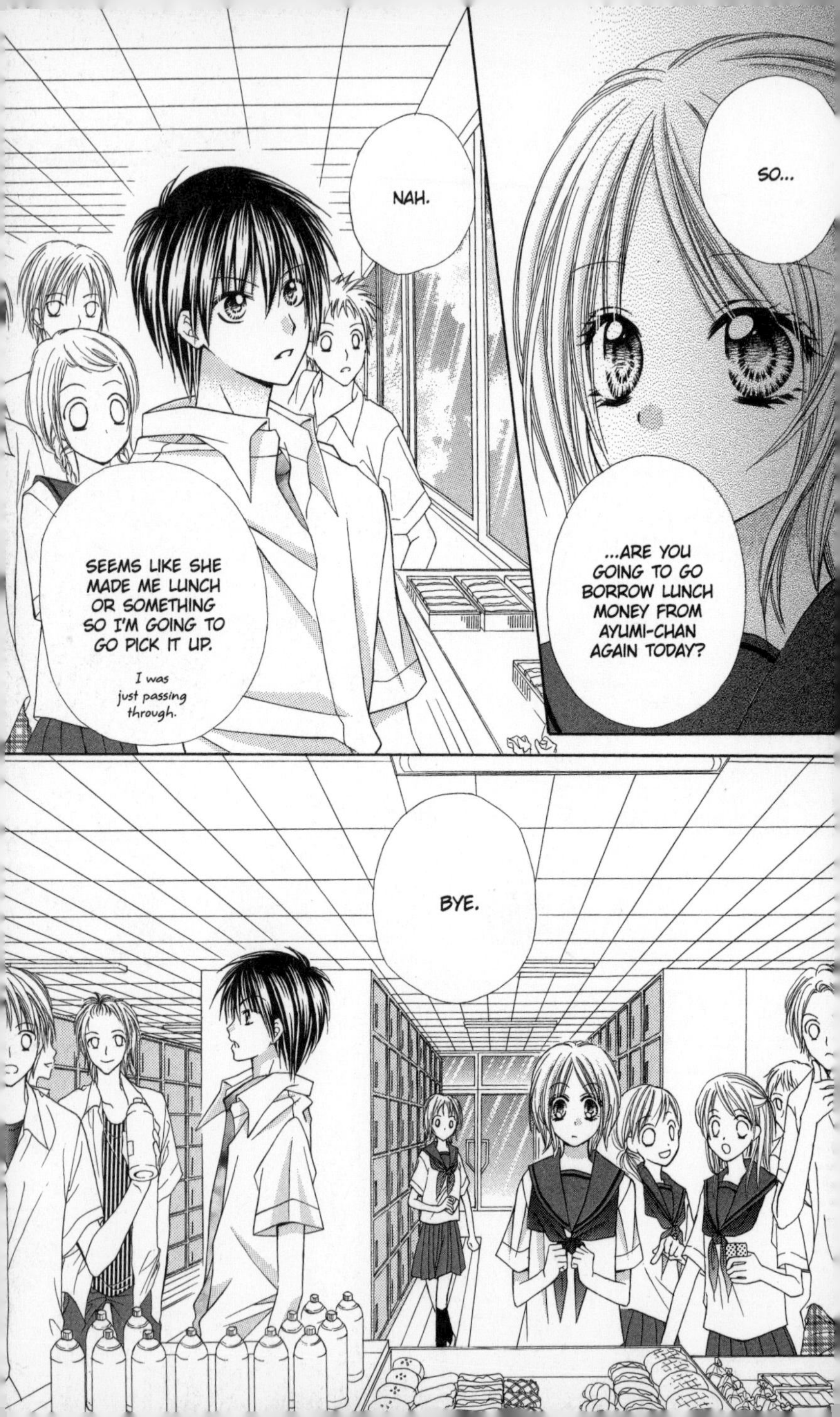
SO...
...ARE YOU GOING TO GO BORROW LUNCH MONEY FROM AYUMI-CHAN AGAIN TODAY?
NAH.
SEEMS LIKE SHE MADE ME LUNCH OR SOMETHING SO I'M GOING TO GO PICK IT UP.
I was just passing through.
BYE.

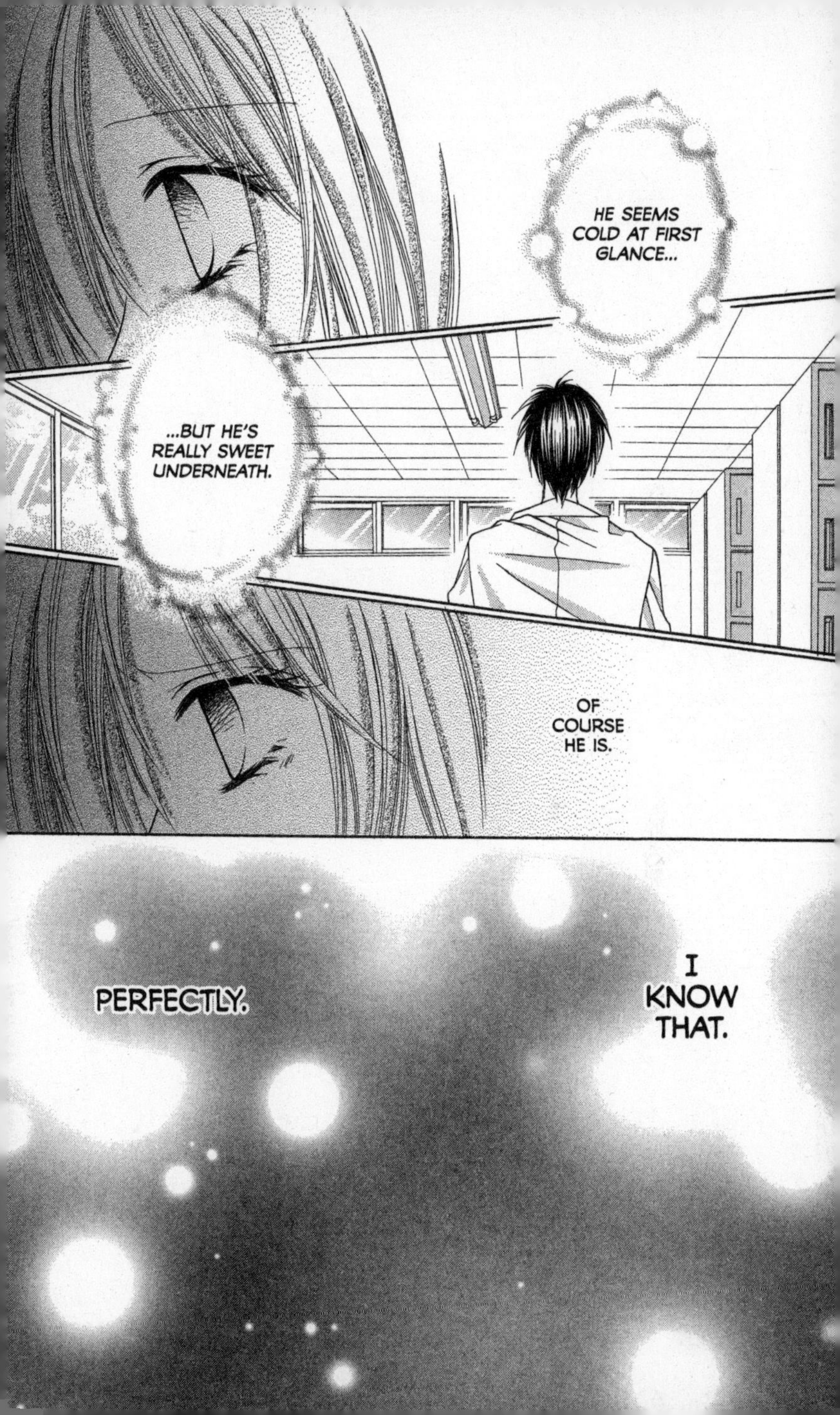
HE SEEMS COLD AT FIRST GLANCE...
...BUT HE'S REALLY SWEET UNDERNEATH.
OF COURSE HE IS.
I KNOW THAT.
PERFECTLY.

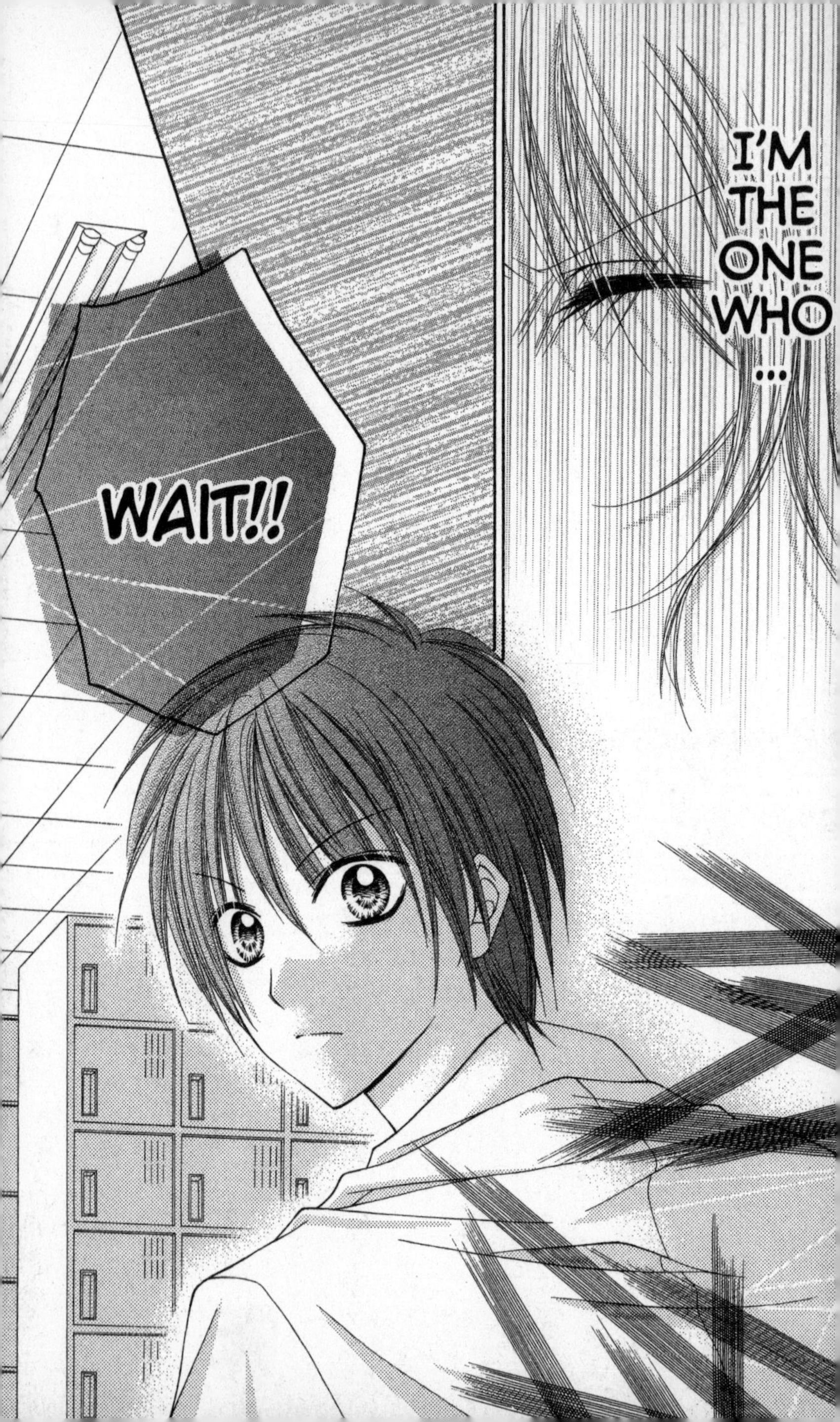
I'M THE ONE WHO ...
WAIT!!

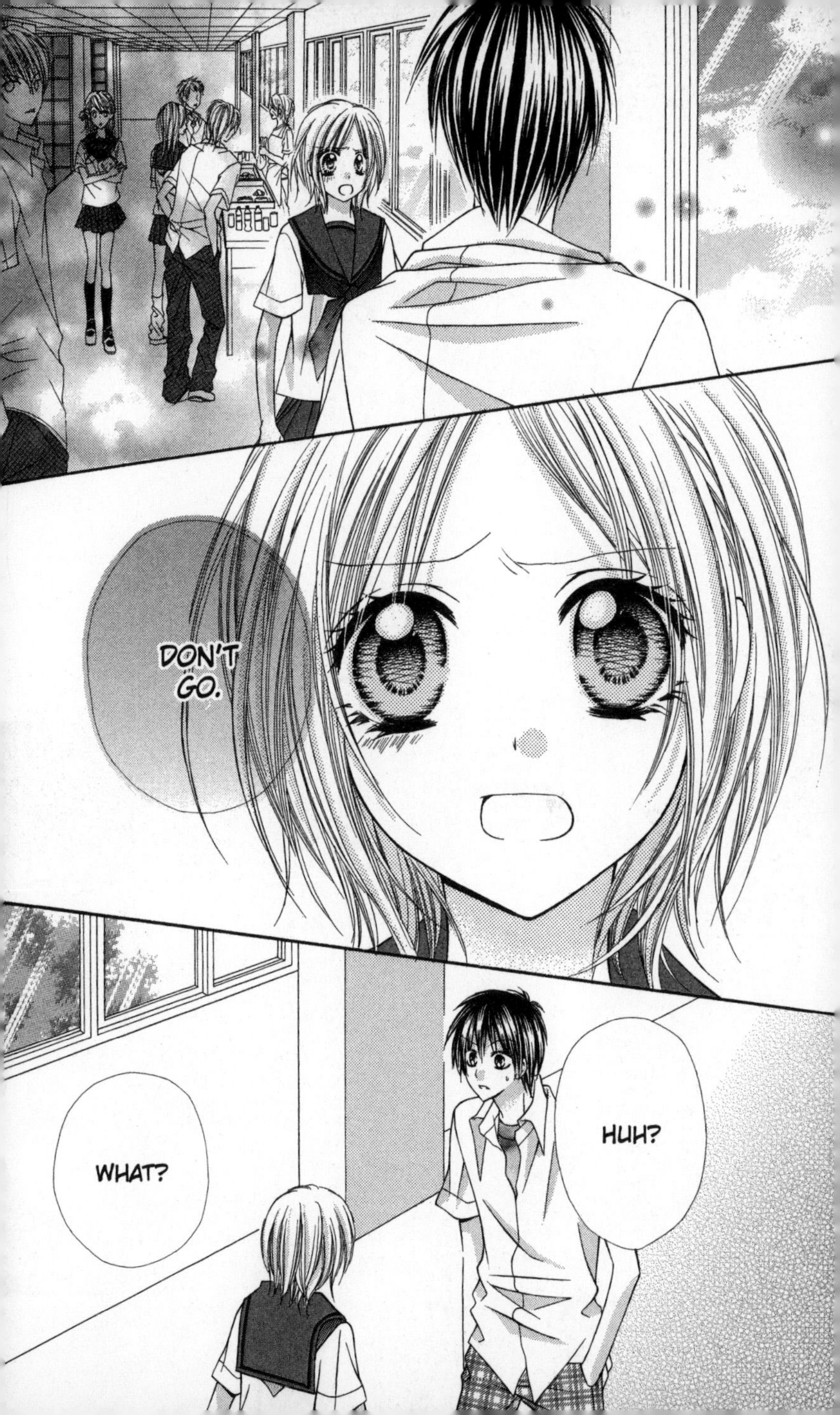
DON'T GO.
HUH?
WHAT?

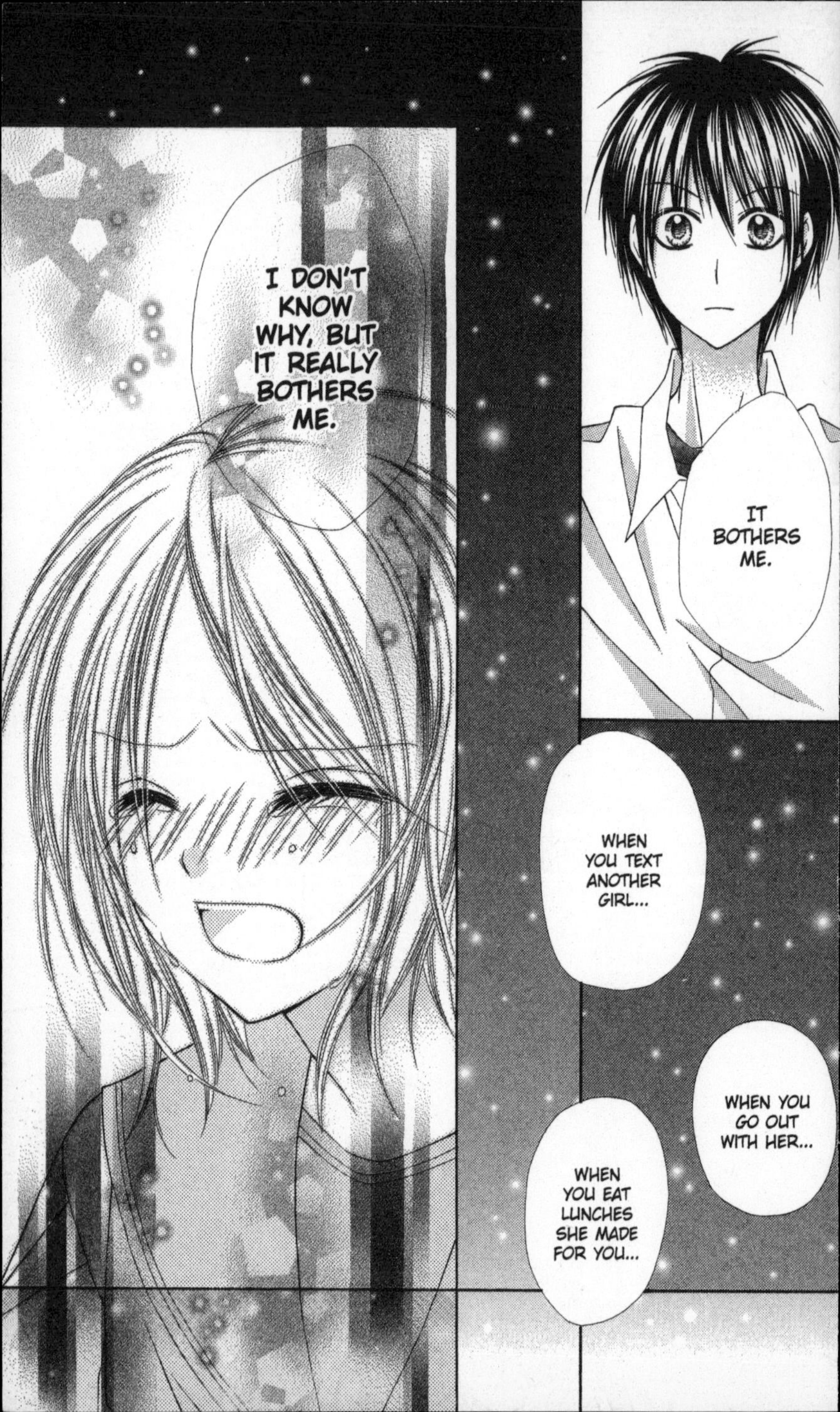
IT BOTHERS ME.
WHEN YOU TEXT ANOTHER GIRL...
WHEN YOU GO OUT WITH HER...
WHEN YOU EAT LUNCHES SHE MADE FOR YOU...
I DON'T KNOW WHY, BUT IT REALLY BOTHERS ME.

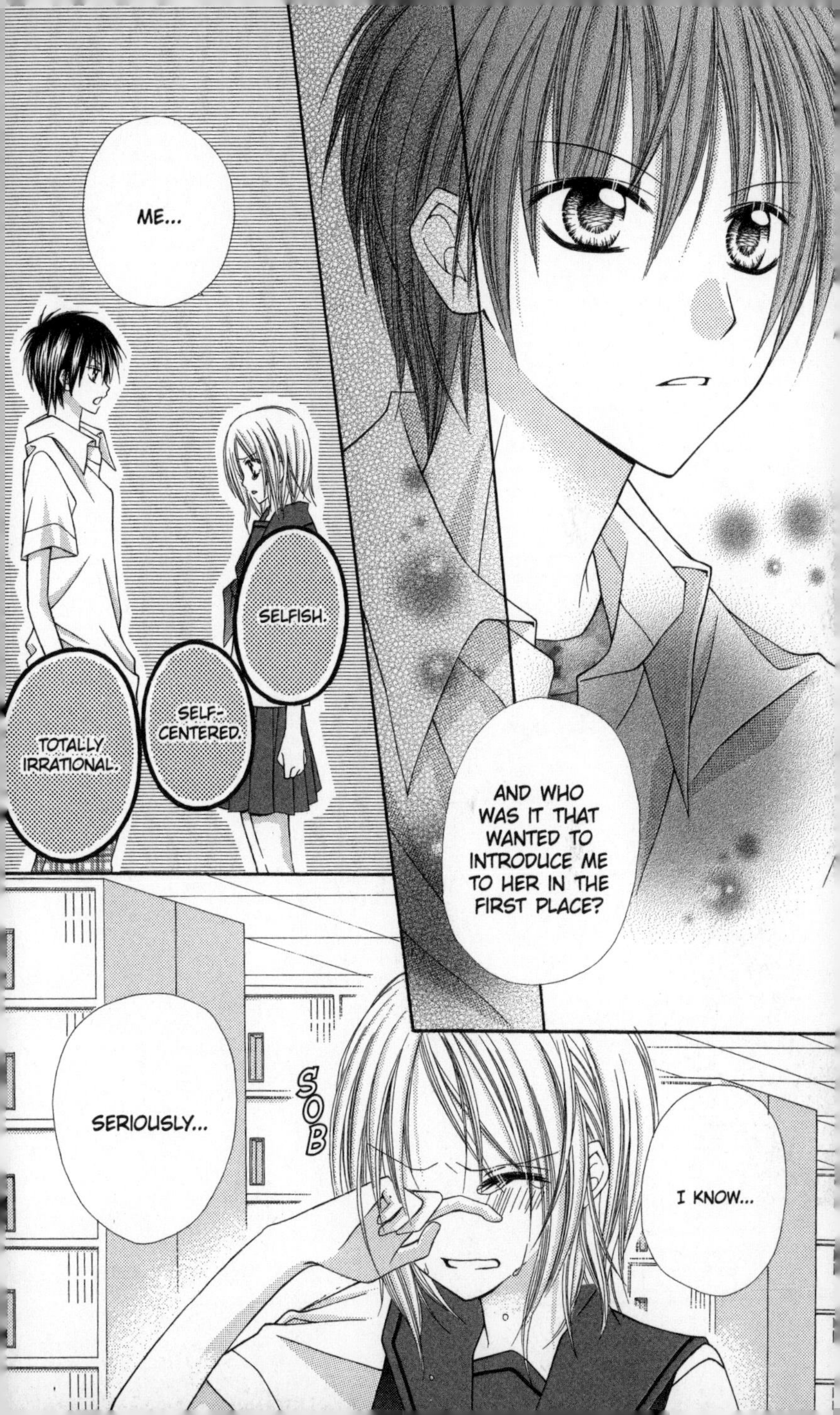
AND WHO WAS IT THAT WANTED TO INTRODUCE ME TO HER IN THE FIRST PLACE?
ME...
SELFISH.
SELF-CENTERED.
TOTALLY IRRATIONAL.
I KNOW...
SOB
SERIOUSLY...

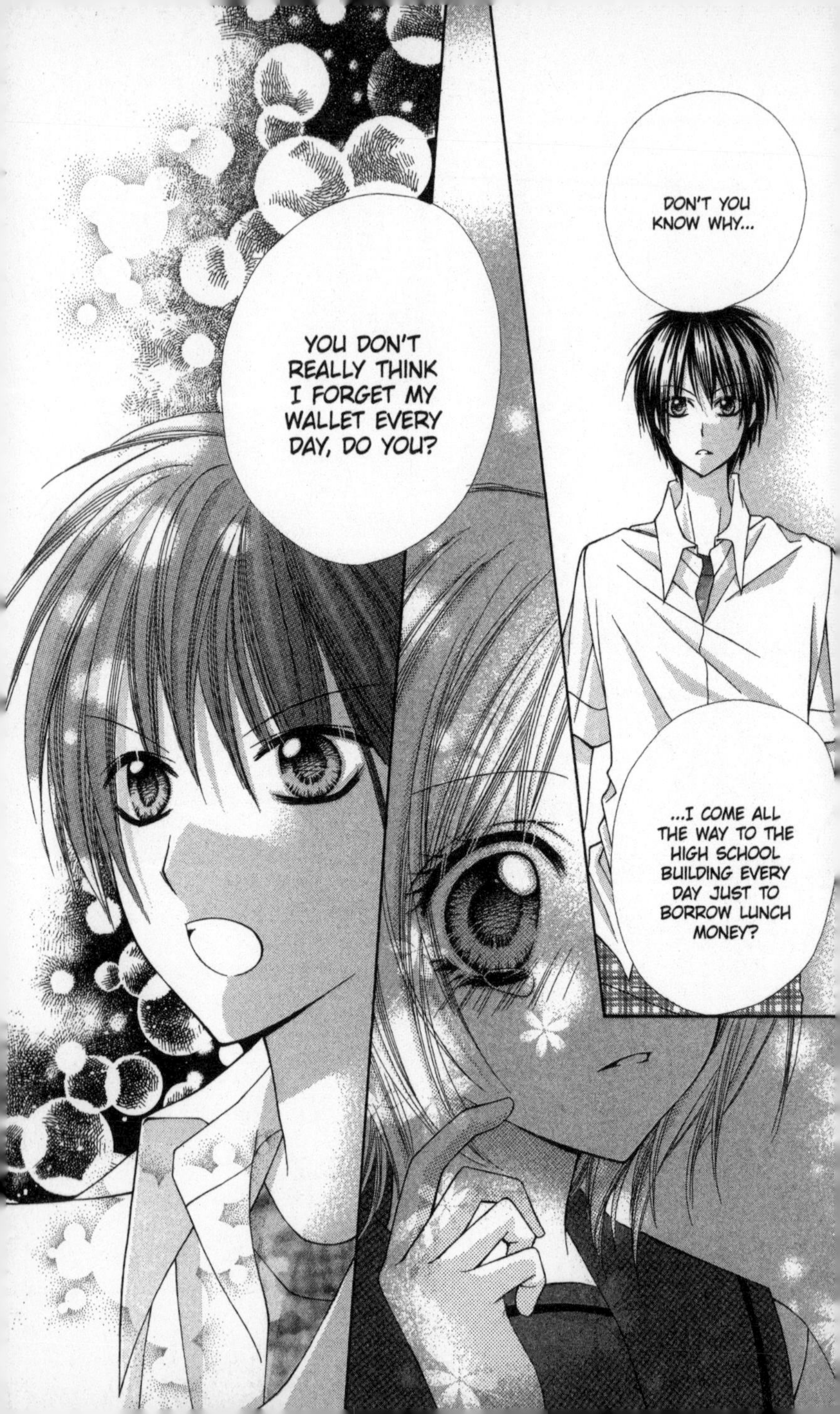
DON'T YOU KNOW WHY...
...I COME ALL THE WAY TO THE HIGH SCHOOL BUILDING EVERY DAY JUST TO BORROW LUNCH MONEY?
YOU DON'T REALLY THINK I FORGET MY WALLET EVERY DAY, DO YOU?

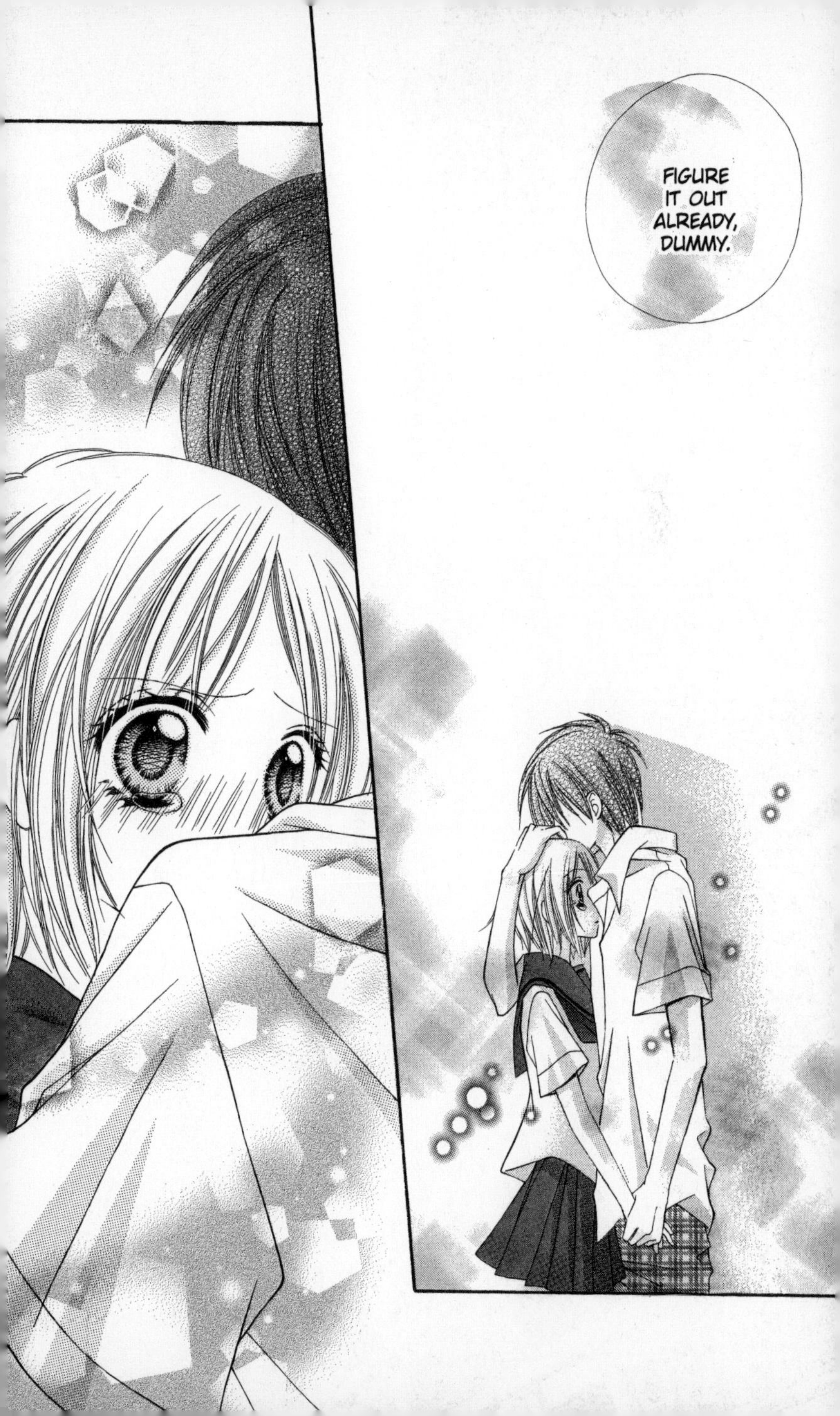
FIGURE IT OUT ALREADY, DUMMY.

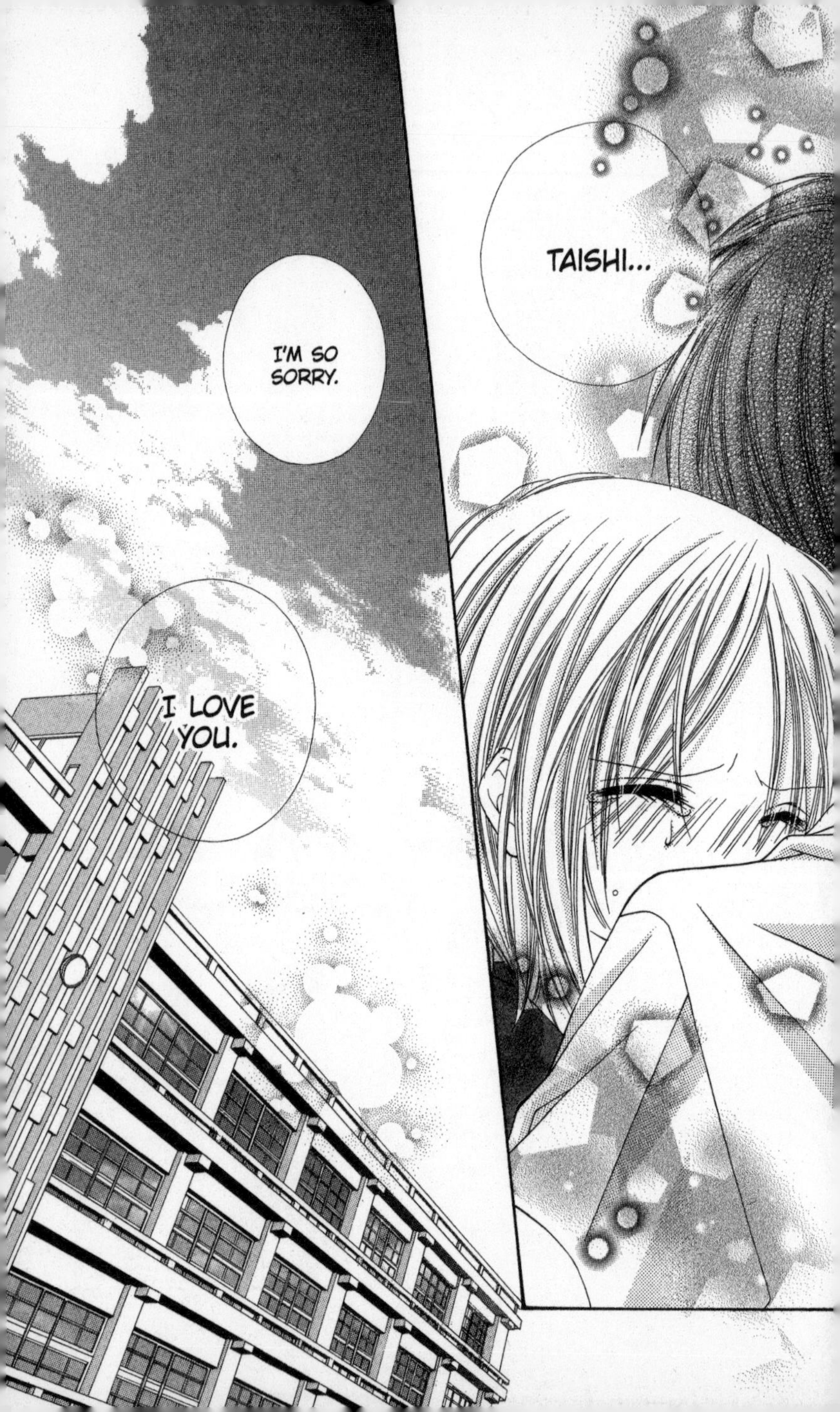
TAISHI...
I'M SO SORRY.
I LOVE YOU.

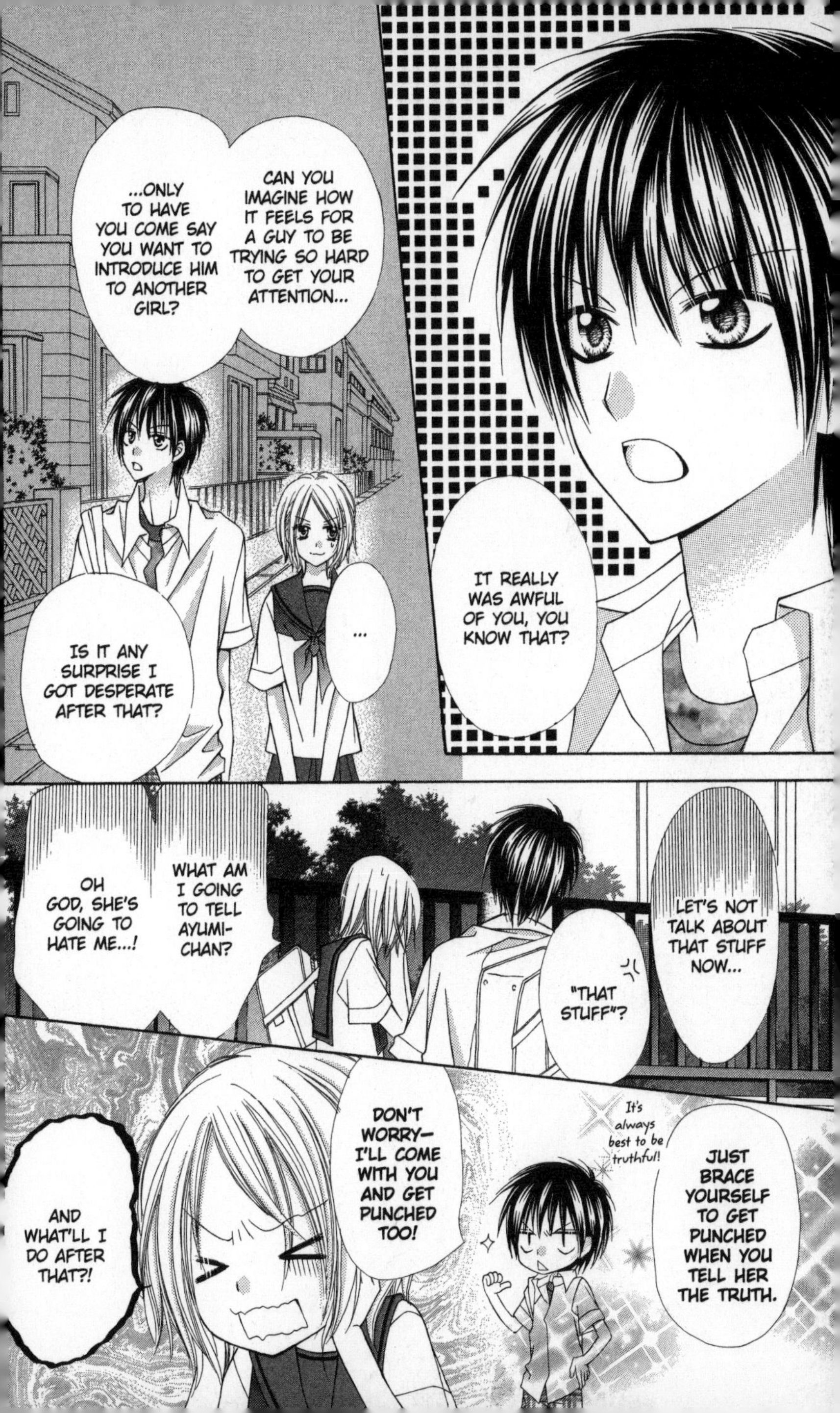
IT REALLY WAS AWFUL OF YOU, YOU KNOW THAT?
CAN YOU IMAGINE HOW IT FEELS FOR A GUY TO BE TRYING SO HARD TO GET YOUR ATTENTION...
...ONLY TO HAVE YOU COME SAY YOU WANT TO INTRODUCE HIM TO ANOTHER GIRL?
...
IS IT ANY SURPRISE I GOT DESPERATE AFTER THAT?
LET'S NOT TALK ABOUT THAT STUFF NOW...
"THAT STUFF"?
WHAT AM I GOING TO TELL AYUMI-CHAN?
OH GOD, SHE'S GOING TO HATE ME...!
JUST BRACE YOURSELF TO GET PUNCHED WHEN YOU TELL HER THE TRUTH.
It's always best to be truthful!
DON'T WORRY— I'LL COME WITH YOU AND GET PUNCHED TOO!
AND WHAT'LL I DO AFTER THAT?!

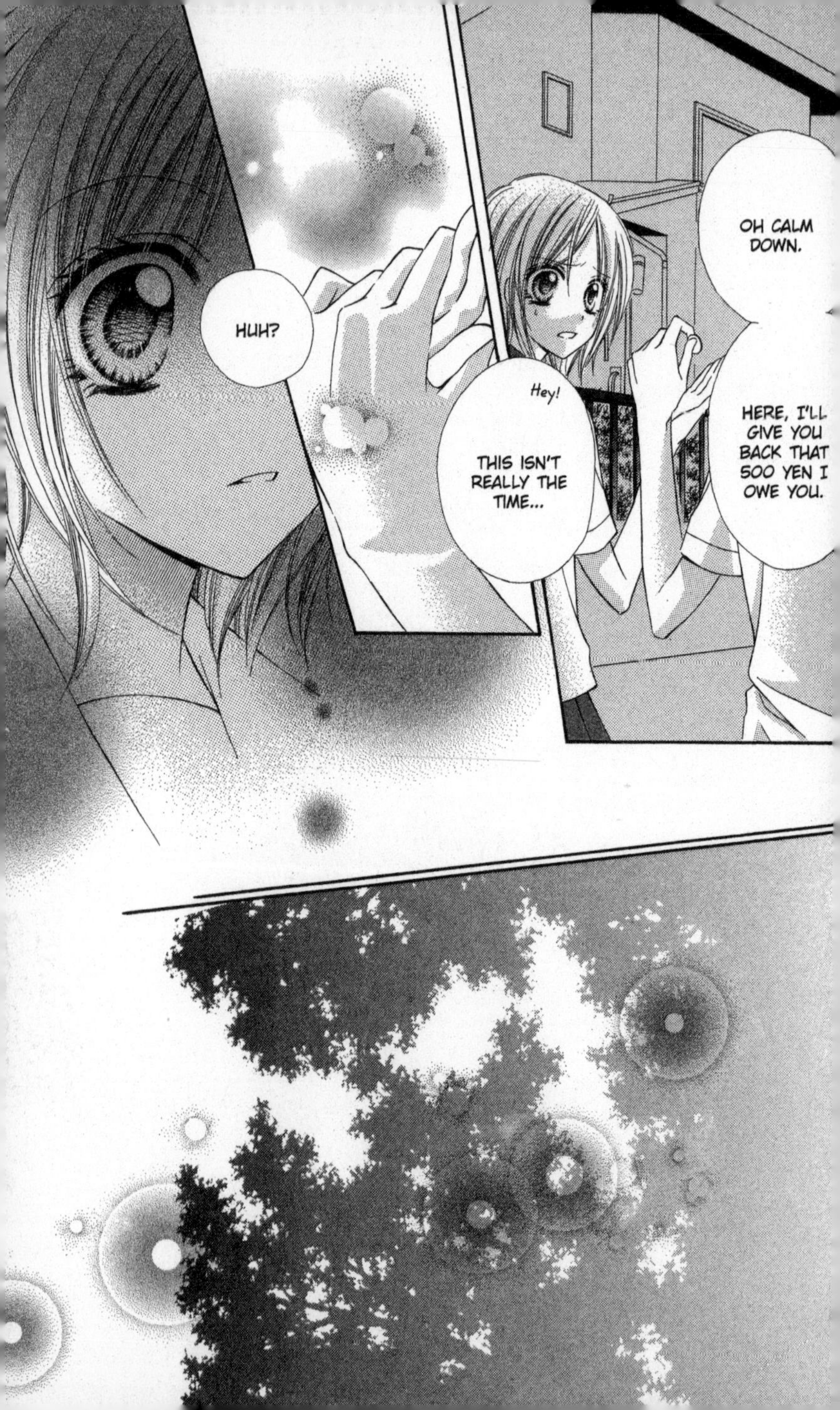
OH CALM DOWN.
HERE, I'LL GIVE YOU BACK THAT 500 YEN I OWE YOU.
Hey!
THIS ISN'T REALLY THE TIME...
HUH?

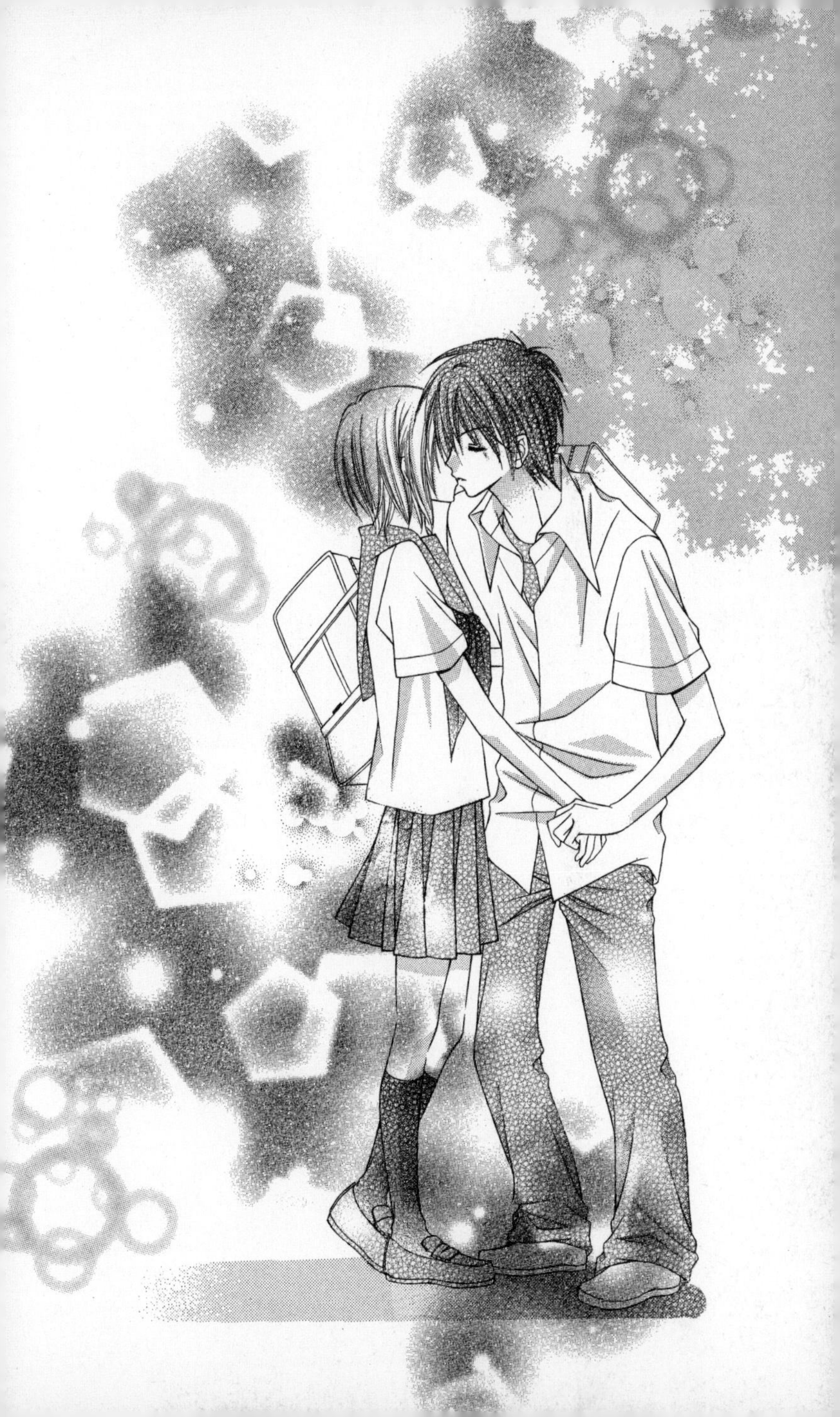

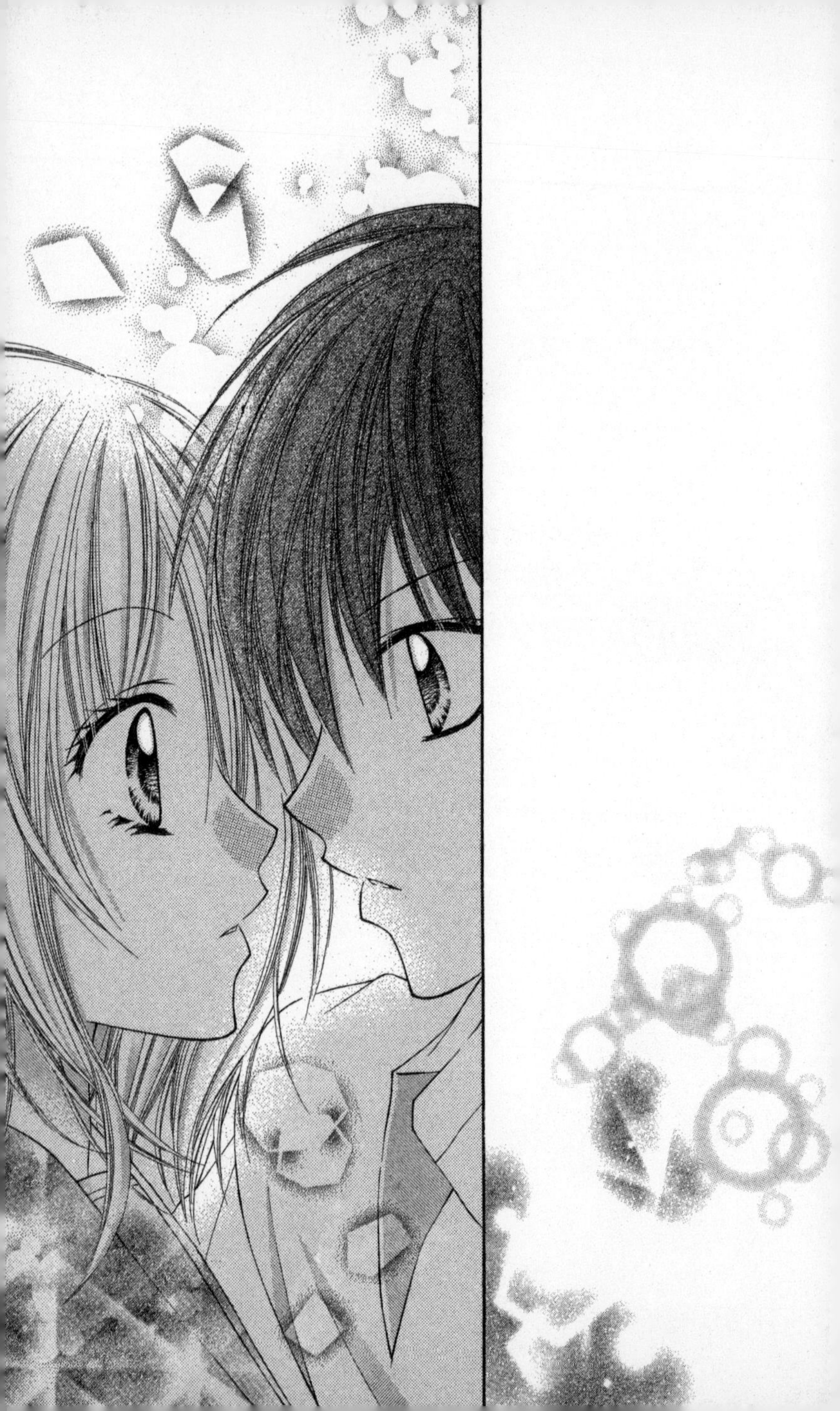

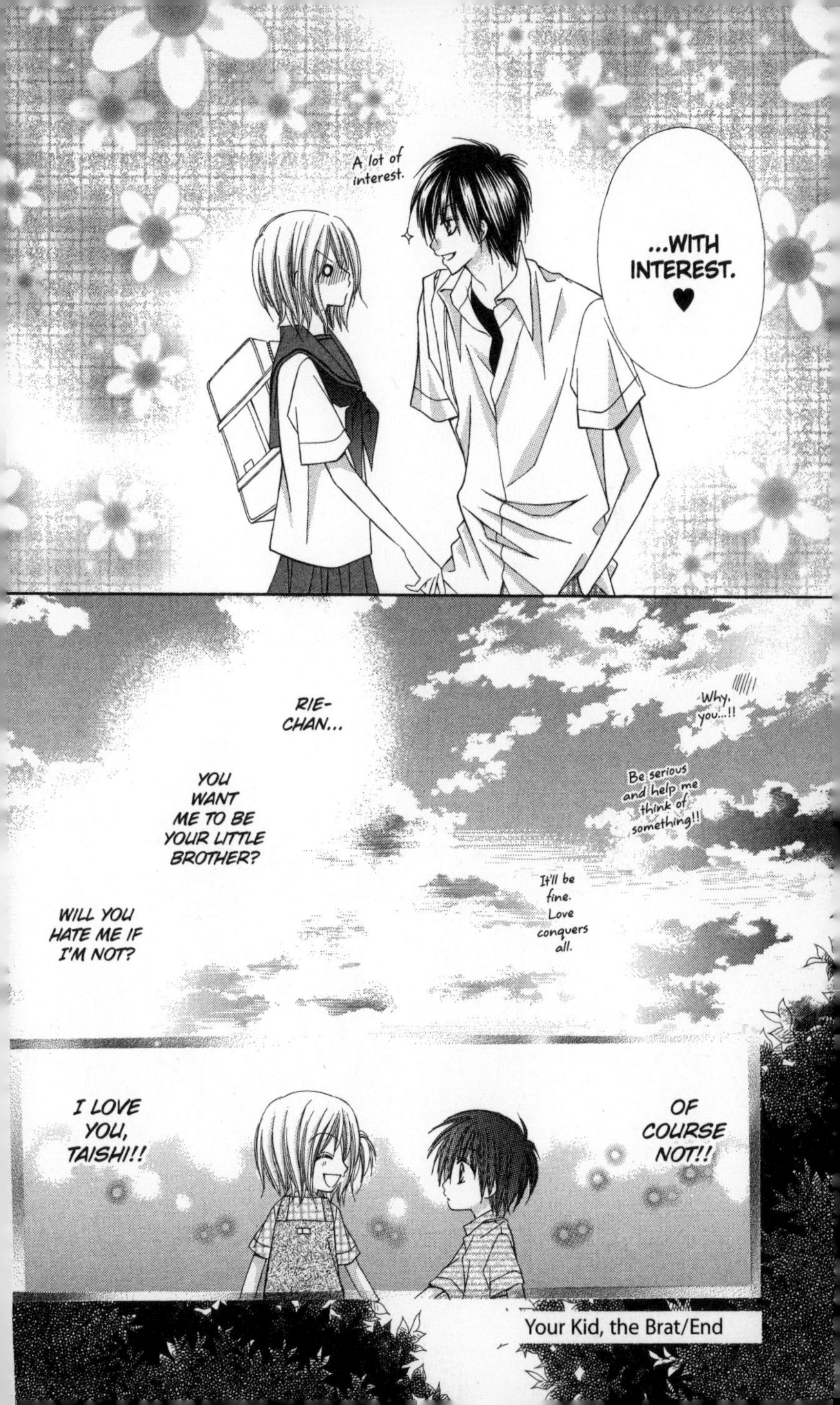
...WITH INTEREST. ♥
A lot of interest.
Why, you...!!
Be serious and help me think of something!!
It'll be fine. Love conquers all.
RIE-CHAN...
YOU WANT ME TO BE YOUR LITTLE BROTHER?
WILL YOU HATE ME IF I'M NOT?
OF COURSE NOT!!
I LOVE YOU, TAISHI!!
Your Kid, the Brat/End

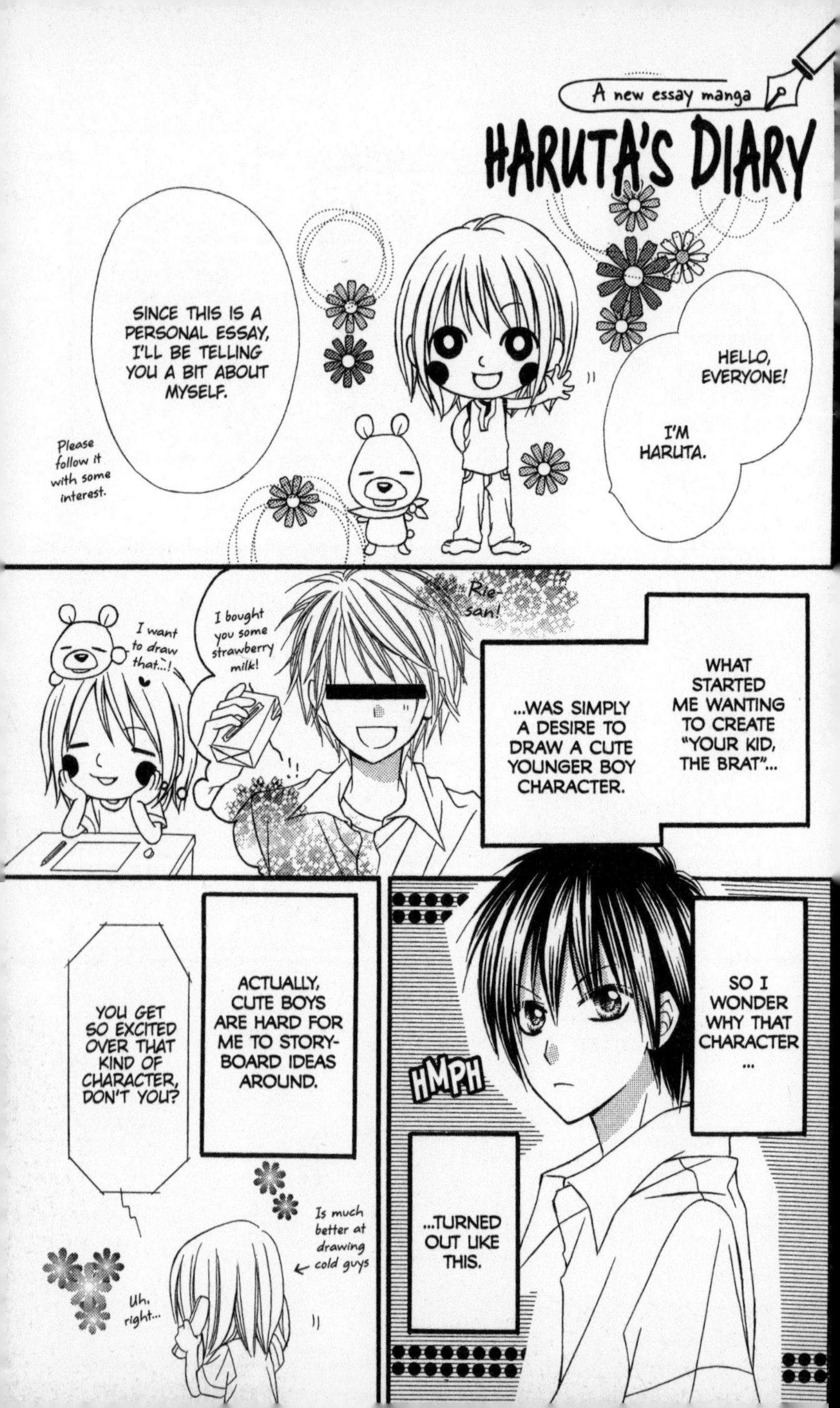
A new essay manga
HARUTA'S DIARY
HELLO, EVERYONE!
I'M HARUTA.
SINCE THIS IS A PERSONAL ESSAY, I'LL BE TELLING YOU A BIT ABOUT MYSELF.
Please follow it with some interest.
WHAT STARTED ME WANTING TO CREATE "YOUR KID, THE BRAT"...
...WAS SIMPLY A DESIRE TO DRAW A CUTE YOUNGER BOY CHARACTER.
Rie-san!
I bought you some strawberry milk!
I want to draw that...!
SO I WONDER WHY THAT CHARACTER ...
HMPH
...TURNED OUT LIKE THIS.
ACTUALLY, CUTE BOYS ARE HARD FOR ME TO STORY-BOARD IDEAS AROUND.
YOU GET SO EXCITED OVER THAT KIND OF CHARACTER, DON'T YOU?
Is much better at drawing cold guys
Uh, right...

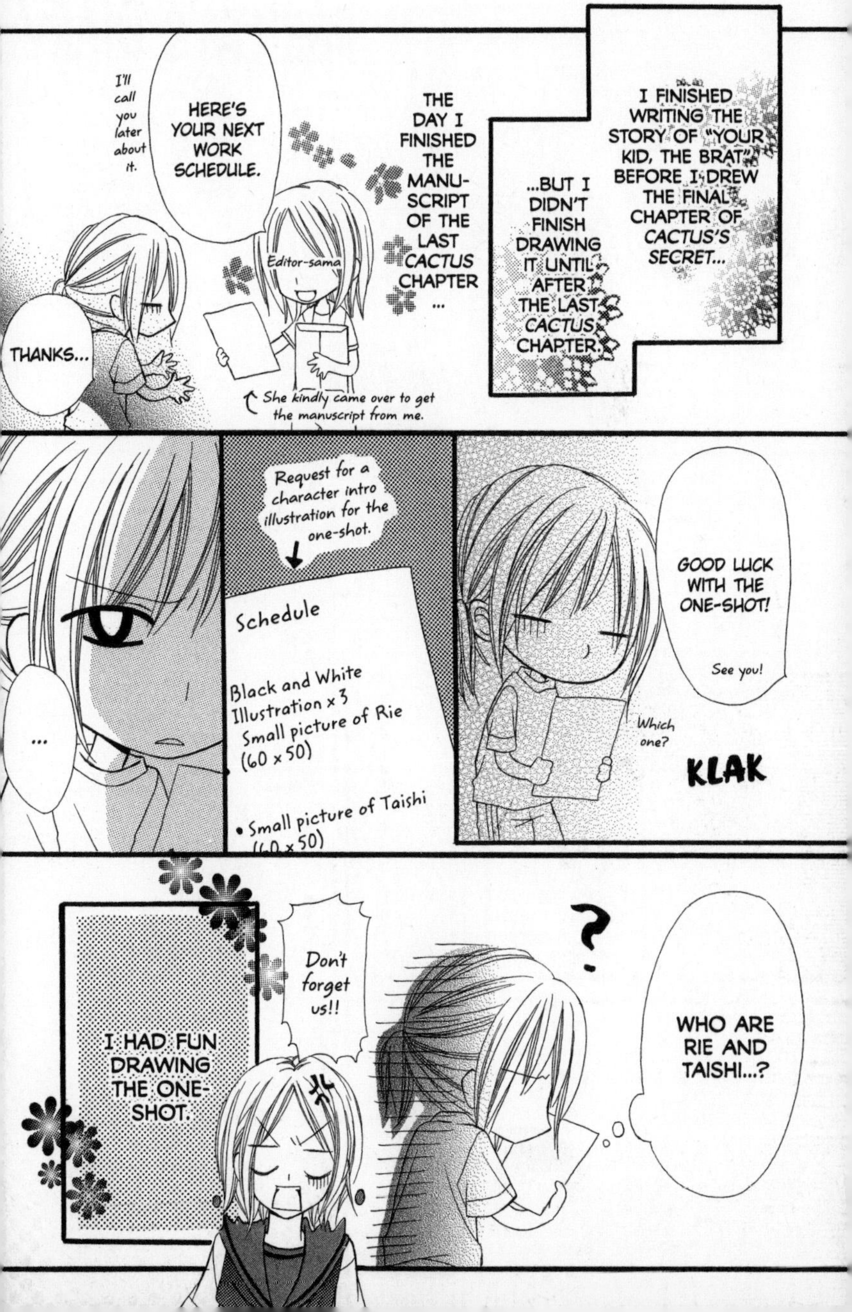
I FINISHED WRITING THE STORY OF "YOUR KID, THE BRAT" BEFORE I DREW THE FINAL CHAPTER OF CACTUS'S SECRET...
...BUT I DIDN'T FINISH DRAWING IT UNTIL AFTER THE LAST CACTUS CHAPTER.
THE DAY I FINISHED THE MANUSCRIPT OF THE LAST CACTUS CHAPTER...
HERE'S YOUR NEXT WORK SCHEDULE.
I'll call you later about it.
Editor-sama
She kindly came over to get the manuscript from me.
THANKS...
GOOD LUCK WITH THE ONE-SHOT!
See you!
Which one?
KLAK
Request for a character intro illustration for the one-shot.
Schedule
Black and White Illustration x 3
Small picture of Rie (60 x 50)
• Small picture of Taishi (60 x 50)
...
WHO ARE RIE AND TAISHI...?
?
Don't forget us!!
I HAD FUN DRAWING THE ONE-SHOT.

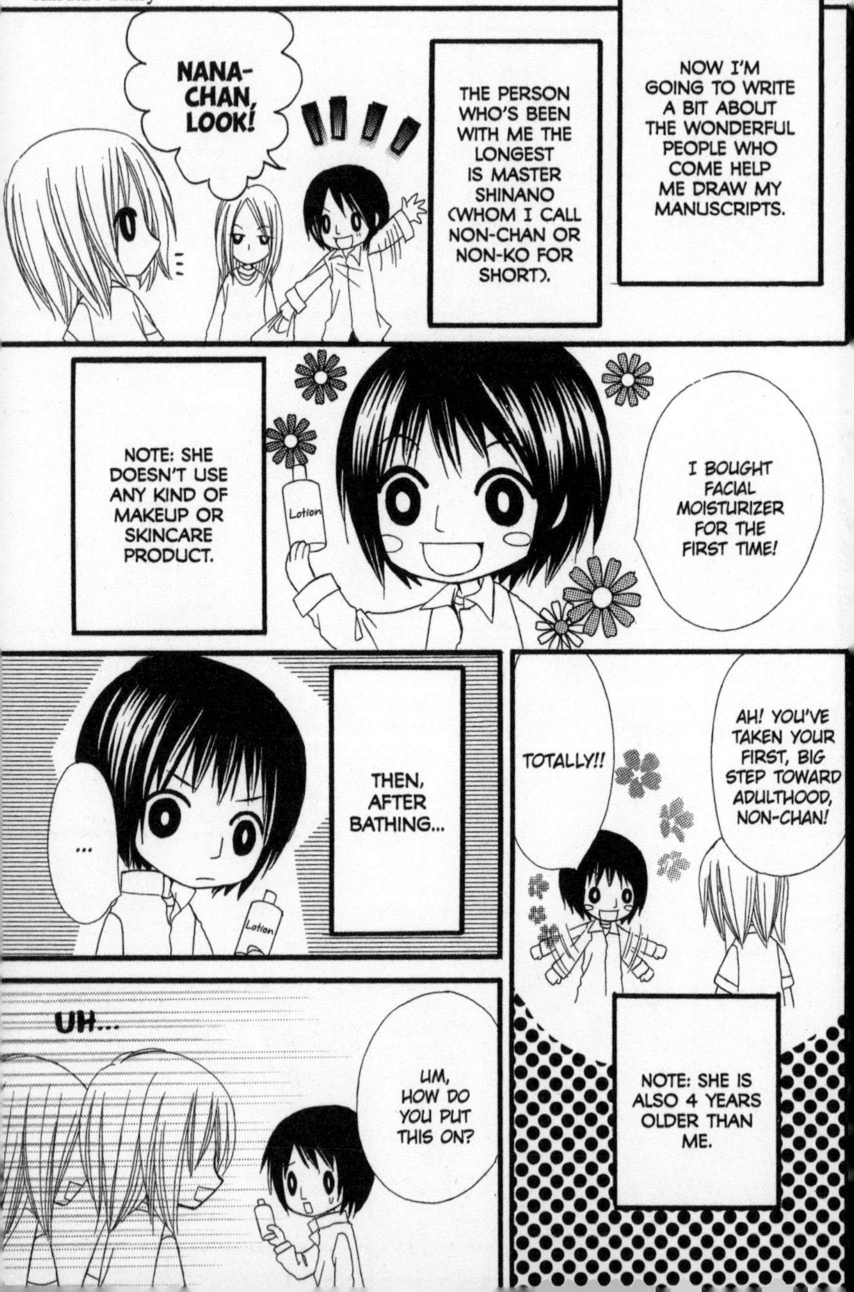
NOW I'M GOING TO WRITE A BIT ABOUT THE WONDERFUL PEOPLE WHO COME HELP ME DRAW MY MANUSCRIPTS.
THE PERSON WHO'S BEEN WITH ME THE LONGEST IS MASTER SHINANO (WHOM I CALL NON-CHAN OR NON-KO FOR SHORT).
NANA-CHAN, LOOK!
I BOUGHT FACIAL MOISTURIZER FOR THE FIRST TIME!
Lotion
NOTE: SHE DOESN'T USE ANY KIND OF MAKEUP OR SKINCARE PRODUCT.
AH! YOU'VE TAKEN YOUR FIRST, BIG STEP TOWARD ADULTHOOD, NON-CHAN!
TOTALLY!!
NOTE: SHE IS ALSO 4 YEARS OLDER THAN ME.
THEN, AFTER BATHING...
...
Lotion
UM, HOW DO YOU PUT THIS ON?
UH...

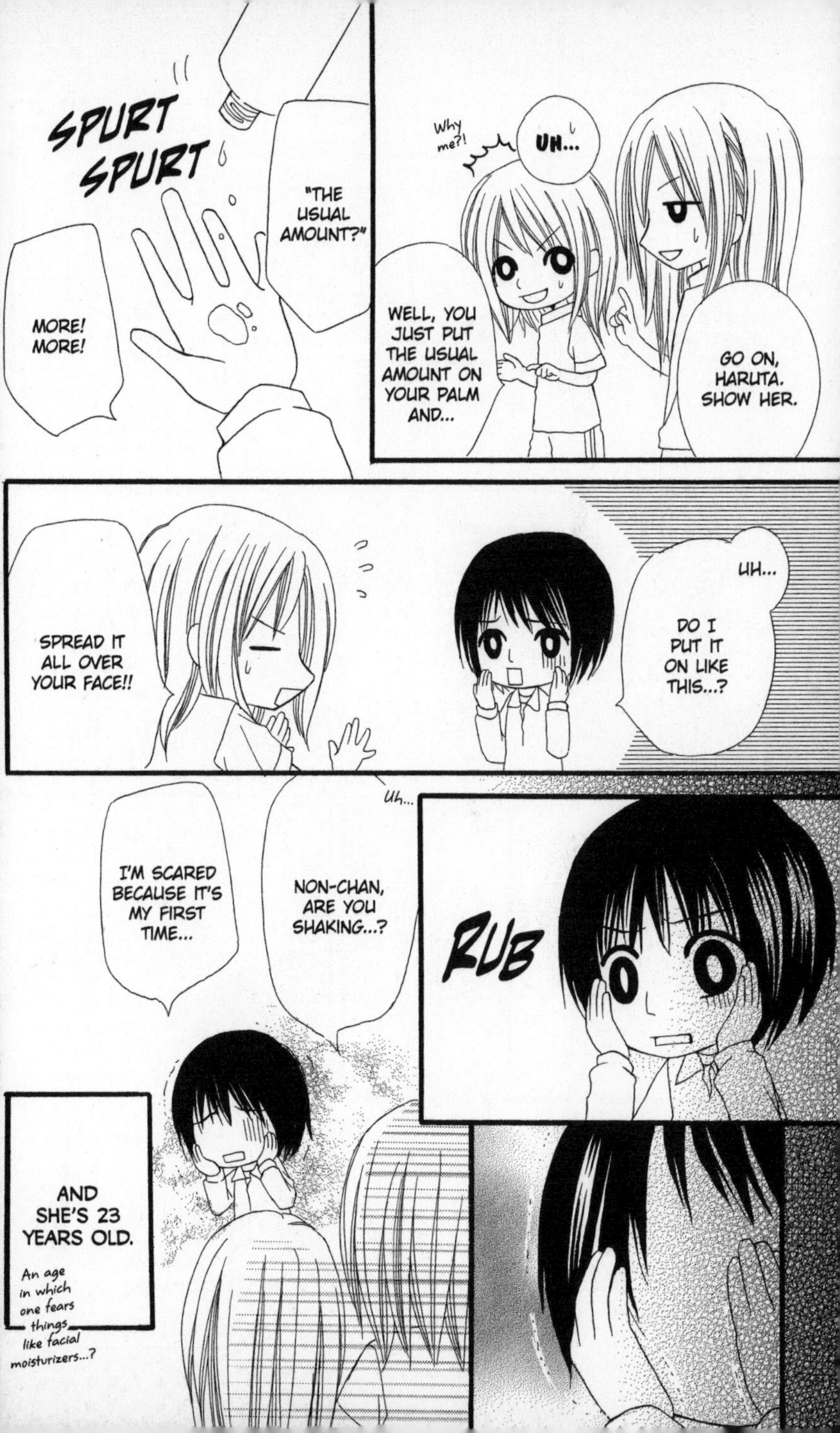
GO ON, HARUTA. SHOW HER.
UH...
Why me?!
WELL, YOU JUST PUT THE USUAL AMOUNT ON YOUR PALM AND...
"THE USUAL AMOUNT?"
SPURT SPURT
MORE! MORE!
UH... DO I PUT IT ON LIKE THIS...?
SPREAD IT ALL OVER YOUR FACE!!
RUB
Uh...
NON-CHAN, ARE YOU SHAKING...?
I'M SCARED BECAUSE IT'S MY FIRST TIME...
AND SHE'S 23 YEARS OLD.
An age in which one fears things like facial moisturizers...?

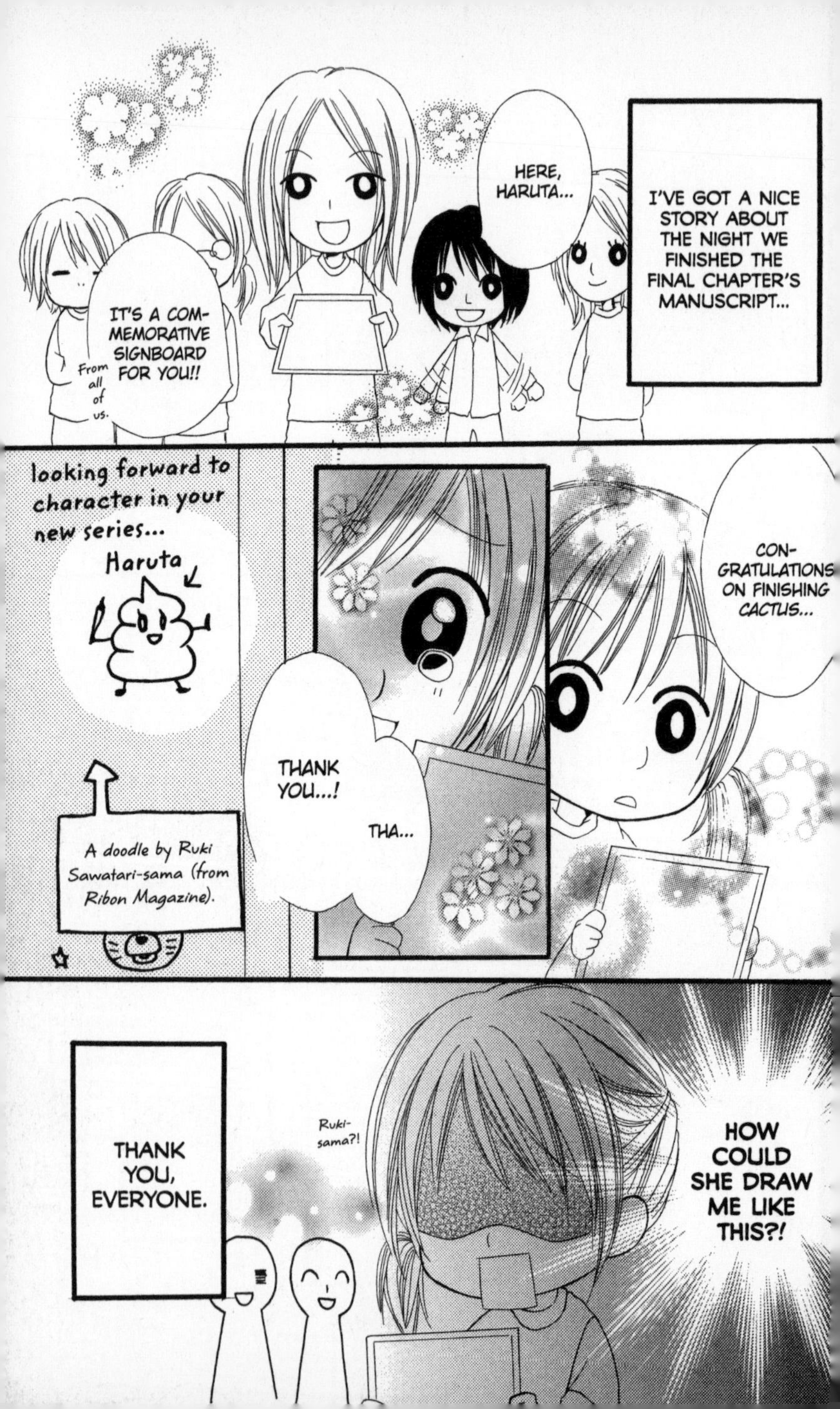
I'VE GOT A NICE STORY ABOUT THE NIGHT WE FINISHED THE FINAL CHAPTER'S MANUSCRIPT...
HERE, HARUTA...
IT'S A COMMEMORATIVE SIGNBOARD FOR YOU!!
From all of us.
CONGRATULATIONS ON FINISHING CACTUS...
THANK YOU...!
THA...
looking forward to character in your new series...
Haruta
A doodle by Ruki Sawatari-sama (from Ribon Magazine).
HOW COULD SHE DRAW ME LIKE THIS?!
Ruki-sama?!
THANK YOU, EVERYONE.

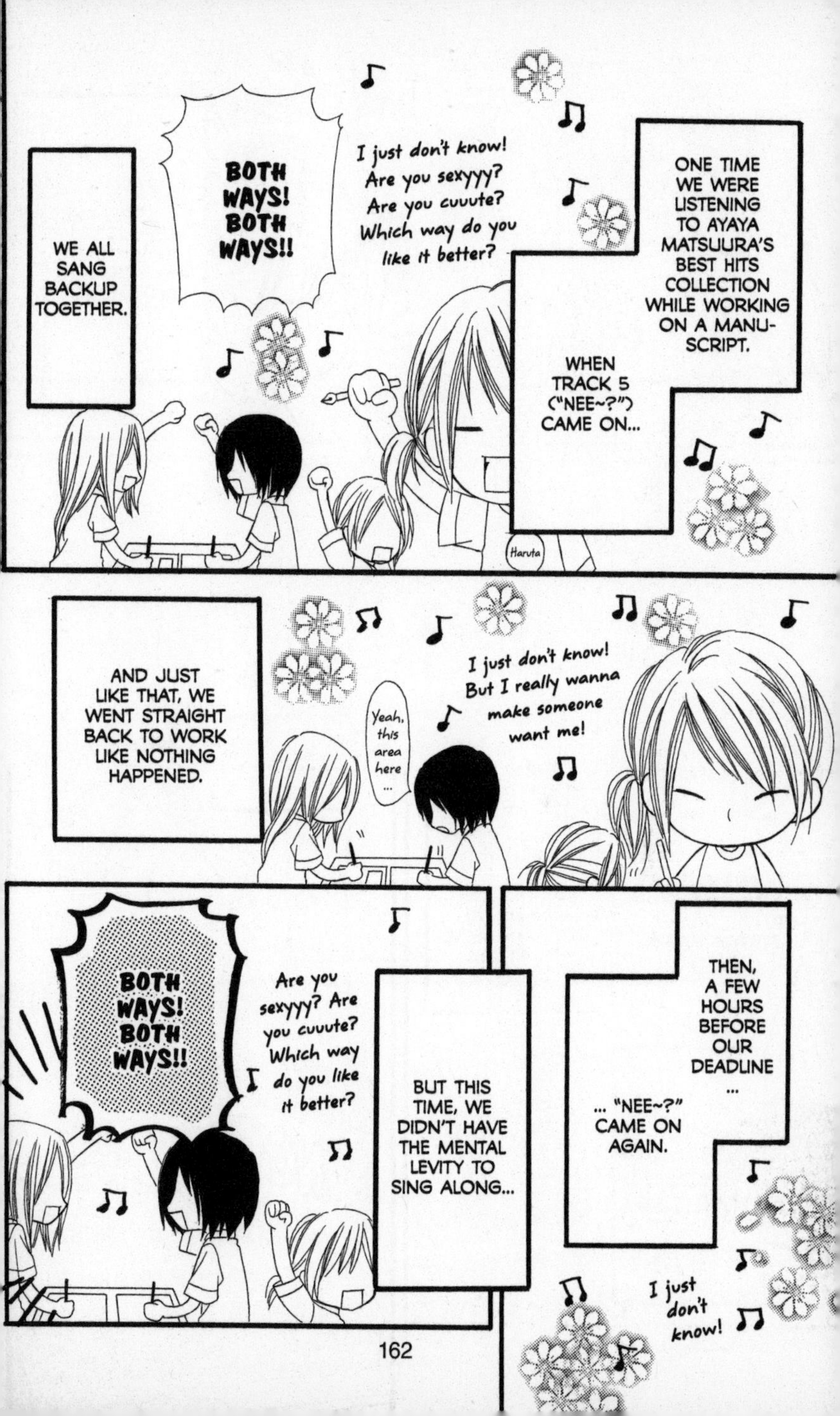

ONE TIME WE WERE LISTENING TO AYAYA MATSUURA'S BEST HITS COLLECTION WHILE WORKING ON A MANU-SCRIPT.
WHEN TRACK 5 ("NEE~?") CAME ON...
Haruta
I just don't know! Are you sexyyy? Are you cuuute? Which way do you like it better?
BOTH WAYS! BOTH WAYS!!
WE ALL SANG BACKUP TOGETHER.
I just don't know! But I really wanna make someone want me!
Yeah, this area here ...
AND JUST LIKE THAT, WE WENT STRAIGHT BACK TO WORK LIKE NOTHING HAPPENED.
THEN, A FEW HOURS BEFORE OUR DEADLINE ...
... "NEE~?" CAME ON AGAIN.
I just don't know!
BUT THIS TIME, WE DIDN'T HAVE THE MENTAL LEVITY TO SING ALONG...
Are you sexyyy? Are you cuuute? Which way do you like it better?
BOTH WAYS! BOTH WAYS!!

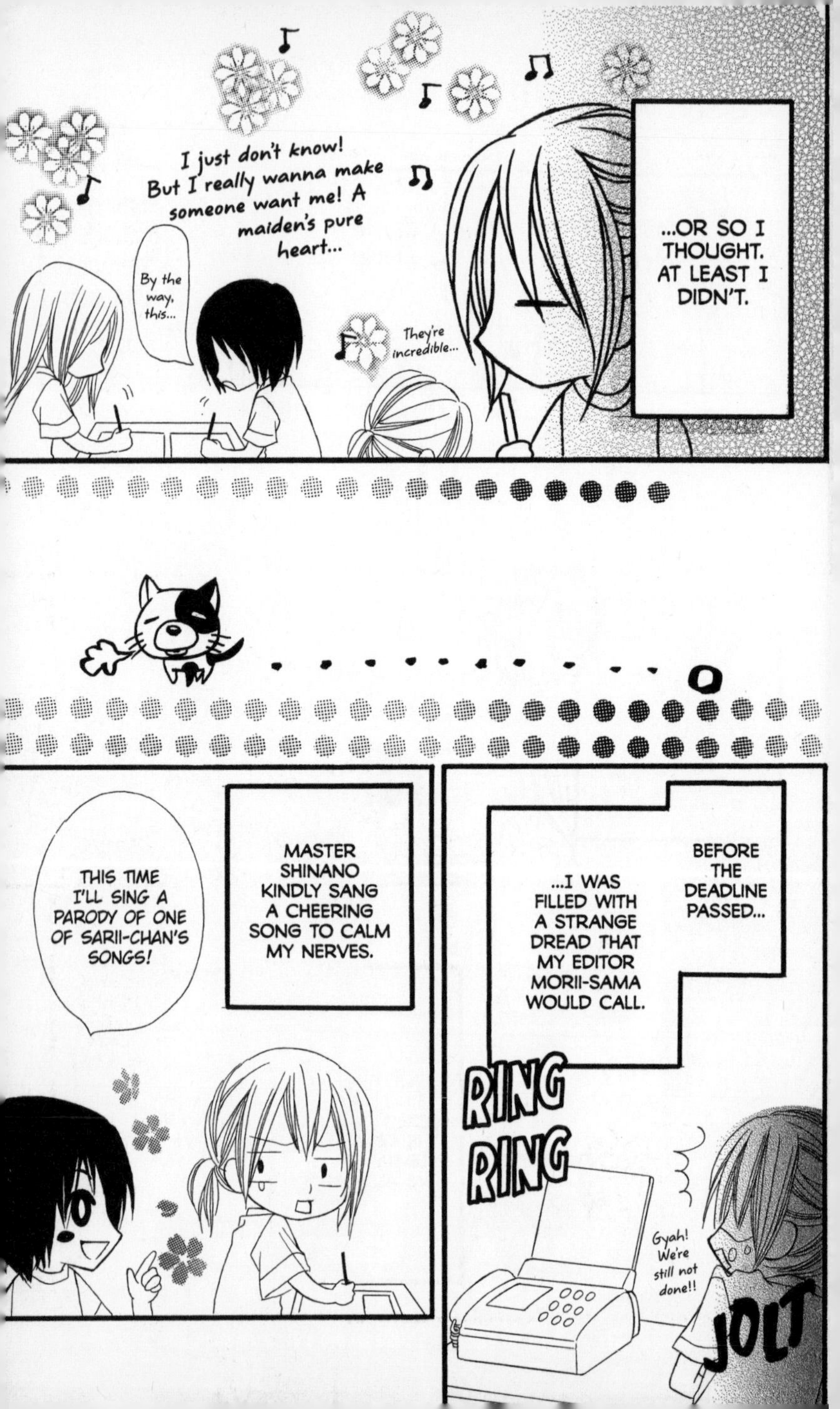
...OR SO I THOUGHT. AT LEAST I DIDN'T.
They're incredible...
I just don't know! But I really wanna make someone want me! A maiden's pure heart...
By the way, this...
BEFORE THE DEADLINE PASSED...
...I WAS FILLED WITH A STRANGE DREAD THAT MY EDITOR MORII-SAMA WOULD CALL.
RING RING
Gyah! We're still not done!!
JOLT
MASTER SHINANO KINDLY SANG A CHEERING SONG TO CALM MY NERVES.
THIS TIME I'LL SING A PARODY OF ONE OF SARII-CHAN'S SONGS!

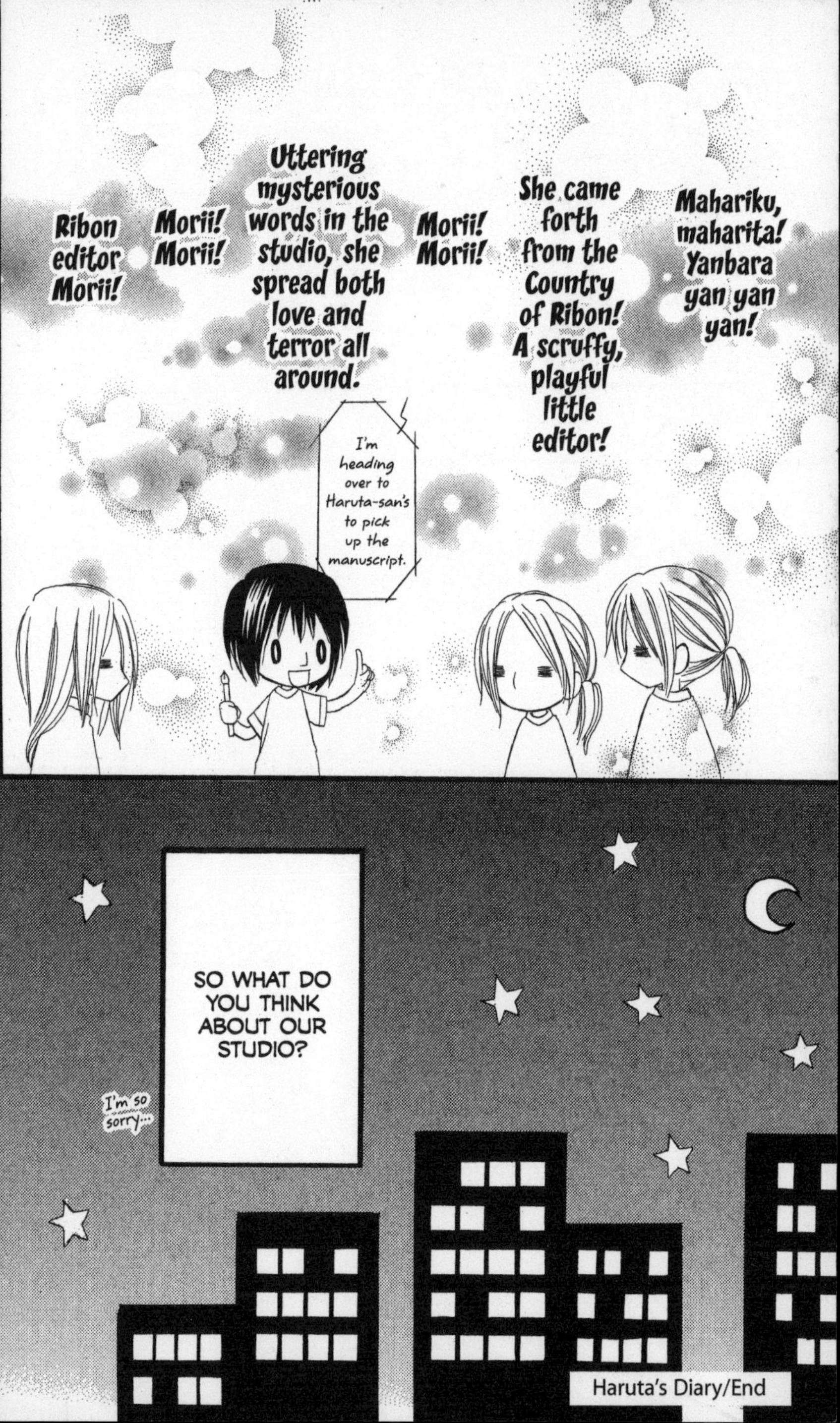
Mahariku, maharita! Yanbara yan yan yan!
She came forth from the Country of Ribon! A scruffy, playful little editor!
Morii! Morii!
Uttering mysterious words in the studio, she spread both love and terror all around.
Morii! Morii!
Ribon editor Morii!
I'm heading over to Haruta-san's to pick up the manuscript.
SO WHAT DO YOU THINK ABOUT OUR STUDIO?
I'm so sorry...
Haruta's Diary/End

A WORD ON CACTUS

Well, looks like we're running out of time now, so the illustrations are just going to be in pencil. I hope they'll turn out okay when they're printed.

- I think I want to take a look back at *Cactus* in bullet form.
- I couldn't say this before out of fear of my editor, but I was working a part-time job during *Cactus*'s serialization.
- I'm so sorry. It was only temporary. Sorry!
- Mayu-pon Sakai came over to help me with a manuscript once.
- Somewhere in volume 2, there's a mob (crowd of background characters) that Mayu-pon drew.
- Those who haven't found it yet, please keep looking!
- I knew the sooner I got chapter one's storyboard done the better it would be—but still, it was extremely late.
- The manuscript was late too.
- There aren't any good points.
- Forgive me, Editor-sama.
- I'll try harder.
- I can't think back anymore.
- The end.

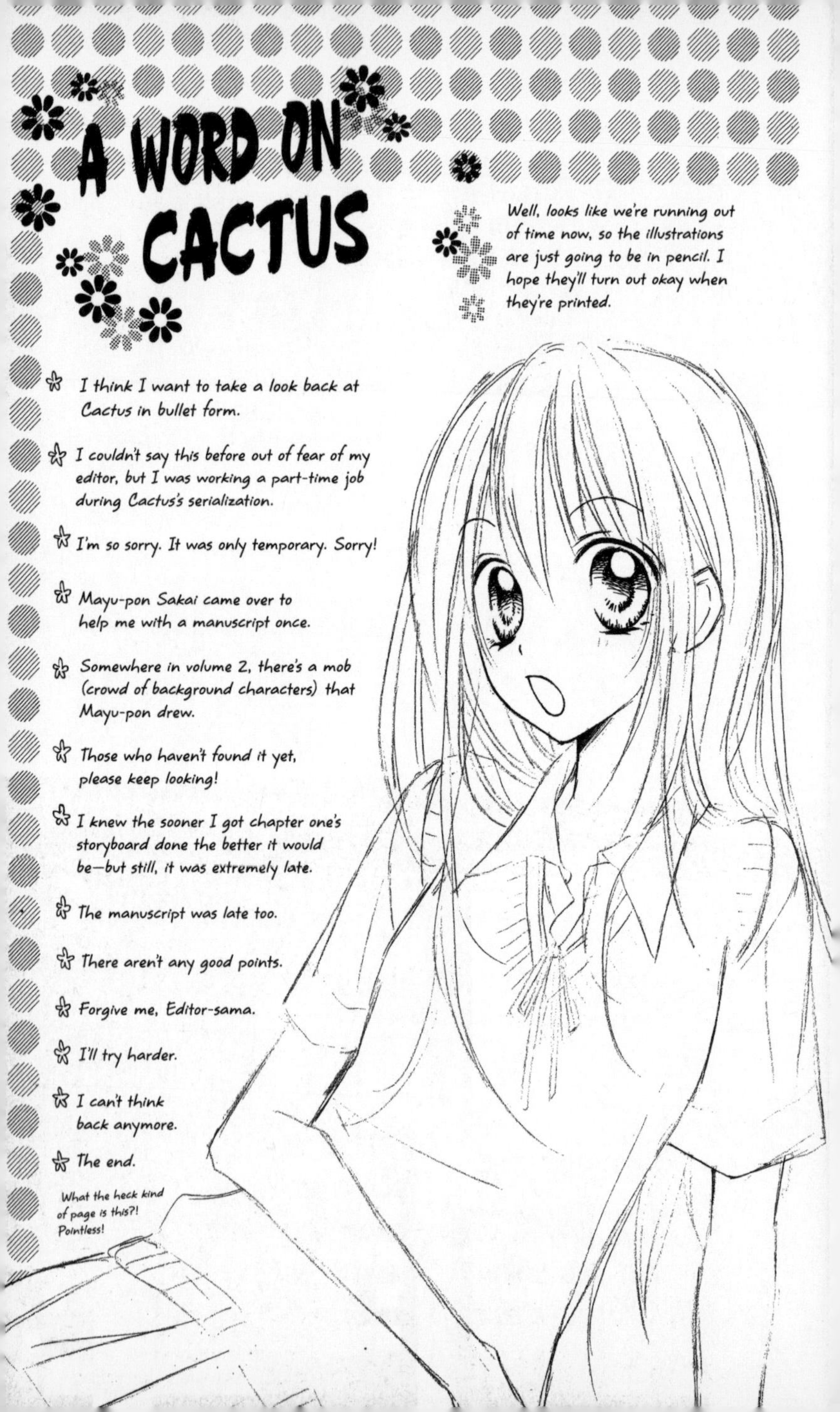

What the heck kind of page is this?! Pointless!

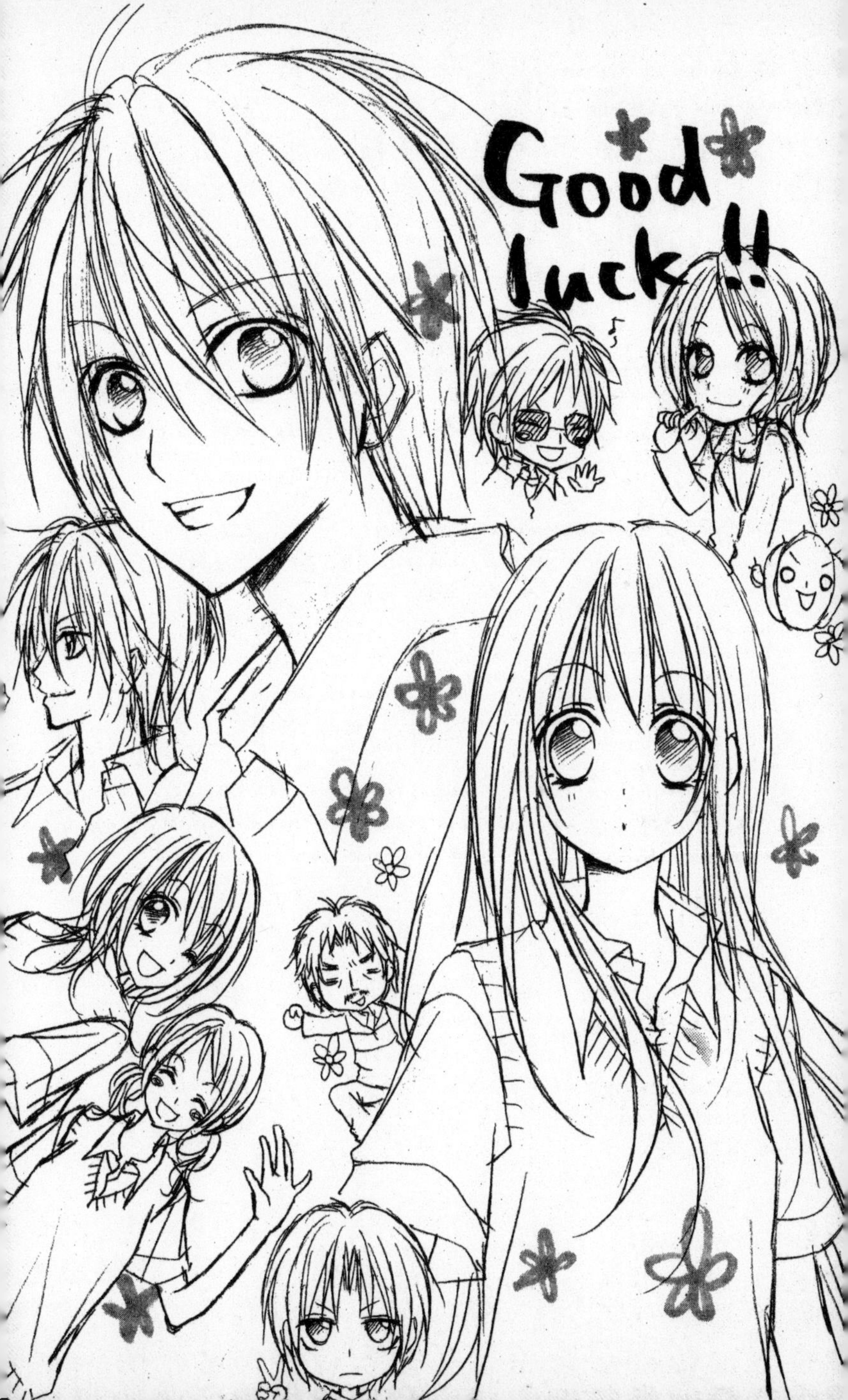
Good luck!!

In Closing...

For some reason it was really fun drawing the sketches on the opposite page. (I wish I could've at least inked them. Sorry! Why am I so bad at time management?) Drawn all together like this, it looks like there were really quite a few characters, huh?

I got a little sad thinking that unless there's some kind of special order, I won't able to draw these characters again for a long time. I guess I feel sentimental because this is the first time I've drawn the same set of characters for such a long period of time.

Miku is so uncute I sort of feel like she was unworthy of being a *Ribon* heroine, and Fujioka was an odd hero to the very end...

But there truly is so much I've gained from drawing these characters. Viewed objectively, they probably seem kind of like good-for-nothings, but to me, they're precious kids who've helped me on a personal level.

Those of you who managed to love them at least a little, thank you so much!

Cactus's Secret ends here, but I hope you'll think of it once in a while and maybe reread it someday.

I guess I'll stop here.

Nana Haruta

Meow...

Special Thanks

M. Shinano
M. Umezawa
A. Ryui
S. Nakano
M. Yukimaru
R. Sawatari
R. Hayase
H. Nozaki

K. Hanzawa
H. Moriwake

and You!

Thank you
for reading.

2005.8
Nana. Haruta

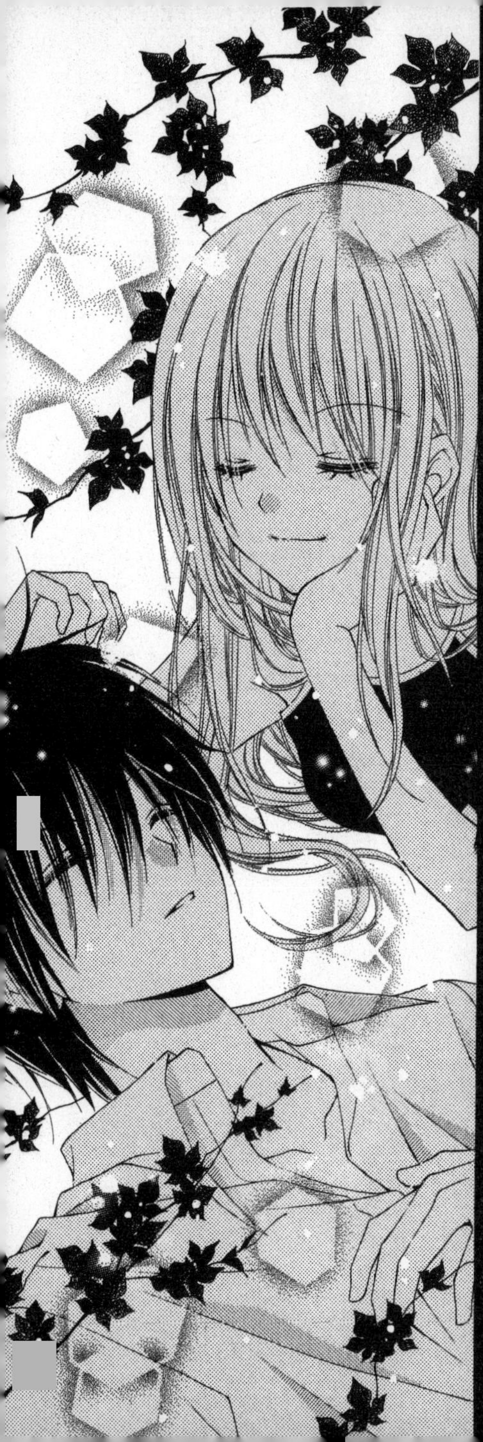

Notes

Honorifics

In Japan, people are usually addressed by their name plus a suffix. The suffix shows familiarity or respect, depending on the relationship.

MALE (familiar): first or last name + kun

FEMALE (familiar): first or last name + chan

ADULT (polite): last name + san

UPPERCLASSMAN (polite): last name + senpai

TEACHER or PROFESSIONAL: last name + sensei

CLOSE FRIENDS or LOVERS: first name only, no suffix

Terms

Onii-chan means "older brother." It can also be used to refer to an older male.

In manga, a nosebleed is a humorous way to depict sexual arousal.

V6 is a popular Japanese boy band.

Obon is a festival in late summer to honor and remember ancestors and deceased family members.

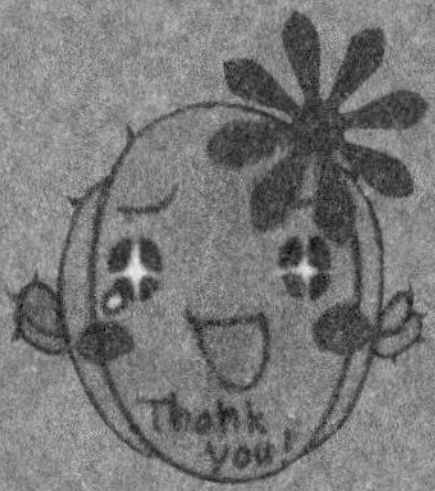
Thank you!

My manga-crafting was hopelessly lousy when Cactus first started running, but it seems to have become not so awful along the way. Maybe all those months of me facing down my own lack of skill and striving to draw the manuscripts weren't entirely in vain. With that thought in mind, I feel happy today.

-NANA HARUTA

Nana Haruta debuted in 2000 with *Ai no ♥ Ai no Shirushi* (Love's ♥, Love's Symbol) in *Ribon Original* magazine. She was born in Niigata Prefecture and likes reading manga and taking baths. Her other works include *Love Berrish!* and *Chocolate Cosmos*. Her current series, *Stardust ★ Wink*, is serialized in *Ribon* magazine.